# THIS IS WISCONSIN

I. Northern Woodland

# This is Wisconsin

## By Robert E. Gard

# WISCONSIN HOUSE
at
Spring Green

By Robert E. Gard

Johnny Chinook
Wisconsin is My Doorstep
Grassroots Theater
Wisconsin Lore (with L. G. Sorden)
The Romance of Wisconsin Place Names (with L. G. Sorden)
This is Wisconsin

For Joe Wilson, hank Ahlgren
and Maryo G. Gard with thanks
for their friendship and help.

# INTRODUCTION

Bob Gard has been carrying on an ardent love affair with Wisconsin ever since he joined the faculty of the University of Wisconsin in 1945. All the while, he has gone about his dedicated task of encouraging the creativity of hundreds of men and women throughout Wisconsin, making the Wisconsin Idea Theatre a viable and inspiring part of the university functions, and helping to bring our university directly to creative people in the arts from one boundary to another. But simultaneously he has been exploring the remotest corners of the state, talking with people in all walks of life, and reaching back into the past for anecdotes, tall tales, and accounts of human achievement and dramatic failure, as well as learning about the present, about the credos and quirks of Wisconsin people today.

He has turned up all kinds of fact and legend — as such books as *Wisconsin Lore*, *The Romance of Wisconsin Place Names*, and others testify — but he has not before given us such intimate portraits of people, past and present, as he does in these pages. He has made no attempt to be comprehensive — how could one book convey all the flavor of our state? — but he has caught here, and often memorably, the people and places he has visited. This book is indeed Wisconsin, authentic, accurately recorded Wisconsin color and drama, fact and fancy, a book meant to bring to every reader something of what it means to live in Wisconsin.

Back in 1948 Bob Gard wrote a book entitled *Wisconsin Is My Doorstep*. This new book is evidence of how well and how far he has got into the house.

-August Derleth

# FOREWORD

There was so much I hoped to put in this book. I expected to be able to tell about the time some quarry workmen discovered a petrified man near Lake Mills in 1903 and exhibited an arm and a leg of him on the streets of Lake Mills. I wanted to include what Russell Hill, county clerk of Barron County, told me about that curious homemade chair in the clerk's office at Barron that once held the county government in its hollowed-out interior. I planned to relate the account of the old mansion at West Algoma that had so much to do with the impeachment trial of President Andrew Johnson. I was eager to include much more of the fascinating lore and legend of the Driftless Area of Wisconsin, or the famous "Ridges" of Door County.

I was distressed to have no space for the interesting material I received from my pal Steve Swedish, Milwaukee musician and entrepreneur, who told me about old theatre days in Milwaukee when the Pabst, the Academy of Music, the Bijou, Alhambra, Davidson, Majestic, Crystal, Empress, and Star theatres were all running full blast. I wanted to tell in detail Steve's story about the night in 1918 that the great French actress Madame Sarah Bernhardt played at the Majestic in a special performance of patriotic French sketches for the Milwaukee French Alliance and that nobody applauded the madame because the members of the French Alliance couldn't understand any French. And I would have loved to tell some of the great yarns of Irma Phillipson and Dore and Gene Reich about nostalgic horse-and-buggy days in the "Athens of America" — Milwaukee. Next time I will certainly get to those. About all I can say now is that I have found Wisconsin a treasure house of comment and of story tellers that can hardly be matched.

I had a glorious time visiting with the Wisconsin people. I only wish it could have gone on and on. To everyone who told me "how it really happened," my intense gratitude; and to those who made the book possible: Dean Joe Wilson, Dean Harold Montross, my friend Walter Bjoraker; my editor, Diana Balio; August Derleth and Professor John Thomson, the Research Committee of the University of Wisconsin Graduate School, the library of the State Historical Society at Madison, the Agricultural and Life Sciences Library, and the other libraries who helped; to my secretary Arnita Ready, and her fine assistant Jo

Ann La Rock of Middleton. I could not have done without them, nor without my wife, Maryo, and my two colleagues Ralph Kohlhoff and Mike Warlum, who took over a lot of my work when I was out gabbing. It takes a lot of cooperation, that's all I can say. And I had better not forget my friend and partner L. G. Sorden, who encouraged me almost every day and added some to my task by suggesting lots of things I ought to include. A few names have been changed, and certain persons disguised to save embarrasment and to protect the innocent!

What I tried hard to do was to let the people tell it. I hope the true flavor of what they said came through in print as it certainly did in their spoken narratives. I met some masterful yarn spinners. If I could only get them all together in one place, what a living and interesting and articulate archives they would be!

What I have personally received out of the whole thing is the knowledge that Wisconsin does have unique flavors; a rare beauty of all the seasons, a unique geography, and most alluring of all, a regional and hard-to-define mysterious sensation that comes to a constant traveler and observer: a far and faint sound from sky and hills and streams and lakes, or perhaps only the echo and memory of many, many things both ancient and new. The mystery, at least, is real to me.

Robert E. Gard
Madison, 1969

# CONTENTS

# Table of Photographs

II. Old Dodgeville Home

III. Tobacco Shed in Early Morning

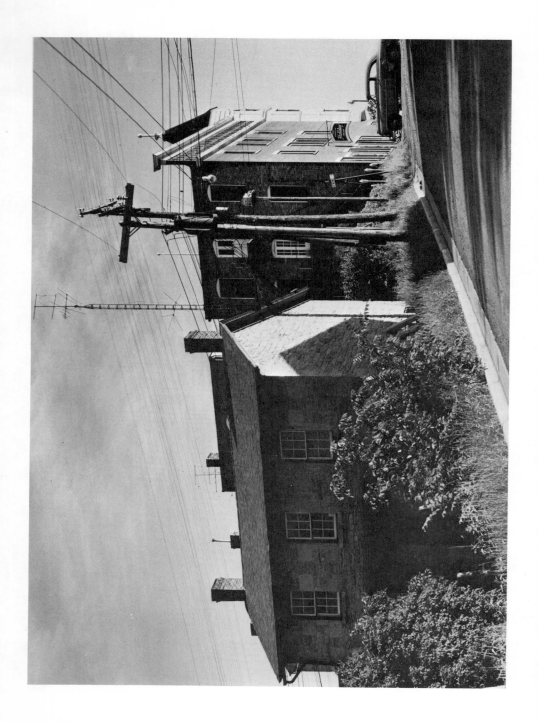

IV.  Old Cornish Cottage in Mineral Point

# PART ONE -
# UPLANDS COUNTRY

V. Uplands Field in Spring

# The Uplands

It was January when I started out to collect the materials for this book. We had been having some unpleasant weather in southern Wisconsin, not very cold but wet and clammy. I had a new pair of overshoes purchased at Cubby Cosper's General Clothing Store in Spring Green, a new pair of long winter underwear, and a new bag that my niece Ellen-Clarke in Detroit had given me for Christmas. It was a particularly fine bag for my purpose, for it was a combination of brief and overnight case, and in it I stowed my small tape recorder, many rolls of recording tape, ballpoint pens, and spare batteries. I was all set to sample the flavors of Wisconsin!

On the Monday morning I started we were having a spell of bad fog in the Madison area. As I had breakfast with my wife, Maryo, I heard the Dane County Sheriff's Department report urging all travelers to forge abroad only if essential. Maryo wondered whether I should go, but I have always responded to fog — it stirs me creatively — and anyway, having waited for twenty-five years to begin the book I had in mind, I considered my travel extremely essential. So I did pack up that morning and set forth in a Ford out Highway 14 toward Cross Plains, Black Earth, Mazomanie, Arena, and Spring Green, hoping to glean on that day some interesting views of past and present Wisconsin in those places. Whenever possible, I would press further afield to Richland Center, Muscoda, Boscobel, Mineral Point, Dodgeville, maybe down to Monroe, and even out to Cassville.

Before I left Madison I had called up Robert Graves, who lives near Spring Green behind Frank Lloyd Wright's great house, Taliesin, and Bob said he would be at his farm around noon. If I dropped by we could have a little drive around the country.

It was a bad day to see the country. Fog in the Wisconsin River Valley behaves in queer ways. It can shut you in completely — impenetrable walls — but then it may open up suddenly, especially in winter. In the clear places you can see the dark etching of the land perfectly, almost intensely; then the fog drops in again and is thicker than ever.

On the January day when I went out to see Bob Graves, the fog descended like a heavy set of gray theatre drapes and held the car and me in our own world. There was only the slushy sound of tires hitting the pockets the melty weather had left in the pressed-snow road.

But I don't really need to see the countryside this morning. A sharpened memory reveals the hills and the valleys to me, and I recall the many summertime trips I have made along Highway 14 and the back roads adjacent; the way the hills looked then: the different shadings of the grasses; the prairie vegetation that still exists on the slopes and along the highways, or along the railroad right-of-way. In summer there are masses of wild flowers, switch grass, and prairie Indian grass, big and little bluestems mixed with the invading cedars. The birds have planted many cedars on the hills — the tall red cedar on the uplands and the creeping juniper on some of the sandstone outcrops. Not so many years ago the hills were almost bare. Now, in places, they are nearly covered again with evergreen, for the cedar waxwings, fond of the fruits of the cedar, have carried seeds far and near.

The hills in southwestern Wisconsin are in a period of change. I doubt that this change is anything new. These hills have been covered with vegetation, then bare, then covered again many times. The north-facing bluffs have birch and red and white oak and basswood; on the south-facing slopes are prairie grasses and bur oak.

In the early spring wild flowers begin to cover the partially balded hills. A succession of flowers will appear in a definite order, until fall.

First come the pasqueflowers in March, followed by buttercups, purple aven, birdfoot violets, catspaw, sheep sorrel, and puccoon. The yellow flower of the early spring is the buttercup, and the waxy petals are like small, hot suns in the prairie grass; when the birdfoot violets come the south faces of the hills are a mass of pale orchid, for the birdfoot violet is never the deep violet of the woodland flower. Mounds of puccoon appear, vivid yellow, along with the yellow wild indigo that in winter turns to leaves gray and stiff, with pods and rattling seeds inside. On the hills there is lupine, blue and lavender, wild bergamot-Oswego tea, and purplish-blue spiderwort in the flat meadows; even a pale bluish-white spiderwort grows along the roadways from Spring Green to Lone Rock.

Along the roadways, also, are day lilies with orange and purple spots, and in low, marshy places and along the Wisconsin River are brilliant scarlet clumps of cardinal flowers that come in late July. Even with all this color I wonder what the look of

2

the country would have been when it was wild and unbroken.

Of the prairies not much now remains. There were once great prairielike sections in southern Wisconsin, and the names still remain of some of them: Arlington Prairie, Empire Prairie, Barnes Prairie, Walworth and Rock prairies, Sauk Prairie, Ridge Prairie, Star Prairie, and many others. And when the early French explorers came through there were flat areas similar to prairies with great herds of game: buffalo, deer, and some elk. The Indians lived well without great effort and with almost no agricultural activity except to pick berries and harvest the Pomme-de-Prairie and nuts. In places the prairie grasses would hide a man walking upright; sometimes even a man on horseback would be almost hidden by the tall wild grasses. On the breast of the prairie were immense groves of oak, like islands.

Surely there is poetry and great symbolism in the remaining prairie elements. Of it all — the wildness, the solitude, and the sway of grasses — tiny plots of prairie alone remain. Often only a scientist can identify the prairie remnants or the prairie plants struggling on hills or "goat slopes."

Once many ancient bur oaks stood in groves in the midst of the prairie. They maintained themselves by toughness and a cork protection that prevented the many grass fires from destroying their vital fibers.

In the ground around these trees of the oak openings were oak grubs, rootings that sent up annual shoots that in turn were destroyed by grass fires. Still the roots and the lower stems clung to life so that, when the settlers came, the grass fires stopped, the grubs began to grow, spoiling the beauty of the oak openings.

The settlers were stirred poetically by the beauty of the oak openings and, being "savanna" people, they made homes near the trees on the prairie. To the settlers, deep forests were full of mystery and darkness, while the open prairie had a loneliness of a different kind. They liked groves of trees from which they might see out at the world.

I pick up Bob Graves at his farmhouse, and the Uplands country, as we drive out of the Wyoming Valley to the high ridge on Highway 23 south of Spring Green, seems to lift with the fog and open out to give a great sense of openness and freedom.

High on a point over the valley, Alex Jordan built his

3

"House on the Rock," a strange ultramodern-Renaissance un-dwelling that sometimes attracts 10,000 visitors on a weekend. Nearby is the Uplands Studio, which the Uplands Arts Council remodeled from a large old barn, with Robert Graves, "the Renaissance Man of the Uplands," doing most of the labor and the design. Far down below in the Wyoming Valley, where the Uplands begins, and on a bank of the Wisconsin River, is the fine Spring Green Restaurant, built by Bud Keland from original designs by Frank Lloyd Wright. Long before his death, Wright himself put up the beams of the restaurant, but the building was not finished until 1967. It was, indeed, completed on the very September evening that Lady Bird Johnson visited Spring Green, and they were still laying the last of the sod as her car rolled up the restaurant drive. That visit in Spring Green has, and will continue to become, a part of the local folklore.

Bob Graves is tall, rapid. I think I could make him up to look more like Abe Lincoln than Lincoln ever looked himself (of course it takes a theatre man to understand what I mean by that!). Bob is moody, individualistic, dynamic. He is a former marine, former oarsman on the University of Wisconsin crew, and when he gets time, a landscape architect who got his training at the Frank Lloyd Wright Foundation and at the University of Wisconsin. Bob is determined that the Uplands will retain its native character and that it will somehow remain unspoiled despite the rapid commercialization that threatens to place hot dog stands, fruit markets, and sideshows all along the beautiful Uplands roads.

I have known Bob since he once invited me to Spring Green to talk about building an amphitheatre where "plays better'n those up at Stratford, Ontario could be going on so folks out in southwestern Wisconsin might see the best right on their own doorsteps!" . . . a philosophy with which I have great sympathy.

Bob lives on the family place, formerly a part of the Wright holdings, for Bob's father, Ben, was farm manager for Wright. Himself a part of Iowa County folklore, Ben Graves was known far and wide as a man you could ride the river with — large, generous, a good manager, and a fine human being. He kept the several thousand acres of the Wright land cropped and fertilized and managed the land in such a way that it not only gave back the harvest of grain and cattle but also preserved the character of Wright and Taliesin, for it was no ordinary farm operation.

Each workday at 3 P.M. work stopped on the Wright lands for afternoon tea, and the hired men as well as the architectural apprentices, who were expected to work in the fields, socialized together.

Bob Graves then is a product of both his father and of Frank Lloyd Wright. Disciple is much too mild a word to describe Bob's attitude toward Wright. Bob was one of those devoted friends who assisted in the Wright funeral in 1959 and walked in the procession that conveyed the architect's body, on a simple farm wagon, to the tiny chapel in the valley near which Wright is buried with only a chunk of field stone, on edge, to mark his grave.

On the one hand, Bob works to make the Uplands an attractive place for visitors, with fine restaurants and accommodations. But — and this is part of his tragic dilemma — though he wants the Uplands to prosper, he also works compulsively to preserve the Wright character of the land, the quiet, poetic loneliness that Wright and his architecture represented.

Bob drives the car and I listen as the university Ford clunks and chunks through slush and hole-riven roads, as we circle and come back above the Wyoming Valley. It was into this valley that the Joneses, Welsh farmers, brought a sense of education, culture, and religion. Born in Richland Center, twenty miles distant, Frank Lloyd Wright worked on his Uncle James Lloyd-Jones's farm and learned many of the approaches to nature that remained his landmarks throughout life.

But I am interested only indirectly in Wright. More, I want to hear the stories, see the people who today throw light on the patterns both past and present in the valley through memories of the past and realities of the present.

"Bob," I ask, "why do you like this country so much? You've told me many times that this valley and these hills were the greatest place God ever made. Now, why?"

"I had the opportunity to work around Taliesin," Bob said, "in the days when Mr. Wright was around, and my father was manager of the farm. I knew well many of the old timers who worked with my father. There was something mystic about it: working in the fields of Taliesin with the students, stopping for tea, and hearing the conversations that ranged over what seemed to me then the whole field of human knowledge. Yet there was earthiness there too, the daily farm life. The smells and feel of toil. Well, after the Korean War and after I had finished a degree at the university, I wanted to come back here. To this community."

"What about the city folks?" I asked. "All the Chicago and Madison and Milwaukee people who are buying up all the land in these hills? How about the big ski hill that Bud Keland is opening right across from your farm. How about all that? Doesn't it disturb your mystic dream?"

"It disturbs me," Bob said. "I looked out of my window one morning and I suddenly saw a parking lot filled with cars. I know it's great for the area . . . new business, and so far we've kept the signboards out; but parking lots are not what I came here to discover, or rediscover, about this country."

We are passing the Wyoming Valley Methodist Church, white, wooden frame, heartland architecture of the 1850s backed up against the hills, a symbol for the whole region. "And this church," Bob said, "where my family went every Sunday, was the center of life, almost. There was a youth fellowship of more than thirty that met on Sunday evenings when I was a kid. Now maybe there will be five come, and somehow I don't feel that my children are getting what I did out of this community. But of course a lot that I got out of it had to do with what people around here thought of Mr. Wright. The idea that Mr. Wright was here gave them something to talk about, always. He was an unfailing topic of conversation. I suppose there's excitement here now, but it's not the same as the excitement that came from his personality, and the apprentices that came from all over the world.

"Then these old codgers who lived around here. Paul Holmes, and an old guy named Ray Winch who lived over by Tower Hill Park, and a lot of others. Salty old men. I enjoyed them very much, and my father enjoyed and appreciated what they had to offer to the whole flavor of the country.

"Over where the new restaurant is, the new Spring Green, that used to be just a coffee place that also sold beer; and on a Saturday evening you could always find these old guys there, gassed up, telling yarns. And old Tracy Hickox fiddling over by the stove. And you know, it's a funny thing, but I believe most of the city people who are buying land out here are hoping to get a sense of the country, the quiet, and the flavors that I grew up with. Maybe they don't articulate it, but they're seeking something unique, and something that is really in and of these hills."

6

Bob Graves believes, among many other things, that the lure of the past is definitely returning to the Wyoming Valley through the yarn spinners. Somehow, he says, it's the tellers of stories that have to make the carry-over between the past and the present so the present knows how humorous, how appealing the past really was.

"It was bachelors like those old fellows who used to work for us over on the Wright farm," Bob said. "We had one bachelor, old Jeff Wilson, an Englishman. He never did wear socks. I remember that about him. He was a big, heavy-set fellow, wore one pair of overalls all summer long. He never washed them or himself either, I guess. We had a purebred Hereford bull, big, gentle . . . pretty much like Jeff. Some folks said they kind of looked alike, actually; and, well, Jeff fell in love with this bull. It was a real affair, I tell you. Every Sunday Jeff would get likkered up, and every Sunday P.M. he would come over to our barn to see that bull, and get on a crying jag. He would set there in the half-dark of the barn, right close the bull's head. Called him Sunshine. That's what he called that bull. Sunshine. Dad would have to go down to the barn and get Jeff out of there and take him home. Used to set there and talk to that bull for hours on a Sunday afternoon."

"You ever hear him talk?"

"Oh, hell, yes."

"What'd he say?"

"Well, things like a fellow would say to a woman, maybe. Tender love things. I mean they were tender, for old Jeff. And then he'd talk about this guy or that guy and what SOBs they were. Then he would get to crying and tell old Sunshine what a terrible time he'd been having, and I swear the old bull would get to crying, too — teacups of water rolling off his cheeks! Pathetic. But it was somebody old Jeff could talk to. Only one he had. Makes a difference, especially out in the country, if you got somebody to talk to, somebody to pour it out to. Well, Jeff had old Sunshine.

"When the Badger Ordnance Works up at Baraboo opened up, Jeff went up there to work. When he had been working there about three weeks, I guess he got likkered up before he went to work one day. Jeff had him a Model A Ford, and he tipped this Ford over so, when the bus to Badger came by, old Jeff was still inside the car. It was raining and the people on the bus got off to help. The bus driver yelled to old Jeff said, 'Hey, there! Can we help you?' and old Jeff says, 'Hell, no. I'm just in here settin' out of the rain.' He wouldn't have a thing to do with any of 'em. So the bus just went on and left Jeff there in the upside down Ford. Shows how independent these old boys were.

"And even in Prohibition times, when even a lot of the best folks up in these hills were makin' moonshine, still they had a rigid set of values. Old Mabel Bennett, ran a speakeasy and made plenty of bootleg. One day Sam Stafford and Harry Pilgrim came over to visit Mabel. Sam had a model A Ford coupe, and while Sam was in the house buying some moonshine from Mabel, Harry stole two fat chickens that was sunning themselves out in the yard. He put 'em in the trunk of Sam's car. Well, Sam didn't know anything about the chickens, and Harry got 'em out when he wasn't looking. Guess there was a big Rhode Island Red chicken feed over to Harry's house.

"Mabel, though, found out about it. Somebody told her Sam had stolen the chickens, so she got the law onto Sam and to save himself he had to tell that it was Harry that done it. The case went to court and Harry got a year in Waupun, just for stealin' two hens. Old Mabel never wavered. Justice was justice.

"Yep," Bob continues, "there is a real streak of practicality in the folks hereabouts. In 1931 Mr. Wright had a whole slew of chickens, and somebody began to steal 'em. Mr. Wright told Wes Peters to find out who was doing it. So Wes and Jerry Caraway set a trap and to their surprise they caught old Joe Maxwell who was hired to be taking care of these same chickens. They caught Joe red-handed with a sack of Rhose Island Reds in each hand. Didn't bother him any. He says, 'Howdy, boys, real glad to see you. Foxes are so bad this summer, decided to carry Mr. Wright's chickens over to my place so I could take better care of 'em.' Mr. Wright laughed fit to kill when Wes told him what happened. Mr. Wright let old Joe keep the chickens. Mr. Wright was like that. Sometimes.

"The first Joneses moved into Wyoming Valley in the early 1860s. They had first settled across the Wisconsin River but found that the land wore out too rapidly there. The Valley was suited to their Welsh temperament and love of hills. It was a large family. Richard, the patriarch, [Frank Lloyd Wright's grandfather] and his sons, Thomas, John, James, Enos, and Jenkin. They were strong, hard-working, religious. They brought the first advanced farming methods into the valley; two of the daughters,

Jennie and Nell, both teachers, brought the first advanced educational methods into southwestern Wisconsin. Their Hillside School offered broad, progressive education in a time when such ideas were mere whispers. The son of their sister Anna and a wandering musician and preacher, William C. Wright, was a lad named Frank Lloyd Wright who finally left the University of Wisconsin to try his luck in Chicago as an architect. He designed his first building for his aunts: the Hillside School.

"There always seemed to be a tragedy connected with the Joneses. In 1913 a threshing crew was taking a steam engine — you know, one of the old kind with high wheels at back and a smokestack in front — up the valley toward one of the Jones farms. They were crossing a little bridge over the creek. The great weight of the engine broke the bridge right in. The engine buckled and the steam scalded two of the men to death. Then James Jones climbed down over the engine, tryin' to help, and he broke a leg. Something happened. He died in a short time. They are buried down next to the chapel near Mr. Wright. The chapel was built by the Jones family.

"One of the hired men at Taliesin would never work in the field back of the chapel. They used to grow tobacco there. One day in the early 1900s they were working in the tobacco field. There was only one cloud in the entire sky. Just one. Blue sky all around. Suddenly a lightning bolt came out of that one cloud and struck one of the workers dead. So this hired man would nevermore work in that field again. He figured it was God's warning to somebody. Maybe him.

"But I tell you, there's a kind of mystery that does hang over this valley. I've heard the sounds from the hills sometimes . . . I dunno . . . "

Now we are sloshing past Trish Carroll's store at Clyde. I never yet saw a smaller place than Clyde, Wisconsin. There's almost nothing to recognize it as a place. Used to be a lot there, but now there is only Trish's little store, which is also a Shell gas station, and a few houses.

"See that parking meter out behind the store?" asks Bob.

"What in blazes is a parking meter doin' out here in the country?"

"Farfetched ideas aren't infrequent out here. One day John Miller, editor of the *Dodgeville Chronicle*, came out to Trish's store. You know, folks like to gather in certain places, and a lot of the country folks do like to come to Trish's place. Oh, they play a little poker, talk about each other. You know.

"Well, John, he drove over from Dodgeville, and would you believe, there wasn't a place to park anywhere around Trish's. John claimed he had to park about a half-mile away. He came storming into the store yelling that he was going to insist on them putting in parking meters. Parking was impossible in Clyde, and so on.

"Trish, she played right along and says that if John could get a parking meter she would put it up. So John got a parking meter, old one I guess, or maybe he stole it, from the city of Richland Center, and Trish put it up back of her store. And you know, damn fools from everyplace would park there and pay money into that fool thing. Trish took quite a little money out of it until somebody stole it one night for the nickels!

"John got Trish another one, and this time Trish had it set in two or three feet of cement. Only thing, this meter is busted and won't take any nickels."

We go into the tiny store to visit a little while with Trish. She is tall, really very beautiful, in her seventies. She speaks frankly on almost any subject and can keep up easily with the men who rely on her for advice on many things. Life in a place like Clyde can be pretty limited, at least it would seem so to me. But Trish Carroll, who has lived in Clyde all her life, has other ideas.

"I'm awfully proud of the people we have here," Trish said, "and I tell anybody that stops. Maybe this afternoon, if you'd stopped here and were going to come in here to live, you know the answer I would have gave you?"

"I don't know."

"This place is just like what you left. A community is just what you make it. If you're liked where you left, more'n likely you'll get liked right here."

"Folks still pretty neighborly around Clyde?"

"I tell you for sadness, for sickness or death, you can't beat the town of Clyde. You went to a funeral, Lutheran, Protestant, Catholic, don't make any difference. If you went to the home in the evening and looked at the crowd, you couldn't tell. Such a good neighborhood and especially in death. Can't be beat. I always say, just like my dad did fifty years ago, 'Treat 'em kindly while they live and bury 'em when they die.' I try to do the same."

10

# Bear Valley and the New York Candy Kitchen

B ob said we ought to take a look at Bear Valley, so after we leave Clyde we come down off the hills and cross the Wisconsin River south of Lone Rock. Just by the Highway 130 bridge, beside the river on the south side, is a cliff that a lot of water drips down. Every Christmastime local folks put a few buckets of vegetable coloring up where it can run down with the water. The icicles hanging to the cliff are therefore of many colors. It's a queer feeling, in a fog, to come around the curve there and see those long, colored icicles.

Ever since coming to Wisconsin I have heard about Lone Rock and the temperature. Said to be the coldest spot in the Middle West, it advertises itself as "The coldest spot in the Nation with the warmest heart." Indeed, many mornings Lone Rock draws the prize for being the coldest place in the United States. Perhaps it doesn't really deserve its reputation. Gaylord Trumbel, chief of the U.S. weather and air patrol station there, told me that one reason Lone Rock is thought to be so cold is that they keep hour-by-hour records and other places don't. "We know how cold it really is," Trumbel said. "They don't!"

Some say Lone Rock — a quiet, very midwestern little town — has a seething undercover life. I wouldn't know much about that except what Helen Silko, who drives into Madison every day from her home in Lone Rock, tells me. As secretary to the Rural Sociology Department (just down the hall from my university office), she has learned a good deal about people, and she says that what goes on in Lone Rock would make very interesting reading but that everybody knows so much about everybody else that nobody dares say a word.

One thing that most folks don't know about Lone Rock is that Charles Lindbergh landed at the little airfield there one day in 1923, when he was a barnstorming young pilot. The Wisconsin River was away up that year and the whole country was flooded. Dr. Bertha Reynolds at Lone Rock village didn't know what to do because she had emergency calls from both Plain and Clyde — really sick people in both places. She got in touch with Lindy, who was very ready to help. He cranked up his plane and took the doctor to both locations, landing in farmers' fields. All patients were saved! Incidentally, Dr. Reynolds was one of the beloved physicians of Wisconsin. She was trained at the University of Nebraska and at the Woman's Medical College in Chicago.

She retired in 1961 and died at 93.

But to get back to Bear Valley . . .

The way folks up in Bear Valley do things now, it's like this; Paul Kooiman of Lone Rock told me this story: Schumacher, who lived in the Crandal House up in Bear Valley, came into a store one day, and Baker, who was operating the store, had a big, live rattlesnake in a cardboard box. Schumacher was pretty much afraid of snakes, and Baker took his rattler and playfullike began to chase Schumacher around the store and finally out into the street. Made Schumacher so mad that he called the Richland County sheriff. The sheriff came over and says to Baker, "You got a snake, a live rattler you been keepin.' "

Baker says, "Yep."

"Well," says the sheriff, "we got a complaint about that rattlesnake and about you chasin' folks with it. So you got to destroy the snake."

"All right," says Baker, "and I know who complained about my pet rattlesnake, the coward! If he's gonna complain about me and my snake to you, sheriff, I think you oughta know somethin' about his still!"

Bear Valley lies north of Highway 14 on Highway 130. It is beautiful farming country, and driving north, through the valley, Bob Graves chats about the region and its charms. It was settled by farmers from New York State, very progressive. For example, they had the first cooperative rural telephone system in the state, and the homes they built are really magnificent!

"Are there any of the old Greek revival style places out here that were so popular in New York State in the 1820s and 30s and 40s?"

"We're coming to one now," said Bob. We passed a lovely white dwelling with the typical doorways and white columns, which I had seen so often far back in the central New York State hills when I lived at Ithaca. I have never forgotten those houses.

"There's a whole lot of fine mansions on this valley road," Bob said. "They're simply magnificent homes! Some of 'em with twenty rooms! Look at the size of that one!" he said, pointing to a rambling brick house that could almost rival some of the great country houses of England.

"Mr. Wright's father is buried up here at the old Brown Church. Interesting story about him. Time of the Civil War, Mr.

Wright's father, who was an itinerant preacher, needed some money to buy his way out of the draft. You know how they were able to do that. So he sold his violin, which was reported to be a Strad, to a settler up here, and supposedly it was still floating around in the vicinity. Well, three weeks ago we found it. It is a very fine violin, but not a Strad. A gal by name of Lorna Carswell in Lone Rock has it now. She was a teacher."

"Does she play the violin?"

"Nope."

"This next house," Bob said, indicating a charming, rambling stone one, "is owned now by a Negro couple from Chicago, people by the name of Vaughn. Some tried a little, locally, to keep them out. Circulated a petition. Didn't get to first base. Folks in the valley were more than glad to welcome the Vaughns.

"Mr. Wright's father, William Cary Wright, came here from Richland Center to preach at the Brown Church. He and his first wife are buried in the churchyard. This is the church right here."

We pull up beside a charming old church, brown, wooden, well over a century old. Tall cedar trees tower over the building.

"Maybe we can see the Wrights' tombstone," said Bob.

And we did locate it — tall, red granite — from the car, but we didn't get out. The day was too messy to go through the fog and wet slush through the old burying ground.

Bob reminded me that William C. Wright's second wife was the mother of Frank, and that *she* is buried in the Lloyd-Jones family graveyard in Wyoming Valley. We drive on toward the tiny town of Bear Valley. As we went, I thought about the New York State settlers and how they came out to Wisconsin, mostly over the old Erie Canal, on to the Lake Michigan shore, and over to Bear Valley and other places in southern Wisconsin. The New York State names thickly sprinkle the Wisconsin landscape; there is even an Ithaca, Wisconsin, about eight miles from the Brown Church, a tiny place, not at all like the Ithaca at the south end of Cayuga Lake in York State so fond in my memory of Cornell University--still the product of a homesick dream, you can bet.

The bar in Bear Valley village used to be called the New York Candy Kitchen. Nobody knows why, unless it was to disguise a speakeasy during Prohibition. If it was, they carried the disguise to absurd lengths. The bar is now called the Valley

Bar, and it is operated by Dorothy and Martin, friendly young folks.

A lot of citizens in the valley gather at the long, golden oak bar with a line of deer antlers behind it. Dorothy, who takes her turn at bartending, is pretty and slender; she sits on a stool behind the bar when she isn't busy with customers, exchanging gossip and information. One can view the main street through the window, but only briefly because there isn't so much of Bear Valley anyway.

Bob Graves and I have dropped in, hoping to get some intimate side glimpses of Bear Valley life, past and present. We have ordered beers, which Dorothy has drawn for us, and Bob is exchanging some remarks with Dorothy when, by some golden chance, two denizens of Bear Valley wander in. They are Otto Schultz and Rudy Dederich, both born and raised in the valley.

At first things are kind of quiet. Bob knows Otto because some time ago Otto offered Bob a chance to bid on eighty wild acres he had for sale. Bob went to Otto's house to talk about the eighty, and Otto's wife told Bob she just that day sold the eighty acres to Otto, her husband! Bob does a double take, but it is the right information. Mrs. Schultz, who is a sharp business women, has indeed sold the eighty acres to her husband on a land contract, no less. She is collecting money from him every month!

Otto orders beers for everybody. We thank him. He digs coins out of an old-fashioned pocket book, the kind with a snap catch on the top. At 67, he has a plump, very round face and a humorous mouth. Both Otto and Rudy are wearing bib overalls, that bear the marks of honest labor. Rudy, broad faced and kindly, is larger than Otto and moves slowly, always with a firm purpose, even when he grasps a beer glass.

Rudy's grandfather was a German immigrant who came to Milwaukee and Madison in the 1850s. In Cross Plains he worked for a time as a wheelwright and bitterly left three children in the Cross Plains Cemetery. He and his wife then moved northwest to Bear Valley, where they found themselves the only Germans amidst a frontier community of Irish and Yankees (mostly from New York State, Herkimer and Tompkins counties).

When Grandpa Dederich tried to buy supplies and some straw to stuff bedticks, the Irish sold him nothing. They did not want to get a bunch of German kids started in Bear Valley.

When he needed lumber to build a house, however, Grandpa Dederich pulled gold coins out of his purse to pay. At the sight of gold, which they had not seen for a long while, the Irish sold him anything he needed.

So there are Irish and more Germans in the valley. Both are Catholic and there is some contention between the groups. At the crossroads Killian Church, south of Bear Valley, the Irish tombstones run north and south across the yard, and the German tombstones run east and west. They wanted divergent ways even in the cemetery! The Protestant church is still called the Brown Church, where Bob Graves and I had stopped.

Rudy tells us these things as we quietly drink beer.

"The valley is a pleasant place," Rudy says. "You would almost think that Bear Creek was coming down through the valley like an artery of nature. And different kinds of trees! So beautiful. Pines and maples and birches, greens and browns and white! Oaks and hickory. You never saw anything like the color out here in the fall. You drive down the valley, you feel like you're in God's own paradise. At least that's the way I feel."

"Me too," Dorothy says. "It's something good and wonderful!"

"Wonderful," says Rudy. "And down south of here is Point Judith. Ever hear of it?"

"No."

"Judith was a McCloud," said Rudy. "Those McClouds. The greatest hunters and Indian fighters ever lived in this country. The early days, this valley was full of game and the McClouds got a good share of it. Even elk in here then. Once when they was coming up through here on a hunt in the 1840s they saw three Indians following them. They laid in wait and watched, and they could see the Indians was on their trail. And when the Indians come along, the McClouds shot all three. One was gettin' away, but they got him too. Then they wrote to Gov. Henry Dodge that they had kilt some Indians. Dodge he come out personally to congratulate the McClouds. Dodge didn't like the red men. But that wasn't the end of it, because the Indians didn't appreciate to have their folks being murdered that way. So one day they come upon the McCloud girl, Judith, out in the open. Started to chase her. Was going to exact vengeance upon the McClouds through the girl, I suppose. She run of course. Was a fast runner. Led the Indians a good chase but finally they was about to take her. She run to the top of a point, a big bluff down south of here, and as they was about to seize her, she jumped over. Some say she jumped into a cave on the face of the cliff, but mostly they say she hopped over and was killed. Anyhow that place is called Point Judith after Judith McCloud. I knew a feller once who said he knew where Judith is buried."

Bob Graves and I listen, drinking beer. The fog outside gets thicker. We are certainly not anxious to leave. Rudy leaves for a few minutes to go to his home, which is just down the street from the tavern, to fetch an item of local history. He has been collecting things and pasting them in a huge wallpaper sample book. The book probably weighs twenty pounds. Dorothy says, with real concern, "I hope Rudy doesn't lug *that* over here. He was sick not long ago."

Rudy doesn't bring the big book, but he does bring a manuscript, his grandfather's own account of his early life in Dane and Richland counties. Someone has translated it from the original German. We all bend over the manuscript, almost amazed at the spiritual strength of the pioneers that led them through the terrible hardships and bitter losses of frontier Wisconsin settlement.

Dorothy breaks the spell. "Ryan," she says suddenly.

Otto instantly swells up like an old fightin' rooster. He takes a large swallow of beer and hollers, "I'll take Ryan on any time! Yes, and anyone else he wants to persuade along! If I so much as spot that son-of-a-gun I will skin him down the front and sew buttons up the back!"

"Just what was your trouble with Ryan?" Rudy asks gently.

"Why it was that gol danged dog," yells Otto. "That no count, yeller, belly-draggin' houn' dog!"

"I didn't know there was a dog involved," says Dorothy.

Dorothy's pretty little daughter comes home from school and Otto waits courteously while the child is carefully taken care of. Then he says, "Another beer all aroun'!" He digs a bill out of his ancient pocketbook.

I have had about four beers, but to decline might interfere with Otto's story, and I did want to know about the dog. We tilt the glasses.

"That dog," says Otto, and he rolls his glass, "there was this auction over by Ithaca. Suggs was the auctioneer. Suggs is good! Can talk the fastest I ever heard except for Paul Kooiman.

16

Well, Ryan had these cows for sale. Said they was fair milkers. Looked like it. But don't ever believe appearances, boys, not when Ryan is around.

"Suggs says, 'Boys, Ryan has got a fine stock dog, and whoever buys the most cattle can have the dog free of expense.'

"I seen the dog. Wasn't much to look at, but you can't never tell a turkey by his wattle; so I says to myself, 'Well, maybe I will get the dog. I always wanted me a good cow dog.' So I buy them cows. Bought thirteen. Was unlucky. And Suggs he says to me, 'Well, Otto, you bought the most so you can have the dog.'

" 'No, he don't' yells Ryan.

" 'Like hell,' I says. 'I bought the most cows.'

" 'You don't get the dog nohow,' says Ryan. 'I want the dog bid too.'

"That's when I seen how Ryan was. Crooked as a blackbird's girdle.

"Suggs says that *he* wouldn't auction off the dog. It was a straight-out agreement. Whoever bought the most cows was to take the dog. Ryan he put on like the dog was his best friend, and he would have to have anyway ten dollars for him to ease his pain at partin'. He put on such a show, cryin' and huggin' the dog that I finally says, 'All right, Ryan, five dollars.'

" 'Ten dollars,' says Ryan, and goes on cryin'.

"Well, I finally give Ryan the ten dollars. I musta been crazy to do it, but I couldn't stand the noise he was putting up. Suggs says it is a shame and a crime and he calls down a retribution on old Ryan. But that Irish — — — don't care. He's away out on the highway to hell anyhow, so what does it matter?"

"Now you sound real bitter, Otto," says Dorothy.

"Bitter? Why I hate Ryan stronger 'n pizen. After what he done to me!" Otto raises his left hand. "See this here hand? Ain't much count. But I can whip any Ryan with my one good hand and come apoundin' him with my bad hand when I get him down."

"Must of been somethin' more to it than what you said," says Rudy.

"There was. Plenty. I taken that dog home and tied him up. And that houn' eat through the rope and run away. Back to Ryan. And I went over to get him and Ryan says I could have him but it would cost me five dollars since he had meanwhile give the dog some grub!

"Well, I called Ryan out right there and offered to fight him anyway, underholts or anyhow. He wouldn't. So finally I had to give him five dollars and I took the dog home. Thought I would try him out with the cows. And you know what? That dog wouldn't chase no cows. Just laid on his belly and howled. So I went and drove the cows up to the barn myself, and when I got 'em in there I seen that they was all dry; not a one had been bred.

"When I see Ryan, and I'm gonna see him soon, he had better look out. I am going to hand him a beatin' that'll last him all of his breathin' life! Timber! Beers for everybody! Timber!"

Listening to Otto talk about Ryan, I marvel at the extension of past into present. The Irish-German feud in Bear Valley is still in high gear!

# Vignettes of a Great Man

Spring Green is a small town of 1197. The main street is lined with old trees, and downtown are low business blocks. The old Meyers Hotel (now the Dutch Kitchen), the Gard Theatre, a Cooperative Farmer's Store, a five-and-dime; several taverns, Buck's Bar, the Corner Bar, Hook's Bar, Cubby Cosper's General Clothing Store, Dr. Jerry Kempthorne's Clinic, a new pharmacy, and a few others. I have always been impressed by the fact that there was in Spring Green no real character of the impulse that created Taliesin, and the whole world of Frank Lloyd Wright, for the buildings are, for the most part, of the most conventional middlewestern design, dull and unattractive. The theatre, however, has a new front designed by Wes Peters, chief architect for the Frank Lloyd Wright Foundation, who also did the Kempthorne Clinic, but that's about all the uniqueness that Spring Green can boast, architecturally. I asked some old timers, Cubby Cosper, Maurice Bernard, and Clarence Hutter, about this one night when we were sitting around drinking coffee at Virgil Steele's in Spring Green. I said that I would have thought that Spring Green might have taken on something of the character of Wright and his work.

"Well," Maurice Barnard said, "a few years back they wanted a new post office here. Come to me and wanted to know if I would build it. I said yes, I would build it on one condition: that I get a good rate of interest and that I not have to bid on it. I simply said, 'I'm not bidding for this thing. You are asking me.'

"Well, it was supposed to be a ten percent deal. Some of the people here wanted the building to be designed by Mr. Wright and asked if I would go along with that. I said sure, but maybe it will cost more money because it would be a nicer building. Well, the man from the government didn't seem to be worried about that. He just said, 'Sure.' So Taliesin, that is, Mr. Wright, drew me a set of plans for a Spring Green post office. Free of charge he drew them. And I took those plans and went to Madison, to the fellows I had been talking to, and I said, 'I'm all ready to go. Mr. Wright has made the plans, and I have everything arranged.' You see, I felt mighty good, because we were going to have a Wright building in Spring Green.

"But this government man said, 'Now hold on. There are now two other fellows who want to bid on this job!' Well, I just turned on my heel and walked out, and that was the end of the Wright post office. I figured if this government fellow wouldn't keep his bargain with me, I wanted no part of him. But I still have the plans over to my house. Yes, I do. And I tell you, the Wright post office would only have cost fifteen hundred dollars more than the conventional one."

Frank Lloyd Wright left a spell over the whole countryside, though, even if the village has no Wright buildings. The merchants and residents of Spring Green and the area love to reminisce about Wright even today, for his presence is still strongly felt. There are all kinds of Wright stories told by the man on the street, or the onlooker, or the small businessman with whom Wright did business. Strangely, though, those who helped Wright most in his bleak years and carried him on their books in Spring Green and Dodgeville are among the most loyal of his backers. A fine lady from Dodgeville, so they say, carried Mr. Wright for grocery bills of more than five thousand dollars. He always paid, eventually, as she knew he would. Etta is now an honored guest at every major Taliesin function.

But without question much of the anti-Wright sentiment that strongly exists in Madison has nothing to do with his reputation as an artist. Rather, it is Wright's reputation as a businessman, and a man of moral principle, that is still on trial. "He never paid a bill" is a statement I have heard countless times, or "You wonder sometimes if God didn't mean to punish people like Mr. Wright for their sins, and he did suffer, heaven knows . . . "

I think most of such comments are apocryphal, or are made out of a sense of wronged virtue or defied convention. Most of the commentators are not those who dealt with Wright but those who have absorbed the stories. In some cases, of course, truth must tell that there is some justice in local criticisms of this man of genius.

I myself am interested chiefly out of a passion for local countryside lore, in which Frank Lloyd Wright certainly occupies a central position.

Maurice Barnard is a handsome man, still very active in business. He has lived all his life in Spring Green, loves it there, and now operates a unique business of renting out bulls to all parts of the country. Cubby Cosper is red faced, black haired streaked with grey, short in stature, strongly made, with humor never far beneath the surface of his eyes and face. He is retiring this year after operating a clothing store in Spring Green for more than fifty years. Both men were friends and admirers of Frank Lloyd Wright. Their stories about him were told to me with love, never with malice or animosity. Clarence Hutter, who is tall and has a weathered face, is a farmer who has lived all his life in the neighborhood.

"I wouldn't say that folks hereabouts didn't appreciate Wright," said Maurice Barnard. "When he had money he paid his bills, and when he didn't have money, well, there are quite a few people who worked for him that never got paid. Of course this community never knew in the old days what a genius he really was. Folks thought he was just an ordinary guy that really didn't know what it was all about. So close to the forest, you know.

"When Mr. Wright's folks, the Joneses, came here to this country they lived near my dad's folks down here at Jonesville. My dad's mother was Jones, and Wright's mother, she was Jones too. I used to drive old Mrs. Wright when I was a boy. My father had a car; Mr. Wright didn't believe much in cars in those days. Mrs. Wright used to tell me all about this, but I was too much of a kid, and my dad, you couldn't ever get anything out of him. He wouldn't even tell you what nationality he was. If you asked Dad what nationality he was, he would tell you that he was a Missouri puke, and I didn't know what that was either.

"The trouble with Mr. Wright and the Joneses in general, they didn't value money. Money didn't mean a thing to 'em. A nice sunrise meant much more. We were very good friends, I and my wife, with Mr. Wright's cousins over there, Dick and Mary Jones. We used to be over there a lot, and Dick never cared for any money. Didn't mean anything to him. He'd sooner stand around and visit with people. The dollar didn't seem to mean anything to those people. They were different from the rest of us.

"But when Aunt Jen and Aunt Nell Jones started the new school over at Hillside, you could tell every student that ever went there. Those students had a certain air about 'em. The rest of us never did acquire it. That school was at least fifty years ahead of any other school around. They put a polish on people that they couldn't get anyplace else. It wasn't just the three Rs either. They taught how to live, how to conduct yourself. We never got that in the public schools. Children came to Hillside from all over. I know my father run a store uptown — a confectionery store — and those kids kind of headquartered there. They would run out of money, and Dad would trust them. They wouldn't pay when they left, but they'd come back the next year, and I've seen some of 'em get off the train and come right to the store and pay up and start over.

"The bigger ones would sneak away at night, weren't supposed to, and would walk over to our house. They would knock and my father would get up and ask what they wanted. They would say that they wanted some stuff at the store; my father would throw the keys out the bedroom window and tell 'em to take what they wanted and keep track of it. That happened more than once. So the Jones sisters were giving those students some good instruction."

Cubby Cosper said, "One time Mr. Wright came into my clothing store to get the buttons sewed on his coat by a lady who lived over in the parsonage; a fellow came in with him, a poet I guess he was. Mr. Wright had some letters, and he was thumbing through them, and he comes to this letter that had real fancy writing on it. Mr. Wright kissed the envelope, and he sailed over in the corner, and this poet run after Mr. Wright, and he says, 'Let me see, let me see!' But Mr. Wright says to him, 'Get away, get away. You've got a lot of crust,' he says. Then Mr. Wright sailed over in the other corner, and he opens up this fancy letter and he starts to read it, and the poet says, 'What did she say? What did she say?'

" 'Says that she likes your poetry.'

" 'That all? No particulars, no particulars?' says the poet.

" 'No particulars,' says Mr. Wright. And he went over in another corner and he opened the window and took some deep breaths and he stayed there for a while, just to plague that poet, I guess. He was a character, was Mr. Frank Wright.

"When my store was where the hotel bar is now, Mr. Wright come and stood and talked. 'Say, Cubby,' he says, 'I want you to get this town to let me build 'em a decent town hall. I would like to design 'em a town hall they could be proud of.' And then he stood there a minute and he says, 'I wish you would talk to Mrs. Meyers and get her to let me design a front on this hotel, tear down this old place,' he says. 'I'd design her a real front.' Well, nobody did let Mr. Wright design much of anything around here. It's a shame. But that's small town life, too."

Maurice said, "Mr. Wright and my father were good friends. Why I don't know. They had nothing in common. Sometimes those friendships develop and there's no answer to it. I was small and could go over to Taliesin. And Mr. Wright had long white hair. Nobody else wore their hair like that in them days. He had Japanese servants around there, and one thing and another, and we were just so struck by the whole thing we just swallered our Adam's apple.

"I worked over there the better part of two years when Mr. Wright was in Japan, building the Imperial Hotel. If you're around Taliesin awhile you get so you like that way of living. I don't know what there is about it. It kind of grows on you. It is a kind of different way of life, you might say. I've always wished that I could be like Mary and Dick Jones, Wright's cousins, and be able to have peace of mind, like they had."

I fumbled with a question. Finally I said, "I wish you'd tell me why there is such strong feeling about Mr. Wright. I've lived in Madison a long time, and I was aware of an antagonism from the very first time I heard of Mr. Wright and Taliesin."

"I can tell you part of that," said Maurice. "I was sitting in the barbershop at Cross Plains one day, and a man who runs a service station there, he cut down on Mr. Wright and his talk bordered on the ridiculous, to say the least. Certainly I suppose some things that he said might have been true, but after he got done talking I told him a few true things, and he said, 'I never knew it was that way,' and I said, 'I knew you didn't.' He said, 'I would like to visit with you again sometime.' And maybe it was just ignorance about the way things really were at Taliesin that sparked so much opposition to that beautiful Monona Terrace plan that Mr. Wright designed for the city of Madison and never got built while he was alive.

"To hear a lot of folks talk, especially those in Madison, you would think that Taliesin was an awful place, where no decent person would be safe. There were people who resented Wright. I think one time, if I recall, he proved the university engineers wrong in regard to stress and strain. Well, maybe this kind of thing had something to do with the bitter things said against him. A lot of folks will resent you if you are better equipped than they are.

"And then there was resentment here that goes a long way back, to Wright's family. The Joneses were lax on their financial obligations. They had some bad financial times. But what folks didn't realize was that the Joneses had something that the rest of us didn't have. Evidently Mr. Wright acquired the most of it or made most use of it.'

"Anyway, there is that rather prominent group in Madison who have got their heads together through hate. Nothing but hate. They would stop at nothing to block Mr. Wright, even going into another state and try to tell them there that Mr. Wright didn't know what he was doing.

"Let's just say that Mr. Wright wasn't always as prompt as he could have been in his financial dealings with people around here. And in Madison too. But again, money didn't seem to mean anything to him. They tell about Jack Schoenmann asking Mr. Wright for some money, a bill that Mr. Wright owed Jack. Mr. Wright says, 'Are you worried about the money, Jack?' And Jack says, 'Well, yes I am.' 'Well,' says Mr. Wright, 'You go ahead and worry, because there is no use of both of us worrying.' "

"At the store I managed for Albert Schwartz," said Clarence Hutter, "Mr. Wright owes us a big bill, and Albert says to Mr. Wright, 'Mr. Wright, could you give us a little money on your bill? We've got to have a little money.'

" 'Why sure, Albert,' says Mr. Wright. He feels around in his pocket and dumps everything he had out onto the table. He had over four hundred dollars. Said he brought it to pay on his bill."

"I think this thing is true about Mr. Wright," said Maurice. "If he made a million today, he'd spend two tomorrow."

"He was a great spender," Cubby said, "no question about that."

"Well, he didn't measure things by the dollar and cents like we do. What he could do in his line of work . . . and you can go where you may, and look about, all this modern architecture has followed right after his . . . every pattern. Every architect has copied his style."

"Don't you think the folks at Spring Green ought to be pretty proud of this accomplishment of Mr. Wright's?" I asked.

"I think that some are. Some are still resentful. They haven't the foresight to appreciate a man who lived in their community."

"Are there any other stories about Mr. Wright that are widely known, things he did?"

"I think that Mr. Wright, deep down, was a religious man,"

said Clarence. "But there were times when he'd talk to you, and if he could get a rise outa you, he liked that. He would shock the socks off of you, if he could."

"My brother worked for him for several years plastering," said Cubby, "and he got along real good with Frank. He said that Frank would come out and talk, and he said that even one of those women who was at Taliesin would come out and help plaster. Eloise Pfister. She was quite a girl too. Worked for 'em for several years. Got paid. That was when Mr. Wright was getting a little more on his feet. "But," continued Cubby, "you are right. In the older days Frank sometimes didn't pay his bills. Those people are still awful bitter. But it was their livelihood."

"Well, to be honest," said Maurice, "Frank did use some folks shamefully. They had wives and kids to support. But Frank was different. If he wanted something he would get it. He had the knowhow that way."

"They claim," said Cubby, "that he was at a big meeting at New York and he was to speak at nine o'clock. He was waiting and waiting and he got pretty impatient. About a quarter to nine he says, 'Well, I'm going home and go to bed! He was a little arrogant, you know. He had a lot of very fancy cars. He was extravagant. He called up a girl one time, she was going to the university. She was taking French, and he spent twenty-three dollars just talking to her. From Spring Green to Madison, twenty-three dollars! He was a spender."

"What amazes me," said Maurice, "is that he had the foresight that he did have. Of course, his two aunts had that too. Had foresight the rest of the people didn't have."

"When Mr. Wright built his home over there, Taliesin," said Clarence, "my father worked over there a lot, and him and a cousin of his by the name of Chris hauled rock for that building. And Mr. Wright had at that time a herd of cows on the halfway farm, between the school and Taliesin. He decided that he was going to sell these cows, so Dad and Chris went over to the sale, like many people do, and this Chris was quite a fellow to have a nip on the bottle, and he had a bottle with him, and he says to Dad, 'Let's go in the cow barn,' he says, 'and have a little drink.' So they went into the feed manger there with the cows and had a little drink; when they were having a second or third Mr. Wright come in. They both knew him real well. Chris says to Mr. Wright, 'Hev a drink, Mr. Wright?'

" 'Oh, my gol, Chris,' he says, 'if I drink that I'd go crazy.'

" 'Then hev a drink,' hollered Chris, 'cause you're as crazy as you'll ever git!'

"Wright just throwed up his hands. He built that house on a pinnacle, you know. Everybody thought he was crazy all right. They didn't appreciate him here at all. And people right in this area, right at that time, they never knew what a genius he really was."

"One time," said Maurice rather sadly, "me and my partner sold Mr. Wright a lot of wood, several cords, and we made a deal with him for five dollars a cord. But when we delivered the wood Mr. Wright said we had agreed to sell him the wood for four dollars a cord. Well, we took that to court, but we never got our money. We couldn't prove nothin'. Why Mr. Wright did that I will never know. And you know something? I love him anyway!"

There is a long silence while we contemplate the fallacies of great men. Helen Steele brings coffee and good chocolate cake. Cubby Cosper feels mellow enough to change the subject from Frank Lloyd Wright to old Bill Scallam.

"They were up at the county meeting in Sauk City, and they got to talking about divorces," says Cubby. "Old Scallam was quite a talker, and he said 'You know, the damnedest divorce I ever heard of happened up in our country. There was a feller named George Rink, had a wife named Mary, and they had a little piece of land there that they hadn't put the wheat in yet, and they wanted to get it in before it rained. One team had gone to the mill and the other had gone after a load of gravel, and they didn't have any horses to put it in with.

"Finally he got the bright idee he would take off, leave only one section on the drag, and hitch Mary up and drag it. So he says he started in the middle of the field and everything was going along fine. Finally on the last row around the outside a rabbit jumped out of the brush and, he says, scart Mary like the devil and she run away and smashed the drag all to hell, and he says now George is suing Mary for a divorce!'

"There was a man named Murphy lived up in Bear Valley. You know, there are a lot of Irish up thataway. Murphy he got powerful sick. All the neighbors got together, the doctor from Loganville was away, and the doctor from Reedsburg was sick or something. Anyway he was away, so they got together to hold a consultation to see what to do about Murphy.

26

"Well, Bill Scallam had been doctoring all the horses and everything around the country, and helpin' out, and so the neighbors says to him, 'What do you think we ought to do about Murphy?' Bill he thought for a spell and says, 'Well, I think you ought to give him a physic.' And so they talked on some more about it, and they asked Bill again what to do, and he says again, 'I think we ought to give him a physic.'

" 'How much shall we give Murphy?' "

" 'Well,' he says, 'why don't you go ahead and give Murphy the same as I would give a horse.'

"So he give Murphy the dose of horse physic and he went home. Bill he didn't sleep very well that night thinkin' about Murphy and how the physic would affect him, so he got up bright and early and done his chores up and he went over to Murphy's. When he got there Mrs. Murphy was out splitting wood for the stove. And Bill says, 'And Mrs. Murphy, did it work?'

" 'Oh, my God,' she says, 'it worked. Murphy went forty times during the night and six times after he died!'

"They told one day Scallam went down the road and it was sleighing time in the winter, and he was going along he noticed up ahead a wagon box tipped clear over. And he says he finally got up there and stopped and went over and up would come the wagon box a little and a voice underneath would say, 'Allllll together, Flanagan!' He said they watched that for a while and every little bit the box would raise up and a voice would holler, 'Allllll together, Flanagan!'

"And there an old boy from Bear Valley he was down underneath and he would push up and holler, 'Allllll together, Flanagan . . .' trying to tip it over. Scallam says he finally went and rolled the box off. Old man never thanked him or nothin'. Just got in the wagon and went on his way hollering 'Allllll together, Flanagan!' "

# Rattlesnake Man

A couple of days previously I had called up Helen Steele, who has started the Winsted Book Shop at Spring Green, and Helen had asked her husband, Virgil, to call up Woody Roberts, who lives south of Arena, and tell him I was coming his way and would enjoy hearing some of his snake-catching adventures. Woody has the reputation of being the greatest rattlesnake catcher in all of Wisconsin, maybe in the United States. Woody told Virgil that it was a real pleasure for him to talk about snakes to anybody, anytime, and for me to come on over. Woody's house sits high, on the edge of a valley; and when I drove up in front I could see the large overalled and mackinawed shape of Woody down by the barn where he was fooling with a silver fox that he calls Randy and keeps in a special cage. This fox won't have a thing to do with anybody but Woody, although Woody may have his eye on Randy's pelt, eventually.

Woody hollers at me (you don't have any trouble hearing Woody) to get out of the car and come on over to his shanty where he has a lot of stuff for me to see.

I never saw such a place as Woodrow Wilson Roberts' shanty, and I guess I never saw such a man as Woodrow Wilson Roberts.

The shanty, which stands just across County Road HH from Woodrow's house, contains mostly rattlesnake mementos, but Woodrow also keeps a bearskin, very motheaten, there so he can tell visitors how he bagged this huge, fierce black bear that reared up right over where he had sat down for a minute to eat lunch. There is a big bear trap that holds an exciting and somewhat unbelievable story in its hungry jaws, several jars of baby rattlesnakes, old guns, rocks with strange fossils, and crazy-looking branches of trees. Woodrow loves every single article in that shanty. He will pick up with great and living care a hunk of tree that beavers have gnawed down, and he will show you a beaver's skull with the great front teeth and the back grinders to illustrate how wonderful nature is.

And nature *is* wonderful, especially when you love it and tell it as Woodrow does, savoring like a benediction every single word he utters. I found him a man of great truth and one of nature's true noblemen in the fashion of course, of the romantic theatre of the great nineteenth century actor Edwin Forrest, who created Metamora, the good child of nature, the noble red man. For Woodrow Wilson Roberts is definitely a romantic figure. If one could get him onto a stage, he would instantly capture the imagination of the American public, and, indeed, it might do something to restore our traditions and belief in ourselves as a people. Everything that Woodrow says is truth to him and wonderful. Life is wonderful. People are wonderful. Animals are wonderful. He loves passionately every animal he kills, every snake he takes for the bounty; he loves it, and I am serious when I say that Woodrow is a man of pure and true love.

Even when he is talking in his natural tone of voice, Woodrow can be heard a half-mile away. If he raises his voice a shade you can easily hear him clear over to Arena, three miles north from Woodrow's farm. This is in the Wisconsin tradition of Robert M. La Follette, Sr., who was born in Primrose Township in Dane County. "Fighting Bob" could stand up in the back of a lumber wagon and be heard by a crowd of five thousand; so could Abe Lincoln, they say. Woodrow Wilson Roberts has even better vocal equipment. You don't need your hearing aid when Woodrow speaks, and he is not even in politics.

When I sat down in the Roberts' clean kitchen, I was surprised to learn that the charming wife of this great snake catcher was deathly afraid of snakes. Well might she be, for Woodrow cherishes the snakes he catches. One night when he and his boy Phil were coming home from town they saw a big rattler crossing the road. "Hold the car, Phil," yells Woodrow, "I will catch that snake." He did and brought it home, put it in a box, and took it down to the basement. Mrs. Roberts didn't know it was there, and one day when she was washing clothes she heard a buzzing sound. Thinking something was wrong with the machine she stopped the motor, but the buzzing continued. Suddenly she recognized the sound, turned around, and saw this big old rattler coiled up right by her foot. She gave a scream, tore upstairs, and handed Woodrow a good drubbing.

Folks around the countryside call Woodrow to come and catch snakes that are bothering them. He has a special pair of tongs made by welding a pair of long handles to ordinary, short plier handles. Then a pair of longer tongs is welded to the snout of the pliers themselves. He is so adept with this homemade tool that he can catch a snake every time he presses the handles together. He doesn't miss.

When I went to see Woodrow, he seemed in especially good form. I just turned on my little tape recorder and let him ramble. This is some of what I got:

"Just wanted to ask you, Woodrow, how you catch these pesky varmints!"

"Snakes, you mean? You're asking about rattlesnakes?"

"About rattlesnakes. How do you catch them?"

"Have me a regular tongs that I had a blacksmith make outta pliers. Nothin' to it at all. Just sneak up and grab 'im behind the head. Then I reach down and pinch 'im right down tight with my fingers, and put 'im in a gunny sack. Hardest part is gettin' 'em in the sack. If you got some in the sack to start with, you gotta watch out because a snake can crawl right up the side of a straight building, or he can go right up in the trees even. That's why It's hard to get 'em into a sack, because as soon as you open the sack up they come a'crawlin'. They'll come right out."

"Now what's the most fun you ever had catching snakes?"

"I could talk to you for days just on rattlesnakes. One day though in particular, me and my brother, we was down on his farm, and I went down over a big rock and I looked down, and my goodness! They was seventeen snakes in one pile! I tell you, that was something to see. Old ones and young ones, and I was killin' 'em that day for the bounty. You see, we have a bounty. Get a dollar apiece for the old ones. It was on my brother's farm and he was so scared of 'em, he didn't want a one of them around so he yells, 'Kill 'em every one!' So I whocked down over the pile with my stick and I killed about six, and my goodness, if one didn't have two heads!"

"Two?"

"They was glued together right at the neck, and their noses looked right out like a crotch. Four eyes and there was two mouths and two separate throats. I kept that head for . . . I had a guy here wanted to buy it from me, but I kept it in alcohol."

"Now you were telling me out in the shack that there were going to be more rattlers in a few years than anybody could handle. What'd you mean?"

"You wait and see, and ten years from now, oh, I tell you now, we'll be overrun."

"But why?"

"There's so much land that the farmers don't pasture. The more land that goes into habitat, so to speak, I mean brush, them snakes will multiply, nobody will molest 'em, except the berry pickers. I know places way back in that is just alive with snakes!"

"Now," I said, "this part right around here, south of Arena, does it have more snakes than other parts of the state?"

"This here country is pretty good. And down by Prairie du Chien that's pretty good too. If I ever get so's I can leave the farms here in April I'm goin' to Oklahoma and get in on some of that rattlesnake roundup, where they hunt 'em for a solid week. The guy that has the most, and the guy that has the biggest ones. Oh! If I ever get down there, boy, that's all I'll do is hunt! Here I don't have much time. I knew a friend of mine went down there and he won the prize."

"When did you first get interested in snakes?"

"Well, I took my first two rattlers when I was pretty young. You know, that was in the depression. You remember that?"

"Yes, sir!"

"I used to work for my neighbor Dodge, for fifty cents a day. Hayin' all day long. Mowing hay. Loose hay. My dad he hunted snakes, but he would never let me go because he said I was too young, see. But I finally got away one day and I got me two rattlers. I took them to Paw and says, 'Paw, there's two dollars!' That's like four days' hard work for Delbert Dodge. Whatta you think of that? And from then on I never quit huntin'. Of course, in them days fifty cents meant so much more than it does today."

"They still pay the same bounty today as they did then?"

"Yes. I believe the best I ever did one day, I told my wife, it was eleven o'clock, I says to her I'm gonna go out and see how many I can get before dinner, and I got me three big old mothers with twenty-seven young ones. I just found the rock by accident. I was walkin' up over the hill and I come right on 'em and I just stood back and looked at that sight, and I says out loud, 'There! That's nature's beauty!' I just marvel at it! And I got every one of them snakes. The small rock, I could poke the stick under, and if there was any under there I could poke 'em out the other side, and that one rock has got me over 150 rattlesnakes! That one little rock! Them snakes they all know where it is, and they go up there and they stay, one rock laying on top of another, just enough cracks so they can crawl under. The sun in the daytime it heats up both rocks and the snake crawls in there about six o'clock and then he's got 'im a warm place to lay and that rock above 'im will hold the heat for quite a while. Just like a shelter."

"Where is this rock, Woodrow?"

Woodrow laughs so's you can hear him clean across the valley. "I don't tell anybody where that rock is! I showed my boy, but that's a good rock. You know I cleaned 'em out. I got 'em about all. This year I never got a snake out of there."

"But there were as many rattlers this year as last year, weren't there?"

"Yeah. I was kind of worried last year we had so much frost in the ground. I thought it might have killed some out; but I don't believe it did."

"Ever been bitten by a rattler?"

"Never been bitten, and I sure hope I don't neither. That is bad. Aw, I often worry about it though. You ever read any of them stories in *Outdoor Life?* It's terrible if you ever git bit. I always carry me a little kit. You know, one of them sharp razor blades to cut and let the blood out if you get bit. Well, anyhow, got a friend up in Plymouth, Wisconsin, who turned out to be a desperately good snake hunter. He come down to hunt with me, and he brought his movie camera. He took some pictures and he showed a whole bunch of film to me one day, and I tell you, a movie camera is so much better, because it will show the snake when you get him on the hook, see; and when you bring him out he is squirming around. That makes him look so much nicer! And then color besides. That's really pretty."

"Woodrow, I've heard it said that a rattler will mate with a blacksnake. That isn't true is it?"

"Boy, I never seen one. I seen blacksnakes right in the same rock with rattlesnakes, but I never . . . Gracious! if they mated, would they have rattles? A lot of people think that a bull snake will kill a rattlesnake, but that's absolutely false. I've had 'em in the same pen all summer up here, and they just get along. They lay right in the same pile."

"Woodrow, how many acres do you have in your farm here?"

"Well, I got me two farms. One's got about 160 and this one's got about 190. And then I rent another big farm. That's why I'm too busy. But now my boy's gonna take over. I got four boys. My boy Phil is gonna be married next month, so I'm gonna rent the farms to him and let him."

"These farms been in your family for quite a while?"

"Well, this farm here has, since 1916 I think it was. I was born in the old log house down here. My dad had so many kids that he couldn't have enough names for 'em. There was nine in our family, and I was born the second of August right when they was cuttin' grain. Dad said to the doctor, 'What should I name this one?' And Doc said, 'Name him after the president, Woodrow Wilson.' Wilson is my middle name. Ain't that a terrible name? Oh, Dad was an old Democrat. You see, he liked the Wilson. I never tell anybody that, but Woodrow Wilson Roberts, that's my name. And it's a long string. Most folks call me Woody. When I was in grade school there was two boys in my class. One was Ray and one was Roy. And me with Woodrow! All them letters! Doc says it wasn't fair!"

"Woodrow, you must have quite a philosophy about snakes and people. What do you think of 'em?"

"Boy, I just love snakes! I don't say that they're not dangerous or like that, but I get a thrill out of gettin' 'em. My boys are just like me. I got four boys, and especially one of 'em — he's more reckless than I am. When he goes with me, why, heavens! I have to give 'im a caution! He goes through the brush just like a wild man. I says to 'im, 'If you do that you're gonna git bit.' We went out one day, out around Highland. Know where that is? Was a good brewery there one time. Real snake country out there. We was killin' 'em that day, and I let 'im take the shotgun. We was cuttin' their heads off with the shotgun, see. That one day we found fifty-one snakes, just about a swill-pail full, the young ones and the old ones. Aw, that was fun! We was out there and we talked to an old couple. They said they was gittin' snakes there in the road; you know if they start findin' 'em in the road, then I try to find the den. There was an old man and a woman there hoeing potatoes and I says, 'Any snakes around here?' 'Boy, I wish you'd hunt 'em,' they says. 'We don't know where they are, but we know we got a big one under the porch,' they says. Well, I tipped up some rocks. They wasn't more'n two hundred steps from where they was hoeing in the garden. Well, I went up there and I seen this skin. If you ever see a skin of a snake laying on the grass, you know that snakes are around there. And I says to the boy, 'Aw! Here's some skins. Look out!' and I looked around below the rock there and they was two great big old females, plumb full of young ones. And I hollers down to the old man and I says, 'Say, you're hoeing pretty close to some rattlesnakes.'

"And he hollers back, 'There ain't any snakes here.'

"But I says, 'They's two laying right here,' and I says to the boy, 'You pick one up and I'll git the other one,' and we both got 'em in the tongs and lifted 'em up.

" 'Keep 'em,' the old man says, 'keep 'em till I come up there.'

"I says, 'We'll bring 'em down.'

"We brought 'em down, and he got all his kids out, we had to show 'em to 'em, and aw! Man, didn't he think that was something? I don't know whose kids they was, but they was a lot of kids around there. He says, 'Come and look at 'em.' I says, 'Just don't step on 'em, that's all.'

"I have knew of two or three in my lifetime that has been bit, but not recently, not around here. In August, you know, rattlers are so much more dangerous. In August they're terrible! You see, they shed. They shed once in June and once in August. And every time they shed they add an extra rattle. You know, a funny thing about it? I never knew this till a few years ago. Before the snake sheds, there will be a skin grow over his eyes. They will be a blue inner skin and when that skin comes off, it'll raise up right on his nose, and within twenty-four hours that snake will crawl right out of his skin, and the skin will all be ruffled up like a sock. That's pretty nice!

"You know they is so many city people will come out and buy a little patch of land high up on the bluffs. Then they will hire me to come in and hunt the snakes out. I just love that. I don't know what I'd rather do! It's my hobby; besides they pay me a lot! Every hill is bought up here. If it keeps on in the next ten years like it has in the past, there won't be a spot where there won't be a good house.

"There was a schoolteacher from Madison. Called me last summer and says, 'Woody, would you know a rattlesnake skin if I showed you one?' I says, 'You bring it out. I'll tell you if it's a rattlesnake.' And you know, it was about the biggest rattle-snake skin I ever saw in my life. Right this side of Dodgeville was where they found it. A picnic table. It was kind of under that. He give me five dollars to go up and hunt. But I'll have to be truthful, I couldn't find the snake! But I got it in my head this spring. Promised 'im I'd come back. He was worried about his kids I guess. But another thing, a snake will get out of your way if it can. You see, I always wear tennis shows so I can sneak up on 'em. If you wear heavy boots that clomp on the rocks, well, you may just see their tail as they go in the hole!

"Rattlesnakes like rocky places then?"

"Oh, yeah. They have to have rocks. That is, in the spring and fall, but in the summertime they're all over. I don't see how the state, now with all the campers, and all the Boy Scouts and all these people taking trips in the woods, if the snakes ever get thick, and they will, then it's gonna be dangerous, because all these kids, they don't know what to look for!

"But a snake hates a dog or a horse. Now my old Shep he will come around a pen where I got me a rattler, and that snake will get mad, and if I pick the snake up then, he'll bite me, if he can. But if the dog ain't around, and if it's a bull snake for instance, I can pick the snake up and wrap it right around my neck."

"Woodrow, what do you think about this southwest Wisconsin country?"

"I just love it! There ain't a place in the state as pretty as right here in southern Wisconsin. I like it because it's home, that's why. Why, if I had time on my hands, which I ain't, if I did though, I'd start out in the spring huntin' Indian arrowheads. Then comes the mushroom season. Then I start huntin' ginsing, later on in the summer. That plant's valuable, you know. And I just love to hunt that because you know in the woods, there isn't much of it and you have to look! Then I do some trapping, and then you got fishin'! I never got time! And then I hunt mud turtles, and then I start huntin' snakes, and in the fall it's deer huntin' and duck huntin', and there's somethin' to do all the time!"

"Woodrow, when do you find time to farm?"

"Now that's the worse of it! I farm real hard while I'm at it, then I take time off. Now I'm going to tell you a story about a fox. Lots of foxes hereabout. And gettin' more! Well, one day a feller give me a fox. He had a baby fox, oh, I'd say it was about as big as a kitten, and we bring it home and put a dog harness on it, and a chain, about three foot long! And I says to my boy, 'Git a washtub and we'll put 'im under that for the night.' And I wrapped the chain kind of around the bumper of the car. Well, we get up the next morning and the little fox was gone. Aw, I felt so bad. He had dug a hole under the tub and had got away with the chain and the harness, and I thought, well, I will find 'im, so we went up and down the road and we looked all over where we thought he'd get tangled up in the fence and no luck. And I felt so bad because I was afraid he'd get fast and starve. So finally I says, 'That's just too bad, but that's the way things happen.' That was about in May and that fall I started trappin' fox, must have been the latter part of September. I set out only a few traps, and the first trap I set was, oh, as the crow flies, maybe about three miles, on a high ridge. I always get a lot of foxes there. And the next morning my girl, she wasn't in school yet, says, 'Dad, can I go with you?' And I says, 'Sure, you can go.' And we went to that trap. We had forgot all about the fox that had got away in the summertime. We went to that trap and I had a nice big red fox. And my daughter saw it first, and she yells, 'Daddy, does all foxes have harnesses on 'em?' And there was my fox that had got away in the summertime. And the chain was missin'. How he ever got the chain off I'll never know! And don't think that a fox ain't smart. He got away with that chain and went about three miles! Didn't know anything about makin' a livin'.

"But back to snakes! The brush isn't so bad as this buffalo grass. They're right in amongst that grass, and in August, when they're havin' their young ones, Oh! you shouldn't go through that grass. Always have their young first week in August. Dens are usually on top of the hill. Right at the very top."

"If you want to see a rattler do you go on top of the hills?"

"The top is the best. I go on the first ledge of rock. But the summer folks wants the rattlers cleaned out. There's several from Illinois I know. They treat me just wonderful. There's one place, a woman from Illinois she called me up, and she told me she thought there was snakes on her farm. I have yet to ever see a prettier place. Me and my boy drove in there. It was the most beautiful swimmin' pool I ever laid eyes on! The water was six feet deep and you could see a penny laying on the bottom! I says to the boy, 'Just look! All this beautiful swimmin' pool and all the lawn furniture, wouldn't it be a shame if rattlers was to come and take possession of all this?' So we went out on the hill, and we never found a snake. I left her a note on the door and I says, 'We hunted it good, and we didn't find any. But I will be back and try again next spring! Wouldn't want no snakes to lay and sun themselves around your swimmin' hole!' "

# Edna

E dna Meudt is decidedly plump; nowadays you would call her motherly or grandmotherly. In her face and eyes there is the poet, and the pride of a poet who has lived a lifetime on a working dairy and cattle farm on Highway 23, south of Dodgeville on the Military Ridge, is definitely there and colors all that she says or writes. She appears to carry the countryside in her soul; her hands are forever fashioning things from Wisconsin earth, or brush, or pine cones, or sticks of dead wood, or seeds. Her house is a cocoon where Edna lives with real things and finds in them the stuff of recreating the past.

Her house is an ancient one as houses go now on Highway 23. The approach is by a long lane, driftbound in winter, for there is no side protection from the winds, and the winds do blow very hard on the Meudt place; once a tornado nearly wrecked the house and barns. But in the winds, as in everything else, Edna hears mystery and magic.

And how could she help it in a setting so fraught with the past, for Highway 23 is a branch of the old Military Road and went directly down to Mineral Point and to the great lead-mining areas.

The Military Ridge, or Road, divides the land between the streams that flow north into the Wisconsin and those that flow south to the Rock and the Mississippi. On the crest of the ridge the Military Road was built in 1835 from Green Bay to Prairie du Chien. It went by way of Fond du Lac, Portage, and the Blue Mounds. The land rises southwest of Madison to the plateau neighborhoods of Dodgeville and Lancaster and rounds over toward Platteville, Galena, and the Mississippi Valley.

It was, of old, an alluring pathway for early explorers and prospectors who saw in it immense possibilities. Official maps of 1835 mark its main trail climbing the summit to Mount Horeb and Dodgeville and west to the Great River, thence forking to the Wisconsin at its westward curve and with side trails down to Mineral Point, Lancaster, and Cassville. The range breaks down abruptly along its high northern flank, into the deep, worn valley of the Wisconsin River, varying in breadth according to the softer or harder contents of the primeval river bottom. Part way along this route the twin Blue Mounds rise like colossal breasts, landmarks from near and far.

Over this road swarmed the immigrants, a surging tide in

the 1850s. Oxen, cows, carriages carrying ladies and gentlemen in silks and tall hats, poor settlers in rags, land speculators, wagons piled with belongings, gold seekers heading west, itinerant editors, politicians, abolitionists, fugitive slaves. An empire moved west over the old Military Road.

And there are still other stimuli that support Edna's sense of poetry and mystery in the land, for in Southwestern Wisconsin the rocky summits of the hills sometimes assume fanciful shapes. Northwest of Dodgeville, for example, I marvel often at the Great Stone Faces of Wisconsin, surely more mystical than the Great Stone Face of Vermont that is so much more widely celebrated, because there are *two* faces in Wisconsin. The Wisconsin Great Stone Face bluff rises fifty feet above a tree-clad ridge. Two faces appear on opposite sides of the rock. Hawthorne told the story of the Great Stone Face of Vermont, but Indians told the legend of the Great Stone Faces of Wisconsin.

Long ago, before the mammoth and the saber-toothed tiger had disappeared from the earth, there lived in the land of the Chippewas two brothers with names meaning the Smiling One and the Complaining One, who were continually arguing about the way each was conducting himself.

The Complaining One could see nothing pleasant or good in anything around him and went about sticking his tongue out at everything he saw. The other rejoiced at every aspect of the world and found pleasure in listening to the song of the birds and in watching the beaver at work.

The way of one brother was so different from the other's that they took each other to task and argued from morning till night. After 100 or 150 years of this, for you must know that people in those days lived much longer than we do now, the Chippewas grew tired of the brothers' strife. Failing to induce them to stop their wrangling, the people in desperation appointed a day of fasting and prayer, to rid themselves of the Complaining One and the Smiling One, although they hated to bother the Great Spirit with so trivial a matter. After the ceremony they went about their various avocations, but in a few days first one and then another noticed the quiet that prevailed. They wondered at it until they remembered that they had not seen either of the quarreling brothers since they had carried their troubles to Manitou. Everyone now went his way in smiles and gladness, and the brothers were soon forgotten.

But in the autumn a great hunt was organized to lay in the

winter's stores of meat and furs, and the tribesmen journeyed to the northland. On the way, to their surprise, they came upon a great rock, which none had ever seen before. On it were the brothers' faces in stone, the one serene and smiling and the other with lowered eyes and protruding tongue, while the hair of their heads had turned to living trees standing upright, giving them the appearance of continuing their old argument.

Gov. Henry Dodge, the Indian fighter, once owned the Meudt farm. He purchased it in 1836, very soon after the Indians relinquished their title. Relinquished is a fancy word for being kicked off, and Dodge was exceptionally good at kicking Indians. John Miller, sage of the *Dodgeville Chronicle*, said that "Dodge was an old Indian fighter; he only fought the old ones." The statement may not be exactly fair, but Dodge was out to get the Indian lands when and however he could, and he invariably congratulated a settler when he had done in an Indian.

Dodge, who in 1836 became first governor of the territory of Wisconsin, had apparently applied for a grant of land (which included the Meudt place) in the names of two of his children, Caesar Augustus Dodge and Louisiana Maddin. They deeded the land (so Edna's abstract reads) to Henry Dodge, 480 acres for the sum of $300.

When I visited with Edna, we sat in her living room, I in a fine old rocker and Edna in her favorite armchair. She had just finished writing a poem about Dodge and said to me, "Maybe you'd like to hear it?"

I am partial to Edna's poems, as well as to the subject of Gov. Henry Dodge. I said I would.

"Then," said Edna happily, "I must tell you, before I read it, that you are sitting in the house that DeGarmo Jones built. He was the shotmaker for Governor Dodge."

"Shot that he made over at Tower Hill?" I asked.

"That's right. Old Helena."

If you want to get a thrill out of the past, go to Tower Hill State Park just south of Spring Green. Climb the steep hill to the tower itself; of course, the modern view tower replaced the old one many years ago. But look across the hills and picture the hive of movement that took place on the hill in the 1830s, 1850s, and 1860s. The idea, of course, was to drop molten lead from a tower, down through a shaft cut for a hundred feet through the rock, and into a spring of cold water at the foot of the shaft. As the lead fell, it assumed a spherical shape. Different grades and sizes of shot could be cheaply manufactured in this way. DeGarmo Jones, as Edna said, was the boss of shot making for old Henry Dodge.

"About three years ago," Edna continued, "an old lady came here from Florida and remarked that ours had been really a grand house in the old days; said that there was an open staircase right *here*, in this room; now can you feature that? So, would you like to hear the poem for our first territorial governor?

"By the way," she said, pausing and fingering her manuscript, "we have had a night visitor here. You won't believe that, but we have had."

"What kind of a night visitor?"

"It won't make any sense to you!"

"Tell me before you read the poem."

"All right, I will."

"We have been here, of course, almost forty years. And back before the war [World War II] I saw this *thing*. It was like a black shadow that came beside my bed. I saw it seven times. Four times I thought I could have been sleeping; but three times I couldn't possibly have been asleep. I have very strong feelings about putting fears into my children, apprehensions and that, so I only told my priest friend Father Dan Coyne, who used to visit here. I didn't even tell my husband, because he would think I was balmy! But I told Father Dan, and he, being a priest, blessed the house. I saw the shadow after that one time but told no one else about it. When my son came home from the Pacific Theatre of War in 1944, he went to sleep in that room. We were terrified in the night to hear a gunshot. My son rushed downstairs crying that this tall black thing had been beside his bed and that he had shot at it with a service pistol. He had never been told what I had seen. So you can take that yarn or leave it. I haven't seen the shadow for years. But the story makes a good springboard for Governor Dodge."

"Just what did the shadow look like?"

"A tall figure of a man, tall and dark. The only place I ever saw it was in that room where Richard was that night; that's where I used to sleep before I moved downstairs. My son, incidentally, described the shadow exactly as I had seen it."

"Is that the shadow-ghost of that old Tower Hill shotmaker who built this house?"

"I don't know."

"Are there any ghost legends around here? I know, of course, about the Ridgeway ghost. Maybe you are seeing the Ridgeway ghost; he's been haunting the old Military Road for about a century and a half now."

"I know it sounds fantastic. But here goes with the poem."

"Shoot."

First Territorial Governor Henry Dodge, 1782-1867

*Is it you, Henry Dodge, "straight as an arrow*
*and as quick" beside my bed, then down the narrow*
*hall of my historic home, in the shattered nights*
*these many years since Bad Axe and Wisconsin Heights?*
*This is the house that De Garmo Jones built — shotmaker*
*of lead, mined from these Winnebago acres.*
*Ruthless chapters: Indians surrendering titles*
*after your illegal possession, miner's rifles*
*in stockade standing the militia off... My abstract reads:*
*"Caesar Augustus Dodge, Louisiana Maddin cede*
*to Henry Dodge for the sum of three hundred dollars,*
*four hundred eighty acres." Hero, non-scholar,*
*sheriff, marshal, Colonel of U. S. Dragoons,*
*your home for forty years, a bargain, is ruins*
*haunted by I know not whom. (Someone destroyed*
*by you? Blackhawk? A Sac or Fox? The deceived St. Croix*
*or tribes at Keokuk?) Dubious honors that spring,*
*1836, you bought this land: The sting*
*of antagonist named Agent for Indian Affairs.*
*"Minersville," "Fort Union," became "Dodgeville" where*
*Wisconsin Territory was made with you its Governor—*
*the honeycomb of politics sealed with Senator.*
*These rolling hills, where agriculture lays a Persian*
*carpet all around, were woodlands once. Versions*
*of history change and love may be the only constant.*
*I do not judge you, Sir, or claim to read the portend*
*of ghosts— a who or why. The Redman, even as you*
*and I, held dear this place, and banished, dreamed these blue*
*blue vistas until death. (We modify the crime*
*and call it patriotism.) Man grows for his own time:*
*in righteous anger to thrash a Grand Jury in court;*
*with vision to legislate for rivers and ports.*
*Are you my guest, a husband, father, Governor Dodge?*
*Come in and rest! Outside they grapple civil gods.*

"Edna," I said, after we had discussed Governor Dodge and his eccentricities, especially his hatred of red men, "Edna, what do you think of this southwestern Wisconsin country? I know you like it, but what does it mean to you?"

"Oh, I don't know. I'm too aware of the past I think. You know, some of us are born to look backward; I'm such a person. I'm always sensing presences. I sometimes think I'm kind of strange. But I love this country, as you said; it's a panorama of so many things, tempered by my memories and my hope of interpreting it. If you go over on that hill over yonder there where my son plans to build his house, you can see forever; it's like that. The people? Well, Cornishmen and Welshmen first, then if you look in the telephone book you'll still see lots of Andersons and Nelsons. North of Dodgeville it's predominantly Norwegian. But there are Irish and Italians too. Gerald Field-house, the nurseryman from Chicago, he's got a summer place over south of Dodgeville. Well, he's making a lifework of collecting a census of this part of the state, every name. He's tracing it. You see, I was born over in the Wyoming Valley. It got dark early at our old home, the sun set about four o'clock, and perhaps that's why I like these hills so much. I can see here. The woods came up near our house where I was born. And such terrible things happened in the valley.

"What?" I asked.

"Well, the Frank Lloyd Wright family murders. Seven, killed by a madman in one terrible afternoon. I was invited to a children's party at the Wright house that very day, and I might have been killed too if I hadn't been late. And I remember the Bront murders. Bront killed his wife and mother and went away, left his little boy there with two dead women. And we had very bad storms, a terrible tornado that took everything we had. And my Aunt Frances, who met her own funeral cortege. How do you explain that?"

"Tell me about Aunt Frances."

"All right. But first I want to tell why I'm a pacifist. Not an active one perhaps, but a real one nevertheless. I never knew why, until I understood why my Bohemian grandfather brought his five sons and two daughters to this country. It was to escape Prussian militarism; antimilitary was bred into me, you see. He had been a miller in the old country, and when he came here he went down to Hyde Mill south of Arena and got a job as a laborer. The mills closed, and he had no experience as a farmer, but he went down there in the valley on submarginal land where nobody, except a Finn maybe, could make a living. So the sons worked out, leaving only the one younger son at home. In the fall, when the boys came home, they would cut wood.

"They had this sister, Frances, very beautiful. They pooled resources to have her picture taken at Dodgeville. Like all girls, she was very conscious of her hair. She went down to the spring and she washed her hair to get ready for this picture. Her mother was very cross about it, but Frances laughed and said that her hair would dry on the way to town.

"She had her picture taken; she bought their groceries; there was a little money left over, and one of the brothers used it to buy Frances a length of calico since it was near her birthday. They started home, and her brother Paul, who was sitting next to her, later said that he thought she felt feverish.

"This was a trip of over twelve miles in a lumber wagon, with a team of heavy work horses, so it was very slow. When they were about halfway home Frances fell asleep against her brother's shoulder. He said later it was a 'spooky' night. They could hear the foxes yapping and fighting, the hoot owls from far away mysteriously adding a chill to the night. And remember, in those days, think what this country must have been at night! Not a light anyplace, narrow dirt roads, horses going by sense and feel and the driver letting the horses take them home. Spooky! Paul said that all the way home he had strange apprehensions.

"Frances awoke all at once, as though she were startled. She grabbed the reins out of Paul's hand and pulled the horses to the left, hard. And the moon had come up by this time. Frances said, 'We have to make room for the procession! It's coming.' Paul couldn't see anything; but Frances said, 'Look! There's Baba [Mama]. She's wearing her veil, and she's in the same wagon with the Aganos, like she was when Papa died.'

"Paul was frightened and jerked the lines away from Frances and got the wagon into the rut again. He got her home as soon as he could.

"Frances fought in fever for three days. My father had to ride to Mineral Point for help, but when he got back, Frances was dead.

"As it turned out, the funeral cortege was just as Frances described it in the lumber wagon on that dark, dark night!"

"So," I said finally, "strange things do happen in the

Wyoming Valley!"

Edna laughed. "Somehow," she said, "the fact that I had these Bohemian ancestors maybe helped me to see the tall shadow I have seen in this house. My uncles told many supernatural tales."

But the lore and lure of the Military Road country always circles back to the colorful figure of Governor Henry Dodge, who mined, it is said, a million dollars' worth of lead in southwest Wisconsin.

The fort and stockade that Dodge built is on the old Raleigh farm just across the fence from Edna Meudt's pasture. They say you can see the outline of the stockade from a plane! Someday I will have a look.

"Dodge had been an Indian agent in Missouri," said Edna. "He knew better than to come up here and take possession of land reserved for the Winnebago. When he was ordered off, he got a whole passel of volunteers — leadminers, wagoners, and they stood the militia off!

"Now the folks who don't know anything about Dodge go up to Governor Dodge Park north of Dodgeville on Highway 23, and they think he was quite a hero. Well, maybe he was, but a lot of poor Indians thought different. Anyway, I wish they had made Dodge Park *here*, where his stockade was. He had nothing to do with that land on Highway 23. Dodge Park indeed!"

# Country Editor

The visit that Lady Bird Johnson paid to the Spring Green area in September of 1967 has already taken its place in the permanent lore of the land. She had several reasons for coming to the village with a retinue of about seventy-five news media people, and accompanied by Orville Freeman, secretary of agriculture, and Roger Stevens, chairman of the National Endowment for the Arts. Mrs. Lyndon Johnson was sincerely interested in people who were striving to improve their surroundings and to give a sense of cultural being to an area. She came partly in behalf of her "beautification" program and partly because she was attracted by Frank Lloyd Wright's residence near Spring Green and by the development of a notable cultural center in a small rural American town by local people. Perhaps, chiefly, she was interested in Robert Graves and his Uplands Art Council, and in the University of Wisconsin Extension, who were cooperating to put on a country festival of arts and crafts out in the hills; she also wanted to see *Hodag*, a rollicking musical by Dave Peterson of the Wisconsin Idea Theatre.

Anyway, her visit gave the local folks a big chance to gossip and comment. I personally think they will never forget her visit.

Go over to the *Dodgeville Chronicle*, for instance.

The *Dodgeville Chronicle* is one of the oldest weeklies in the state. In 1858 a printer named Hoxie, passing through Milk Valley, was forced to stop because of impassable roads. (There just may have been some hootch mixed up in it too.) He gave up his journey and stored his printing press in the barn on the old Ruggles farm near Ridgeway.

When a group of Dodgeville men — Sam Hoskins, S. W. Reese, Nicholas Arthur, Jacob Miller, Henry Madden, and B. F. Thomas — heard about Hoxie's misfortunes, they scurried over to Ridgeway, bought the press, and started a newspaper. They hired Francis J. Rowe of Mineral Point as editor, and on August 19, 1858, the old press rattled off the first edition of the *Iowa County Advocate*, parent of the *Chronicle*.

John Miller, who until recently was editor of the *Chronicle*, sat with me at a table in the print shop. John is about 65, short, stocky, shrewd, very friendly, always smiling and luring you on to make a statement that he can give a humorous twist to. Folks in Wisconsin have enjoyed his line of light chatter and homey satire for years.

Lady Bird was to visit a farm near Clyde owned by a young farmer named Joe Johnson. After the farm visit she was to have dinner at the new Spring Green restaurant and then attend a play at the Gard Theatre in Spring Green village. It was about as gusty an event as the area had ever had. Old John was eager to get in on the fun. Readers throughout the whole region were asking him about Lady Bird. When was she coming? What for? Would they get a chance to shake hands? Things like that.

"Well," John said, "When I first heard about Lady Bird comin' out to Clyde, I contacted various people, such as Congressman Vernon Thompson, to see about getting a pass to attend this farm visit. After a lot of red tape I got a call that come in here to the *Dodgeville Chronicle*. I wasn't in the office when the call come in. Somebody come runnin' down to a bar where I was, yellin' that I had a call. Says it was from the White House! Left a message. 'Have old John Miller call the *White House!*' Me!

"Well, if I'd been there in the office and had answered the phone I would have made a crack about a Dodgeville practical joker. You know, we got a plenty of 'em out here. The funny thing is, I didn't really need a pass to get to the Johnson farm, because Joe Johnson's place, where they were going to visit, adjoins mine. I could have come right down the ridge row. But the thing that impressed me about the visit was the way the reporters covered it. A lot of 'em had never been in a barn nor seen a cow, and being a country boy, when there's a lot of visitors come in a barn, especially a strange barn with strange cattle, you try to stand in front of the cows because things will happen and quite a few of the writers got it, if you know what I mean. Lady Bird didn't get it, because they kept her in front of the cows. But you know how it is with cows on a cement floor?

"Orville Freeman, he asked Joe Johnson about prospects for young farmers. I guess Orville thought that Joe would say that every young feller ought to get out to the farm. But Joe he said he thought the prospects weren't very good. In fact, Joe advised young fellers not to go into farming. Orville didn't have anything to say for a moment, but our Wisconsin boys always say what they think no matter who's present. Joe's got him a nice place, but it is hill land after all, and even with a good herd like Joe's it's hard going. And then Joe's got a lot of fancy equipment, glass silos and such, and these things cost big money. Joe wasn't kidding when he said the prospects weren't too good. Fact is, lot of the money for improvement comes from government loans. Joe said the prices weren't very good, and the investment was too heavy.

"Then the writers were always complaining that there weren't enough telephone booths. Incidentally, they had a direct wire from Dodgeville to the Johnson farm, and also one to Wright's house and one to the Spring Green Restaurant, and they had a girl sitting here in Dodgeville all the time, so they could get a direct wire into Washington, or so Washington could call out to Dodgeville."

"John," I said, "You were present at the farm visit?"

"Oh, yes, I was there. And this gal from the White House — she was one of Liz Carpenter's assistants, I guess — she told me that my pass which I got from the White House wouldn't get me into the restaurant, or into the theatre in Spring Green. Well, I up and told her that I was a director of the Uplands Arts Council and a friend of Bob Graves. 'Oh,' she said, 'how many hats do you wear? You're in everything.' 'Just about everything except that stuff in the barn,' I told her. And she laughed and says that those Johnson cows at the barn are not as ladylike as the ones down on the Johnson ranch in Texas. She says that Lady Bird can go into the barn any time she likes and the cows won't ever raise a tail."

"Is it true, John," I asked, "that Mrs. Joe Johnson didn't wear any shoes during the visit?"

"That's not true!" John cried. "Mrs. Joe Johnson had on her tennis shoes. And I tell you she done right. Some folks around here figured Mrs. Joe Johnson should dress all up, high heels and such, it being her farm and all, but Mrs. Johnson is a real helper on the farm. She helps with the milking and such, and tennis shoes are the most practical things to wear, because you can just take 'em and toss 'em into the washing machine. Mrs. Johnson said that Mrs. Lady Bird would surely want her to look about as she did around the farm, and she didn't wear no high heels. And I admire her for it. So did Lady Bird, I guess. Newspapers all over the country remarked about Mrs. Joe Johnson and her tennis shoes.

"But folks were quite impressed," continued John. "Up until the time that Lady Bird came here, the most noted persons who had visited Clyde were Congressman Thompson and Lt.

Gov. Jack Olsen, both great fellers, by the way. Before them, the Clyde folks had never seen anybody higher than the sheriff, and him infrequently.

"It impressed folks at Clyde quite a bit, having all those dignitaries. Can tell you a story connected to that. You know, I said my farm is right there at Clyde, and I had built me a new dam. It wasn't much, but I saw a chance to get some high-up folks down to Clyde. Clyde has always been a sort of Democrat's hideaway, but in order to get some Republicans to Clyde I invited Congressman Thompson and Lieutenant Governor Olsen to come out and dedicate my dam. They come! Even the small places ain't too little for Wisconsin Republicans to take a notice of! And we must have had two hundred folks out at my place. Just a visitin' it was. No speeches or anything like that.

"Well, down at the Clyde crossroads we have Mrs. Patricia Carroll. Old family in Clyde, her pappy ran a general store there for fifty years maybe. And Trish she's got a little store and Shell gas station there now. They sometimes refer to Trish as the mayor of Clyde. She plays a hot hand of poker. And she says, 'Now, John, who're we going to have next? We went pretty high with Lieutenant Governor Olsen and Congressman Thompson. I think a lot of both of them fine men, but who's next? Let's keep the ball rolling,' Trish said.

"And I says to Trish, laughing, 'Well, we ain't had the president yet!'

" 'You wouldn't try to get that poor busy man,' Trish says.

" 'Nothin' to keep a citizen of Clyde from askin' him,' I says. 'Joe Doyan down here's got a new waterin' tank. We could dedicate that!' So when Lady Bird was here I told Trish, 'Well, LBJ couldn't come himself, but he sent his wife!' After that Trish kidded about it, and she says, 'Who's next?' And I says, 'You want me to get the Pope?' Trish didn't answer nothin' to that."

John went on to tell me about the Dodgeville money.

On August 29, 1963, a man or woman unknown put into the post office mailbox a big handful of letters addressed to different people in and near Dodgeville. The unusual thing about the letters was that they contained money. Some had a twenty dollar bill, others had a hundred. There were a lot of surprised Dodgeville folks when the mail came. Some of them figured that it was just manna from heaven and didn't say much about it. Some others decided that they ought to try to find out why some person unknown was sending them a windfall. The postmaster finally came over to the *Dodgeville Chronicle* and told John that the letters had gone out and that people were asking him what it was all about. The postmaster was disturbed because folks seemed to think that maybe the post office was handing out the free money. They couldn't think of anybody else in the whole of Iowa County who might do such a thing, and since the postmaster represented Uncle Sam, they figured he must be the one. He rapidly said it wasn't.

John, who had left Waukesha County a dozen or fifteen years ago to become a country editor, saw the news potential in a hurry and slipped a little note into his weekly chatter column for the *Dodgeville Chronicle*. All he said was that somebody in Dodgeville was handing out free money. The little item started a kind of minor news cataclysm. Dodgeville folks immediately shifted their suspicions to John and for a while he had lots of offers of marriage and other arrangements; several folks who were drawing relief money thought it would be a lot easier for them to just come over to the *Chronicle* office and get a few bills from old John. John maintained stoutly that he hadn't done it.

Then the suspicion shifted to George Page who ran a local store. George was having wife trouble, and she and her lawyer instantly developed the idea that George was doling out his money so he wouldn't have any to make a settlement when his wife got the divorce. George appreciated the thought but went out of his way to show that it really couldn't have been him. The wife's lawyer didn't believe it and started an injunction to prevent him from handing out any more mazuma. For a while George had trouble getting enough money out of the bank to pay for his cakes!

The papers and news magazines picked up the story, and for about two weeks Dodgeville was national news. It became known as that little city in Wisconsin where such a spirit of good will and neighborliness existed that you just got a mailbox full of hundred dollar bills every day. Many individuals packed up and made a trip to Dodgeville to look it over with intentions of moving there. Industries down on their luck looked into the terrain around Dodgeville. The chamber of commerce thought Dodgeville had hit the jackpot, and old John Miller garnered some really nice checks from *Newsweek* and *Time* for stories he filed with them. Unfortunately, the bonanza petered out, entirely because the mysterious donor stopped sending any money. When the money ran out, folks lost interest.

I found the story of the free money very interesting because Dodgeville is about the least likely place in the state where such a thing should happen. Dodgeville folks are conservative usually. They go overboard for a thing like their high school basketball team, which won the state tournament back in 1964 (they still have a sign on both sides of town advertising that glorious victory), but Dodgeville people aren't much in the habit of giving away dough. It is a typical middlewestern town of fine respectable people, and they save their money in Dodgeville.

# The Cattle Buyers

The cattle buyers of southwestern Wisconsin gather in the auctioning pavilion at Richland Center. Paul Kooiman, manager of the pavilion and a chief auctioneer of the area, has invited me to view the festivities from the cattle floor, below the auctioneer's stand. Above us the seats bank upward sharply like a very modern theatre, a space stage, or perhaps a glimpse of the old Globe Theater of London if one is extremely fanciful, only now the players are cows and sheep and pigs.

The buyers are a colorful lot. Most of them wear bill caps, some with earflaps tied up; they all wear work clothing — overalls, usually with bibs, and heavy winter jackets and boots with pants tucked in top. Their faces are weathered and they are a talkative and jolly bunch. Mostly they are commission buyers for many different kinds of interests, for southwestern Wisconsin is more and more a cattle country. More dairy stock used to be sold, but now that dairy farming is so much more efficient, a farmer has time to run a bunch of beef cattle too or more hogs. A buyer may be commissioned to purchase feeding stock, may represent a packing house, or may speculate for himself.

It is constant activity. Inside the vast and coldly dark cattle pavilion one hears the bawl or lowing of cows and calves, the grunt and occasional angry squeal of hogs, the blat of sheep, the cries of men, the sharp snap of the small lashes the drivers use to control animals, the banging of heavy gates, and, at last, always amplified these days, the unbelievably rapid chatter and lingo of the auctioneer.

According to Paul, the famed eighteenth century English scholar, Dr. Samuel Johnson, was one of the best auctioneers, at least in his time. I was amazed to hear him cite Dr. Johnson as we stood on the sawdust-covered floor of the pavilion. Paul said that Johnson had one great philosophy: "to make a sale, convince the buyer that he's going to reap the profits of his action, that it's not just the pig or the cow that's important in the long run; it's the golden harvest the buyer is going to reap if he takes advantage of the wonderful opportunity the auctioneer is giving him!"*

"The important thing," Paul said, "is that it doesn't matter what you're selling — an antique commode, or a bunch of little pigs that you are going to raise up to be big pigs and resell. The important thing is not to sell the *means* but to sell the *end.*

You've got to convey, impress, by some kind of an electric process that you are going to reap the riches if you buy those pigs."

An ancient cow was driven into the arena. The young auctioneer glanced at her, and with a comical expression he shouted, "Boys, lookey here! A fine milker! And in the prime of life. Take her home, boys. She will be an inspiration to your whole herd! Somewhere, this old girl has discovered the secret of the fountain of youth! A mysterious herb in Sam Maxwell's pasture! Demonstrate that a cow can live to be one hundred. You'll make your herd a sight happier one, boys, if you take old grandma here home. Now, what am I bid? Do I hear ten dollars?"

"Looks like what she needs is a shot of Spanish Fly," hollers a big fellow, red faced, in a heavy checked mackinaw. The crowd howls.

"This old girl don't need no Spanish Fly," said the auctioneer, "she'll take 'em all on, anytime!"

The ancient cow was sold for some trifling amount, and a young heifer was driven in. She stared at the crowd, backed away, put her head down, and pranced around the ring. The gateman flicked at her with a short whip that had a little snapper on the end. The heifer bawled loudly.

"Now this heifer, she's a fine one, boys. Listen to her beller!"

"Can't tell," shouted someone. "Is she bred?"

"You bet," cried the auctioneer. "Due to come in in April."

"Better let old Higgins take a look. He can tell about them things," cried an elderly humorist.

"All right, Higgins," the auctioneer called to a powerfully built, low-slung man, "how about it? Is she bred?"

"Yep," yelled Higgins. "She's been to the dance!"

General merriment. Then the auction gets serious. I listen and can't follow the patter of the auctioneer at first. It is unbelievably rapid. He hits a price word, $10.00, $9.20, or some such, and between he fills the gap with auctioneer's jargon, meaningless to me, but the buyers understand perfectly what he's saying. They listen, impassive, and sit so quietly that I cannot really see movement; but the auctioneer, keen eyed and very alert, sees the flick of a hand, a finger, or the slight nod of a head, which indicates a bid.

There is absolutely no phonetic way to reproduce the lingo of a good stock auctioneer. You can hear it and recognize it, but you'll have to take my word that it's mighty hard to do and takes long training. You just watch the upper lip of a cattle auctioneer; you never saw a sewing machine shuttle move any faster.

Paul told me about an auctioneer who knew the curious ways different buyers have of bidding.

"One day he was conducting a farm auction," said Paul, "and there was this tractor. The owner said to get as much money as he could for it, at least $1,800. The auctioneer started in and was going good. He felt somebody slap him on the leg and figured that was just some buyer's way of bidding. He kept working the price up, and the slaps kept coming. He got it up to $1,700 and knocked it down to the buyer who'd been signaling bids by hitting his legs. He turned around to look at the buyer; what he saw was a big farm dog sitting there, slapping away with his tail. 'First time I ever sold a tractor to a dog!' he said."

The buyers make modestly good livings. Sometimes they will buy more than a hundred head of stock in a day and collect $1.00 per head commission. Higgins, who is from Ithaca, told me that he made a good living, and his wife is also getting $2.70 an hour as a machine operator at the Badger Ordnance Works. Together they make a nice income.

Guys like Higgins work hard because order-buying cattle for somebody else is a big responsibility. If you buy a man a poor bunch at a good price, he will likely be mad at you. He'll pay more, without griping, if the stock is good.

"Haven't seen your friend since you hit him," Paul says to Higgins.

"Nope!" Higgins says, "He ain't been back."

Higgins got into a fight in Ithaca one night when another fellow accused Higgins of cheating at cards. The fellow said to Higgins, "I'm gonna whip your ass!"

Higgins says, "It'll take you a while!"

Higgins hit the fellow, and he goes sliding across the tavern floor and bangs up into the juke box. Higgins had knocked him cold, but he picked him up and set him on a chair. The guy came around, looked at Higgins and said, "I suppose you're satisfied." Higgins replied, "Well, you oughta be!" Higgins was a little concerned. Thought they might drag the law in, but they didn't.

Paul told me a story about one of these cattlemen and his brother. The game warden was after them for trapping beaver out of season. They were running hard as they could and when they came to Willow Creek, they crossed it on a log. When the game warden crossed on the same log, the boys turned it over, dumped the warden into the creek, and took off for home. They were wearing full beards, and when they got home they both shaved. Warden was mad as hops, but he couldn't identify 'em!

*Dr. Johnson, when he was auctioneering off the Old Anchor Brewery in London said, "We are not here to see boilers and vats, but the potentiality of growing rich beyond the dreams of avarice."

# Julia's Grandfather

Standing in a prominent triangle of the city of Janesville is a twenty-room mansion that boasts of having Lincoln as its guest on the nights of October 1 and 2, 1859. Grave and stately in its quiet dignity, the mansion, built in the manner of an Italian villa, is pointed to by residents of Janesville as the home where Lincoln was entertained on his last visit to Wisconsin.

The mansion, built by William Tallman and completed about 1857, is still a marvel of the architectural accomplishment of that day. Immense, high-ceilinged rooms with richly scrolled friezes; bronze candelabra ornamented with colorful statuettes; the beautiful spiral staircase up which Lincoln walked the nights he was a guest; the lavatory inlaid with gold in the bedroom where he slept — all are viewed by the modern builder with amazement and appreciation, especially when he learns that all of this material, even every brick, was hauled by team from Milwaukee over roads that today would be called but trails. The white enameled woodwork, still of a beautifully smooth and lustrous finish, unchecked and unchipped, is the original coat put on three-quarters of a century ago.

Lincoln's stay at the Tallman home resulted from the efforts of the Republican Club of Janesville. Having learned on a Saturday morning following his appearance at the state fair in Milwaukee that he was to speak in Beloit that afternoon, the club asked Lincoln to speak in Janesville that evening. Several staunch Republicans in the Janesville vicinity had heard the debate between Lincoln and Douglas at Freeport in August of the year before and therefore wished particularly that their friends and neighbors have an opportunity to hear this powerful and dramatic Illinois orator.

Lincoln accepted their invitation and, after delivering his address at Beloit, drove to Janesville. He recognized the route now known as the prairie road, as the one he had traveled twenty-seven years before during the Black Hawk War and talked freely about the war to his companions: A. A. Jackson, Daniel Wilcox, and J. H. Burgess.

With this introduction which I learned from different sources, I went to see my friend Julia Mailer, whose maiden name was Hanks. Her grandfather slept in the same bed with Lincoln during that Janesville visit. It is one of Julia's favorite stories, and she likes to tell it when she can find time from her vital job of lending plays from the library of University Extension.

I go into the library on a March morning and sit down near Julia's desk. We always exchange some banter, compare notes on various infirmities, and then settle down for a good talk. Although I have heard her tell the Lincoln story many times, today I want to record it in her own words. As she makes ready, I can't help thinking that she is still, though near retirement age, one of the beautiful women of Madison, as she has been since her student days at the university when she was considered the belle of Langdon Street. Beautiful clothes always, a stylish hair-do, a friendly smile, and a life dedicated to the welfare of Wisconsin's theatre lovers. What more could anybody want?

"All right," Julia says, "I'm ready."

"Shoot."

"Well, it was 1859, perhaps in the month of October. Lincoln had debated in the area, at Freeport, Illinois, the year before and Mrs. Tallman of Janesville, whose husband was a banker, thought that Lincoln might be a 'shirt tail relative' of the Hankses through his mother, Nancy Hanks. A Hanks herself, Mrs. Tallman probably thought it might be courteous to invite Lincoln, if he was ever in the area again, to come to Janesville and visit them.

"Mr. Tallman issued the invitation and Lincoln did later come to Janesville. My grandfather told me this story many years ago and I used to be kidded dreadfully when I was a child in school, because when I told the story the kids would say, *Oh, yes!?*' However, this is the way my grandfather, Lucien Hanks, told it.

"He was also staying at the Tallman house as a guest, because he was the nephew of Mrs. Tallman. He had been born at Mystic, Connecticut, and had his schooling there. His parents were dead, and as a young man of sixteen he was wondering what the future held for him. He needed to seek his fortune and wrote his aunt at Janesville, because 'west' was where all the young men wanted to go in those days. The Tallmans, of course, invited young Hanks to come to Janesville.

"Mr. Tallman was a very prominent citizen in the city, and his wonderful house, which had just been completed, was already famous in the whole area. Mr. Tallman was engaged in many business projects, and one of the spots he had in mind for my grandfather was in the Janesville bank. My grandfather soon went to work there as a teller.

"At the time, he was living in the Tallman house and occupied the guest room. When Mr. Lincoln arrived he immediately noticed young Lucien Hanks and the beautiful daughter of the house with whom my grandfather was much in love at the time. Lincoln saw what the situation was and had a gay time teasing the youngsters, and after dinner Lincoln said he was tired and believed he would retire. He must have been aware that there were more guests than beds in the house, because he said to my grandfather, 'Young feller, where are you going to sleep tonight?' Grandfather replied that he was going to sleep down in the living room on one of the couches.

"Mr. Lincoln would have none of that, and he said to my grandfather, 'Well, young man, do you kick?'

"My grandfather said, 'No, Mr. Lincoln, I don't think I do.'

" 'All right,' Mr. Lincoln said, 'you just come upstairs then and sleep with me.'

"I guess grandfather wasn't too keen on that, but Lincoln insisted, and so after a while they went up to bed.

"My grandfather often said to me, 'Did *I* kick! Lincoln kicked all night long. In fact he kicked so hard with his long legs and size thirteen feet that I had to get out of bed around three o'clock in the morning. I spent the rest of the night on that couch in the living room.'

"In the morning, while the family were awaiting breakfast, Mr. Lincoln had not appeared. Mrs. Tallman said, 'Lucien, you better go and see what's happened to Mr. Lincoln.'

"So my grandfather went to the foot of the stairs; they are still there in the old mansion, and whenever I go down there I often think of that story, my grandfather standing at the foot of the stairs, looking up. For here came Mr. Lincoln, his feet in white socks and with no shoes on. He smiled at my grandfather and said, 'I don't seem to have any shoes, Lucien!'

"Of course they had been taken by a servant to clean, and hadn't been put back at Lincoln's door. Lincoln wasn't the least bit bashful. He came to the dining room table and sat down in his sock feet. After that everybody felt real comfortable and homey, and Lincoln knew that he had some strong friends up in Wisconsin!"

(Julia says it may not be true, but I have also heard that Lucien Hanks was fond of telling how he was in Washington one day after Lincoln was elected. He suddenly came face to face with Lincoln on the street and Lincoln stopped, grasped Hanks by the arm and said, "I recognize you!"

"Yes, Mr. President," said Hanks, "I was the young man you kicked out of bed in Janesville in '59!")

"Later on," continued Julia, "my grandfather after his sojourn in Janesville came to the bank up in Madison. This was the old state bank owned by Samuel Marshall. He became president of this bank around the turn of the century and he told me about the great panic of 1907, which caused a hard run on the bank.

"My grandfather came down to the bank one morning. I remember it, as a girl; it had a long passageway at the back of the bank where his office was situated. There was always a lovely coal fire back there in the wintertime, and it was in winter when this happened. My grandfather got to his office, stirred up the fire, and sat down at his desk; as he did so the cashier came running in.

" 'Mr. Hanks, there's going to be a run on the bank. People are collecting at the front doors! What shall I do?'

" 'How are we fixed?' asked my grandfather.

" 'We probably have only about five thousand dollars in actual cash.'

"In those days the cash was always sent down to Chicago when it got collected in any amount. Very little was kept in Madison, perhaps for fear of bank robbery.

" 'Very well,' said my grandfather, very cool, 'I tell you what to do. Go back to the cash desk and bring all the silver dollars you can find here to me.'

"The young cashier went to do as ordered while my grandfather stirred up the fire some more. He took the big fire shovel and, when the dollars came, he dumped a whole lot of them on the shovel and put the shovel into the fire.

" 'We'll heat these silver dollars,' my grandfather said, 'until they're red hot. Then I'll bring them into the lobby. We'll throw 'em on the cashier's counter, then we'll open the doors, and you can tell the people that we're making the money as fast as we can and not to worry! This will, I'm sure, slow 'em down. They can't handle the silver; it's too hot, and they'll pass the word along that there's no cause for worry. The bank has plenty of money. They're making it now!'

"That was how Grandfather Hanks stopped the run on the Madison bank!"

58

# The Thirteenth Century

The thirteenth century has some interesting implications for Wisconsin. One day I am at Okauchee and I hear a strange tale about an artist named Prof. Vladimir Shamberk.

In 1928 the professor is commissioned to paint a portrait of the president of Czechoslovakia, Dr. Thomas G. Masaryk. While working he has time to wander about the streets of Prague and to the surrounding villages that he had known as a young artist. Just before dusk one evening, he enters a little chapel in the village of Rakownik, and he is surprised to see above the altar a most unusual picture of the Holy Virgin. He stands for a long while looking at the picture; something about it will not let him depart. He asks the custodian of the chapel about the history of the painting.

On July 5, 1297, the painting had been brought to King's Hall Monastery in Prague by King Wenceslaus II, ruler of Bohemia. King's Hall was a great Cistercian establishment, founded by the king, which for hundreds of years harbored the royal tombs. At King's Hall, nobles, princes, kings, and queens knelt to pray at the altar with the strange, quiet face of the Madonna gazing down upon them. The painting acquired through the centuries a reputation for bringing special favor to those who worshiped before it.

Then came religious war in Bohemia. The Hussites destroyed the monastery in 1420, and the precious painting was removed to Karlstein Castle. In 1445, when peace was restored, the Cistercians began to rebuild their monastery, and the painting of the Madonna was again placed in King's Hall. It remained there until 1785 when Joseph II, son of Maria Theresa, dissolved the monastery and almost wholly destroyed the Cistercians. The painting finally was taken to the small chapel in Rakownik.

Standing in the small chapel more than one hundred years later, Professor Shamberk is so affected by the painting that he buys it from the officials of the chapel, who can use American money. Upon returning to America, he presents the sacred painting to the rightful owners, the Cistercians, who have established at Spring Bank, Wisconsin, the first such monastery outside Europe.

The brothers invite the professor to make his home with them and to paint the saints, which is his chief mission. He inhabits a small stone house on the monastery grounds where he paints all summer long in 1928, always influenced by the old painting of the Madonna.

Three years later, the professor receives the greatest commission of his life. The head of the entire Cistercian order, the Rt. Rev. Maria Franciscus Janssens, has visited the monastery at Spring Bank and seen the painting of the Madonna. He arranges for the professor to travel to Rome to paint the Holy Father, Pope Pius XI, so that the portrait of the Pope may also hang in the chapel at Spring Bank.

It was the ancient painting of the Madonna that brought about his good fortune, thinks the professor, and subsequently he has indeed a useful life. Some of his paintings sell for as much as twenty thousand dollars!

The thirteenth century, which symbolized so much that was created by the hands of man to the honor of God, reached also to Monroe, Wisconsin.

There, one day, I meet an interesting man named Lee Lamboley. Lee, a successful businessman and major real estate developer, owns a packaging company and other enterprises. Some years before he suffered a nervous breakdown from overwork and has had to take a layoff.

During that period, he becomes interested in creative writing. At the University of Wisconsin years before, he came under the spell of a professor of medieval history, Robert Reynolds, who has opened the doors to the past in a way that Lee has never forgotten. He decides that he will attempt to write a novel about the thirteenth century and the Gothic cathedrals that so well illustrated the aspirations of men in those times.

Lee will center his novel on his favorite historical character, Bishop Hugh of Lincoln, England, who stimulated the building of the great cathedral there.

He assembles a private library, the finest medieval library in the state, with the exception of the University of Wisconsin's. He reads everything he can find on the subject of the thirteenth century, and particularly about Bishop Hugh. For three or four years he writes every day, all day long. He creates the character of Bishop Hugh again and again. He writes perhaps a million words, but something is missing. "What is wrong?" Lee asks.

"Perhaps," I say, "you are writing too much. Perhaps you should select more carefully, take those facets of Bishop Hugh's character that will make your story go ahead faster. Dramatize the whole thing."

"There is too much," he replies, "too much that interests me. I can't stop."

For a period I drive down to Monroe almost every week, and we sit in Lee's living room and talk about his work, which never seems to get near completion, or we simply sit quietly. I have stopped being a mentor to Lee. I know that he no longer needs any guidance that we can give him. He needs help beyond instruction or criticism. His doctor is concerned.

"Lee absolutely must finish the novel," his doctor says. "He must finish it to overcome his fear. If he can finish the novel he will probably be completely well again."

"If I could only visit Lincoln, England," says Lee, "and see the cathedral that Bishop Hugh built. If I could only do that I think that I actually might finish the book."

Lee has not been far out of Monroe since his illness and fears travel. Since university days, he has wanted to visit England, but he has always been too busy. Now, at last, it seems the time. He overcomes his fear. His wife Orene, is eager for him to go, and they make preparations. I have never seen Lee so happy, so completely sure that he will now be successful, that his book will really be completed. I too am sure, and I tell him that the book will have a great sales potential. It is a deep book that creates scenes of medieval Europe in a wonderful way, and it tells an inspiring story. The last thing Lee says to me before they leave Monroe is, "I'm really going to do it. I'm going to see Lincoln Cathedral!"

Two days out of New York, at lunch on the liner *France*, Lee suffers a heart attack and dies. His manuscripts and notes lie today in Monroe, waiting for someone to complete this wonderful story of the thirteenth century. I used to think I might take a crack at it, but I know I couldn't do it. I, too, have never seen Lincoln Cathedral . . . .

# The Aroma of Cheese

I am real fond of that country south and west of Madison, over in Green County. Every time I go over that way, out Highway 18 west of Verona, and turn south and cut through Primrose Township to Mt. Vernon near where old Bob La Follette was born in 1855 in western Dane County, I think about the Norwegian and the German pioneers coming into that country and how their hearts lifted when they saw the gentle land rolling and green. And the Swiss coming into the land south of there and liking that because it reminded them of parts of their homeland. The small towns, Belleville, Monticello, and New Glarus, which is becoming a center of Swiss culture. Everybody ought to see the new chalets down there and visit the old homes and see the fine collections of Swiss objects that are left as memorials. While you're down there on Labor Day weekend, stop and see the Wilhelm Tell pageant, a festival that goes on day and night. The highlight of the whole event is Schiller's *Wilhelm Tell*, presented outdoors in German and English on the Herb Kubly farm, with a fine herd of Brown Swiss cows taking important parts in the play along with the village folks, some of whom have been playing the same roles for most of their lives.

Herb Kubly has made New Glarus his permanent seat now — it always was in fact — but he does most of his writing there, and New Glarus folks are very proud of him.

Yes, and if you're driving on to Monroe, stop for some beer and a fine Swiss cheese sandwich, the best Swiss cheese sandwich for fifteen cents anywhere in the United States. Do some visiting with your friends, and don't forget that Monroe is very cheese conscious. One day in Monroe I heard a yarn that demonstrates how jealously the cheese tradition is guarded. As background, I'd better say that Monroe has long been famous for its various makes of cheese, among which Limburger has held an esteemed position.

In the early days of Monroe, those citizens not so fond of cheese held their noses when the big wagons loaded with Limburger passed through the town; some citizens even demanded that the cheese wagons discover some other route to their destination than that around Monroe's town square.

However, with the increasing prosperity brought about by cheese, the odor of Limburger became respected, even hailed with delight, and disparaging remarks were almost unheard of, until one day in 1935.

On this January day, Monroe's postmaster, John Burkhard, sat in his office, basking in, and perhaps warmed by, the golden era and aura of Monroe cheese when suddenly an assistant entered bearing a package.

"John, look!" cried the assistant, shaking with excitement.

"What's wrong?" asked Mr. Burkhard, reaching across his desk to spread a cracker with golden Limburger.

"This package!" cried the assistant. "This package of Limburger sent to Independence, Iowa, by the Badger-Brodhead Cheese Company. It's been returned to us by the Independence postmaster."

"For what reason?" said Mr. Burkhard.

"For the reason," shouted the assistant, "that it smells too bad to keep in the post office. In fact, Postmaster Miller writes that this package of Limburger made one of his rural carriers so sick he was laid up for several days!"

"Let me smell the package," Mr. Burkhard said. He took the package of cheese and sniffed it carefully. "I can discern no odor whatever. Can you?"

"There's a bit of fragrance about it," said the assistant. "But why not? It's Limburger! The King of the Cheeses!"

"Exactly," said Mr. Burkhard, getting up and pacing around his office. "Limburger asks no odds of anyone. It creates its own exclusive atmosphere."

"It may be," said the assistant, though probably not believing what he said, "that there are some who don't exactly like the odor of Limburger."

"Green County folks," said Mr. Burkhard solemnly, "don't value books for their covers, people for their faces, nor good cheese for its smell. Return the package to Postmaster Miller immediately."

"Okay, John," said the assistant.

So a short time passed and one day the package returned again to the Monroe post office. "Postmaster Miller, of Independence, Iowa, says," stated the assistant, "that he has returned the package as unfit for delivery and trusts that we will dispose of it."

"He does?" cried Mr. Burkhard. "That's almost treason! Send my secretary in here!" And when the secretary was ready, Mr. Burkhard dictated a stout reply to Postmaster Miller. "Limburger," he stated, "has every constitutional right to travel through the U. S. mails. You, sir, are undoubtedly lacking in esthetic values."

The reply, of course, was duly received. The Iowa postmaster, who proved to be a former newspaper editor, was able to retort in kind.

"You mean *anesthetic values,*" he countered, "and I am fully appreciative, if you please."

"This," said Mr. Burkhard reflectively to his staff, "has gone far enough. It's a matter for Washington. If Limburger can't travel through the mails, our whole civilization is on the rocks. Take a letter to Postmaster General Jim Farley in Washington. He'll settle this fast enough!"

So off went the letter to James Farley in Washington and back came his reply: "I'm sorry," he wrote to Mr. Burkhard, "but at this distance I can't tell whether the cheese smells bad or not."

"We'll fix that," said Mr. Burkhard. "Do up a package of Limburger and send it to Mr. Farley. Let him decide for himself."

And off went a carefully done up package of Limburger to Washington. For a time nothing was heard. Then word came in a roundabout manner. Jim Farley was himself under attack by Huey Long, and the newspapers saw in the cheese situation opportunity for a few humorous remarks. One editor wrote:

"Green County, Wisconsin, Limburger has at last accomplished what Huey Long has not succeeded in doing — getting Postmaster Jim Farley out of his comfortable office."

Burkhard naturally refused to believe this nonsense. "Certainly," he cried, "there must be somebody in Washington with a normal sense of smell. We'll contact the second and third assistant postmasters general."

Meanwhile the newspaper wits continued to have a field day. "Jim Farley is facing a strong issue," commented a New York paper. "What a day for hydrogen sulphide," added another.

In Iowa, Postmaster Miller remained firm. "Limburger shall not pass!" he cried. "The U. S. postal service has withstood many attacks. But it has never *smelled!*"

Burkhard's faith in home industry, however, was to receive reward. A letter arrived from the second assistant postmaster general, Harlee Branch, in Washington. "I have carefully sniffed the package of Limburger cheese you sent to this office," he

64

wrote to Mr. Burkhard. "It has no offensive odor, in fact, has no odor unless held directly under the nostrils. You have wrapped this cheese in wax paper, tin foil, brown wrapping paper, and heavy paper on the outside. Wrapped in this manner you have the authority of this office to send Limburger through the mails. To my knowledge, Postmaster Miller, of Independence, Iowa, is the only one who has complained."

"The battle is over!" cried Mr. Burkhard. "Long live Limburger!" And then he became solemn. "There is, however," he reflected, "one person in the country who has not been converted to an affection for this wonderful cheese: Postmaster Miller of Iowa. Something must be done immediately!"

After thinking the matter over, Mr. Burkhard decided to challenge Mr. Miller to a duel, a cheese-sniffing duel. "I will meet you at the St. Julien Hotel in Dubuque," he wired, "on Saturday, March 9. I'll bring the lunch, and that means the best Limburger in Green County, to convince you to the belief that Limburger is actually a fine dairy product, not to be discriminated against because of smell."

Mr. Miller, who was equally eager to do battle, accepted. His telegram read: "If Julien objects, strongly suggest contest be held in tannery. No smells barred. Winner takes all. Limburger has no terrors for me since I lost my sense of smell ten years ago, but Monroe seems wrapped up in it. I take it each man furnishes his own weapons."

The entire cheese industry waxed jubilant over the ensuing publicity. "Cheese-sniffing duel of the century to be held," screamed the headlines. The radio commentators and the comedy programs took up the farce. Orders for Limburger poured into Monroe. John Burkhard was the hero of the day. "I am hopeful that this publicity will be the turning point in the Limburger cheese industry," stated one official. Newspapers gleefully recalled that affairs of honor were usually held in the morning, but because Dubuque was approximately halfway between Monroe and Independence, and each duelist would need to drive about seventy miles, the duel would be held at 2:30 P.M.

Mr. Burkhard, fearful that Mr. Miller could not withstand the terrific ordeal, assembled an old gas mask, a spring clothespin, and smelling salts in case of an Iowa emergency.

"We will win!" said Mr. Burkhard. "We must win for the honor of Monroe cheese!"

Reporters swarmed to the scene, and many colorful accounts of the meeting were given. Perhaps the best of these was written by the great *Milwaukee Journal* reporter, Richard S. Davis:

"The correspondent is sending this dispatch from the dueling grounds: Parlor B in the Hotel St. Julien, Dubuque. On every hand is evidence of the historic contest between Chevalier J. J. Burkhard, postmaster of Monroe, Wisconsin, and Leftenant W. F. Miller, acting postmaster of Independence, Iowa. It has been a duel to the breath and everywhere is spent ammunition.

"It was Leftenant Miller, away back there in January, who voiced the insult to Mlle. Limburger. He said bluntly that she smelled bad, and that he would no longer permit her to hang around the post office. He said, moreover, that she was improperly dressed and that she was contaminating the less flamboyant parcels in the vault.

"Mlle. Limburger was sent back in disgrace to Monroe from whence she came. But again she ventured into the office of the sensitive Leftenant Miller and again she was ordered out as a wanton and malodorous baggage. The second affront occurred February 28.

"This was altogether too much for the gallant Chevalier Burkhard. He challenged Leftenant Miller to a duel to be fought hand to hand with rye bread sandwiches, on neutral ground. The place was Dubuque, and the hour was 2:30 P.M. Saturday. The appointed moment coincided nicely with lunchtime. The contestants were on time to the second.

"The injured party, Chevalier Burkhard, appeared with a considerable company of Monroe citizens with Colonel Ralph H. Wenger, of the Badger-Brodhead Cheese Company, as chief second. Leftenant Miller was accompanied only by his two sons and J. H. Levin, of the post office construction department. Major Levin acted as second for the independent gentleman from Independence.

"Neither contestant wore armor of any sort, except an opulent napkin placed immediately below the second chin. Both were standing stoically as they advanced to shake hands. A hush fell upon the gathering of Monroe, Independence, and Dubuque citizens, flanked by the correspondents and photographers who had been tipped off on the date.

"The formalities over, Chevalier Burkhard drew his knife and cut a thick slice of Badger Brand. He placed the aromatic ammunition upon a slice of rye and thrust it into the dauntless right hand of Leftenant Miller. General Anton F. Schrup, post-master of Dubuque, who was serving as referee, spoke the signal that had been agreed upon; 'Allons, Messieurs,' said General Schrup. 'Go to it!'

"Leftenant Miller took a large and manful bite. His grim expression changed. He took another bite and a smile appeared on his ruddy countenance. He took a third bite, which meant the end of the sandwich, and his battle-scarred face turned positively beatific.

"In the meantime Chevalier Burkhard had been loading again, and when Leftenant Miller completed the final swallow, another charge was given him point-blank. Again he took it full in the mouth, and again he gave every evidence of full enjoy-ment. It was apparent that this would be the most one-sided duel in history.

"A third time Chevalier Burkhard loaded and fired with perfect aim. A third time Leftenant Miller took three bites, making nine bites in all, and the cheese disappeared beneath his waistcoat.

"The Independence traducer then held up his hand in token of surrender. He was still smiling broadly, but looked a trifle dry. He moved slowly to the center of Parlor B where many bottles containing restoratives had been placed in case of casualties, and proposed a toast to his conqueror.

" 'Chevalier Burkhard,' he said, 'your honor, and the honor of your girl friend, Mlle. Limburger, is avenged. I pledge my word that never again will I say or do anything to reflect upon either of you. Chevalier and Gentlemen, I give you a cheese that is a cheese!!'

"All the tenseness of the occasion disappeared with Leften-ant Miller's acknowledgement of defeat. Onlookers who had been holding their ears, if not their noses, promptly relaxed, and the rest of the meeting was nothing if not jovial.

"A good many of the bottles on the table in Parlor B contained the famous liquid companion of Mlle. Limburger, Herr Pilsener. The two were the life of the party. Even Leftenant Miller was never without one or the other on his lap.

"Further to add to the triumph of Mlle. Limburger, Che-valier Burkhard and Chief Second Wenger spoke eulogies to the 'living cheese.' Both eloquent gentlemen declared that every other variety is a sissy. They lauded the scent of Mlle. Limbur-ger, her beauty of complexion, and her firm yellow body. It was enough to bring blushes to any heroine.

" 'The reason Mlle. Limburger bears her own perfume,' said Chief Second Wenger, 'is just this: Within her tender skin . . . rind to you roughnecks . . . is whey. The whey ferments and that makes the aroma. It is just a natural process like the distilling of perfume within the rose. Other cheeses don't have Mlle. Limburger's fragrance because they lack whey.'

"Then he discoursed on the garments worn by Mlle. Limburger when she journeys through the mails. No fashionable lady has such lingerie. First there is parchment, then manila, then tin foil, then a filmy label, then a wax paper wrapper, and finally a parchment coat in lieu of mink.

" 'In lieu of mink,' murmured Leftenant Miller, 'to retain the . . . that is, er . . . I mean to retain the unsurpassed fragrance.'

" 'Precisely,' said Chief Second Wenger.

"But all the same, the other Chief Second, Major Levin, of the post office construction corps, took the correspondent aside. He said: 'We are now building a new post office in Independence. It will be a modern and beautiful edifice.'

" 'What will be its special feature?' asked the correspondent.

"Major Levin paused and smiled. Then he said impressively, 'A smell-proof vault.'

"Henceforth when Mlle. Limburger arrives from Monroe, Wisconsin, she will be royally received in Independence, Iowa. It's a grand idea for a lady so renowned."

VI. Early Firehouse

# PART TWO -
# The FLAVORS OF
# RIDGE AND WATER

VII. Washington Island Shore

# The Bitters Society

Washington Island has the only Bitters Society in the world, as far as I know. The island's getting to be a pretty sophisticated place these days with Paul Rutledge as full-time physician and a big new community center as well as a new marina and Norse motel complex building down at beautiful South Point. But the Bitters Society transcends all periods and cuts across every aspect of island life. I don't know what Dr. Rutledge thinks of the society as a plus on the side of island health, but society members consider their organization the veritable fountain of youth. In Bessie's place they will tell you about the society like this:

Old Tom Nelsen, who started Nelsen's Tavern on Washington Island, before he came to this country worked at an angostura bitters factory in Europe; of course he developed a liking for bitters himself, and he found out that it had a pretty good wallop too.

The label on the bottle says 50 percent alcohol — that's equivalent to 100 proof whisky — so during Prohibition, angostura bitters became a medicine, not a liquor. And during Prohibition old Tom got himself a druggist's license and dispensed bitters in place of liquor.

If the boys couldn't get any whisky, they could always get themselves looped on Tom's angostura bitters. They say that all you've got to do, if you want a good cheap drunk, is to take a bottle of beer and three shots of angostura bitters and you're all set. If you can walk home, you're doin' well.

The people who make bitters say Washington Island is one of the few places in the country that buys it by the case! Washington Island is known as the bitters capital of the world for more is consumed there than any other place in the United States.

Many a Washington Island sailor, and quite a few island boys do go on the lakes to work, will roll into a tavern on the mainland somewhere and holler, "Hey! Give me a shot of angostura bitters!" Bartenders will look at them and ask, "You say *bitters?*" And the Washington Island boys will say, "Angostura!" They will finally give it to them! And up and down the bar the customers will gather round to watch. "It's good!" the boys say. "It has a better flavor than whisky!"

There's about a hundred different kinds of herbs in it, good for gravy seasoning, too.

Old Tom Nelsen never really got so old that he couldn't be in the bar. He got a couch and lay down behind the bar when he felt tired. He lived into his nineties because, he said, he drank some angostura bitters every day. Washington Island folks were so impressed the way old Tom lived so long that they do their best to follow his example. That is why they have a Bitters Society on the island.

The headquarters are, naturally, Bessie's Bitters Bar, for Tom is finally gone now. Bessie is Tom's daughter-in-law.

To be a member of the Bitters Society is really pretty easy. All you have to do is down a two-ounce glass of angostura bitters. Then you wet a thumb and make your print on a card. You are then a card-carrying member of the Bitters Society.

I have been a member of the society for a long time now. The first time I went into Bessie's, back a few years, I was with my friend Wilson Trueblood, who may have been one of the charter members. Anyway we were standing in Bessie's place, up to the bar, and I had just become a member, and was wondering how my stomach was going to feel, when an old fellow next to me — don't now recall his name — thought, I guess, that I was acting like some kind of a hero, just from drinking the bitters. He says "You like to make like a hero, do you? Hero of what? War? Love? It ain't so hard to be a hero nowadays, anyhow. The movies will make a hero easy, or TV. Or you just set and holler louder than anybody else and you'll be a hero with a bunch of girls tracking you around, too. Heroes! Why, there ain't many today that can bear pain or suffering. Soft, yep. We're soft all right. I seen a lumberjack once in a camp up Vilas County, cut his foot nigh off with an ax. Seen it couldn't be fixed so he just hacked her off the rest of the way and come acrawlin' back to the bunkhouse carryin' his foot along with him. Says he didn't want to leave her there to freeze. Now I call that heroic behavior, gentlemen. Ain't no real brave ones any-more.

"You take old Bob Noble of Washington Island. You been here on the island, boy? You ain't no boy, I see that, but still you ain't a real man! Not no man like Bob Noble was. Know what Bob done?

"Well, you heard of Death's Door, ain't you? Water be-tween Plum Island and the mainland, Door County. That's the

Door. Right unpredictable waters, boys. You heard of it? How all them Potowatomi Indians drowned in there? Swamped the whole bunch of 'em, four, five hundred anyhow, and they was drowned, all of 'em. Well, ain't no matter now, but Bob Noble, he was a man, one of them heroes; even if he didn't save nothin' but himself.

"One morning, December 31, was 1864, Bob set out in his old scow to row from Detroit Harbor to the mainland. Death's Door was full of floatin' ice, but Bob shoved himself along right well till he was opposite Plum Island. Sudden he was in the midst of thick ice. Way it is in the Door, seems like clear sailin' then, Wow! she closes up. Well, Bob he got to Plum Island all right, but she was deserted. Nothin' living was there. Tried to build him a fire. Was forty below!

"Was an old lighthouse on Plum Island. A ruin, but Bob he went in there. Finally he got a fire goin' with the one or two matches he had; but snow slid down from the old clogged chimney and swamped it out. Bob waltzed and frisked around all night long. Had to. Would have froze.

"Morning, Bob hadn't et or slept for a day and a night. Decided he'd better turn back to Detroit Harbor. So he set out in his scow, and had went maybe a quarter-mile when the ice got him again. So Bob rips out the seats of the scow, made him some snowshoes, and set out a foot over shiftin' ice.

" 'Course the ice gave way with him and into the water he went. You ever been cast into Michigan water, boy? When she's forty below? You ain't? I guess you ain't. But Bob Noble, he was different stuff'n you. Swum back to the boat. Was froze nigh solid. Ice everywhere on him. Like one of them iron suits. But old Bob he stamped and howled around and seen that he couldn't walk, so he flung himself on his belly and started slidin' himself along on the ice.

"Ice busted and Bob was in the waters, tryin' to hold on, slidin' off of the ice cakes; and then his arms turned into big hammers of ice, and Bob used 'em like hammers, breakin' the ice ahead of him.

"Was crawlin', swimmin', pullin' himself along, for five, six hours; and he made it across to Detroit Harbor. Ice was firmer there and he got to Washington Island. Found a fisherman's shack.

"People ought not to have used kerosene to soak him in. Kerosene has a lower temperature than water and water would have helped save his feet and hands in my opinion. Brought out the frost! But they soaked him in kerosene. 'Course his feet and fingers was ruined.

"But wasn't no doctor on Washington Island, and no way gettin' Bob to the mainland. Had to wait till June he did, with feet and fingers rottin' all that time.

"Come a doctor from Kenosha in June. Hadn't no doctor tools. Cut off Bob's fingers and feet with a butcher saw. But that didn't stop Bob neither.

"Old Bob he got him some wood feet and a couple of hooks for hands and went back to work. Was a well driller, he was, and run the ferry over to Sturgeon Bay, too.

"You know, boy, what become of a hero like Bob?

"They put him in the poorhouse when he got old and he couldn't lick that. The poorhouse finished him. I'm tellin' you true. Old Bob Noble was a hero. Ain't that so?"

# The Islanders

I have come over to Washington Island on a cold February morning, driving from Sturgeon Bay to Northport where the Washington Island boats put in when they can't use Gills Rock; the Gills Rock side, I have seen, is completely frozen in. The trees stand blackly silent and tall at the peninsula's end, and the road is deserted, not a person or a moving vehicle visible as I turn from Gills Rock to Northport in the early light. The desolate Northport wharf is covered with thick ice.

I know that the propeller on the Washington Island Richter Ferry, the *Griffin*, has had an encounter with a hunk of ice that got stuck and that a blade of the wheel has been broken. While the *Griffin* (so named by Arnie Richter after the schooner of La Salle, some say, sunk in Death's Door in 1679) is in Sturgeon Bay getting a new propeller, the *Ranger* carries valiantly on.

The *Ranger* is a fishing tug, and she really isn't equipped to be a ferry. She is low inside; forward is the fish-handling equipment. At the port side an old coal stove reddens and smokes. Center is the big diesel engine, enclosed, and behind is the steering gear.

The weather is very cold, seven below at present. It is beginning to snow, and I have been waiting at Northport for the *Ranger* for about two hours. I am well iced.

Mrs. Arnie Richter told me, when I called her last night from Sturgeon, that the *Griffin* is laid up but that the *Ranger* will definitely be over to pick up mail and some freight and passengers. A young soldier and his bride, both Washington Island natives, a trucker from Illinois, and I are the only passengers. I have left my car near the ferry landing at Northport, and now we are aboard the *Ranger* where I happily nurse the coal stove while milk cans are put aboard. A snowmobile owned by the trucker, who is going over for a winter holiday, is hoisted up on top, on the deck; some plywood is stowed; propane gas tanks are clanked in; and a batch of soil pipe is tossed up with the plywood. The *Ranger* is pretty well filled with these items. The young soldier, sturdily built, easily handles the heavy gas tanks, and I lend a much less sturdy hand with the ten-gallon milk cans, which fortunately are empty.

On the way over from Washington Island the ice, they tell me, has been bad. The Coast Guard launch from Sturgeon Bay that was formerly kept at Plum Island has been pressed in to help break a way, and the steel hull has ripped the ice, or the powerful propeller has thrust the launch right up on top of the ice so that the weight of it breaks it out. The *Ranger* has gotten through.

Now, after the freight has been loaded, the cakes have welded together again, and the *Ranger* presently knocks into the ice. I am amazed that the wooden hull of the fishing craft will take the pounding.

I never cross the Door in good weather or bad, without feeling a sense of romance, partly from the name itself, I suppose. Death's Door has a mystic and somehow a final symbolism. But half the pleasure of a Richter Ferry ride is the romance, and when a storm is really blowing and the stubby boats "stand on their beam ends" with vast dashes of spray against the cabin windows, and here and there a sick, sick face, the old stories of the Door and its hazards seem somehow more real.

According to the late Hjalmer Holand, peninsula historian, and Conan Eaton, contemporary historian, the Door got its name in the following way: When the Winnebago Indians came to Door County Peninsula, they found it occupied by the Potawatomi, who offered to share the land. The Winnebago refused and attacked the less numerous Potawatomi at every chance. The Potawatomi withdrew to the islands, but even there they were not safe from invasion by the Winnebago. The islander Indians planned a surprise counterattack across the water and sent three spies ahead to kindle a beacon to guide their canoes to safety.

The spies were caught. Under torture one finally told their secret plans. The Winnebagos lit a fire one dark and windy night on a steep bluff, which offered only danger. Meanwhile, they dispatched a canoe detachment by a roundabout route to attack the islanders' camp.

As the misdirected Potawatomi urged their canoes toward the fire, a great increase in wind and waves cut off all choice of turning back. Their frail craft were broken against the rocky bluff. Some braves drowned; the rest were soon tomahawked by the waiting enemy.

For their part, all the Winnebagos in canoes were swamped by the seas and drowned in the passage. Their tribesmen waited at land's end a full day until the wrecked canoes washed up on the shore. They took this loss as an omen that they must never again try to cross the Door of Death, as it was afterward called.

Out the *Ranger's* port I see fantastic and beautiful patterns of jagged and broken ice. When the cakes have frozen together it is a puzzle of abstract shapes. Far out is a stretch of open water, and I wonder why, since the temperature is below zero. "Current," somebody says. "The winds make a strong current through the Door, and if the wind would start suddenly to blow hard from the northwest, all this ice would go out of here."

Over near the horizon and stretching away between Plum Island and the mainland is what appears to be a great wall of snow and ice called the bridge. It forms that way and acts as a barrier so that passing over the ice is sometimes possible.

We bang and crunch our way into the dock at Washington Island. Out across the ice are the two old car ferries that Ed Anderson, the island potato king, purchased for twenty-five thousand dollars apiece to store his potato crop in. Everybody who comes to the island wants to know what those huge boats are doing there.

The *Ranger* has a little trouble getting up to the dock. Ice has to be broken and cleared out. But eventually we are tied up, and I climb out over the milk cans. Percy Johnson, town chairman of Washington Island, who works for the ferry line, is waiting for me in the ferry office. Percy is large, friendly, and competent. He has been a good chairman, getting a number of things accomplished for the island, including a fine new community building. They have needed that for years. I sat in the warm office and Percy did some talking.

"Lots of times," he began, "these ice conditions get really rough. Sometimes it has taken as much as eight hours to make a crossing. One winter about three years ago we had a boat comin' back from Northport just about dark, and it got a big ice cake in the wheel. Couldn't back up or go ahead. Had to call the Coast Guard. They come out here and freed her. Course if there wouldn't have been no Coast Guard boat the ferry would have stayed there all night. Things like that are kind of hectic.

"You have to remember that the ferry is our lifeline. If we don't have a ferry service, boy the island is up against it. All our supplies come over on the ferry. Even the milk goes now. All the milk from the farmers goes across every day, and of course then the ferry brings the milk cans back.

"The Door really isn't such a dangerous piece of water. It scares people when they hear of Death's Door, but actually it's not so bad. It was the old sailing boats that really had problems."

"I guess the people remember those Potawatomi and Winnebago Indians that Hjalmer Holand said were drowned in the Door," I said.

"That's right, and the boys on the ferry boats really have to answer questions. Everybody wants to know why it's called Death's Door. 'Is this really the Door of Death?' 'Do all ships that sail here run great danger?' "

"How long has Arnie Richter been running the ferry?"

"Since 1940. He bought it from the original owner, Bill Jepson. Arnie has done well with the ferry. Bill Jepson, he did well, too. Only thing was, he had wife trouble and got divorced, and the lawyers and the courts sort of left old Bill stranded.

"He had a boat called the *Welcome*. Was a wooden craft, square sterned, and she'd carry about twelve cars, the small kind, Ford Model T's and A's and such.

"Arnie took over the ferry in 1940 and made a success of it. He had all our boats built: the *Griffin* was built in 1946, the *Richter* in 1942, and the *Voyageur* in 1960. He's a good employer. Men like to work for Arnie, and generally our men stay a long while."

"Was gonna tell you," says Percy, now telling how independent island folks really are, "I got an old uncle, dead now, but when he was eighty years old this new Social Security thing come through where they could get this thirty-five dollars a month after seventy-two. He wouldn't even take that. That independent! 'I've gone all my life on my own way. I'm gonna go the rest of the way!' That's how independent they are.

"One old guy out here, he could have been getting a pile of money all this time through the veterans. He's entitled to it. All he had to do was go down to Sturgeon Bay and sign for it. He could have been getting, gee, seventy-five dollars a month or something, for years and years — ten, twelve years back. He won't. That's how independent they are."

"Who supports some of these old timers who haven't got anything left?" I asked.

"They take care of themselves. Anyway, they are so interrelated, they always got some family here. Actually, they're self-sustaining. It doesn't take too much to live over here. They saved their money. They work a little, too. Cutting wood, to save fuel bills. Electric bill is small, all they need is a few light bulbs."

Thorsten Williamson, director of the CAP office on the island, comes in. He certainly must be one of the strongest men on the island, and Washington Island has a long history of strong men. Thorsten is built like a heavyweight wrestler, a walking oak tree. He is going to take me over to see an old-time fisherman named Albert Goodmander, who lives over on the other side of Washington. Albert, retired now, has the reputation of knowing many things about the island, the Door, and the olden days. We climb into Thorsten's CAP carryall and drive over to Albert's.

Albert, in his eighties, greets us warmly at the back door of his pleasant dwelling. He acts as though he is really glad to have callers. We go into his living room and he doesn't give me much time to get ready.

"Where's your home town?" says Albert, looking at me very brightly. "Where you from?"

"Madison."

"Oh."

"I'm from the University of Wisconsin."

"Oh."

"I've been interested in the island. Been here many times. Came over on the *Ranger* today."

"Yep. Ferry busted down. They got to use that *Griffin* boat because she's the only one with a single screw. Got to use a single-screw boat in ice."

"Was asking something about an old timer I heard about once in Bessie's Bar. Bob Noble. Ever hear of him?"

"Yep. Knew him."

"Was quite a man, I hear."

"That's right. At one time he was quite a man."

"Big fellow, wasn't he?"

"Had been. Had been a big, strappin' man. And he had a case on this schoolteacher here. I forgot just who that was. Tried to think who she was. Well, Bob he tried to cross the Door on foot on thin ice. Fell through. It was cold! Managed to get out and crawled up on the ice, was on Plum Island. Managed to get back froze. And they cut both of his legs off, at the knee. He was tough, strong, hardy. Big feller. Went back to Sturgeon Bay and started in the implement business. Told lots of stories. Had a couple of wooden legs."

"I was thinking, coming over on the *Ranger* today, what it would be like to be out there in that water where it isn't frozen.

Be a cool bath!"

"Yep," said Albert. "Remember one time we left the island, were going to Chicago. George Hall was captain of the Coast Guard station, and they had a little boat here that was built at Sturgeon Bay. She was a pretty good little iceboat, but she was small, and a bunch of us . . . there was thirteen of us, nine from the island, all going to Chicago. They bucked ice until they come around the south side of Plum Island, for three hours, and couldn't make no headway, so there were two Coast Guard guys with us, and the mail carrier was a feller by name of Christenson, and we got out on the ice there and we walked to the south end of Plum Island and across over to the mainland And the Coast Guard men they had canes or sticks and every time they would stick them in the ice they would go right through and water would shoot up. It happens like that, that the Door will freeze over with one or two or three inches of ice and a swell comes down the lake and mows everything right down. There was thirteen of us. That's an unlucky number. But we got acrost."

"Did the ice crack?"

"Oh! Roar, you'd think there was a regular thunder storm!"

"Is this Door particularly dangerous?"

"Sure. It's a passage, you know, and it gets awful rough and a big swell comin' out. Course they exaggerate a little bit, but the Indians when they were fighting here, a tribe would come here and get drowned in the Door. My dad came here in 1872. Came to Milwaukee in 1870. And then mother came over in 1872. Well, then they lived on Detroit Island for two years. You seen that long island there, didn't you? Well, they lived there for a couple of years. Then they moved over to Washington. If you notice when you come up the main road where they're building the community house, they lived near there."

"Your father a farmer?"

"They owned a forty. But he wasn't no farmer. He was from that part of Iceland there where they fished. About all he knew. Got a job in Milwaukee right away, on Jones Island. Was a big fishing place them days. Feller by name of Hen Allen, Russian-Finn, I guess, had him a little fishing boat. Lake was full of fish then. Then they moved up here after two years. Them days the bay was just loaded with whitefish."

"What kind of folks lived here on Washington Island then?"

"In the seventy's there, along the shore, they were mostly all Irish. They lived right on the edge of the beach, and they would pull the boats out nights. And one time Rock Island was really a town before this here was. There was Indians here then. They disappeared, too. Mostly the Washington Island Indians went up north when they left here. They liked it better up in Michigan. There was an awful lot of half-breeds."

"Why did the Icelandic people come here so much in the early days?"

"There was a few came here, and my folks was some of the first ones. Then they flocked here. They came because there was so many Icelanders here. But there was much more that left here when they seen what it looked like. They went on out west and took up homesteads."

"Well, there must have been a lot of fishing here, in the big days of fishing."

"Sure. Didn't need a very big rig, you know. Not too many nets. Boats were small and all sailboats; but they were mostly Irish here at that time. Feller at Rock Island named Severs. Had been a druggist in England. He was one of the first to start fishing out of Rock Island. They said he left a family in England. Don't know how true that is but sure married another woman after he got on Rock Island. Little vessel come along pickin' up fish. Left him there. Then he got married to another woman by name of Boyce, and they had one child. And he got to be our town clerk and was postmaster for years and years. Funny how things happen, ain't it? So that made the fourth wife. Jessie Miner told me this. Must be a woman I missed in there somewhere."

"Went off and left him, eh?"

"Not the last two. One got to be crippled up and she was a dope fiend for years and years. Then he married another one named Rittenberg from Egg Harbor. Have to have women here. Washington Harbor was a big fishing place here, and there was others all along the island."

"Was this a pretty wild place those times?"

"You get a little whisky . . . them Irish was as bad as the Indians. They liked whisky better'n they do beer. Every Fourth of July was a big celebration. They would go out on the lake on the third of July so they could get a good start. After they'd get ashore after dinner, they would open up the beer keg. Generally started out with beer. Ended up with whisky."

"Lot of excitement?"

"Oh, boy!"

"Lot of fights maybe?"

"Oh, fights! Turrible! Would lay around like dogs. Next day, Fourth of July ... worse! Was another bad place down West Harbor there ... big Dutchman there. Had a big factory at Sheboygan. Herman [The Dutchman] came up here. Biggest store on the island at that time. Now it's different altogether. Yeah. Then there was old Hutchins; he was an Englishman. Good education but a terrible drunkard. He left his family in Canada someplace, got a job on a sailing boat, and he was drunk all the time, so when they got up in the Door here, the captain sent him ashore in the yawl boat. Dumped him off there. It wasn't any real addition, because the Irishmen was all drunk there anyhow. Hutchins' home town was Hull, in England. He said.

"Then he straightened up. There was a woman here that preached out in the Baptist church. She belonged to the Salvation Army. She came here from Gills Rock, and she converted old Hutchins."

"She converted Hutchins?"

"Old Hutchins, yeah."

"What happened to him after that, then?"

"Well, he was gettin' quite old, then. Eighty years old. But he's got a grandson, real good preacher.

"Old Hutchins said he had danced with the devil for years and years and years. Now, he said, he was gonna dance with the Lord!"

"What did Hutchins look like?"

"Well, he was tall. Pretty near six feet tall. Long beard. But that beard never hurt his drinkin' none."

# Captain Jack

After we left Albert's I drove one of the CAP cars over to Martha Stelter's Holiday Inn. Martha's cherry pie, made of island cherries, is perhaps the best I have ever eaten and she is a remarkable women in other ways: a fine hostess, a musician, and an artist. I first met her years ago when she was trying to become a writer, a conference at Green Lake I think it was. So I always stay at Martha's when I go over to Washington Island.

Now I wash up a little, because Thorsten Williamson has invited me over to his house near the ferry dock for dinner. His wife, Mae, has fixed an Irish stew, which doesn't have much cultural significance because Thorsten is Norse and Mae is Mexican, a fortuitous combination that has led to a good marriage and fine children.

After a fine dinner Thorsten had a happy thought. "I'll call up Capt. Jack Hagen," he said. "Jack has lived all his life on the island and has sailed most of his life. He runs a party fishing boat now. Knows all the good fishing places around the islands. If Jack will come over he can tell you some great yarns."

Jack was happy to come and arrived presently. He has slightly gray hair, a face as strong and chiseled as Dick Tracy — a tall, handsome, powerful Irishman, and proud of it. He has been a Great Lakes sailor, a farmer, and now, in the summer, he makes a living chartering his boat for fishing parties. He gets comfortable in one of the easy chairs, and when I tell him how I am trying to get some slants on the informal and romantic lore of the islands a glimmer comes into Jack's eyes.

"Well," Jack said, "we had a strong man around Washington Island named Allen Bradley. An Irishman. He was known as the giant of Hedgehog Harbor because he once lived at Gills Rock and it was called Hedgehog Harbor! Some of the feats of strength he performed were quite unique. In fact, one of them finally appeared in Ripley's "Believe It Or Not." There was a store down in Washington Harbor they called the Furlong Dock. Folks used to get their flour, salt, supplies there. One day when Bradley came down to get some supplies the storekeeper told 'im, 'Bradley, if you can carry a barrel of flour home on your back without stopping, I would give you the barrel!'

"Mr. Bradley was a poor man, and this was a chance to get some free flour. So he put the barrel of flour on his back himself, 496 pounds, and he started off. On the way up from the dock he had to climb the first hill, a pretty steep one, and then it was uphill for the next half-mile, and just before coming to the Bethel church, there is a real steep hill, and about halfway up that one they said one of his friends came along, and Bradley passed the time of day with 'im. Must have been quite some while because Bradley was a very courteous man and didn't want to walk off in a hurry from anybody.

"Anyhow he continued on his journey and carried the flour to his home. It was a distance of three miles. And Bradley never took the flour off of his back, or never stopped until he got there."

"Jack, do you happen to know what year this might have been?" I asked.

"That would have to be right around 1880," Jack said. "The island was pretty young then, too, and that was when the Furlong Dock was going pretty strong. Well, one of the other feats that Bradley performed, Grandfather Koyen was tellin' me, was when they were putting in the Furling Dock. They had a big log to get into place. And they said there was ten men strugglin' with that log to get it into place. It was going to tie in a corner of the dock.

"Those ten men couldn't get it put into place. Bradley happened to come down there just before dinner, and he was watching them, and the men couldn't do it, and it was lunch time, so they dropped everything and went off to eat lunch. When they came back to go to work, why Bradley had put that log into place. By himself.

"Another time he was in Sturgeon Bay and there was a schooner anchor on one side of the street. They said the anchor weighed eleven hundred pounds. So they bet Bradley that he couldn't carry it across the street. He shouldered that anchor and he carried it from one corner of the street to the other."

"Some boy," I said.

"You're right," Jack said. "Some boy! He was a big man, over six-foot-six, and broad as a farm door. Once he carried a 240 pound man for about a quarter-mile with the fellow hanging onto Bradley's beard. Course, back then the fellows were all pretty husky, because they worked hard, and I guess got simple pleasures out of being strong, or of admirin' somebody who was. Something to do, you know? They would start telling some things. My uncle was working for Al Schousley. They were running a freighter between the island and Green Bay, and of course the farmers would ship their cream to the factories in Green Bay, and they would send it by this little freighter. So one day a bunch of the boys were standing by the warehouse and Clyde was there (my uncle) and they bet Clyde that he couldn't take two ten-gallon cream cans in each hand — four ten-gallon cream cans — and carry 'em from the warehouse and set 'em on board the *Wisconsin.*

"Now Clyde had to carry them a distance of seventy-five feet, and these were full. So they took up a collection. Wasn't much any one of 'em had, but together they made up quite a purse. So Clyde says, 'All right, put your money up.' And Clyde took up those ten-gallon cream cans, two in each hand, and done 'em one better, he took and set 'em up over the boat's rail with one hand. He took and set the four of 'em up there. That man weighed 170 pounds. So he carried 200 pounds in each hand, and imagine gripping those two handles together. You're familiar with a cream can, you know what that is. He just lifted 'em up four feet in the air to set 'em on that rail. You wonder how, wouldn't you? He's living out in Arizona right now. Yeah. And when you look at 'im you wouldn't think that he could lift any more than anybody else, because he was slender built, but he had great big hands and big arms and he was wiry. But he was powerful; he would take a full barrel of gasoline and lift it aboard the boat. That's 550 pounds. Just roll it up and set it up, 'stead of bothering to use the sling.

"But there's a trick in that too. You get down and get the barrel onto your knee, and then you roll the barrel up your leg. But it still takes a lot of strength."

"I would think it would."

"Now when I was on the Door County board we were sitting and talking up in Sturgeon Bay about feats of strength; one of the fellows from Bailey's Harbor said the town chairman they had a few years before would take a sack of marrowfat peas, 140 pounds, grab it in his teeth, and shoulder it. Imagine that, grab it in his teeth and toss if over his shoulder!

"An' I dunno, used to talk about splittin' wood and so forth. I know Grandpa Koyen was tellin' me about Grandfather Garret, one used to walk to Green Bay on the ice. Said he was a powerful man, said he was walking along through the woods one day, and he came up to these guys that were cuttin' wood an' he picked up the ax. Said, 'You got a pretty good ax here,' and he swung it into a tree, right up to the eye, and they couldn't get it out. Hadda go get a sledge to knock it out! Grandpa said that he was just terrific. One of the boats came in, a steamboat, had a little boiler then, and they wanted two cords of wood in less than four hours. He had to cut it with an ax and deliver it. He had to go to the woods, cut that, and deliver it to the boat in four hours.

"He says, 'I'll be there with it,' and he was.

"He cut that two full cords of wood with his ax and delivered it. He said in less than four hours."

"A cord of wood's a lot of wood, isn't it?"

"That's right. That's a pile four feet high, sixteen feet long, and four feet wide. It's four by four by sixteen. He cut two of those in four hours and delivered it. But as my grandpa said, when he swung the ax it went in up to the eye every time. Wasn't no little ax like you have nowadays. He said he had about a five-pound ax he used.

"Never seen nothin' like it, Grandpa says, way he could swing. He could cut a tree down a lot faster than anybody could saw it down. My Grandfather Koyen he knew what he was talkin' about. He said it was unbelievable."

I had heard that at one time there was a considerable Irish settlement down at Washington Harbor. There had been, so Albert Goodmander said, some wild doings down there.

"Ever hear of the Irish settlement?" I asked Jack.

He laughed. "I was born down there."

"Were you?"

"Sure. Even though I'm only fifty years old. My grandparents lived there. There was four houses, and I can remember them myself. A couple of 'em were two-family dwellings. And that was called the early settlement. Too bad those buildings weren't preserved. The construction was different. And there was the 'white house' there and it was the first frame dwelling in Door County out of sawed lumber. I used to play in that. I remember when Annie Einarson was still living in it. But of course those Irishmen were pretty tough!"

"That's what I hear."

"Oh, they had the Irishmen's war. At one time there was a kind of excursion come over from Escanaba. I think there was around fifty people. They brought their own beer with 'em. They were having a big outing. Don't know what organization it was. There were three or four fish boats, I guess. Anyhow, they started beering and gambling, were havin' themselves a time! An' a lot of these Irishmen joined 'em and started getting pretty well oiled up, if you want to put it that way, an' began to fight. And Willie Whitman was the constable, and they called Willie to come to stop it. When these Irishmen seen Willie acomin' they took in after him and they chased him up a tree. And he stayed there.

"An' I can't think of the feller's name now, might have been Tom Guinan. Anyhow, he picked up a club and he hit an Escanaba man across the eye, and the guy went up the road hollering at the top of his voice: 'Boy! I got mine, boys! I got mine!'

"And old Charlie McDonald, he knifed a guy in the arm."

"This Irishmen's war, it was really a liquor war, eh?"

"Well, they call it the Irishmen's war. An' I guess the fellows from Escanaba, when they seen what they had started, packed up their gear and took off. The damage was done then though. Old Tom Guinan, he was quite a tough man. Once he had a guy down on the floor of a tavern and he took his thumb and gouged the other feller's eye out, and they grabbed him, and Tom he let a lingo out of him and says, 'If you hadn't pulled me off, I'da got the other eye too!'

"That's the way they fought. It was a way of life with those Irishmen."

"Was this about the same time as Bradley?"

"No. This was later. About 1900 was the Irishmen's war."

"These Irishmen were mostly fishermen?" I asked.

"Yeah. Fishermen, and involved in this, too, was the Barnson brothers, the Helgesons — they were Icelanders but they must have had the fighting Irishmen's heart, I guess, because they surely did fight all the time.

"We could to on to the Barnson boys, Johnny and Sivert, and Bess Helgeson. They fished together, they drank hard, moonshine, and they could always tell when those boys got drunk on the lake. Sivert, he could swim, and Johnny and Bess they couldn't swim, and even if they were out in the lake ten miles Bess and Johnny would try to throw Sievert in over the side. Make him swim ashore. Sievert would jump up on top of the boat to get away from 'em; folks could tell when the boys had been having a party, because here would be Sievert standing up on top of the boat, and he'd have a club in his hand, and if they tried to get up to get at him, he would club 'em across the fingers. Keep 'em down.

"One day Sievert got even. He was the only one who could run the engine, so they got about three hundred feet from the dock coming in and they were going to throw Sievert overboard as usual, but he stopped the engine and jumped overboard. They couldn't start the engine, and there was an offshore wind and they went drifting out in the lake."

"Were there any famous female characters?"

"Oh, yes. Take Idy Richter out here, she was just a good picturesque woman, about six feet tall. Went right on the lake with her husband and worked right along with him. Her and the boys. They had this point, right out here across from Thorstens, and the ferry dock. They call it Richter's Point. There was two sons, Earl and Roy. Both gone now. Were first cousins to Arnie who runs the ferry now.

"Well, strange things happen on these islands. You know, on Rock Island, one of the original members of the Boston Tea Party settled out there."

"Really? What was his name?"

"Kennison. I think he lived to be 120 years old. The saying often crops up, you know: one man can raise and take care of eight children, but eight children can't take care of one old man, not when he's old and feeble they can't spend the time on it."

"That's the truth."

"Well, this old tea party man was the same way. He had twelve or thirteen children and he ended up in Chicago. Incidentally, in one of the Chicago parks there's a monument to him. He went down there and he exhibited himself as the last remaining member of the Boston Tea Party, and of course charged a little bit, and that's the way he kept himself out of the poorhouse. His kids never done a thing for him.

"And say, you know there was a railroad one time on Washington Island?"

"A railroad?"

"Yep."

"Really? Where?"

"Over on the east side. Believe it or not. Lot of folks don't know that. Wish I could recall the number of board feet. I'm gonna find that out. Number of board feet they took out on a sleigh load. Was big. They had a load of logs on there one time that Grandfather said was unbelievable. But they used to carry water and ice the trail so they could put a load of logs on, sometimes sixteen feet high. Would have an overhang so the logs would hang over ten feet or so.

"Well, they figured they ought to have a railroad to make the logging easier in soft weather when couldn't use the sleighs. So they made the rails out of hardwood, and the ties just cut, and the railroad was about four miles long. They started out just about at Jackson Harbor, and they had wheels made that would fit on the wooden rails, and they would pull these cars with oxen. Didn't have any steam. Just oxen. A train pulled by oxen. Even today I can take you out in a section where the ties of this railroad are still there. Of course the track is gone but the corduroy is there. Had to keep the rails on level ground, so they had to meander around in the woods for the level spots. Was kind of interesting. Grandpa talked about the size of the trees. You know, you walk around the woods today you see a cedar tree about eighteen inches in diameter you think that's a pretty big cedar. But he told me on the fraction, out where Hogg Island Park is now, they sawed cedar trees in there six feet in diameter. He told me the number of ties they got out of one log and it was fantastic.

"Wasn't there a lonesome pine or somethin' out here" Thorsten asked.

"That tree was about seven feet in diameter. Lightning struck that. It was in Arnold Wickman's. It's a shame when you stop to think of it. On the farm where I'm livin' right today, when they cleared that it was some of the finest pine in the area. They just cut it down and put the torch to it, just to get rid of it. Pine that were four or five feet in diameter. In there one of the logs, when they were skidding one time, was so big that when they hit a side hill it rolled down and took the team with it. Couldn't stop. Miracle neither of the horses got hurt. Six feet in diameter and eighteen feet long that log was. My dad always told about the time the Barnson boys got tangled up in a drinking brawl; that was in West Harbor right below my place. Old Freiberg lived there. He had a glass eye and Bess Helgeson hit him in the eye and busted his glass eye in his head. Never hurt him. My dad was witness to that. They had old Hutchins, as they called him, by the beard, and they were pulling him along the ground, using old Hutchins for a sled. This Johnny Barnson he was just a little guy, not over five-foot-two. Good puff of wind you'd think would blow him over. He weighed about 115 and Dad said that here was Johnny astraddle of old Hutchins and he was layin' there and Johnny had a hardhead rock that weighed about fifteen pounds, holding it right over Hutchins' head, and had his sleeves rolled up and was shaking this hardhead right over Hutchins' eye and yelling, 'Forty-eight inches of muscle! Look uh that!' If he'd have dropped that hardhead he'd have smashed old Hutchins' head.

Jack chuckled, muttered, "Yep, that was a way of life! Those old fellers knew how to live!" And pretty soon Jack began to talk about courtin' in the olden days on Washington island. From what I hear, a lot of courting goes on on the island now. But Jack said that in the olden days it was even more strenuous.

"My uncle, Charlie Hagen," says Jack, "they didn't have cars, and o' course they worked! Younger generation don't hardly know what it is to work hard today. But where I live, I'm on the west side of the island, Uncle Charlie and my dad used to cut cordwood on the east side of the island. That was a distance of four miles. They used to get up before daylight and when they got out to the woods they could just see to start cuttin'. They'd cut cordwood all day long and would walk home in the dark.

"Old Uncle Charlie he would have to do a little courtin' so he would walk out to see Thora, who later became my aunt. She lived four miles out toward Jackson Harbor. He'd walk out there, spend the evening with her, walk home, and come after midnight and get up and go out and cut cordwood all day. I wonder if the youth of today would think that the girl of today was worth it? What would they say about that down at the university at Madison?"

"I guess most UW boys would let the girl walk the four miles to see them," I said.

"I guess they would," Jack said.

"There would not be so many marriages or even so much courting," I said.

"No money neither," Jack said. "Now this is a story about courting that my uncle used to tell. He used to saw about them good old days, you know, when you had to walk your girl along the road. He said you would walk them real fast and get them tired, then you could just ... well, you know ... them anywhere. Just some of the attitudes of the old timers."

"Hasn't changed much," Thorsten said. "Not the attitudes anyhow."

"Could have been kind of a male fantasy, too," Jack said.

"Knowing my uncle, I guess it was more talk than anything else. But I don't know anyway, courting here on the island wasn't near as interesting as moonshine making."

"I didn't know there was ever much drinking here on the island," I said, just to get Jack stirred up, though I knew there was plenty of drinking at the Bitters Bar and other places.

"You don't know much then," Jack said. "During Prohibition I would say that about every home place, one in four anyway, had a still on it, and maybe they wouldn't sell, just make their own liquor for parties and so forth, you know. I can remember my cousin Emery talking about parties down to Bennie and Nelse Jensen's. They were two old Norwegian bachelors that lived by themselves and they always made wine. They made brandy too. They had a cherry orchard that they never used for anything else. Used to make their own moonshine, too, of course. A bunch of the guys would get together and they would go out there. They had the wine right out in a barrel, and you had a cup and you'd just dip it out of the barrel. He said of course the end of the evening the barrel would be gettin' kind of low and he said you'd have to hold your teeth together to strain out the ladybugs! But he says we still drank it, and enjoyed it!

"Some of them made their own beer. One of them was talkin' about coming into Tom's Bar one time. They used to really spike that stuff, and of course they'd get kind of wild, and get looped up pretty well, and instead of opening it, you know, he'd hit the bottle a crack on the bar and the yeast would pop off and the cap would hit the ceiling, and they had a pail just to catch the home-brew! The island was ideal for moonshining because the feds had to come across on the ferry and folks would get tipped off. They could smell a fed, even smell him coming across the bridge at Sturgeon Bay, and they'd call up and warn the island boys. So they'd take all their stuff and hide it.

"One of the fellows who made it was Charlie Smith, quite a picturesque character. A butcher. His son and another fellow started a golf course. The number one hole was at the entrance, across from the farm, and they always said very few guys got by the seventh hole because here was Charlie with his jug, sitting in the lee of the granary waiting for 'em!

"They'd sit there and most of the golf players would get barreled up and they never finished the course. Maybe that's why golf never done so well here on the island.

"How they camouflaged the likker making — they hid it under the pretense of boiling fish guts. You see the fish guts would camouflage the smell of the mash; so they had a hole dug near this pan where they boiled the fish guts and they had the mash buried down in that hole underneath there. Here was these rotten fish guts and no fed could ever smell the mash! Never wanted to after he smelled those fish guts!

"One of the parties one time, one of the guys had made some beer that was extra strong; so when Hank Gufteson came walking up the lane why here was George Nelson laid out, and Gufteson says to one of the guys, 'He sure must have made a hog of hisself!' 'No,' they said, 'he only had three bottles of beer!'

"Gufteson says, 'Ha! He's a sissy!'

"So they give Hank three bottles of beer and laid Hank out alongside of George. Nobody could drink more than three bottles of that beer that Arnold had made!"

I had heard of a trial held in Milwaukee where a Washington Islander was tried for moonshining. I couldn't recall that anything much had happened to the defendant, but I asked Jack about it.

"Oh, yeah," Jack said, "he's still living. That was Herman Magnusson. He got reported for making this booze you know, and my brother-in-law was workin' down at one of the cottages and this guy came and wondered where Herman Magnusson lived. And my brother-in-law never give it a thought. And when this guy went out to Herman's it was the noon hour, and Herman was in the shed stirring his mash. And he heard a click. He turned around and here the fed had taken his picture while he was stirring the mash! Caught old Herman with his pants down!"

"Was he ever tried?"

"Yep, he was brought to trial. Never came to nothin'. He was paroled in care of one of the . . . wouldn't care to say who it was . . . he's quite high up in the government service."

Jack has got a charter boat service and he does a lot of fishing off one of the docks that was built for the use of the schooners they had around here. It's right across from the harbor. Jack said, "I was talking with the son of the former owner of the dock and he says that some of those schooners were a hundred, two hundred feet long. They'd come right in

Detroit Harbor and go over to this area where I fish. Those schooners were shallow draft, only drawing a couple of feet. They were all wood. Floated up like a cork! Way they'd work it, they had the dock in close to shore where they put the cordwood and so forth, and then out from shore about three hundred feet they built another crib and in the winter that crib was about fifty feet by fifty, and anyhow that crib—they would drive their teams out on the ice and they would load that crib up with cordwood, high as they could stack it. They would come in in the summer, load up at the dock, and they would put all they could on without scraping bottom, then they would go and stop at the crib and top off their load, and off they'd go!

"You see, Art Hanson's father, who had the dock out in Jackson Harbor, his dad used to run a schooner, a little floating store. And he used to travel up and down the shoreline of the county selling his goods right off the boat, and because transportation was slow there was docks built, one at Detroit Harbor, one at Washington Harbor, and there was a place for a dock at Jackson Harbor. The Furlong people came up from Milwaukee and bought up all the shoreline they thought it was possible to put a dock up on, on the north side of the island. They had a monopoly. They used to control it. They had this dock in Washington Harbor, and all the produce had to go across that dock. They collected a dockage.

"The farmers one time tried to build a dock up in Washington Harbor, and they said it was awful mysterious how that dock went out one time in a storm. Found out afterward that some guy had been paid to do some dirty work on it. But there was wagonloads of potatoes lined up to load on those schooners on that dock for a distance of one mile, one team behind another. They would load, schooners would come in, cattle led up to be put aboard, put about eighty head of cattle on one schooner. A lot of potatoes here then.

"Speak of people being hardy, Ben Johnson, he had relatives in Escanaba, that's thirty miles, and went over to Escanaba, and visited his sister and he came back late that afternoon. He dogtrotted. Never walked. Could cover ground like a horse. Just died here a couple of years ago, ninety years old. Just took off acrost the ice by himself.

"Kind of deviating now, but speaking of fishing one time a seal got away from one of the zoos in Chicago. A couple of old-timers here, Jake Young and John Larson, went out fishing, rowed out, and set their nets. First thing you know this thing come up and stuck up his head alongside of the boat. John he seen this and hollered! 'It's an otter!' But old Jake he says, 'Chiggers! It's a wabbit!' They dropped their nets and headed for shore.

"Different now. When I was a boy the Hagen family was here, six families on the island, and at Thanksgiving or Christmastime we had to go to each member of the family for a meal. The parents would play cards, and we had our sleds and we had the greatest time there was. We didn't ride in a car neither. Rode in a sleigh with sides and blankets on it. We would leave soon as my father was done with the milking and went down the side of the island. Weather never stopped us. Midnight we came home. Cars is too fast now."

Captain Jack told me about the hazards of carrying mail across the ice.

"Great-grandfather Garret carried the mail between Green Bay and the island, back and forth; he'd leave on a Monday morning, walk on the ice to Green Bay, pick up the mail, and bring it back. Once a week he would make that trip; of course, that's a distance of close to a hundred miles.

"I mean he was a welcome sight to all the folks. He was quite a big man; I've seen pictures of him. He used to pull a sleigh. He didn't take any load of packages though, only a bundle of letters and the likes of that.

"He had his route laid out, so about every thirty miles or so he would stay overnight at one of the places along the shore. He would drop off mail at Sister Bay and Fish Creek and all the places along the peninsula.

"It's a little different than nowadays. When you think about it you wonder if it was worth it, but it was a way of life and they were happy with it.

"That was the earliest method hereabout of carrying the mail. Then they went on to the carrying of mail by horse. I have heard lots of stories of when Pete Anderson used to carry the mail. The mail would come down to Ellison Bay or Sister Bay, and Pete would take the horse from the island and drive down there in the morning, pick up the mail, and come back the same day.

"They used to tell how that horse was so well trained that in the wintertime, goin' across the ice, the cracks would open up, maybe six, eight, ten feet wide, and Pete used to carry planks in his sleigh that he would lay down. Three planks. The horse would walk the one in the middle and the sleigh would come acrost on the other two. Times he would have 120 feet of water under him. Nervous work for that horse and Pete. But that horse was so well trained that he would do it.

"One time Pete was comin' back from gettin' the mail on the other side; the ice started to break up. Pete ended up on an ice cake, him and his horse and sleigh, adrift out in Death's Door. And Lucien Boscha, who's living right today — he was one of the captains of the ferry line for years — was with Pete.

"While they was drifting out there, of course, the Coast Guard seen what had happened. But at that time they didn't have any motor-driven boats or anything like that. They had a big surfboat which took quite a bit of time to row out there.

"Before they got the boat launched, Molly Boscha, who was Lucien's mother, called up the Coast Guard station; was worried why Pete and Lucien wasn't back yet, and she says, 'Say, have you seen anything of Pete and Lucien?'

"Reb, he was the man there, says, 'Oh, sure. They're right here in front of the station.' Course he didn't tell her that they was floating on a cake of ice. Wouldn't want to worry her unnecessarily.

"So anyhow, before the Coast Guard boat got out there, that ice cake was breaking up. Originally it was maybe a couple hundred feet square, and by the time they got out to the men to tow 'em into shore the cake had got so small, the horse tried to crawl up into the cutter and set with the men!

"That horse got kind of nervous when his feet started to get wet. Anyhow they grabbed into the ice cake, and the Guard towed the horse and sleigh and the men in and everybody was safe. That's some of the experience that comes with island living sometimes!

"And sometimes they would just set and visit with the greatest tall yarn spinner the island ever knew. Hans Hanson, known as Hans Mads.

"Aw, wish I could think of the stories. You know, Uncle Hans he was always up to every occasion. One summer when he was puttin' up hay--he really had hay that year. He had so much hay he didn't know what to do with it. But he says, 'I know what I'll do,' so he went ahead and did it. He filled up the outside of the barn, and what was left over he put on the inside.

And that way he got his hay up.

"Then he had a fish that he caught one time and he didn't want to eat it because it was such a pet. So he took it home and put it in a bowl, and that fish got to be such a pet and went with Uncle Hans wherever he went. One day Uncle Hans went out fishing, and when he came home he was really feelin' bad, because that little fish fell out his pocket and drowned.

"He had a cat he used to tell about. He said that cat was really ugly. Anybody that came walkin' up to their place, why that cat would reach out and claw him on the leg, you know. So Uncle Hans had to get rid of that cat. He didn't know what to do, so he finally took 'im down to the lake and threw 'im in. Thought, 'I'll fix him.' Well, Uncle Hans came home there was the cat. Had beat Uncle Hans home. Just as ugly as ever. So he thought, 'Well, I'll fix that cat,' so he took the cat down in the woods and cut his head off. He didn't go right home. He went around and stopped off at the neighbors and when he come home, there sat that cat on the gatepost with his head in his mouth!"

# Master of Rock Island

A remarkable man named Chester Hjortur Thordarson once owned Rock Island. He was famed as an inventor of electronic devices and when he died in 1946 his ashes were returned on the Washington Island ferry. When the urn arrived, Arnie Richter had no specific instructions as to what to do with it, and nobody else seemed to know, so the urn sat on a shelf at the ferry dock for a number of years. Finally, the urn was buried in a bramble patch, for the old cemetery on Rock Island was quite overgrown then, and Thordarson's marker, when I saw it, was a small piece of lake stone lying flat. It seemed a humble ending for the man who had made the first million-volt transformer and had exhibited it at the St. Louis World's Fair of 1904. But perhaps it's not so bad to finally come home again, no matter how.

Thordarson left Iceland in 1873, when he was five. To people in Iceland, America was almost an unknown country. By 1870, a number of families had gone from Iceland to the United States, and most of them had settled on Washington Island, in Lake Michigan, off the northeastern coast of Wisconsin.

The Thordarsons had little, but it was enough to carry them as far as Milwaukee. There, while the father was still planning what to do and where to settle, he died unexpectedly. With four children on her hands and absolutely no money, the mother was left to manage adventures in a strange land, among people speaking an unfamiliar language.

Their first home was on a farm in Dane County. Here Thordarson's education, such as it was, began when he learned his letters during a couple of summer sessions. That was about all the schooling he managed to get for a good many years. Icelanders are by nature and tradition, however, a very literate people. It is still said that if they are going on a journey they may sell their clothes to obtain money, but they will take along their books.

After living in Dane County for two years, the family moved north to Shawano County among the pine woods and near the Menominee Indian reservation. Here they had several other Icelandic families for neighbors and felt somewhat at home. But it was difficult to make much of a success farming the pine barren. The people became dissatisfied and decided to move farther west. Rich lands could be had cheap from the government, it was said, in North Dakota. They decided to go.

The families that were going did not have money enough for everybody to make the trip by train, so only the women and small children went that way. The men followed by wagon with the household goods, farm implements, and livestock. Thordarson was thirteen years old at the time, the youngest member of the wagon party.

It took two months to complete the thousand-mile trip. Most of the time they walked. They reached the Red River Valley in North Dakota and found land fully as rich and as cheap as they had hoped.

But North Dakota was practically unsettled then. From the new home it was forty miles to the nearest railroad station. For five years Thordarson never saw a train. The soil was deep and fertile but virgin to the plow. Many times, in turning over a new field, the plowshare was thrown out of the furrow by striking the half-buried skull of an elk or a buffalo.

In this remote region young Thordarson passed the intensely formative years from thirteen to eighteen without any formal schooling whatever. He was forever asking questions of the world about him. Among their books was one written in Icelandic and called "the blue book" for its blue paper cover. It was a treatise on physics.

During the long North Dakota winters, when there wasn't much work to do beside cutting firewood and feeding the cattle, Thordarson studied this book. In it he found for the first time the definition of a scientific experiment. "An experiment," the book said, "is a question that we place before Nature; and she always answers in a most direct way. If the answer is not what we expected, it is because we did not question correctly. After making several attempts, we learn to question more directly, and the answers we get from Nature will be more to our purpose."

He had always been asking questions of nature. He now decided that he must somehow become a scientist. One section of the book was devoted to electricity, and that subject particularly fascinated him. He made up his mind to learn all he could about it.

By the time he was eighteen, one of his sisters had married and had gone to live in Chicago. There were free public schools in Chicago, and undoubtedly there were also places where a great deal could be learned about electricity. His elder brother was running the farm. Thordarson left for Chicago and started to school. He was placed in the fourth grade among children of ten. In two years he passed through four grades, but he never got beyond the seventh. At twenty he went to work. This enterprising man went on to invent and manufacture some of the pioneer electronic developments. He had more than one hundred major patents. His Chicago firm was at one time very important in manufacturing transformers and other equipment. An official of General Electric once said that if Thordarson had wished to exercise really big-time business methods, that his company today might have been larger than General Electric!

For all his success in electronics, however, Thordarson never forgot his Icelandic background. About 1900 he and his wife began visiting the Icelandic colony on Washington Island and soon they wanted island property of their own. In 1910 he bought most of Rock Island from Rasmus Hanson of Jackson Harbor. He added some small tracts to the 661 acres purchased from Hanson and paid for the entire acrage only $5,735. The only part of Rock Island not owned by Thordarson was the lighthouse reservation.

He built cottages, greenhouses, a water tower, and a residence for workmen. To protect plantings from deer he built an immense fence mounted on a stone wall around thirty acres. He placed bronze plaques on stones, engraved with quotations from literature. Finally, to house a great Icelandic library that he had spent years collecting, he built the Rock Island boathouse.

The boathouse, constructed of lake stone, took masons three years to complete and cost Thordarson $250,000, not counting the cost of employing a wood carver for several years in Chicago to create massive tables with legs and tops carved with Icelandic runes and scenes from Icelandic folklore. These tables, chairs, and a great desk along with a fireplace large enough to serve a dinner in, were the showpieces of the library. The valuable book collection was moved from Chicago to Rock Island in 1941 just five years before Thordarson died; after his death many institutions competed for the collection. The University of Wisconsin was able to obtain a one-year option, and the university regents eventually purchased the library for $270,000 plus a $30,000 broker's fee. It was the most important collection the university library ever purchased, and apparently the collection has increased many times in value since its purchase.

The great furniture, sadly, is no longer in the boathouse.

The desk and the chairs and tables are in a warehouse at Roen's Shipyard in Sturgeon Bay.

When the state of Wisconsin purchased the island in 1965 at a cost of $225 per acre for the 776 Thordarson acres, there was no clear understanding about the furniture. Presumably the furnishings of the boathouse belonged to the Thordarson heirs. The state, when asked whether it wished to purchase the pieces, at that time was not interested or able to give a clear answer. I expect that the state hoped that the furniture would simply remain in the boathouse where it belonged. It did not. In the spring of 1966 a barge belonging to Roen came to Rock Island. The furniture was loaded aboard and transported to Sturgeon Bay. All efforts to get it returned to the island have so far failed.

There are many Thordarson legends. Sometimes he was inhospitable and warned off visitors to the island with a shotgun. At other times he was unbelievably generous. He even built a cottage for his friend Mayor (Big Bill) Thompson of Chicago and royally entertained his other friends such as Erle Stanley Gardner and Clarence Darrow. There is a story that once when Thordarson could not find a particular book at the public library at Sturgeon Bay, he whipped out his checkbook and made a substantial gift to the library on the spot.

His tenure of Rock Island was very fitting. There had been some very interesting individuals and yarns there before him. The old lighthouse built in 1836 and put into service the next year is not only the oldest light in Wisconsin and the first on Lake Michigan but also the oldest house in Door County. David E. Corbin was the first tender. He was a War of 1812 veteran and he tended the light until his death in 1852. The light guards a vital shipping lane between Rock and St. Martin's islands, Michigan.

The island, known by the French as Potawatomi Island or Louse Island was probably the first place in Wisconsin visited by white men. Nicolet possibly stopped there in 1634. A somewhat mysterious early resident was a John A. Boone, supposed to be a brother of the famous Daniel. Among a number of Illinois settlers, called "the Illinois Colony," was that old man named Kennison who was the sole surviving member of the Boston Tea Party.

# The Man Who Loved Roses

Three Wisconsin men are very important to an understanding of man and his environment. All three created magnificent careers out of their love of nature, and the relationship of nature to man and to man's happiness.

One of these, of course, was Frank Lloyd Wright. Another was John Muir, raised on a Wisconsin farm near Portage, who became the father of our national parks system. The third was a dynamic man, burning with a drive to teach the value of a balance in life, an understanding of the forces within man that make him seek for fulfillment in an understanding of nature, and in a closeness with the earth. This was Jens Jensen.

I met him one Sunday afternoon many years ago at the Clearing near Ellison Bay in Door County. I was new to the state, and I had heard of this remarkable man who was trying to create a study center where any sincerely interested person could come to learn about plants and trees and the whole ecology of the region.

He came out to the yard before the main building, a tall man, very neatly dressed, very dignified, with clear eyes and firm steps though he was then in his late eighties. He inquired about my interest in the Clearing, and I explained that my work in the arts, and in literature, was closely allied to the people of Wisconsin, and that I wished for them a more complete expression of their relationship to places intimate to their lives. He sat down on the steps, I remember, and we talked, such talk as I would have expected from him.

"It is, simply, that nature's mystery is the deep truth in all wild, chancy, random, natural things; there is bonding and coalescence, improbable and unbelievable, but durable and real. It is purpose made sensible, love bringing focus to love."

He wears a white beret off the forehead, a loose plaid work shirt, a white jacket, and dark slacks. He has gnarled, muscular hands (on one a large wedding ring), a full white mustache, and snow white, bushy eyebrows; his nose is prominent.

As he talked that day, I thought of his writing, and how the wild prairie rose symbolized the whole process of nature.

"This," he wrote, "is the story of the prairie rose that is an unalterable part of the land of which you and I are part. The prairie rose is found growing along farmers' fence rows, creeping along the roadsides, and over railroad right-of-ways, in abandoned farm yards, or wherever man permits it to grow and sing of our great heritage.

"During childhood's days I have walked barefooted through fields of roses, their briars tearing my legs and leaving scars far in the long winter as reminder of summer glories. Gone are those roses and my childhood, but their fancies still remain. No other flower links my past to the future, no other flower is as much a part of my childhood memories as the wild rose, its sweet essence growing far into the tomorrow, awakening an exuberance of living thoughts."

Today, February 9, 1969, Jens Jensen is long gone, and I am seeking more shafts of light upon him as a character and an influence. I am going into the office of the Wisconsin Farm Bureau Federation where a remarkable woman is working to carry on the Jens Jensen ideals. Her name is Mertha Fulkerson.

The Farm Bureau is a busy place. It is men, largely, in the corridors, men with briefcases, with hurried assignments. As I wait at the desk in the corridor it seems strange to me that I am here, in this busy Madison building, hoping to recreate the spirit of Jens Jensen. Yet perhaps it is not so strange, for Jensen was primarily a farmer. His, at the last, was a rural ideal. Education for rural people, for everyone of course, but without the farm folk he would have thought his experiment at the Clearing in Door County, a failure.

Presently Mertha Fulkerson appears. She is a tiny woman, yet there is great strength in her. We retire to a corner of the lounge, and after a bit she begins to tell me about the man she worked with so many years, and for whom, in spirit, she is still working; as she explains it, the Wisconsin Farm Bureau has accepted the Jensen philosophy and is really making the Clearing possible.

"We make it a point," Mertha said, "that every student at the Clearing works. He does something to better the environment. We have only week-long classes now; in Jens Jensen's time they were one month. One day of that week is turned over to doing something for the Clearing, because it was Jens Jensen's philosophy that you are really not a part of something unless you have contributed toward its development. So the students go out in the woods, not to cut trees, because we want the woods to tell their own story in their own way, but we will help the trees along by pushing down old trees, breaking up the branches, and scattering them so they deteriorate faster. This kind of work the students have helped do all these years.

"The Clearing, I might say, is a peaceful spot, one where intense introspection, meditation, and deep thought may be done. It lies in a heavy woods near Ellison Bay in Door County, and passing on Highway 42 going to Gills Rock, you would never know the Clearing is there, unless you have knowledge of it.

"We never hire anyone to do this work, because we feel it must be done by someone who has a feeling for the woods, for nature.

"The state of the woods, after all this student attention, is very interesting. When I first came to the Clearing in 1935 I used to say to Jens Jensen, 'You know, they're lovely, but they're shallow. The trees are so spindly. There's no feeling of maturity.' He says, 'Oh, give it time. You'll have to wait. These woods have been cut over, burned over, and you have a result.' But he says in time nature will take care of that.

"I didn't quite believe him. I didn't think it would happen in my lifetime; but each year I'm amazed how mature the trees are getting, and where there were birches, and poplar, and trees of that type coming up every place, we now have maple and beech. It is all moving faster for a climax."

"Mertha," I said, "does the personality of Jens Jensen still hang over the Clearing? Do people, when they go there understand anything about this man?"

"It's a very interesting experience," she replied. "Before he passed on, you often thought, well, when he goes who will carry on that spirit that he so definitely permeated the Clearing with; and I often worried how to keep that spirit alive. It was the thing that made the Clearing very important to people. But there again I have seen that there is no place you can go at the Clearing that you don't feel that Jens Jensen is close by. Many of the students come to me after they have been with us a week and say, 'Although I've never met the man, I think I know him.' "

"How do you remember him, Mertha?"

"His appearance was that of a good many men of his age. He was tall, stately; he had a definite personality that stood out. Many men of that time were of that nature, what you would call a self-made man. Many people said he looked like Mark Twain. Many said he looked like Schweitzer. He was quite a dresser. He always felt that any special occasion needed special dressing, that that was one way of showing your appreciation of an event. If we had a party at the Clearing, he might spend half a day deciding what was the appropriate thing to wear to give it the dignity it should have. He made no rules, however, for others. His example rubbed off. No one would appear at dinner without at least washing their face, or combing hair."

"How did he acquire the Clearing, and how did he begin to develop it with this philosophy of nature and conservation?"

"Well, he bought the Clearing back in 1919. He sent two young men east, all around the Great Lakes, and one west. And it was in 1919, when these men had returned and had reported on different areas, that he went to Door County. He had never before visited Door County, and before he left that trip he had bought the first acreage. He didn't start to build, however, until 1935."

"When he sent those young men to search for a school location, where was he then living?"

"In Chicago," Mertha said. She paused, leaned back. "He was at his height in landscape work then, and many things happened that kept him from building the Clearing as soon as we wanted."

"What did he have in mind when he sent these young men to search?"

"Well, he had in mind just what the school is today. He had in mind an educational center where people could come and where the wilderness spoke louder than anything man had to say. He always called our professors the applesauce. They were the things that brought the students to the Clearing. The wilderness, however, was the textbook. It was from the woodlands that they got their real thoughts."

"Did he conduct some of the classes himself?"

"Every morning, Jens Jensen would conduct a class on the out-of-doors. A class in ecology. Now one person or another does the same thing. The group was always working in these classes. But they would always end up by sitting down someplace and having an argument on the real purpose of life, and I remember very distinctly a student asking a question. Often Jens Jensen would pretend he didn't hear. But he never forgot the question. He waited until the proper moment, when an example was apparent. Then he would tap the student on the shoulder and say 'You remember when you asked me about this?' and he would then point out the living example.

102

"He never liked to answer a question without having some proof.

"I came into the project the day we came up to Door County to plan classes. I came in March, a cold drizzly March day in 1935. We opened the first class in June of that year. We had students, but we had no buildings. So I was sent up to find some contractors and somebody who knew how to put up logs.

"I see today many of the effects of the Clearing. You know, Jens Jensen was part of that movement they called the Chicago school. It was just a group of men who believed in the fundamentals of your environment, the effect on your thinking. Frank Lloyd Wright was one of those, Carl Sandburg was one, Vachel Lindsay, Harriet Monroe, all of these people had that influence of a new world opening up, and its influence on the lives of people. And I see the results now, very much so. Lots of the confusion we have in the world today — that may be a result of the imperfection of our relationships with places and people, and a deep enough probing of our roots. Eventually, I think the confusion will settle down to a real American culture.

"Jens Jensen was born in Denmark, in that part of Denmark that came under German rule, and he had to join the royal guard of Germany. After he had served his time he decided he did not want to live under German rule. That's why he migrated to America. That was back in the 1880s. He had been born on an old estate and had been trained as a farmer. He was to take the old home. Because he migrated his father had to sell the homestead, because the other brothers had been trained for other things.

"He landed in Chicago. He was trained as a farmer, but he started to work with the Chicago Park System as a laborer. From there he advanced from laborer to superintendent of a little park, and advanced to superintendent of Humboldt Park, and then he became superintendent of the whole west park system. He laid out Columbus Park, Douglas Park. He redid Humboldt Park, built conservatories at Garfield Park, and before he left he made a survey and drew up the plans for the forest preserves of Cook County. He used to speak to women's clubs, Rotaries, churches, lodges — every place he possibly could he spoke on the forest preserves of Cook County. There was a referendum and two times it was down, but the third time it passed, and the forests became an actuality.

"When he came to Door County he was seventy-five. He

just turned his work over to the boys in the drafting rooms and told them, 'I'm getting old, and I must be busy on the Clearing.'

"If you look back over his work, he was always much interested in conservation. He would hire a whole crew of secretaries to push through a bill he believed in. His whole attitude was: here is something America must not lose, this untouched wilderness that we have possessed. Very few countries have had this and it is a precious thing, telling us a bigger story than mankind can ever tell. Our files are full of letters from people who say that their time spent at the Clearing has given them a new outlook on life.

"After Jens Jensen died in 1951 at the age of ninety-one, I was sure that we would have difficulties. He held the Clearing and its work together. We had an opportunity to turn the Clearing over to the American Audubon Society, but I knew that Jens Jensen didn't build an Audubon camp. He had human motivations in mind. He wanted to effect a change in society, to better the lot of man by showing him himself and his role in relation to trees and flowers and other men. I said to myself: Jens Jensen thought that rural people were important. We must get the help of someone or some agency that is interested in rural people. That's where the Farm Bureau came in. I had a good neighbor, a farmer who was a fruit grower across the road, and I went to him. He told me about Farm Bureau and helped me get an appointment with the Farm Bureau Board. It turned out that they were interested. And they have been so ever since."

Mertha Fulkerson was born in Indiana, had her schooling there and then went to Chicago, close to Jens Jensen's studio. She grew familiar with his work and remained his assistant until his death.

"Jens Jensen and Frank Lloyd Wright did many jobs together," Mertha said. "Jensen would do the landscaping for Wright buildings. I would call them friendly enemies. When they did a job together they fought from the beginning. We hated to see a Wright job come in, because the fight started immediately. Jens Jensen always upheld Frank Lloyd Wright and felt that the world was too long in accepting what he had to offer."

Jens Jensen is buried in Chicago, but his influence will be felt in Door County so long as students continue to come to learn his philosophy at the Clearing.

# Sister Adele

Whenever I go up to Ephraim in Door County I always stop by to see my friends, Dave Stevens and his wife, Ruth. I've been going to Door County now for quite a few years. Dave has a beautiful spot on the side of a hill above Eagle Bay and a house that is, in part, one of the earliest farmhouses on the peninsula. I think it was Dave who first told me about Nils Otto Tank and his great experiment to bring a colony of Moravians to Green Bay in 1840 to live in absolute bliss and complete happiness. Tank, a Norwegian, had a lot of money and bought a great tract of land that he intended to divide up among the people who came with him. Only trouble was, he didn't get around to dividing it up soon enough, and some of the Moravians, believing that he intended to found an old style feudal community, left Tank at Green Bay and sailed up the Bay to found the Moravian colony at Ephraim. It was one of these Moravian families, the Amundsens, who once owned Dave's place.

When he was an instructor at the University of Chicago, teaching students Milton in the earlier decades of this century, Dave heard that the Amundsen farm was for sale. He'd been bringing his family to Door County, and now he could buy some property, if he could find enough capital. He got several of his friends to take a portion of the large lake frontage that stretched back up the beautiful wooded hill, and Dave kept the old Amundsen farmhouse and spacious grounds for himself. Dave left Chicago in 1930 to become director of the humanities division of the Rockefeller Foundation in New York, but he kept the place in Ephraim, and it was Ephraim for which the Stevenses lived throughout each winter in New York.

Dave is rightly known as the grandfather of the American theatre because, as Rockefeller Foundation representative, he greatly assisted so many young men and women who later became famous in theatre. I received my first fellowship through Dave, and when I went to New York about 1940 for the interview he spent very little time on the matter. He only said, "How long is it since you have seen your mother?" I replied, "About two years." "Then go home," said Dave. "Go home and see her. Then come back and we'll fix up the fellowship."

Dave is retired now, and he and Ruth live full time at Ephraim. Whenever I get the chance I drive up there and go scouting around Door County. I was with Dave the last time I visited with Hjalmer Holand, who also lived near Ephraim, and from Holand we heard again the story of the discovery of the mysterious Kensington Rune Stone, and about Holand's championship of this strange artifact which had been found on a farm in Minnesota, presumably a Viking record of an unbelievable trip to inland America in pre-Columbus days. I also heard first from Holand the tender tale of Adele Brice and the hardy Belgian settlers who had such terrible hardships in the early days of their pioneering on the peninsula. The Brice story is so interesting that I must give it special space. It went like this:

Everywhere in the Belgian settlement on the Green Bay peninsula in the 1850s, the people were dying of Asiatic cholera. Strong men, apparently well at night, would be found dead in the morning, the skin on their faces turned black, their eyes sunken into the sockets. It seemed that pioneers had brought destruction to the new country. There was great sorrow.

The people stopped coming from Belgium. The Wisconsin pioneers were left alone, and from one sorrow they went to another, for after a time there was no food. The men sought work in the faraway cities, walking the whole way to Milwaukee. The women were left alone in the wilderness, lonely and afraid.

In the Brice family cabin Mama Brice was very much afraid when the wolves howled at night. "Oh, the wolves," she would murmur, "Always the wolves! Why did we leave Belgium? Why did we leave home?"

But in the Brice household there was the daughter, Adele, a simple Belgian girl of eighteen who had faith.

"Do not fear, Mother," she would reply. "The wolves will not hurt us. God is with us."

"We do not even have a church. Only at Bay Settlement, ten miles away, is there a church. Why did we leave home!"

But Adele only said, "Some day we will have a church, Mama."

There were other sorrows to come. In 1857 came a financial crisis that stopped the work in the cities. The men came trudging home, worn out, discouraged. When Papa Brice came home, Mama could only ask, "What will we do now, Papa?"

"We have plenty of timber," replied Papa. "But we have no oxen, no horses. We cannot move the timber out. In Green Bay they said pine shingles might bring $1.50. If we cannot move the logs, we can at least make the shingles!"

Oh, there were hard times! Belgians young and old became shingle makers. Father and mother sawed the trees into eighteen-inch bolts. The children split them. Father shaved them down and bound them into bundles of shingles. Then, the bundles were carried to the lake shore, miles away, by hand. A day's wage was so very little, but the families were kept alive. Their needs were few. Gunny sacks there were for clothing, and wooden sabots were used in place of leather shoes. The problem of bread was worrisome to Mama Brice.

"Bread, Papa," she would say. "We must have bread."

It was indeed a problem. Wheat was sown among the forest trees and cut and threshed by hand. But, because the nearest gristmill was fifteen miles away, the wheat, so carefully grown, was put in a bag. The bag was then tied at the open end, and the other end was made into a hood, which Mama put over her head. The bag on her back then, she trudged all day through the forest, her feet bare, and her wooden shoes dangling from a cord about her neck, for the shoes must be clean when she made her appearance at the mill. When she returned there was flour, but there was also great weariness. "Papa," she would say, "I am so tired, so very, very tired. Papa, has God forsaken His people?"

"Sometimes it seems so, Mama."

Mama sighed. "If we only had a church nearby where we might worship!"

"The Belgian settlers are talking, Mama. They're saying, 'Let us return to Belgium.' Mama, shall we leave Wisconsin?"

"It seems that God has forsaken us," said Mama sadly. "I will return if you wish."

"Here we have land," Papa said. "In land we are rich as the landed gentry in Belgium. But in everything else we are poor. I am ready to return, Mama."

But in that household there was also the girl, Adele.

"Mama, Papa, do not give up," she pleaded. "Stay! God has not forsaken you."

"And why has He not?" said Mama, "There has been no sign. There has been only starvation, sorrow, weariness."

"What could you know of the ways of God?" Papa said to Adele. "You, a girl!"

"Even the priest at Bay Settlement is discouraged," said Mama.

But Adele only said simply, "I do know, Mama. Have I

ever feared the forest? Have I feared the wild beasts? When I walk alone in the forest, the trees whisper to me. Always they whisper that God is near. Mama, Papa, it is very wrong to doubt God."

"You are a good girl, Adele," Papa answered wearily. "But your dreams are not enough."

"Let me go to Bay Settlement tomorrow, Papa. Let me go there and pray for all of us. Please, Papa."

"But Bay Settlement is a long way. Ten miles through the forest."

"Let me go. Please let me go, Papa."

"It can do no harm," Mama said. "Let her go. Her prayers may bring us luck."

"My prayers will be answered," said Adele. "I know they'll be answered."

"Go if you like then," said Papa. "But start early and return before nightfall."

"Yes, Papa."

So this young girl set out for the settlement. And for what follows I must ask you to believe, as I believe, for there was only goodness in the heart of this child.

As she walked the trees whispered to her, the birds sang; indeed, as she walked near them, they seemed to be singing for her alone. The sunlight filtering through the leaves made strange patterns on the ground. The streams tinkled in their beds; of such things are visions made, perhaps. But certainly in the being of this young girl there was no thought of vision. There was humility and prayer, the forest was close and friendly about her, and indeed God seemed very near; yet of heavenly symbol there was nothing. The forest was to her as always, and the fingers of the wind touched only as usual; still, as Adele climbed a little knoll, exactly there in the space between the trunks of two white birch trees appeared a blinding white light. Surely such a light as one had never dreamed before. As Adele cowered breathlessly before it, her lips moving in soundless prayers, her ears were hearing unworldly music.

When she dared at last to raise her eyes to the light, it had changed. Indeed, it had taken a definite form; between the two trees, there in the lonely forest, stood a marvelously beautiful lady clothed in dazzlingly white garments. Her eyes were deep and dark, and she smiled radiantly and kindly upon the girl who now knelt before her. Adele only whispered, "Oh . . . oh . . . oh."

It had happened before. Joan of Arc saw visions and rose to be a leader of her people. The early French settlers in the valley of the St. Lawrence were comforted by a report that the Virgin had appeared among them in a vision. Here, in the Wisconsin wilderness, a simple Belgian girl had seen a vision of the Holy Mother. Would she, too, be the instrument through which her people might regain faith and courage?

These things were not in Adele's mind as she hurried on to the church that Father Daems had built at the Bay Settlement. She was only a frightened child seeking explanation for what she had seen. At the church, trembling, she told her experience to the priest.

"My child," said the priest, "are you certain you saw what you describe?"

"I did, Father. I did. You must believe me!"

"I believe you, Adele," replied the priest.

"What shall I do, Father?"

"You must have courage, Adele," said Father Daems. "If ever the vision appears before you again, you must say, 'In the name of our Lord, who are you and what do you wish of me?' Do you understand, Adele?"

"I understand, Father, but to speak to the Virgin . . . Father, I couldn't."

"If the Virgin appeared to you, Adele," said the priest kindly, "it was for some very great reason. Do not be afraid then. Rather give thanks that you, a poor settler's daughter, should be the subject of this visitation. Will you do this?"

"Yes, Father," whispered the girl. "But I'm afraid!"

So Adele turned back home, and as she walked the forest seemed to become still. There was no wind in the trees. No birds sang. The streams were hushed. Adele knew only her trembling heart pounding harder and harder as she neared the little knoll with the two white birch trees standing still and straight. As she climbed the knoll her knees became weaker and weaker, so that before the two trees she sank to her knees. And slowly, as Adele raised her eyes, the vision was there again before her — the beautiful lady in white, the same smile.

"Who are you?" whispered the girl. "In the name of our Lord, who are you and what do you want of me?"

"I am the Queen of Heaven," said the beautiful lady, "who prays for the conversion of sinners. Do you the same; for through you will come the salvation of your people. Through you the instruction of the children. Through you the faith of your people will grow strong again."

The vision faded away, and Adele ran home with the news. The story spread through all the Belgian settlements.

Of course not everyone believed. Adele's parents believed, for they knew Adele, and they knew she could not lie. But there were others.

"She had a dream" said one neighbor. "She was always a dreamer, that Adele."

"Always walking alone," said another. "Always talking with the birds and the animals! What might not such a one imagine?"

But there were others, perhaps the ones most lacking in faith, who saw here an answer to their prayers. A sign. Indeed, most of the settlers believed in the miracle, and the simple girl became a great teacher.

She went from home to home, from neighborhood to neighborhood, restoring the faith of the parents and instructing the children. The people accepted the story.

And this belief became dominant. From far and near, from Green Bay and the distant cabins in Union, Brussels, and Gardner in Door County came people to look upon the holy ground where Adele saw the Virgin. That same fall, the settlers built a chapel on the very spot and a schoolhouse close by. As the settlers regained their faith in God and the new country, their condition began to improve.

Still, those highest in her church did not believe Adele's story. The bishop did not believe. "It's a myth!" he roared. "An imposition! Adele Brice is an ignorant girl with a sensational story!"

Adele was denied the Holy Sacrament and treated as an outcast from the church but this made no difference to the Belgians. They did not waver in their faith but gathered in large numbers to worship at the "Chapel of the Holy Virgin." August 15, the day of Adele's vision, was regarded as a holy day when pilgrims from distant states came to pray. With triumphant faith the crippled were able to walk out whole, leaving their crutches behind.

Finally there happened a great event that forced the church to recognize the mighty faith of Adele Brice, Sister Adele.

It was October, 1871. There had been great changes in the lives of those Belgian settlers. How Papa Brice loved to tell of his good fortune!

"Mama," he would say, "we are as rich as Belgian gentlemen! We have a sawmill and a gristmill. We have cows, Mama. Are you not glad we did not return to Belgium as you wanted?"

"It was more you than I who wanted to go," Mama would reply.

"Oh, you forget so easily."

"I do not forget that our strength is in God. I do not forget that, Papa."

"No," answered Papa, "we do not forget. Never again. There is but one worry now. The forest is so dry this fall. So very, very dry."

No rains fell. The nervous settlers could see at nightfall flashes of red flame far away, and the whole skies were deadened by smoke. On Sunday, October 8, 1871, the terrible tragedy struck. Folks afterward called it "Saddy" October 8, for it was the saddest day the Belgians ever knew.

In the morning the day was quite ordinary. Some smoke was in the air. In the afternoon the wind came up fresh and strong, but in the evening the air was very still. Then, out of nowhere, came a great gust of wind followed by a great roar. The flames shot up and up. Great trees came crashing down. Birds screamed and wild animals bounded into the clearing, mad with fear. Out of the sky came a whirlwind, a tornado of flame, falling in great clouds out of the sky, on the homes of the people, upon them, destroying everything. Only one thought was in the minds of the people: "It is the end," they shrieked. "The end of the world!"

There were many tales of sorrow. At Williamsville, ten miles south of Sturgeon Bay, sixty settlers were burned to death as they huddled together in the middle of a three-acre field. "Holy Mary, Mother of God, pray for us!" they cried. "Pray for us. Help us!" And so they called and prayed until the terrible flame crashed down upon them.

Everywhere there was terror. Homes, barns, granaries filled with the fruits of a summer's toil were utterly destroyed. The cattle, so newly purchased and so prized by these agricultural folk, were burned to crisp while fleeing through the woods. The plow handles were burned in the furrow; the logs in the corduroy roads were consumed.

Sister Adele, with her little church and school there on the spot where she once saw the Virgin, was in the very path of the raging flames. The good sisters, who had come to help Sister Adele with her sacred work, were huddled about her as they watched the great flames creep nearer and nearer.

"Sister Adele," said one, "should we not go now before it's too late?"

"Should we not, Sister," pleaded another. "Let us go. Please, Sister Adele."

"We are the servants of the will of God," replied Sister Adele. "We will stay. This is holy ground."

"The air is so hot and heavy. We can hardly breathe."

"Have courage. God is with us. Come, I will lead you in song so that God may know we are not afraid. Sing! Sing, Sisters!"

As they sang, one of the sisters gave a great cry.

"The flames! The flames! The flames are upon us!"

"They will not touch this church," said Adele quietly. "Let us finish the hymn."

It is true that when the mighty flames reached the tiny wilderness chapel, they divided, passing on either side of the chapel and school; neither was burned, and none of the Sisters of Adele was injured.

When the bishop heard this he was no longer able to withhold his blessing. "I believe that Sister Adele's vision was true," he stated. "I hereby restore her and her following to the Holy Sacrament."

And though the people suffered, and hundreds died in the fire, they had learned their lesson. No more did they cry to return to the Old Country. The first was the will of God; was not the sparing of the chapel witness that God was with them still? The ways of God are wonderful and strange. Not theirs to question. They would submit, but they would never again lose faith. Homes could be rebuilt, new mills erected. They would get more cows. The main thing was courage, yes, and thankfulness for the freedom of the new land. It would take work, but what Belgian is afraid of work?

Through the following years the Belgians worked and prospered. Among them, so long as she lived, was Sister Adele, the girl who one morning saw the vision of the Holy Mother appearing between two tall white birch trees, "who through her vision restored the faith of the Belgian folk in the Wisconsin wilderness."

# Dorothy

The play Dore Reich of Milwaukee and I wrote for Green Bay's centennial in 1948 recounted the story of Nils Otto Tank and the Moravians. The Green Bay Community Theatre produced the play, I remember, and the day before it opened we went over to the old Tank cottage, west of the railroad tracks, still wondering whether we would shock the old boy by putting him on the stage. I had the feeling, even then, that Green Bay was going to outstrip even the wildest dreams of pioneers such as Morgan Lewis Martin, who dreamed of a great waterway with Green Bay at one end and New Orleans at the other. Actually, Martin put his dream into gear and caused the early building of the old canal at Portage connecting the Fox and the Wisconsin. Or, I wondered then, suppose Tank had really been able to form the perfect society he dreamed of: men and women sharing, working together in peace for the good of all. Would his dream have ever equaled the frantic excitement of a Green Bay Packers afternoon? And nowadays, with a major university building at Green Bay, and with the Packers where they are, Green Bay is manifesting all the signs of being a city much larger than it really is. It is blessed somehow with a favorable location and an adventuring heart.

One of the places I enjoy visiting in Green Bay is the home of Jack and Dorothy Carey. I like to drop in there once in a while to hear Dorothy, who is a long-time member of the Wisconsin Regional Writers, tell a few Wisconsin yarns. I stopped one evening on my way to Door County, and after a delicious fondue dinner, during which I stabbed myself in the hand with a fondue fork, Dorothy began to yarn about that little boy at Greenwood, south of Montello, who wouldn't tell a lie.

"There was this little boy from south of Montello and his name was Emmanuel Dannan. He was supposed to have been born in England about 1843. When he was about two his parents brought him to Milwaukee. Shortly after they had arrived both the parents died, and the little boy was placed in an orphan asylum.

"It happened that there was an uncle living near Montello, and he took the lad. For a little while everything was fine, but the boy had bad luck again and the uncle too passed away.

"About the same time that the uncle died, a certain Samuel Norton and his wife came to Montello from Illinois. Since the

Nortons were going to farm they thought the boy would be of help to them. They took him in and gave him a home. They were, however, very cruel, and he was often beaten. The boy never complained though. He had had a lot of hard knocks and was willing to take whatever came.

"When the boy was eight a peddler came through the country one day and stopped at the Norton home. The Nortons, thinking no one would ever know, slew the peddler for his goods and horse. Unfortunately for them, someone did see the crime: the boy, Emmanuel Dannan.

"The Nortons were instantly fearful that he would tell about the crime. They talked for a long while to Emmanuel and forbade him to say anything to anyone about what he had seen. Emmanuel refused.

"Norton, furious, tied the lad to the corner of the log cabin and beat him for two hours. Always Emmanuel said that he would tell the truth.

"At the end of two hours he was dead.

"The foster parents were tried for Emmanuel's murder and found guilty. After seven years of imprisonment, they were released upon their promise to leave Wisconsin forever.

"In the meanwhile Emmanuel had been buried in Greenwood Cemetery about ten miles south of Montello. The boy's death had attracted national attention because of its terrible nature, and because it became known that he had died in behalf of the truth.

"Several groups set out to raise money to erect a suitable monument. The total amount collected was $1,994.94. The fund was so promising that someone suggested the fund raising be extended into the eastern states; enough money might be obtained to provide a most unique memorial for Emmanuel. They hired a promoter who said he could raise more money.

"He didn't raise an additional penny. He did, however, submit a bill for expenses. The amount of his bill was $1,994.94, the exact amount of the memorial fund.

"For over one hundred years Emmanuel's grave lay known but unmarked. In 1954 local newspapers revived the yarn about the boy who wouldn't lie. The Montello Granite Company donated a six-foot-high red granite monument for his grave. At its dedication on May 2, 1954, hundreds of people paid homage to the orphan boy who valued the truth more than his life. On his stone are these words: Emmanuel Dannen 1843-1851, The

Boy Who Would Not Tell A Lie.

"And speaking of cemeteries," Dorothy went on, "how about that old Belgian cemetery over near Brussels? Ever been there?" I never had.

"Back in 1866, many Belgian emigrants settled in Door County. They were a devout people and built the Church of St. John the Baptist, a few miles north of the present town of Brussels. At the time the church was built, the settlers also set aside land for a cemetery.

"They were dismayed to find, when they went to dig the first grave, that the ground was so rocky that nothing could be done. There was only a very thin soil above solid rock. Blasting powder was the only way they could provide graves.

"This was all a great shock. They couldn't change the location of the cemetery, because the ground had been consecrated for this purpose. So they decided that if they could not bury their dead in graves under the surface, then they would haul in soil and bury them above the surface. Thus they built a wall six feet high surrounding the cemetery. Hills and knolls in the vicinity were scraped level, so that enough soil could be had to fill the enclosure. Still they had not enough soil, so every time there was a burial additional earth was hauled in to cover the coffin. They said, at the time of the establishment of the cemetery, that it stood above the level of the surrounding fields, looking much like the first story of an Egyptian pyramid.

"Well, the old church is gone now, and the cemetery is, or was, owned by William Robillard. It is next to a cherry orchard. Brush has so overgrown the old burial ground that it is almost obliterated. It can be found, though, and if you inquire where the old Church of St. John the Baptist stood, you will find the old cemetery where the dead were buried 'above ground'.

"Something else about cemeteries," Dorothy continued, "my great-grandfather, Robert Laurie, and his wife, Katherine, came over from Scotland in the 1840s. They were city people, having lived in Glasgow and Edinburgh. They came to Door County and settled near what is now Sturgeon Bay. It was quite a change for them. They sent out east for their clothes and even to London; yet they lived in the simplest style. They did strive to keep some of their 'city folks' ways despite their surroundings!

"After the Civil War, Robert Laurie purchased a horse from one of the returning veterans. They called the horse 'Old Nick' and he became a family pet. They never worked him in the fields, and all he had to do was pull the family into town once in a while in a very fancy buggy that Robert Laurie had shipped from Milwaukee.

"The rig was used by many of the neighbors, too, for funerals, especially, and Old Nick got pretty used to going to the local cemetery. Got so he kind of liked to hang around looking at the gravestones and occasionally takin' a mouthful of the sweet grass that grew there, just munching and brooding — very fitting for a thoughtful horse in a cemetery.

"One day the family couldn't find old Nick. He had disappeared, a new experience, for he had never run away or caused trouble in any way. But old Robert Laurie got to thinking about Nick and the kind of horse he was. Finally he said to the others, 'You wait here. I just might know where Old Nick has gone.'

"Robert Laurie went where Old Nick had taken so many others. To the cemetery. And when he got there he knew that it was Nick's last trip, for he had gone there to die."

"Ever hear about the horse cemetery?" Dorothy asked.

I never had.

Dorothy claimed that in 1945, while clearing an area for U. S. Highway 45 between Fond du Lac and Oshkosh workers were surprised to run into a tombstone in a clump of old lilac bushes.

Curious, the road crew tore away the vines covering the crumbling stone. They hoped to find the name of the person buried there. To their surprise they found not one but four occupants of the grave — all horses.

The headstone had been placed there by Joseph Kinsman, a pioneer farmer, in memory of four horses he had buried between 1849-65.

Clearing the inscription the men read the ungrammatical but sincere tribute:

"Here lies Tom and Bill
They done their duty
with a will.
Also
Doll and Kate
As true and faithful
as their mates."

Above the lettering was an etching of a weeping willow tree, a sign of sorrow much used in those days. In addition, on both

116

upper corners were bas-relief portraits of Tom and Bill's heads.

The Wisconsin Humane Society learned the story of the pioneer farmer who loved his horses so much. They put up a new stone with the inscription:

"In memory of an early Wisconsin
Humanitarian Joseph Kinsman
Who buried four horses here
Between 1849-1865.

Wisconsin Humane Society
Milwaukee, Wis.
1945"

The old headstone was then laid flat at the foot of the new stone for Kinsman, the man who truly loved his horses.

# Legend Magic

I can never travel Wisconsin without feeling the spell of ancient Indian places and legends. I think the earth, now so constantly shaken by motor traffic, must still give emanations of the older peoples and their tragedies and hero tales. Everywhere I go I listen for the tales handed down from long ago.

There is an old hotel at Butte des Morts not far from the place that the old Indians called the "Hill of the Dead." At this hotel I have often had good food, drink, and companionship. The last time I was there was with John Kuony, director of the Paine museum at Oshkosh. After dinner we went out to the location of the Hill of the Dead and here we saw how it had been cut through and cut again. First by the North Western Railway, which constructed a pile bridge across Little Butte des Morts Lake and made a deep cut through this point about thirty feet from the mound. They excavated and removed the gravel of the point over an area of about five acres to a depth of about twenty feet; with this excavation went the famed Hill. The skulls and bones of ancient kings of glory were strewn along the right-of-way for miles. Early doctors often resorted to the mound for skeletons. The highway makers also later desecrated the ground.

The old tradition creates a tale of how the Fox Indians, demanding tribute of all travelers who passed the lake, finally became such a nuisance they could no longer be tolerated. A Frenchman, Moran, concealing soldiers in his bateaux as though they were merchandise, came to the shore near the point on signal from the tribe. As the Fox crowded on shore to receive their presents, up rose the Frenchmen and slaughtered them, while a detached body made a detour to the village and killed the remaining men and women among the burning wigwams. The legend ascribes the origin of the Butte des Morts to this event and the burial of the Fox tribe.

Like the story of the "Lost Dauphin" it is fixed in the legendary lore of the romantic Fox Valley. Standing up boldly in view of all travelers up and down the small gem of a lake to which it gave its name, the Hill could be plainly seen in settlement days by pioneers of Neenah and Menasha on the opposite bank of the lake. Twelve feet high, sixty feet long north and south, and thirty-five feet wide, it stood in the middle of a wide prairie three hundred feet back from the lake shore on a point of land that was thirty feet above the level of the lake. It was the only high land on the west side of the lake.

I cannot go to the little place called Ahnepee in Kewanee County without remembering that it means "Land of the Wolf" or "River of the Wolf." Many times I wondered how it got this name; finally I heard the legend, as told by Old Katoose, ancient chieftain of the Potawatomi, and handed down by others. It is a tale that applies to the Door-Kewaunee Peninsula, Upper Wisconsin, and the lower part of the Upper Peninsula of Michigan.

There were many wolves in those days, but none like the great gray wolf Ah-ne-pe. He fed upon women and children. If a Potawatomi girl strayed into the forest when we made our camps, she never returned. If a child played in the bushes when we came to this river, he never returned to his mother. Even our hunters sometimes came staggering back into camp with their clothing torn and the blood running from red wounds. They had seen the great gray wolf; he had come upon them like the rushing wind, from a thicket, or pounced upon them like a spirit in the darkness, and their arrows were as broken reeds and their axes refused to do their work.

A great fear came over all the red people; surely this gray wolf was an evil spirit. The forests were deserted, the red deer ran swiftly away, and even the black bear left his haunts and no longer strayed here. The tribes paddled their canoes swiftly along the shores lest night should overtake them in the land of the wolf.

When the children cried at night and a long wailing sound came from the woods, the women would say, "Hush, it is Ah-ne-pe, the gray wolf. He will eat you." And so in all this land around us no hunter built his fire, no creeping thing was in the forests, and there was only silence, a silence broken by the cry of the sea gull by day and by the howl of the big gray wolf at night.

Now in a great village of the Potawatomi far to the south there lived a mighty hunter. No man in all that land so swift of foot, so sure of eye, so strong of arm, so keen upon the chase as the great hunter Sha-hoka.

Sha-hoka was yet a young man, but he took no wife and his wigwam was empty. The Potawatomi maidens threw love sticks at him but he made no sign; the sticks fell to the ground and he passed on. Sha-hoka was a man of iron and there was no little bird singing in his heart, only laughter when the red blood ran from the wounded bear and he shouted, "Ho, shebah, Sha-hoka will eat you," as he gripped the savage beast with his bare hands and bore it to the ground. No hunter was so mighty in all the land as Sha-hoka.

Far to the north, beyond the lakes, there lived a maiden in the land of the Chippewas, the daughter of the chief Os-a-ma-kee. One day, walking in the birch woods beyond the lake, Sha-hoka met this maiden, and the heart of the strong man became soft, soft like a woman's, and he went to Os-a-ma-kee and said, "Give me this maiden to wife."

Os-a-ma-kee replied with great laughter, "Does the wolf's daughter mate with the rabbit? Does the eaglet take to husband the catbird? Does a Chippewa maiden carry water for a dog of a Potawatomi?"

Sha-hoka, in great anger, replied, "There are many lying Chippewas, yet I have killed more bear than there are Chippewas in all the land. With my naked hands I have strangled more wolves than the Chippewas ever saw running through the forests."

"Go and kill Ah-ne-pe, the gray wolf," sneeringly replied the chief and he walked away.

Now Sha-hoka had heard of the big gray wolf who had his den by the black river near the big lake, and he had long wanted to hunt him. But the words of the chief made his heart sore, and for days he was like a sick man as he lay by his campfire. His hunter's hand was weak and his warrior's heart was afraid. Such is the sickness of the heart which may come to even a great hunter. But one day the maiden stole to his lodge and she said to him, "Go and kill Ah-ne-pe, the gray wolf," and she fled frightened back to her village.

Then up sprang Sha-hoka with a glad cry: "I will kill this Ah-ne-pe, this eater of women and children, this slayer of men, and the Chippewa maiden shall live with me in his den."

And Sha-hoka went forth into the forest and he found him a strong bow of an ash tree that bent to the west when the wind blew strong from the north. From the hide of a red deer he had shot in the light of the full moon, he made strings for his great ash bow. An ancient arrow maker filled his quiver with arrows so big and heavy that only a very strong man could shoot them. Then Sha-bah, the medicine man made him a medicine to make the heart bold and the arm strong. No man but Sha-bah in all the land could make this great medicine. Then

120

he set out for the land of Ah-ne-pe, the gray wolf.

As he walked through the forests carrying his mighty ash bow, the great bear cried to him, "Kill me; I am good to eat," and the red deer shook their antlers at him and refused to run away, and the squirrels mocked him, and the crows called to him that they would pick his bones, but he gave no heed to them and hastened on.

When he finally came to the land of Ah-ne-pe there was a great stillness; no squirrels chattered in the trees, no birds sang; only the pines whispered together and the waves of the lake lapped the white stones.

Sha-hoka now stole through the forests of maple and beech and birch with great caution; he looked into every thicket; he crept upon every fallen tree; with a hunter's instinct he knew the sound of every crackling twig. He came to the river, black and flowing silently between banks of beech and birch into the big lake. Here he made his campfire. The first night he heard no sound, and the mournful silence of the frozen night had something about it terrifying and strange.

For many days and nights he camped here by the river, and he watched and listened and waited, waited with the patience given only to great hunters. Little by little a big fear possessed him, a strange fear which he had never felt before: the fear of the dark, the fear of the loneliness, the fear of the deserted wood, and the fear also of the weird wolf, the horrible prowler who had driven every living thing from this land.

One night the sun went down red and the sea gulls came a little nearer to the white shore and Sha-hoka said, "The gray wolf will do some harm tonight." He wrapped himself in his blanket and lay at the foot of an upturned tree, but no sleep came to his eyes. Way in the night there came to him from the distance far up the river the long howl of a wolf, like the wail of a child for its mother, like the voice of a demon seeking for evil spirits, like nothing else Sha-hoka had ever heard in all his life in the woods.

But the hunter uttered a kind of grunt of joy and he said, "This wolf has the mind of a man; he is afraid of Sha-hoka; he bids me to go away and to leave him in peace."

For many nights after that Sha-hoka heard the great baying of the big wolf begging him to go away and not to kill him. One day, while creeping near a huge thicket, covered with dead leaves, a monster beast, entirely gray, jumped up and ran away like the wind. Sha-hoka with a mighty cry set out in pursuit of it. Through the forests they ran; the tall trees sped by, limbs tore his hair and bruised his flesh, blood spattered from his torn hands and feet; but always he kept in view the leaping gray monster with red tongue and fiery breath.

The gray wolf ran directly toward the river . . . the little river where it joins the big river, and as they came to the water, Sha-hoka shouted, "Ho, Ah-ne-pe, you have not the mind of a man. You are but a cowardly wolf with the spirit of a rabbit."

The gray wolf heard him and saw the glittering water ahead. With an ugly snarl it turned and rushed directly upon the hunter, with red eyes and horrid gleaming teeth and fiery breath. It came on with leaps and bounds, scattering the dead leaves, eyes gleaming like two stars, its back arched with bristling hair.

Sha-hoka stood still, threw away his bow, and seizing his ax, awaited the rush of the demon beast. With a mighty leap it sprang upon him. The hunter struck with his ax and a blinding stream of red blood spurted upon his face.

Then he seized the wolf with his naked hands at the neck and together they struggled in a mad embrace, biting and tearing and throwing the dry leaves up in clouds where they fought.

It was many hours after when Sha-hoka awoke. When he opened his eyes the sun had gone down and the woods were growing dark, but he lay with his head upon a quivering gray mass. There was no beating of its heart and no breathing in its throat. Ah-ne-pe was dead.

Sha-hoka returned to the land of the Chippewas and he carried with him the head of Ah-ne-pe, the gray wolf. Coming to Os-a-ma-kee, he threw the head of the wolf at his feet and said: "Chippewa, here is the head of Ah-ne-pe; Sha-hoka, the Potawatomi hunter, gives it to you."

Then Sha-hoka took the daughter of the chief by the hand and he led her back through the woods to the land of Ah-ne-pe, and when they had found the den of the great gray beast there they built their lodge and there they lived.

And now that Ah-ne-pe was dead, the red deer returned to the woods, the bear found their old lairs, the squirrels again chattered their quarrels in the woods, and the birds once more sang there.

# The Oneidas

West of Green Bay, Highway 54 runs through a hilly area that has a soft, romantic look, or it did one misty day when I came up over a hill to the village of Oneida.

I was interested in the Oneida Indians, partly because they were the group led by that strange man, Eleazar Williams, from central New York to a new home in Wisconsin. At the top of a hill above the village stands a large, stone Episcopal church, with a smaller parish hall across the road, and here I sought someone who could tell me about the Oneidas, something of their history and their lore, and perhaps, if anybody cared nowadays, something of the relationship between the tribe and Eleazar Williams.

In the CAP office, which is in the parish hall, a pleasant Oneida lady answered my question instantly. "Oscar Auchiquette," she said.

"Where is he to be found?"

"Start out on 54 back toward Green Bay. Go about a mile. You'll see an icy road off to the left. Down in the valley you will see Oscar's house, next to a log cabin which is very old. I will see whether Oscar is at home."

She called, but Oscar's line was busy. I was soon to discover that Oscar Auchiquette is one of the busiest men in the whole region. His phone is hardly ever quiet.

I found the neat white house set beside a 150-year-old cabin, and in the yard I found Oscar himself, ruefully looking at the injured door of his car, which he had recently banged against a tree. He is a sturdy man in his late sixties with fine eyes and a clear, loud voice.

I said merely, "I want to talk to you about the Oneidas," and he replied, "I'm happy to see you. Come in. It is very important to talk about the Oneidas. We want many people to know about our tribe. I have tried very hard to keep its history alive."

We went into Oscar's living room in which there are many comfortable chairs. I sat in one near the telephone so I could hand it to him when it rang, for Oscar has a game leg and cannot rise easily. The phone rang a lot — all kinds of requests for Oscar to come to this meeting or that, or inquiries about the evening course that he is teaching in the Oneida language, or messages from the Green Bay Human Rights Commission. But we got a lot said, anyway. I just let Oscar talk.

"I am happy to have this opportunity of relating some of the history about the Oneida nation, in the state of New York as well as Wisconsin. It is very important that the history of the Oneida nation be made public. This would help to change the attitude of some of the white people toward us Indians.

"Let us go back to about 1390, and even before. Now before 1390, as far as I know, we were known as the Iroquois. In 1390 Hiawatha organized the five nations, and since then we Oneidas have been known as the Onaya people. Onaya means stone.

"Originally the Oneidas were Mohawks. But the Mohawks divided into two groups — one group was Mohawk, the other was the Stone People. The name for Stone People was Onaya, but this was mispronounced by the French as Oneidas. Some called us 'standing stone people.' The stone is granite, supposed to be a sacred stone with us.

"The Oneidas were a member group of the Iroquois. The Tuscorora Indians were admitted into the league in about 1720. After that we became six nations. The other nations were the Senecas, the Mohawks, the Oneidas, the Onondagas, and the Cayugas.

"Now we come to Eleazar Williams and his part in the history of our people. He was raised in eastern New York State, up on Lake George, by an Indian family — Mohawks — by the name of Thomas Williams. One day, so we Oneidas have heard the story, two white men came to this Indian couple with a little baby boy. They made arrangements for this couple to take care of the baby. That's about all we know about that early experience of the little boy, but he was very sick and the Indian couple cured him of his illness. They had another son as well, but this adopted boy was made to believe that the Indian couple were his real parents.

"The two boys were sent to school, and the Williams boy wasn't as interested as the new boy in schoolwork. The real son went back home to his parents. Eleazar Williams stayed in school, and no doubt became very well educated. Then in the War of 1812 Eleazar Williams was in the services of the United States, and he was in command of six hundred Iroquois; of this six hundred there were twelve Oneida women who fought in the War of 1812.

"Williams, who spoke the Mohawk language fluently, was also very much interested in religion, and in 1818 he became the missionary for the Oneida nation. He was the only white man, if we must call him that, who was interested at all in educating the Indians. He was a very religious man, and in about 1819, he became a missionary. He taught the Oneidas the Bible and he taught them in their own language, because he was able to speak Mohawk fluently; Oneidas can understand Mohawk.

"The older generation were really well versed about the Bible, because they were taught in their own language, and at the same time, Williams taught the Oneidas English.

"Now the Ogden Land Company of New York was then interested in the lands owned by the Oneida nation in eastern central New York State around Oneida Lake. That is a beautiful part of the country, and the Oneidas were proud to be the owners.

"I have a copy of the claim that we would like to have against New York State. There are about five or six million acres that we feel we were much underpaid for. We only got seven-hundredths of a penny an acre for some of it, and the Ogden Land Company turned right around and sold the Oneida lands for many times as much. We do have a claim pending in the Indian claims commission, but we also have a contract with a group of attorneys at Syracuse, New York, who would like to sue the state of New York, and they are now asking the federal government to represent the Oneidas against the state of New York.

"Through the treaty of 1794, known as the peace treaty, friendship treaty with the Tuscororas and Oneidas; and we have fought in every war this country has ever had, on the side of the United States. This is very important for people to know, the great record the Oneida nation has for its fellow men, the white men. They fought for them, with them, in all the wars. I doubt that there is another nation that has the record that equals that of the Oneida nation. If the public could only know the history of the Oneida nation, I think they would be proud of us, as well as we Oneidas are proud of our history.

"Now then, the Odgen Land Company was interested in the Oneida lands, and in those days we had nine chiefs for the Oneida nation. Since Eleazar Williams was their missionary, he also acted as interpreter in business affairs for Oneidas. The Oneida nation would not sell their lands in the state of New York, but the Ogden Land Company and other real estate men were interested in purchase and did everything they could do to discourage the Oneidas from remaining in New York. They wanted the Oneidas to move to the state of Wisconsin. I don't know how they got the information that they should move to Wisconsin, but the Indians were told that in Wisconsin there was all kinds of game. In fact, since Eleazar Williams was the chief interpreter, he did agree with the chiefs that they didn't want to move; but life got more and more miserable, so finally Eleazar Williams, as I understand it, did advise the chiefs that maybe it would be better if they did move to Wisconsin. But first, he said, the Oneidas must look at the land and see just what kind of a deal they could make here in Wisconsin.

"In 1820 the first group of chiefs came with Eleazar Williams to Wisconsin and talked with the Menominee Indians and the Winnebagos, who owned the strip of land from the Milwaukee River to Iron Mountain, Michigan.

"It was agreed that the New York Indians would purchase five million acres from them. Here the history becomes cloudy. No one knows who made the agreement or took the money that we are supposed to have received from the Ogden Land Company and paid to Wisconsin Indians. Who handled the money? The government, the Indians, or Eleazar Williams? Who paid that money to the Menominees? There is no record. No receipts. I wish to say here that I am supposed to be the walking encyclopedia about Oneida history, but I can find no record of who received the money from the Oneidas.

"I am not sure whether the government was represented when we sold our land to the Ogden Land Company. Then, Eleazar Williams was accused of being bribed by the Ogden Land Company and persuading the Oneida chiefs to purchase land here in Wisconsin, and move to Wisconsin.

"Later, Eleazar Williams was excused of this blame. The chiefs themselves decided it was better to move here to Wisconsin, so in 1823 the migration really took place. The first chief who came with the group had the Indian name of Skanandoah. His name would be Elija Skanandoah; so he and Eleazar Williams led the first group out here. I have somewhere the exact figures of the first Christian party. They were all Episcopalians.

"Now let me go back on Christianity, to 1390, when there never was a white man here in our country. At that time the five nations believed in religion. They believed in superhuman power. Why? Because they had a name for God: 'He Who Holds the Skies.' They had six seasons at which time they gave thanks to He Who Holds the Skies for all the things that grew here in our country. And they also believed in forgiveness and repenting, or forgiveness for all the things they might have done. They all form a circle and hold hands and ask Almighty God to forgive them. I want to make this very clear that there never was a white man here, for they already had religion before a white man ever stepped in our country.

"So when Eleazar Williams became missionary in 1819, the Oneidas had long ago accepted this white man's religion.

"In 1702 some of the Oneidas were converted to the white man's religion. You must know that not all the Oneidas were Episcopalians. Some had refused to accept Christianity and remained pagans, but in 1823 even those accepted Christianity and were converted to be Methodists. So the second group that came to Wisconsin in 1823 were Methodists.

"These Christian parties were known as the Orchard Parties. The Oneidas were great in planting fruit trees; that's how they came to be called 'Orchard Indians.' You notice the many fruit trees here now. So in 1823 the Oneidas came to Oneida and settled here in Duck Creek. The first Orchard party settled in the north end of the reservation of eight by twelve miles, as was set aside in 1838. That was the final agreement made in 1838, even though we had purchased five million acres. We ended up with land eight miles wide by twelve miles long. The first group naturally settled on the north end. The second group came later and had to settle the south half of the reservation. There had been a friction between these two groups, the Methodists and the Episcopalians, because the Methodists felt they were given the leavings of the reservation. To this day it shows up a little here and there, in the generation in their seventies and eighties, and there are some still living at this age. And this feeling comes from these old generations. Some of the young generation don't know anything about this, but I notice it, since I have been holding office for the Oneida tribe since 1934. Every now and then I hear that this friction still exists.

"I meet so many government officials, and it is news to them to know that we have two groups here that do not work together as they should.

"In 1823 we had Eleazar Williams for our missioner. I wish to give him credit. There never was another white man interested to educate us Indians. He set up the Oneida Mission Day School where he taught up to about fourth grade. Eleazar

Williams was with us until about 1845, and during this time he taught the Oneidas religion and music. He was well versed in music, and he had made some translations. He taught many religious hymns of the Episcopal church. Oneidas are musically inclined. And recall, singing may have been the only means of recreation at that time. He got good attandance. The Indians gathered here at the church and exchanged news and opinion; we have quite a number of Indians here who have very good bass voices — I think this is lacking with the white people. We can sing really well, and we can sing loud!

"Now we still have wakes here. It used to be that the corpse was brought back to the home where we have the Indian wakes. This was carried on in a very nice religious way. So now nobody speaks out loud. It is all in a whisper to show their respect to the deceased and his family. They do not knock at the door when they come to the wake in the evening; they walk right in. A chairman is appointed for the evening. He calls on different ones to make a speech, and it is always about the Bible. Also we are not to say anything unfavorable about the deceased's way of life. We must only talk about the pleasant things that he did.

"As to our singing, it is all Bible words, and we truly believe in our faith. We're not only using it as a cover. Some of the religious hymns that we sing were translated by Eleazar Williams into the Oneida language. One is the 'Te Deum' used as a sacred hymn for the Oneidas. It is only used on Thanksgiving, Christmas, and Easter and on Bishop Day. In 1939 a folklore project was set up here, sponsored by the University of Wisconsin. Since I was one of the two who were considered the best spellers in phonetic alphabet in our language, I was selected to make the transliteration from the Oneida Indian hymnbook written in Mohawk sounds, which was carried from New York to Oneida. In 1940 I made the translation into the new alphabet.

"Eleazar Williams was our missionary from 1823 until about 1848. He died at Hogansburg, but his corpse was brought back to Oneida here and buried near our church in about 1950. The Oneidas quarried the stone for our church, native limestone. My father was a foreman in quarrying the stone. I think that right here is a great record again for the Oneidas, but not a thing is said about the work of the Indians. The priests are given all the credit for what has taken place here in Oneida. It is the

Oneida Indians who were responsible for civilizing our own people. Williams was the only white man, as I've said, who really helped us get education.

"In 1848 Williams left us, and others took his place. Always, one or two get a superior education, and by 1870 we did have some well-educated persons, but instead of helping us they defrauded quite a few. In 1887 the Allotment Act became law; through two Oneida Indians and others, the law went through so that the reservation of 65,000 acres was broken up and allotted to individuals. Those who were not twenty-one received around twenty-six acres, and those older received forty acres if single; a married couple received ninety acres.

"Now this land was still held in trust by the federal government; in other words, it was exempt from taxation. Again these educated Oneidas worked with the superintendent and managed to get another bill passed in Congress whereby the heirs of a deceased person could sell his allotment. In 1906 this act really began to decrease our tribal lands, because much of the land could then be sold to white people.

"From 1823 on, the Oneidas were self-supporting through hunting. The women did the garden work. The men provided the meat.

"In 1918 the government made a taxable deed, except for a few who were old or uneducated, whereby the individual owners were able to mortgage, sell, or do otherwise. Immediately they started mortgaging their land and forgetting to make payments. Quite a few acres were sold for taxes. The white men took advantage of it and paid the back taxes and took the land; after four years they could get what is called a tax title deed. Some Indians mortgaged their land for a team of horses, which maybe were supposed to be four years old and turned out to be eighteen years old! The real estate men of Green Bay and West De Pere really took advantage and laid low for Indian lands. One eighty-acre section was sold, I think, for eighty dollars.

"In 1918 the Oneidas lost a lot of tribal lands. Finally many Indians were left with nothing. Then they went up north, around Tigerton, where they could cut cordwood for maybe a dollar a cord, and that's how they made their living. They started to move out of Oneida, because there wasn't any more game or timber. This migration started soon after 1918.

"In 1929 it was reported that the Oneidas were ninety-nine percent landless. In other words, we might have had about 100 acres of tribal-owned land. In 1934 the Indian Organization Act came into being, and we had factions here who were very excited and said that they were going to take shotguns, round up all the white people who had taken over the Oneida land, and march them down to Green Bay. The tribal chiefs were not recognized after 1900 by the Indian bureau, so there was a self-made chief who was telling the Oneidas that under the Indian Organization Act the government was going to move them out of Oneida, up north somewhere, where there were rattlesnakes. 'If you accept the Organization Act you will be moved.' But that was not true.

"Actually, under the Indian Organization Act, the government will buy land wherever the Indians wish to live; later on we accepted the act, and we have our own government. We have been able, also to get back about twenty-five hundred acres owned by the tribe and exempt from taxation. We assign this land to individual Indians. Also, we own some land inside the city limits of Green Bay, and we want to work with Green Bay to better ourselves. We want to create employment for our people, and to show that we are a dependable people with a great tradition.

"I don't know what Eleazar Williams would think if he saw us today. We have only a few Oneidas who can do bead work. Only one lady can make the husk rug out of cornhusks. We have a group of Indian dancers, but they were taught by white people, a priest who only wanted to satisfy his own curiosity. We make the Indian corn bread from white Indian flint corn. I have a mortar here with which we hand-grind our corn. One lady bakes corn bread one day a week.

"And when the wild geese fly high, we Oneidas think it will be very cold weather; when they fly low there will be a mild winter. I told a senator from Oklahoma that when a robin sings there will be rain before twenty-four hours, and there were a few other things I told him. I said, 'The only things which we Oneidas cannot forecast, nor tell, is when the federal government will pay us our claim!' That must have been twenty years ago, and we still didn't get our claim, but the money is now set aside for this five-million-acre claim; maybe, some day, the Oneidas will be again a landed people.

"I only wish that Eleazar Williams was here now. He would be helping us to fight our battles and to give us even better education."

# Was There a Bourbon Among Us?

And now we come to the Eleazar Williams part of the story that Oscar Auchiquette has only hinted at. It is certainly one of the great tales of the state and bears telling many times.

Years ago, while I was a resident of New York State, wandering around into strange corners, I heard many tales about a strange personality named Eleazar Williams, an Episcopal priest* who worked with the Oneida, Stonebridge, and Brotherton Indians. When I moved to Wisconsin, I found Eleazar again or, rather, relics of him, for he moved with his Oneida Indians to Wisconsin where he married a beautiful fourteen-year-old half-breed, Madeline Jourdain, at Green Bay, and took her to a small cabin south of De Pere on the banks of the Fox River.

Here they raised a family, and here Eleazar watched a fantastic tale come into focus, blaze bright, and then die away, leaving a broken, discouraged, and impoverished man and a whole network of belief and disbelief in the tale; it continues in disjointed phases of belief and disbelief to this day.

At Lost Dauphin State Park, south of De Pere, is a metal plaque that relates that at this place once lived Eleazar Williams, known as "the Lost Dauphin." The plaque doesn't say he *was* the lost dauphin. It merely asks, Was he the lost dauphin? The cabin has been restored, but the logs are the same ones Eleazar used to build the place. The land was once owned by the Gillespies of Green Bay, who were certain that Eleazar was not what people said but a much greater figure. In fact, the State Historical Society almost lost the land for the park because they could not quite accept the authenticity of Williams as a prince.

Folks around De Pere are rather passionately fond of Eleazar and tales of the dauphin, and the legends, to many of the older folks, have grown into fact. The story really falls into two parts.

## PART ONE
### The Story of the Poor Dauphin

Sometime in the thirteenth century, a group of buildings was erected in the northern part of Paris as the quarters of those

---

*He was never ordained a priest and had only deacon's orders, says Dr. Gilbert Doane, specialist in Episcopal church history in the Middle West.

crusading knights known as the Knights Templars. In the middle of the group stood a great tower, four stories high with turrets at each corner, the keep of the castle and known as "the Temple."

During the French Revolution, at 7 P.M. on August 13, 1792, the king and queen of France, Louis XVI and Marie Antoinette, the king's sister Elizabeth, and the two children of the royal family, princess royal and little Louis Charles, were imprisoned at the Temple. The little crown prince, heir to the French throne, was known as the dauphin. All of the possessions of the royal family were taken away, and they were treated like common felons.

At first the royal prisoners were allowed to be together and could walk quite freely around their prison, but when the Commune gained control over the National Assembly the imprisonment of the royal family became extremely strict. Four members of the Commons were selected daily to guard the dauphin, and two slept in the chamber of the king. None of the guards was ever allowed to serve more than once, and these four special guards were employed in addition to the regular turnkeys and guards of the Temple. One of the regular Temple guards was a shoemaker named Simon.

In the early part of January, 1793, the king was removed from the Temple, tried before the National Convention, and found guilty of conspiracy against the liberties of France. On January 21, 1793, the king was sent to the guillotine. After the king's death, the royal party, largely in exile, declared that the little dauphin was now king of France. He was called Louis XVII.

The dauphin's mother and his aunt continued his education in prison, but at about 10 P.M. on July 3, 1793, six months after the death of his father, six men burst into the quarters of the family and read the following order: "The Committee of Public Safety has ordered that the son of Louis XVI be separated from his mother and placed in the most secure apartment in the tower."

A heartbreaking scene followed, but there was no mercy shown. The young king was dressed and taken to the part of the prison formerly occupied by his father. At half-past ten the dauphin was committed to the care of the ignorant shoemaker, Simon, who was to be the boy's tutor and guardian.

Simon, who called the boy "the damned wolf cub," beat

him and forced him to do the vilest work, and the dauphin became the servant of his brutal jailer. His food was reduced to barely enough to keep him alive.

The boy never again saw his mother, Queen Marie Antoinette. On the night of August 2, at one-thirty in the morning, five police came for Marie Antoinette in a carriage and, escorted by twenty mounted gendarmes, conducted her to the Conciergerie.

She was given only the mockery of a trial. Evidence against her was cited by Simon from a document that he supposedly compiled from statements made by the boy. The queen was sent to the guillotine on October 16, 1793.

About this time there was a rumor that the dauphin had disappeared from the Temple. The rumor started because Simon kept him shut up on the second floor, fearing that the boy's tears would soften the hearts of the soldiers on guard. The population believed the rumors were true, and that the dauphin was no longer in the Temple. To prove that the rumor was false, the members of the Convention had the child led into the garden to show him to all the guards. The eight-year-old boy cried out there against the treatment he was being given. To avoid further rumors, Simon thereafter often brought the prince to the guardroom on the first floor.

Simon resigned on January 19, 1794, and he and his wife moved out of the Temple prison. Before he left, Simon insisted that four members of the Council inspect the prince, to be assured that he was still safely in custody. The four men did inspect the room and the person of the dauphin, found him in good health, and granted Simon a release. They then took over custody of the child. From that time on, the slightest sign of compassion for the prince was considered a crime against the state.

It was decided that Simon should have no successor and that the child should be placed in solitary confinement; for two days he was in the charge of the guards, while a special room was being prepared.

The door to the boy's anteroom was cut down, breast high, and was grated from top to bottom with iron bars. A small door or wicket was made, fastened with an enormous padlock opening upon a shelf where the food for the dauphin was placed. He took what he wanted from the shelf.

On January 21, 1794, the dauphin was locked alone in his

bare room. He had neither fire nor candles. The shutters of the room were closed. The room had light only from a lamp hanging outside, which shed a few gleams through the grating, and for more than six months there was no fresh air let into the room. No one ever entered it, and no one spoke to the child except to tell him to go to bed. He had no playthings, no way to amuse himself. For food he had thin soup with pieces of bread broken into it, a small amount of beef, a loaf of bread, and a pitcher of water.

The municipal guards changed every day and arrived separately about midnight. When each guard arrived he would insist that the wicket in the dauphin's door be opened, and that the child come to the wicket so they could see him. The wicket opened with a great noise of rust and grating.

Because of the harsh treatment, the child became very thin, apathetic, and unable to change his bed or clothes or even to wash himself.

After the fall from power of that strange and terrible man Robespierre, the Reign of Terror phase of the French Revolution was over. Barras became dictator. He visited the Temple prison and discovered the conditions that existed there. In the escort with Barras was Citizen Laurent, a member of the Revolutionary Committee of the Temple Section. Laurent had gained the confidence of Barras, and on the recommendation of Barras, Laurent was appointed keeper of the children of the ex-king. Laurent was a small man, unmarried, and lived with his mother and two young sisters. He was well educated, had very refined manners, and was fond of flowers.

Laurent arrived at the Temple on the evening of July 28, 1794, but it was not until 2 A.M. that the guards conducted him to the room of the Dauphin.

Laurent was horrified at the terrible stench that came from the room. The municipal guard called loudly for the dauphin at the wicket, and finally came the boy's feeble reply, but he would not come into view.

Next day Laurent sent a request to the Committee of General Safety that an examination should be made. He was, of course, obliged to use the greatest caution, because any show of sympathy for a member of the royal family was still regarded as a criminal action.

Laurent's request was heard by the committee, and on July 31, 1794, several members of the committee and several guards went to the Temple to see the condition of the little prisoner. They called to him at the wicket, but he did not answer, and workmen were sent for to unfasten the door.

When the door creaked open finally, they saw a terrible sight. On a dirty bed, covered with a filthy cloth, lay a child of nine, motionless, his neck bent, his face wasted, his cheeks tinged with green. His head and neck were covered with sores, and his wrists and knees were swelled and yellow. The nails on his fingers and feet had grown to a great length and were as hard as horns. His hair was stuck together with a scurflike pitch. Bugs and lice crawled all over his bed, and there were many large, black spiders.

The committee asked the boy many questions, but he answered none of them. His only words were "I want to die."

Laurent pleaded with the committee to be allowed to send for some warm water to bathe the child's sores. It wasn't that they were not humane men, it was simply that the committeemen were afraid for their lives. They refused.

They did consent, however, to have the wicket and the grated door removed; the coverings of the windows were partly taken away to give more light, and the room was cleaned. Laurent had a clean bed brought, changed the clothes, and gave the boy a bath; a woman called Mother Matheu cut and combed his hair. The head was so sore and tender that the combing took many hours, and finally a physician did come and treat the great sores on the boy's neck.

Laurent himself was allowed to visit the dauphin only at mealtime, and once in a while he was able to take the lad to a platform near the top of the tower for a walk. But the prince remained very weak and said hardly a word.

A man named Gomin was now appointed by the Committee of General Safety to assist Laurent. He arrived at the prison late at night, but Laurent took Gomin at once to see the prince. He spoke to the child but the prince would not speak to him.

Now the prince had cleaner quarters, but still he was kept a solitary prisoner. The boy was alone from breakfast time until 2 P.M. and from then until 8 P.M. when a lamp was lighted outside his chamber. He was then given his supper and left alone until 9 A.M.

All the keys to the prison were locked in a cupboard in a guardroom on the first floor. The cupboard had two locks, each with a different key, and each key was carried by a different guard. The cupboard could not be unlocked unless three men were present.

Gomin was refused permission to take the prince out into the garden, but the boy finally was given a few toys, a couple of packs of cards, and at last some books. Yet the prince grew weaker. Tumors came on his legs, but the sores cleared on his face. He begged to see his sister, the princess royal, who was kept prisoner in a room above him, but they were never to meet again.

Laurent now retired from the prison work, and a new person came to take his place: Citizen Lasne became the new superintendent of the Tower. He was terrified at the condition in which he found the prince. "I recognized him perfectly well [for Lasne had formerly been a guard at the royal palace before the Revolution]. His head had not changed. It was still beautiful, but his chest was contracted, his arms and legs emaciated and weak, and his right knee and left wrist were covered with enormous tumors."

The boy eventually responded better to Lasne than to anyone else. The new superintendent played cards and dominoes with him and brought him books.

But early in May, 1795, Lasne and Gomin believed they must inform the government of the prince's condition. They wrote, "Little Capet [the Bourbon family name] is dangerously ill."

There was the usual long delay. Several days passed. Then M. Dusault, an eminent physician, was appointed to attend the prince. He came at once and made a long and careful examination. The prince was suffering, he said, from a family disease of which the prince's brother had died. Dr. Dusault prescribed a medicine and recommended that the boy be moved to the country. No heed was paid to his suggestion.

The princess royal, upstairs in the prison, begged to be allowed to nurse her brother, whom she knew was ill. Her request was refused.

On May 30, 1795, when one of the guards on duty asked Dr. Dusault whether the child would die, he replied, "There are many persons in the world who hope so." These were the last words ever spoken in the Temple prison by Dr. Dusault. He himself died a few days later.

There were many attempts made to show that the doctor was murdered. Some said that the Royalists had poisoned him to prevent his disclosure of a startling fact: *that the child he had treated in the Temple was not the dauphin.*

Others said that the doctor had administered a slow poison to the child, and he himself was killed to prevent his disclosure of the crime.

On May 31, an artist, M. Bellanger, visited the dauphin. Bellanger was one of the commissioners on duty at the prison. He asked the prince to allow him to make a sketch of his face, and later this artist sculptured a very fine bust of the prince from the sketch. M. Bellanger found the condition of the child extremely distressing. Gomin took the dying prince to a large, light room, free of bars. Yet, even that night the rules of the Temple were not relaxed. The child remained alone from 8 P.M. to 9 A.M.

"I am always alone," the dauphin said to Gomin. "My dear mother is in the other tower." The prince never knew of the fate of Marie Antoinette.

The symptoms of the child's illness became alarming, and the end came at 2:15 P.M. on June 8, 1795.

Gomin went at once to notify the Committee of General Safety of the dauphin's death. The meeting of the committee was, however, over for that day and Gomin was instructed to keep the news secret until the following morning.

At eight o'clock June 9, four members of the committee came to the Temple to make sure that the dauphin was really dead.

They were shown the body, but they were indifferent. "The event is not of the least importance; the police will receive the declaration of death; the burial will be without ceremony."

Everyone present, who had seen the dauphin when he was alive, was asked to view the body and identify it. Everyone present vouched that the body was that of Louis XVII.

The testimony that the body was indeed that of the dauphin was sworn to by at least twenty persons. The next day the body was viewed again, and again the death was verified. At 7 P.M. on June 10, 1795, the body was placed in a rough coffin and taken to the Cemetery of St. Marguerite accompanied by gendarmes and a small detachment of troops. The coffin was deposited in the common grave without religious ceremony of any kind. The grave was filled up, and the soil restored to its former level. Not until then did the police withdraw. Two sentinels, one at the gate and one in the cemetery, remained on guard for two or three days.

A year later, after the accession of Louis XVIII, when the monarchy was finally restored, a search was made for the boy's body that it might be placed in the royal sepulchre at St. Dennis, but the body was never found.


## PART TWO
### The Story of the Poor Missionary

On April 24, 1814, the restoration of the Bourbon dynasty in France was celebrated with great rejoicing. Louis XVIII, with his niece, Madame Royale, daughter of Louis XVI and sister of the dauphin, landed at Calais on their return from exile. On the same day, Napoleon was beginning his exile on the island of Elba, and in America, on the shores of Lake Champlain, a young man by the name of Eleazar Williams, commanding the U.S. Secret Corps of Observation in the war that began in 1812, was riding from Rouses Point to Plattsburgh bearing latest news of British invasion to Commodore McDonough.

Eleazar Williams was, everyone thought, the son of Thomas Williams, a chief of the Mohawk Indian nation, but some persons noted that the youth had no Indian characteristics. He appeared to be French, or Spanish, and was well received by French persons in Plattsburgh, home of many French emigres, some of whom were highly born.

After the War of 1812, Williams became an Episcopal missionary, serving first the Indians in New York State; when certain parts of the New York tribes were sent west to Wisconsin, Williams went with them as their spiritual leader. It was said that Williams had ambitions to establish a great Indian empire in the West, with himself occupying a central position. Such an empire never materialized, but Williams remained in Indian work, living south of Green Bay, on the west bank of the Fox River near what is now the city of De Pere.

Nothing was said about his parentage until 1841 when a notable visitor from France came to Green Bay. The visitor was Prince de Joinville, son of Louis-Philippe, king of France. He was seeing the American West, supposedly, just as his father had seen it years before, and was, indeed, tracking over the same route taken by his father.

De Joinville was a young man of twenty-three when he made his famous American visit. He was a sailor and commanded the frigate Belle Poule of the French Navy. He had already served his father well, as special diplomatic agent to several foreign countries; in 1840, it was de Joinville who was sent to St. Helena to bring back to France the ashes of Napoleon. Although this mission was full of danger, for there was still deep feeling in support of Napoleon in France, the young prince carried the mission through successfully and deposited the remains of the Emperor Napoleon with pomp and ceremony in the tomb at the Invalides. When he went to America, many may have thought he was on the lookout for important French exiles.

At Mackinac in Lake Michigan, de Joinville told the captain of the steamer that he particularly wished to visit with a man named Eleazar Williams. Strangely, Williams was also in Mackinac, having arrived there on Saturday, October 16, to preach a sermon on Sunday evening at the Fort. The regular steamer for Green Bay with the Prince de Joinville on board put into Mackinac on Monday. Captain Shook of the steamboat *Columbus* said to Williams, "The prince has asked to see you," and Williams went forward to meet the famous young man. According to eyewitnesses, the prince showed great interest in the missionary. Williams journeyed on to Green Bay on the same steamer, and during the trip the prince and Williams conversed many times.

When the boat reached Green Bay, the prince invited Williams to join him for supper at his hotel, the Astor House. The missionary declined, saying that he must go instead to the home of his father-in-law, Joseph Jourdain, and that he would return later to speak with the prince.

About ten o'clock that same evening Williams did return to the hotel, and in a room adjoining the one in which the prince was entertaining his guests, a very famous interview supposedly took place. Williams recounted the interview in his diary, and several persons of high reputation reported that Williams and the prince actually did meet.

In his diary, Williams recorded that the prince made wonderful revelations to him: that he was actually the son of Louis XVI and Marie Antoinette; that he was the poor prince who had been the prisoner so cruelly treated in the Temple; that he had been taken from the Temple and carried to America by faithful old servants of the royal household; that his history was known by the present king of France, Louis Philippe; and that he,

Prince de Joinville, was commissioned to make Eleazar Williams a generous offer.

The prince asked Williams to sign a document stating that Williams would renounce all claims to the throne of France; if he did so, a splendid estate and establishment would be provided for him in Europe or in America, as he preferred.

Williams, dazed and bewildered by this news of his royal birth, refused to sign away his birthright. The prince grew very angry, pointed out that the missionary was a poor man, living in miserable conditions, and that it would be utterly impossible ever to make good his claim to the throne. Williams, however, absolutely refused to sign his name.*

The following day the prince and his party left Green Bay. At De Pere the prince went again to see Eleazar Williams, and Hannah Sharpe, whose father drove the prince in his wagon to visit Williams at his cabin, said that the prince returned very discouraged and full of pity for the missionary.

It was not until 1853, however, that the story of Eleazar Williams was made public. Between the time of the prince's visit and 1853, twelve years, Williams discussed the strange circumstances with the Rev. John H. Hanson, another Episcopal clergyman. Hanson became extremely interested in the case and apparently had a sincere regard for Williams. Hanson determined to do what he could to make Williams' claim to the French throne valid. He searched for all scraps of information, both in America and in Europe, and in 1853 he published a long article in *Putnam's Historical Magazine* called, "Is There a Bourbon Among Us?"

Hanson thought that there was, and that the Bourbon's name was Eleazar Williams. His story was fantastic and unbelievable, yet he had found witnesses who swore to the truth of much in the article.

According to Hanson, it was the shoemaker-jailer, Simon, who arranged the plot to save the dauphin and free him from the Temple. Probably it was on January 19, 1794, that the escape from the prison was accomplished. "On that day," wrote Madame Royale, who was imprisoned in the room above him, "we heard a great noise in my brother's room below, and we supposed that he was leaving the Temple. We were sure of it

---

*Eleazar Williams' diary is preserved in the library of the State Historical Society of Wisconsin.

when we looked through a hole in the sun-blind and saw a great many packages being taken away. On the following day we heard his door open, and believed that they had put some other prisoner below."

There was, of course, still a child in the Temple. Plots and counterplots were constantly being carried on all through the Revolutionary period by royalists, and many credible Frenchmen testified that Simon secreted in one of the bundles the eight-year-old dauphin, substituting in his place a boy from the charity hospital.

Hanson found many items which did not fit at all with the straightforward account of the imprisonment and death of the dauphin at the Temple. He found significance in the coincidental fact of Dr. Dusault's death and certainly it was strange the doctor should suddenly die just before the prince did. He found conflicting evidence in the testimony of the doctors who performed an autopsy on the body of the dauphin. They could *not* swear, Hanson wrote, that the body they examined was that of the prince. He cited a police order that had been issued to arrest any person or persons traveling the highways with a boy of the age of the dauphin. There had been an escape from the Temple; several children were actually arrested. Hanson pointed out the curious fact that the name of the dauphin was omitted from the list of dead members of the royal family when memorial services were held.

The dauphin, he said, had been brought to America by two old servants of the royal household, the Jourdains. The couple had with them several articles bearing the crest of the royal family, and Mrs. Jourdain had once been the personal maid of Marie Antoinette. These articles were sold in New York.

The couple had with them also a mysterious boy, a child of about ten or eleven who had some illness, presumably mental. Indeed, the boy appeared to be an imbecile. Hanson then related that the Jourdains had traveled north from New York to Lake Champlain and to the St. Lawrence Valley.

Between the years 1795 and 1800, many refugees from France went to the Lake Champlain and St. Lawrence valleys. One of these was Peter Sailly, who had been a member of the personal bodyguard of Louis XVI. It was Sailly's firm belief that the dauphin had been brought to America and placed with an Indian tribe on the shores of the St. Lawrence. Sailly was one of those who strongly supported the theory that Williams was the dauphin.

At any rate, Hanson claimed that the Jourdains had deposited the young prince with the family of Thomas Williams at Caughnawaga, and later Mrs. Williams, the Indian wife of Thomas, gave a statement, taken down by an interpreter, that Eleazar was indeed her fourth child. But another statement was later written down in the Mohawk language that "the names of my children were Peter, Catherine, Ignatius, Eleazar (adopted), Louisa, John, Peter, Hannah, Rhoda, Charles, and Jarvis."

The church register at Caughnawaga has the baptismal record of all the children of Thomas and Mary Ann Williams, but no mention is made of Eleazar.

The greatest stumbling block to the theory that Williams was the little prince was that Williams himself had no memory of his life in France. Hanson attributed this to the harsh treatment of the boy in prison, which indeed rendered him unable to speak and so unbalanced his mind that he gave the impression of being an idiot; it was in this condition that he was deposited with the Williams family. How then, did it happen that Eleazar Williams, grown to manhood, was a person normal in mind, with an excellent memory?

Hanson found witnesses who swore to a curious event. One day when Eleazar was about twelve years of age (possibly a year or two older since Williams himself did not know the exact date of his birth), he struck his head against a rock while swimming. Witnesses said that a remarkable change occurred in the boy. As if by a miracle, his mental facilities were restored, yet he never spoke about a life in France. That part of his life was entirely blocked off.

In supporting his case that Eleazar Williams was the true and lawful dauphin, Hanson made some convincing points. His features, he said, were certainly not those of an Indian. Indeed, several noted painters testified that the Williams face was a Bourbon face and that his manners were as delicate and refined as those found in a royal court. At school Williams appeared to remember flashes of noble buildings and had nightmares about terrifying scenes. Once when Williams suddenly saw a portrait of the Revolutionary jailer, Simon, he cried, "I know that face! It has haunted me all my life!"

Then there was a Frenchman named Bellanger, who related, on his deathbed, that he had helped the dauphin escape, and that he was living in America under the name of Williams.

142

Three famous doctors examined Williams and pronounced that he was a European, not an Indian. They said that scars and other indications showed that he had suffered impure air, bad food, and mental strain when young. They confirmed that he had an inoculation scar like the dauphin's and that he also had a scar over the eye where Simon was said to have struck him.

Others, however, had equally good proofs that Eleazar's claim was a hoax. Certain individuals who had lived with him claimed that he was lazy, fat, crafty, and unscrupulous. On evidence supplied by Williams himself when he applied for membership in a Masonic order, there was a five-year difference in the age of Williams and the age of the dauphin. Thus, Williams could not possibly have been the dauphin.

The most convincing evidence of all, though, was the testimony of Eleazar's own mother that he was her true and lawful son. Later, according to Hanson, she altered her statement to read "adopted son," but the opponents of the dauphin theory claimed that she was very confused when she made the second statement and did not rightly understand the significance of it.

Furthermore, Eleazar could read French, after a fashion, but could not pronounce it at all. If he were indeed the dauphin, the antagonists argued, would he not have some knowledge of pronunciation, particularly since the dauphin had a rather extensive education?

Finally, Col. H. E. Eastman reported that he wrote a romance about the lost dauphin, casting Eleazar as the lost boy. According to Eastman's own testimony, the book was written many years before the dauphin theory became known, and it included all the details of the Williams-dauphin story. He gave the manuscript to Eleazar to read, and Eleazar kept it. This manuscript never has turned up.

For a time the dauphin story had wide acceptance. Williams had a real following. A group in New York State, in order to give him a dwelling in keeping with his past, built him a "French chateau" at Oneida, New York.

But the fever died soon, and Williams was never able to sustain his claims; and fewer and fewer believed the story. He sank into ever deeper poverty and discouragement, and finally retired to the chateau where he died, a terribly unhappy man who really believed, at the end at least, that he was the true and rightful heir to the throne of France.

# Utopia

In the spring the country up toward Green Lake and Ripon is almost beyond description — the soft atmosphere of the land and sky; the rolling earth and the way the hills come down to the edges of the green-blue lakes; old houses nursing memories of large families in those days when families did the farm labor. It is a utopian sort of country, and I can understand, going toward Ripon on a warm spring day, how a group of Kenosha farmers in 1844 might well have believed: if utopia is possible on this earth, it might well be created here.

Folks at Ripon still yarn about the "long house," and they have a lot to say about how it came to be built. They tell about the nineteenth century Frenchman, Francois Marie Charles Fourier, who said that sharing the wealth would solve everybody's woes. They tell about that Kenosha group (Kenosha was known as Southport then) led by Warren Chase, who thought that Fourier's ideas were excellent and ought to be tried out in Wisconsin.

It was in 1844 that a land agent got the first group of Kenosha farm folks located up where Ripon now stands. They had sold stock at $25 per share and bought some beautiful land. The twenty people who went first named the location of their colony Ceresco, after Ceres, goddess of agriculture. They also built a house 32 feet wide by 208 feet long. Take twenty apartments, each twenty feet in length, arranged in two rows with a corridor between — pin them together, and you have the long house, a frame building with the architecture of a string of boxcars. But since there were no boxcars around when the long house was built out in the country in 1844, let's say that it looked like a sheepfold. And it was a fold, for human beings.

What made the old building in Ceresco Park at Ripon notable is that it was a shell of dreams, but of dreams that were realized. The Yankee farmers from Kenosha were one of the few nonreligious groups in the world ever to have made communal living a success. The long house standing at Ripon today is not the original.

At the end of seven years the community divided about $40,000. There never were any serious quarrels or scandal within the group. It was finally disbanded for the simple reason that while Wisconsin Fourierites had enjoyed their seven years' experience in communal living, they decided that they liked living out in the world better. Taking his share, each went back to the individualistic life.

The name "long house" was a little unadorned for the founder of the utopian movement, Fourier. In Fourier's scheme every such communal building was to have been a "noble palace" and was called a "phalanstery." Those who lived in it composed a "phalanx," the unit in Fourier's plan for reorganizing the world.

It seems a bit ludicrous to think of a group of shrewd Wisconsin farmers putting up their scythes at noon and telling each other that it was time to go up to the phalanstery for dinner. No, it just couldn't be done; they had to say "long house."

Fourierism was the technocracy of the 1840s. An enticing cure-all for the ills of society, it was brought to the United States from France during a depression period on this side of the water. The depression that started in the winter of 1836 was a bad one. In fact, it was so severe that, in the early 1840s, it was said that one could go from Albany to Buffalo and not find six businessmen who were not bankrupt. Naturally everyone was thinking on subjects ordinarily left to statesmen and financiers. In debating clubs, in country stores, and around the family dinner table, discussion centered on a solution to the depression. Most radical of all the cures proposed was that of Fourier.

News of Fourier's scheme was brought to the United States by Albert Brisbane, a young man from New York who had been studying in Europe and had heard Fourier lecture in Paris. Fourier himself looked like Dante and had pinpointed pupils in large gray eyes and a lion's mouth that curved down at the corners. A young engineer, he worked during the French Revolution in a shipping house at Marseilles, where immense stores of rice had rotted while hidden away from the starving population. It became the duty of young Fourier to see that this spoiled rice was secretly cast into the Mediterranean. While occupied with this work, he became convinced that something was wrong with the social order. He began a series of studies that finally yielded a philosophy all his own.

The universe was governed by laws, he said. It was up to man to discover those laws. Apply them and social harmony would reign. Fourier denied that labor was a divine punishment imposed on man. Labor ought to be made attractive, he said. This was a brand new idea, and one that impressed other thinkers of the period as gigantic.

Shops, he declared, ought to be very different places from

the wretched shambles where manufacturing of the period took place. He went so far as to say that they ought to be actually "elegant."

There ought to be rotation of labor. No man ought to have a solitary occupation in which he lived and died; that was petrifying to both mind and body. Man should choose his work, changing from one order of labor to another as often as he wished. Thus the benumbing influence of labor would be avoided. Individuality was by no means to be curbed, and ownership of private property was not to be done away with. Labor was to have short sessions. The entire working period of man's life was to be only about ten years.

The only means of attaining a normal social organization was by association of human beings in both labor and interest. The social and productive life of man ought to be identified. That meant collective living, but collective living organized on what Fourier said were strictly scientific principles.

The living unit was to be a community of about two hundred persons to be called a "phalanx." In this number, he said, every order of talent was apt to be found. He believed, for instance, that any phalanx could produce opera better than that of Paris.

Twelve phalanxes made a union. A number of unions, in turn, formed a district, and so on through provinces, nations, caliphates, regions, and continents, up to the final organization, which was the world itself. Each of these was to be governed by a republican ruler, elected annually with the "omniarch," the ruler of the world at Constantinople, which was to be the ultimate capital of the globe.

Fourier was dead when his plan for reorganizing the world was brought to the United States. "Headquarters" in New York was a room where pamphlets on the subject were on view. Lecturers talked to interested groups about the wonders of Fourierism; the most important convert to the theory was a young editor named Horace Greeley.

One Saturday night, while on the train between New York and Boston, editor Greeley read pamphlets in which was set forth Francois Charles Fourier's new economic system. By the time the train had pulled into the Boston depot, he had become convinced of the soundness of Fourier's theory that individual effort was a great economic waste as compared with communal effort. He agreed with the Frenchman that industry ought to be made attractive and that labor ought to be divided so that every person performed the order of work that he enjoyed.

Curiously, one idea that particularly impressed the New York editor was the advice to do away with woman's never-ending toil in the kitchen by the simple method of having community kitchens.

Greeley's conversion to the scheme led to the adoption of the theory by the entire Brook Farm community, an organization of idealistic and dreamy folks in which the editor of the *Tribune* was a leading spirit. It also brought about a daily column in the *New York Tribune* devoted to the exposition of Fourierism. This column was largely responsible for the Wisconsin tryout of Fourier's plan.

A debating society called the Franklin Lyceum, composed of pioneers who had settled in Southport (Kenosha), read about Fourierism in editor Greeley's paper. One evening in November, 1843, its members held a debate on the topic, "Does Fourierism Present a Practical Plan for Such Reorganization to Society as Will Guard Against Our Social Evils?" Before January 1, 1844, members of the lyceum had formed the Wisconsin phalanx, and Fourier's dream plan was about to be put to the test. They sold the stock, and the experiment was ready to go.

Where should the colony make its experiment? With a Green Bay land agent, officials of the phalanx tramped for two weeks over central Wisconsin. The leader was Warren Chase, who had $800 in his wallet to pay for the selected land. A tract in a beautiful valley in Fond du Lac County, in what is today Ripon, was selected.

In the meantime, back in Southport, other members of the phalanx were busily preparing to take up community life. One Monday morning the advance guard, composed of nineteen men and one boy, set out for what was to be the phalanstery. In the cavalcade were thirty-four horses, eight yoke of oxen, and thirty-eight other cattle. They traveled six days, making camp each night beside the trail. On the seventh day, May 27, 1844, they set up their tents in the lovely valley that was to be the scene of the Fourier experiment.

These nineteen men included Warren Chase, Alexander Todd, Jerome C. Cobb, Jacob Beckwith, Nathan Hunter, John Limbert, T. V. Newell, H. G. Martin, Lester Rounds, Laban Stillwell, James Stuart, William Dunham, Joseph S. Gracy, Carlton Lane, George H. Stebbins, Seth R. Kellogg, and Chester

Adkins.

Since spring was well advanced, there was no time to be lost if there were to be crops that year. And before winter there must be houses. So, while half the group went to work breaking up the sod of the prairie, the others dug cellars, hewed oak timbers, and rived out shingles, all by hand. One of the number, who had been a Scottish sailor, did the cooking, and the meals were eaten in the open. On the Fourth of July they dedicated a flagpole and ran up a star spangled banner. By this time twenty families were occupying the half-finished houses.

The dwellings were standard, each twenty by thirty feet and divided into several apartments, so that more than one family lived in each. These houses, connected in 1845, formed the famous long house. Members ate at a common table. Board was figured at sixty-three cents a week the first year. It never exceeded seventy-five cents a week.

There was a faithful attempt made to carry out the plans of Fourier, however complicated they might be. Besides actual hours of labor performed, there was an allowance for skill, so that some of the highly skilled workmen were able to score as many as 25 hours of labor in a twenty-four hour day.

In the winter of 1846 a charter was obtained from the territorial legislature, and by the close of the next year the population had increased to 180; the annual dividend was 7.25 percent.

Expense accounts in the phalanx were carefully kept, and at the end of a year it was known exactly how much it had cost to produce a bushel of wheat or corn or a yearling heifer. One-fourth of what they called the "new increase" was added to the capital, and three-fourths was distributed for labor in proportion to the number of hours each member had worked. Everyone drew stock or cash on settlement day in proportion to his credit on the daily record.

The first year, the president reported, phalanx workers performed 102,760 hours of labor, besides spending considerable time in the practice of both vocal and instrumental music. They also indulged in cotillions, especially on the occasions of the three weddings that took place in the second summer of the phalanx.

What really killed the phalanx? It was financially successful and its members did not quarrel; there was no dispute over the kind of table set; the members were free to prepare meals in their own quarters if they chose (which ultimately most families did).

The Wisconsin phalanx died of a too-ordered life. Existence was too simple; there was not enough adventure in it to suit the Wisconsin farmers, their wives, and their children, once they had cut down the trees, made the prairie into fields, and finished the long house. It died of the disease that Fourier had said was brought by one order of labor performed day in and day out. Strange that they did not foresee that a community as well as an individual may succumb to monotony.

# Independence

One day when I was going through Winneconne, I saw Jim Coghlin's sign on his real estate office and figured it was time to go in and ask about the great sovereign state of Winneconne. Jim obliged, with the help of the local newspaper, the *Winneconne News*.

From the viewpoint of its size, it really isn't hard to understand how the State Highway Department forgot to include Winneconne in the highway maps of 1968. That did happen, however, and for a little while Winneconne enjoyed the most fame it probably can ever hope to have. Not only did it become world famous, for one day it enjoyed the unique status of being the only sovereign state within the state of Wisconsin.

The incident began on the cold Monday morning of January 16, 1967, when a Milwaukee printing salesman, calling in the village of Winneconne for the first time, asked the news editor of the *Winneconne News*, "Where's Winneconne? I can't locate it on the new Wisconsin road map!"

The following Thursday the editor published four short paragraphs in his column, "Look Out Below" by C. O. Little did he know that he was igniting a fuse for a tremendous series of events. The fuse was worded this way: "Guess what? Would you believe that the village of Winneconne is no more? The state mapmakers must have been napping when they should have been mapping — they completely eliminated the village from the new Wisconsin road maps. They were gracious enough to leave the dot where Winneconne used to be, but the name was lost somewhere between Omro and Butte des Morts."

After reading of the curious omission, the officers of the local chamber of commerce, with Mrs. Vera Kitchen as president, went into emergency session and drafted a letter to Gov. Warren Knowles asking what had happened. On January 21, 1967, Governor Knowles wired James P. Coghlin, village president, and Mrs. Kitchen the following apology: "Deep regrets over the elimination of Winneconne from the maps. Apparently the State Highway Commission 'goofed' — it won't happen again."

This attempt to appease, however, caused a ripple of indignation to ruffle the hearts of the citizens of Winneconne. Bill Schlapman, president of Colt Manufacturing Co., picked up the ball on the next pitch when he remarked at a chamber of

150

commerce meeting, "The omission of Winneconne from the maps has placed a financial burden on the village as a resort area!" This threat to the economy of Winneconne (the name means "place of skulls" in Indian lingo) cemented determination to fight for Winneconne rights.

Don Lewis of the *Milwaukee Journal* produced a green sheet story and things began to happen. A group of Oshkosh citizens, headed by Dick Rutledge, Tom MacNichol, and Les Farrow, visited Winneconne to lend the support of their famed metropolis to its tiny neighbor. A committee under the leadership of Mrs. Kitchen was established and known as "Vera's Kitchen Cabinet." All meetings were held in secret and by candlelight.

The Winneconne story broke nationally and internationally on Thursday, March 16, when a resolution was presented to the Winneconne Village Board calling for immediate action and urging all men "of good will, who have faith, hope and charity, to establish forever the right of the village of Winneconne to refuse disfranchisement by the state of Wisconsin for any cause whatever." The slogan "We like it . . . where?" was officially adopted.

It was widely recognized that if the village no longer existed fisherman could not know where to fish, industry would not know where to locate, and employees could not know where to work! Many poems were written about the situation, for example,

Wisconsin must have had a mental lapse
To take Winneconne off the highway maps.

How to put Winneconne back on the map became a burning question. Fierce debates were held, and finally a contest was started on the subject, with the winners to receive a wonderful all-expense weekend in Winneconne. The hapless Knowles, trying to quiet rebellion, was made chairman of the contest.

The winners of the contest were two Wisconsin girls, Janice Badtke and Kay Klipstine, who resided in Washington, D.C. Their brilliant suggestion showed a tremendous grasp of statesmanship and of American history. They wired: "Secede and declare war." The wording of their suggestion gave a distinct sense of grandeur to the Winneconne Village Board. "Winneconne secedes from and declares war on the United States, proclaiming the Republic of Winneconne. Authorities to seize federal property, detaining postmaster as enemy alien; request U.N. peace commission to prevent border hostilities, preserve

Winneconnian territorial integrity, close port of Winneconne to U.S. shipping, enforcing twelve-mile limit."

With a vast feeling of destiny, Coghlin issued the following proclamation:

I do here and now proclaim that an act of secession has taken place. The sovereign state of Winneconne does in fact exist, and is directed by the proclamation of secession, approved by the village board, Thursday, July 20, 1967. I accept the appointment and the responsibilities of president. To effect continuity of government I shall here and now appoint the staff necessary for the conduct of business:

| | |
|---|---|
| Prime Minister | Vera Kitchen |
| Secretary of State | William Schlapman |
| Secretary of Defense | Horace Saunders |
| Secretary Treasurer | Dorothy Nimmer |
| Secretary of Maps and Publications | John J. Rukauf |
| Secretary of Long-Range Planning | Tom Hendry |
| Secretary of Short-Range Planning | Lynn Ihrig |
| Secretary of Imports and Exports | J. P. Gruwell |
| Secretary of Security | Garnet Peterson |
| Secretary of Highways and Byways | William Krings |
| Secretary of Foreign Contacts | Orville Hintz |
| General Services Administration | Evelyn Corcoran |
| U.N. Ambassador | Sarah Schneider |
| Special emissary to Norway | Ben Bockin |
| Attorney General | Melvin Crowley |
| Postmaster General | Henry Luebke |
| Admiral of the Navy | George Kontos |
| General of the Air Force | Gaylord Tyres |
| Honorary Citizen | Richard Rutledge |

The Department of Heraldry of the new state came forth with a national banner, which they described with immortal eloquence:

The flag of the sovereign state of Winneconne, which can possibly be changed to read "the sovereign state of Where-econne," is a magnificent creation, the result of the power of several combined brains of the realm. At the upper left corner, all on a field of azure, is the Do-Do bird ... a bird, say these great heraldic designers, as extinct as Winneconne will be, unless it is put back on the map. Then at the upper right stands a skunk rampant, tail araise ... symbolically interpreted as nobody wants Winneconne ... or "we stink." At lower left is a triumphant spray of poison ivy, adopted as the Winneconne state flower, for obvious reasons. And finally at the lower right a sheepshead ... a scorned fish, taken off the fish maps, just as Winneconne was taken off the highway maps. Alack!

And meanwhile, back at the capitol, a saddened Warren Knowles worked hard on "An Ode To Winneconne," hoping thus to mollify the citizens. He read the ode aloud to Att. Gen. Bronson La Follette and Lt. Gov. Jack Olsen in the washroom on July 25:

*About Winneconne's secession I have no fear*
*Because I knew you would like it here.*
*With the highway department I will negotiate*
*To place Winneconne on a map of the state.*
*I will send you a flag of the Badger State*
*To replace the temporary flag of Winneconne state.*
*Congratulations to the Kitchen Cabinet,*
*You have proved to the world that Winneconne has it.*
*What has been done has been done —*
*All is forgiven. Just pass a resolution,*
*And come back to heaven. You'll like it here*
*And will know very quickly,*
*It's the best darn state of all the fifty!*

The governor read with a slight quaver in his voice, and what the poem lacked in literary merit he more than made up in deep feeling and expression. His two listeners applauded politely.

Failing to reach the sensibilities of the Winneconne populace with his verses, the governor finally sent a barbed communication to Mrs. Kitchen: "Why don't you try having a contest to see which pilot can locate Winneconne from the air; and you might consider suggesting that the astronauts use Winneconne as their next landing place. If they require water, have them try Butte des Morts." The governor's communique caused a flurry of indignation within the Kitchen Cabinet.

At almost the same time a letter was received, addressed to The high Lord Mayor of Winneconne:

Protector of the Sovereign State of Winneconne
Formerly located in Winneconne, Wisconsin.
Your Honor:

We extend our greetings to you and wish to offer our humble services in assisting your plight, on the adverse problem inflicted on the proud people of your fine domain. If it is your intent to arise against the evil and Yankee government of Knowles and his accomplices we stand ready to assist. We are prepared to offer the full and united legions of the United Klans of America, and Daughters of the Confederacy, and any other worthwhile group that will foster dignity of states rights and the return of solace and peaceful government to your community. Among our members we honor the names of Harry S. Truman, George Wallace, Barry Goldwater, and Henry Miller as several of the true Americans that comprehend these problems. Give 'em hell, Coghlin, and we'll be up there to lead the charge next summer. The South and Winneconne will rise again. Signed, Colonel Beauregard, C.S.A.

President Coghlin also received this letter:

Dear Sir:

We are a group of Marines now serving in South Viet Nam. Today we read of the valiant stand taken by the brave citizens of your fair state. Since we feel that you have exemplified the highest spirit of Americanism we would like to apply for residence in your state. Many Marines from other states have received state flags. We would feel most honored if you could find it in your heart to send us yours. We would be especially honored if Miss Winneconne would deliver the flag in person.

Signed,
Eleven Marines in South Viet Nam

Now beside himself and overwhelmed with the gravity of the situation, Knowles sent a desperate wire to President Coghlin, who was basking in the glory of his newly established seat.

Have received proclamation for secession, passed July 21, 1967. Stop. Convinced your action is serious threat to well being of the entire state of Wisconsin. Urge the village council to reconsider and and rescind secession decree. Sincerely hope accord can be reached and that youth of National Guard Troops and Civil Defense Volunteers and other law enforcement agencies will not be required to reverse this act of rebellion. I will negotiate directly by phone from temporary command post at Camp Ripley, Minnesota. By the way, where is Winneconne?

Signed, Warren P. Knowles

Nothing, however, could stop the drive for liberty and justice. A "Declaration of Independence" was issued by President Coghlin, and a fund-raising project was immediately established to seize and place a toll on the bridge over the Wolf River at the village edge. Toll keepers were instructed in a special bulletin to be courteous and happy, and to let off anyone who seriously objected to paying a toll to support the new state, since Winneconne did not wish to seem to be in the same unfavorable light over taxation as the state of Wisconsin. Toll keepers were urged, however, to try to elicit tolls by rhetoric rather than force or bullets. They were only too happy to comply.

Funds to the extent of at least ten dollars were obtained in this forceful and direct way. Some supporters from abroad even sent dollar bills pinned to pictures of skunks, Winneconne's state animal.

Meanwhile floods of telegrams and letters were pouring in. The mayor of Valparaiso, Indiana, a former citizen of Winneconne, offered to intercede to get Winneconne admitted to the state of Indiana. President Lyndon B. Johnson offered to use his influence to admit Winneconne to the state of Texas. Winne-

154

conne citizens were left limp with the burst of support.

Euphoria, unfortunately, must end. At 4 P.M. on the first glorious day of independence, Governor Knowles, grey with worry and bitter in defeat, for he feared the bikini-clad legions of Winneconne maidens who threatened to march upon him and who constituted the bulk of the Winneconne army, capitulated. He telephoned President Coghlin and suggested a negotiated return to the state of Wisconsin, fully conceding all demands.

A great cheer rent the Winneconne air, and the populace, weary from the cares of sovereignty and celebration, thankfully returned to be Badgers once again.

# The Marsh

There are many marshes in Wisconsin and a good bit of swampland. Sometimes developers have seen great potential for canning and truck vegetable operations in these lands, but somehow most of the schemes haven't worked out. Some of the marsh lands are said to be "bottomless," and the state highway boys, when they were building Interstate Highway 94 from Madison to Milwaukee, had real trouble with a marsh near Lake Mills that seemed pretty nearly bottomless.

I love the marsh lands. I go sometimes to a place near Madison, a sort of swale where there is a growth of cattails and stiff marsh grass; the ground there has a springiness as though all underneath are coils and coils that reach down to the core of the earth. It is very pleasant to walk upon this springy carpet and to feel the grasses against my body, to break away the head of a brown cattail and let the airy white fluff float away. I have walked in this place in summer when the red-winged blackbirds were nesting nearby. The birds clung to the tallest cattails and gave their angry cries; one afternoon two of the birds came at me, descending and dashing upward again, and the blood flowed a little from a cut one of the birds made at the back of my head.

And I never tire of the great Horicon Marsh.

Along in September the wild geese really begin to arrive at the Horicon Marsh. This marsh, so famed in Wisconsin story and legend, is located in Dodge and Fond du Lac counties and lies to the north of the city of Horicon. The south portion includes 10,794 acres and is known as the Horicon Marsh Wildlife Area. It is state owned and administered by a crew of the Wisconsin Department of Natural Resources. The north portion is owned by the U.S. government and is called the Horicon National Wildlife Refuge. It contains 20,924 acres. The state and federal men get along fine except on certain matters of wild goose management. More about that presently.

Certainly no sight I can possibly think of rivals the mighty flocks of geese that inhabit the cornfields and pastures along Highway 49 east of Waupun at the north edge of the marsh in late September and in October. It is thrilling to watch these great birds in the fields, feeding or seeming simply to stand, taking it easy, and to see them suddenly move and rise in such unbelievable numbers that the breath quickens, then stop as they come powerfully through the air above, to wheel, and return, or to circle higher and higher and away to locations that they must have planned, but which can only be guessed at by the viewer.

I could spend all day watching the geese; many persons do. An inn at the northeast corner of the marsh is a delightful location to sit with a drink, to have a leisurely dinner, and watch the birds coming and going. It releases great tensions in me, and I can understand the restlessness and longing that poets have attached to the wild goose for centuries. I would love to spend a vast amount of time at the marsh, except in mosquito time, for the marsh is certainly one of the most lively skeeter spots in the state. But looking across it in winter, for example, I always respond to the sense of wildness, different shades of the vegetation, the tops of muskrat houses, which in places seem innumerable, the ever-present wildlife. I recall that the glaciers made the marsh when the Green Bay Lobe of the ice scooped out an egg-shaped hollow, which measures fourteen miles from south to north and three or four miles from east to west. Huge hills, or drumlins, were placed haphazardly around the depression when the ice retreated, and water filled the valley to make a lake of fifty square miles. Silt from the Rock River washed into the lake, and decaying vegetation displaced the lake waters. A marsh was formed.

Before the white man came, the Indians built their villages and buried their dead at the edges of the marsh. Effigy mounds, representing at times the game the red man hunted, ring the marsh. His tools and arrowheads are still being exposed by the plow. Then came the white trapper, followed by the settler. The Indian vanished and the marsh became subject to the white man. In the areas above the marsh the settlers turned woodland into farmland, and as crops increased and markets grew, a need for water power and transportation developed.

A dam was the answer to these needs. With brush, logs, stones, and mud a dam that provided power for a sawmill and a gristmill was built at Horicon in 1846. Nine feet of water backed up behind the dam, forming a lake reputed to be the largest artificial lake in the world. The lake became famous for its bass, pike, pickerel, and bullheads. It also supported a large number of game birds and animals.

The lake had a short life. In 1858 two lake-edge farmers filed suits against the owners of the dam and won their suits.

Other water damage suits followed. The result was the removal of the dam in 1869. The waters of the lake drained away and the area reverted to a low, shallow marsh and again became a great waterfowl area. Finally in the 1940s the marsh became the property of the state of Wisconsin and of the federal government, as it is today.

Blackhawk, famous chief of the Sauks, led his shadowy band north in 1832, and concealed them somewhere in the area, perhaps for a time in the swamp itself; nobody knows for sure. If they had stayed hidden for a while longer, possibly the battles of Wisconsin Heights and of Bad Ax, so disastrous for the Sauks, would never have taken place. Anyway, the legends are rife.

Seeking word-of-mouth information about the marsh and its lore, I arrived at the state headquarters near Horicon quite late one afternoon in February. I started with one of the young research specialists named Jim March.

"Jim," I asked, "what happens when the wild fowl migration starts into the marsh in the fall?"

"Generally it starts slow," he answered. "Last year we had quite an influx of geese all at one time. It went from around 13,000 birds to 90,000 birds in two or three days. This isn't common. It was a spectacular migration."

"What causes that kind of spectacular migration?"

"It's usually the weather up in Canada, in the breeding grounds."

"I was talking with an Indian this morning up at Oneida, Oscar Auchiquette. He says that the Oneida Indians have this superstition that when the geese fly very high the winter is going to be real hard."

"Well, it is the weather that moves the geese out of Canada and off the breeding grounds. And it's what moves the birds out of here eventually. If it gets cold, or snows hard, it gets deep so they can't find food."

"You have any problems of management when so many people want to come in here to see these birds?"

"Just the sight-seeing crowd up on Highway 49. They have plenty of traffic problems up there. Takes about a half-hour to get across there in the fall of the year. They may have to prohibit parking on the road."

"Are there any peculiar habits of the geese that are unique to the area? I've noticed how tame they are, for example."

"This is true. They don't really have their fear of man, as

158

they did when there were fewer birds. These geese have pretty well adapted to man. Hunting is the big mortality factor, but they don't have the shyness of a smaller number of birds. Some of these birds, a whole lot of them in fact, never even get shot at."

"Does every bird that comes to the marsh get enough to eat?"

"Basically the birds get enough to eat. This is one of the conflicts here, of course: where he gets it. When he starts feeding on the private lands, and swinging into the standing crops, that's when we get the depredation problem. These birds are in the best condition of the year when they leave here."

"What kind of problems do you have with the local farmers?"

"There actually is damage done. This past year, because the fall was dry, the farmers were able to get their crops out. There were only three or four goose damage claims. In a bad year, when it is wet and the farmer can't get in to harvest his corn, well, the geese may get into the field and gobble half of it up."

"How does the farmer substantiate his claim?"

"Well, the farmer calls up, and either a state or a federal man will go out. He will try to scare away the geese. We have scare devices, and try to move the birds out of the field. Then the farmer files a notice of claim, and we have to go out and evaluate the loss. They agree on a figure."

"Federal or state claims?"

"State. The federal government doesn't pay any type of damage. Federal crop insurance doesn't cover goose damage, and that is limited to $1,500 in any one farm or any one claim."

"Even if the geese clean up a whole farm, it is only $1,500?"

"The legislature has set the amount of the damage claim. It used to be only $750."

"What other kinds of wildlife are there?"

"Ducks, some raised here in the summer, and muskrats. I believe they trapped about 30,000 muskrats a year ago. And there's deer in the marsh. We have a deer hunt here every year. There's a heron and egret colony. And we have all the other marsh birds, rails and gallileau and coot and this sort of thing. Lots of fox, too, raccoons. The most unique are the herons and the egret colony. The marsh was designated at one time as a duck-producing area. But it probably doesn't produce as many ducks as it might. Still, in some good years there may have been up to a million ducks on the marsh."

"Any special yarns about the marsh?"

"We have a fellow down at the shop named Eddie Lechner who's lived around here all his life. I bet he could."

I leave the office and go down to the shop. I find Ed Lechner building a large box. He is a big man, very friendly, perhaps in his early sixties, dressed in khaki. We go to the back of the shop, and he waits for me to speak, wondering what I am after. "If you've got a minute," I say to him, "I want to ask you some questions about the marsh. I hear you've lived here a long time."

"I've been around here working for the conservation department approximately sixteen years. But I've lived on the marsh ever since I was eight years old."

"You must know it about as well as anybody here."

"I've trapped and hunted every year since I was a young man."

"March, up at the office, was telling me that last year there was a terrific migration of geese."

"Total, about 200,000 Canada geese."

"Why'd they all come last year?"

"Truthfully," Ed said, "I believe it was because the flock had been building up for several years. The hatch last year was real good up in the Goose Bay, Hudson Bay areas."

"When it's big up there the migration is big down here?"

Ed walked across the floor and scraped with his toe at a lump of grease. He got it up and deposited it in a waste can. "The first refuge manager we had here — his name was Watson Deed — started to develop this marsh to encourage the geese to stop. We never shot any geese here in the fall of the year. The only time, years back, when any geese were shot was in the spring of the year. 'Course that's now against the law. If a man got a goose in the fall of the year — this was before the refuge was developed — it was really something, really out of the ordinary. Now it's very, very common. When they started to develop this refuge we had three, four hundred Canada geese, then it built up every year. Us native fellows we could go out and hunt any farm on the east side of the marsh just for the asking. There was no cost. No charge. As the flock got bigger, then the interest started taking ahold, and more people came out, and began to lease this land, and pretty soon we fellows, the native,

160

we were outside lookin' in.

" 'Course today, with the tagging system, you can, if you're lucky, get a tag to shoot one Canada goose."

I was very interested to know whether the development of the refuge had caused many problems in the area. Ed thought that it had. "The flock," he said, "when we had sixty or seventy thousand, was pretty well under control, but as the flock has gotten larger the birds started to get out into the farmer's fields. The state and the federal governments cooperate with the farmer. We have these scare-away guns, and we set them out if a farmer calls and we try to keep the geese out of the corn. We were fortunate last fall. The weather cooperated a hundred percent. Farmers were able to pick their corn. Once they open a field and they get rainy weather and a farmer isn't able to pick it, then the geese get right in there. After they're in there once, there's nothin' in the world that's going to keep them out. Big problem. I tell you, a goose can rattle the corn off of an ear faster'n you can talk. Pick it clean.

"Year before last we had rainy weather, and the geese got in there and they just started walking in between our scare-away guns. Didn't bother 'em at all. Make quite a bang, too.

"You know, it's real interesting. Some time ago I read in the *Milwaukee Journal* about this fur buyer at Portage . . . fergit his name. He was a Frenchman; big strong feller . . . "

"Pacquette," I said. "Name was Pierre Pacquette, was Indian interpreter and trader at the Portage in late 1820s and early 1830s."

"Right. And this Indian that killed him because of some raw deal or something, fergit what, well, that Indian should have migrated here to the Horicon Marsh. We have Indian graves on the east side of the marsh. The museum has booklets on some of these graves. This man, Dr. Bruder, from Milwaukee, he is a dentist and a smart boy, well, he come out here and studied a lot of these graves, and when they built County Trunk Z, this is on the northeast side of the marsh, the county widened this road, and got into these graves, what they call the moundsmen. Fact there's one farmer had two copies of those booklets that Dr. Bruder wrote. Name is Augie Kalterman. I went to see him about this stuff, wanted to get some dope, and he says, 'Ed, I'll let you read them, but I won't let you take 'em home. I showed 'em to a guy one time and almost lost 'em.' Well, I offered Augie a hundred-dollar bill to let me take 'em home. He says,

'No you set right here and read 'em.'

"These graves, 'course, as you probably know, are in the shape of some animal, or turtle or bird."

I asked Ed whether he had ever heard that Blackhawk came up into the marsh when Generals Henry, Atkinson and Henry Dodge and troops were hunting him.

"Seems as though I heard of it," Ed says, "but I never read anything about it. But these graves on the northeast side of the marsh, they were laid down about seven hundred and fifty years ago, according to this booklet. But then the graves down further, in the southern part of the marsh, like on the Muche farm and the Cook farm over here, and over here on Indermuerle Island, some of these graves are younger. You can find relics and arrowheads and people are still going around picking them up."

Ed thinks that the development of the marsh has caused some problems, but that it has also done a lot for the community.

"Ah," he cried, "better'n a million dollar business! It's terrific. Sight-seers. Bird watchers, tourists, hunters, fishermen, photographers, and all different schools come from Milwaukee, Racine for tours, education."

"What do you like best about the marsh?"

"What I like best about the marsh," Ed said, "is just to get out there all by myself, do a little hunting, or do a little trapping, and you feel relaxed; you're all alone and you see these birds, and to be truthful with you, if I don't ever shoot another duck or another goose it isn't gonna bother me. At the present time I'm beginning to feel that the hunting pressure is just getting too great. Too many people, and what're you gonna do?"

"In the earlier days when you were younger, were there any local characters who lived in the marsh and knew it quite well, before the governments took it over, I mean?"

"Oh, yes. Several of our real old duck hunters are Bill Zerning and Albert Zerning, and of course there were the Strooks, John Strook, and there were the Prowatchke boys. These were real old-timers, and they still remembered the Indians. In fact, old Bill Zerning, and this was some interest to me, when I was a real young man, Bill had Indian ponies. He had a little milk route and these were the days when you had a milk can in the center of the wagon, and the people come out of their houses with a pitcher and Bill would fill their pitcher for them. These Indian ponies, Bill said that they were from the tribe off of the marsh. This is true. In fact, the last of those ponies died here several years ago.

"And then, we also had two hermits. They lived on the east side of the marsh. They were the Strellow brothers. They were really characters. In fact I remember one of 'em, they tell that he walked to the World's Fair at St. Louis in 1904. He wouldn't ride with anybody. And he walked back. They were real, real old-timers. In fact, the old foundation of their place caved in there. Had a few acres of land; it's now kind of a parking lot. We still call the hill Strellow Hill."

"Ed," I asked, "was there any one great hunt that you remember in here?"

"Yes, there was. When I was a real young man, 1924, we had a cloudburst, and the dam went out. This dam was there for the mill. My uncle owned the mill. Uncle John. And we had a lot of water on the marsh. Hunting was terrific that year! And then in 1928 we had a lot of water, and that year also was terrific hunting. Duck population is down, you understand, in a dry year."

I asked Ed about muskrats. "Muskrats are cyclic," Ed said. "Last year they were terrific. 'Course this year the boys have done real well. We still have some ice trappers out. But I'll tell you one thing that might be of interest. When I was a young man I would go out to the Greenhead Club, and there was old John Strook, and there was the Clark boys, there was the Yanzen boys, and the Zerning brothers, had a little shack out there and they would do a lot of hunting. Of course I'd occasionally get a chance to go bog hunting with these fellows. And when they'd go up into the bay there was no outboard motors. This was all done pushing. And you tell the young fellers today! And these old-timers would get up at three o'clock in the morning to get the best blinds up into the bay. They would push the boats up there. Nobody pushes anymore. Use a kicker. I still think we should go back to hunting the marshes with skiffs, 'stead of these big boats and outboards.

"They scare a lot of the ducks off of the marsh, before the hunting season opens. They are up there building their blinds months before the season opens.

"When I was a young man, we used to be able to shoot fifteen ducks, and we had these live decoys, these English callers, this is all done away with. 'Course it's understandable with the amount of hunting pressure. We have hunters from all over — all the cities, rural areas, you name it. And we have some women hunters. In fact, when we had check stations some years back, when we had the blinds in the refuge, the blinds were set up by the state and run by the state, it was first come, first served. We had 114 blinds to start with and we wound up with 106. We had quite a few women hunters."

"Are the mosquitoes bad in the marsh?"

"Really rough. And the flowers! You never seen anything like the wild flowers in and around the marsh. The lilies, the Mayflowers, trillium, violets, feather-leaf, honeysuckle, huckleberry, marsh hyssop and we have all these ferns in the ledges. I tell you, it's really beautiful here."

I went back up to the main office to see James Bell, director of the state refuge. I found him, like Ed, extremely enthusiastic about his work, and about the whole atmosphere of the marsh. Once I got him started, he just kept going because there was so much to tell. Bell, a graduate of the University of Michigan, is still a young man, though he's been at the marsh since 1952. He wore a red plaid shirt, khaki trousers, work boots. And he sat back very relaxed at his desk. Behind him, on the wall, was a dart board with a single dart, which, no doubt, he used to decide the day's activities.

Bell explained that he loved the natural state of the marsh and found it constantly beautiful. "It's been changed somewhat by man," he said, "the drainage ditches, and the dam at Horicon that floods it; and you have the tree and shrub plantings all put in by man, but they blend in well with the natural setting. Since a hundred years ago, if you want to go that far back, there have been radical changes in the marsh. Originally this was a marsh as a result of the glacial action. Then man built the dam for a gristmill, pretty close to the site of the present dam, and as a result it went back to lake again. Then drainage interests in the early 1900s decided that the marsh could be reclaimed for agriculture. So they drained it and after they did, you could go out here . . . the old timers used to go out to this point here to cut marsh hay. Then, to get better hay they would burn the marsh over periodically, and the fire would burn down into the peat; sometimes you couldn't stand the smoke in Mayville or Horicon. Then it was reclaimed after the drainage project proved a failure, and the state and federal governments purchased the land, and the dam was built in Horicon to flood it.

" 'Course it has silted in a lot over the years because of erosion and the watershed.

"The patterns of wildlife have changed, too, especially as concerns the Canada goose. In the 1940s, for example, only a few hundred geese flew over, much less stopped. We know back in the early days, the late 1800s and early 1900s, geese used to breed in here. Disturbances drove them away, and they went up Hudson and James Bay area to breed.

"The geese now stop here because of three things: protection, food, and water. After the federal government purchased the refuge at the north end, they began planting food — corn, rye, buckwheat. The first thing they did was to close the area to hunting. The geese had sanctuary. And that helped, and they began to stop here in ever-increasing numbers. In 1950 they built the dyke across the south end of the refuge, then the geese had all three requirements. We are at the point now where the geese have become a terrific problem; we'd be much happier here with 50,000 geese instead of the 170,000 we had last fall. The federal people figure that food for 50,000 geese is the limit they can plant in the refuge. The geese now consume the food in the refuge very quickly, then they go out and feed in the farmers' fields, and this makes the farmer mad. Years ago, before we had the quota system, farmers could get rid of them by hunting. Farmers on the periphery of the marsh had quite an income renting their land to hunters or leasing blinds by the season. The price kept going up, up, and up as the goose hunting got better.

"In 1959 or '60 the federal government felt that the marsh was being overshot and they assigned a quota, not only to Wisconsin but to Illinois. The last two years the quota has been 20,000 geese for the whole state of Wisconsin so that only so many birds can be taken and the number of hunters is limited, and the farmers aren't getting that revenue that they formerly had. They see all these geese here — more than ever — they can't shoot anymore, and they find it hard to understand, because the birds leave here and go to Illinois and are taken down there; they get right unhappy sometimes."

I asked Bell whether the Horicon Marsh was different from other marsh areas in the country.

"Well, it all depends on the type of refuge you're talking about. If you're talking about a waterfowl refuge in this part of the country, Horicon would be pretty much typical. Depends, too, on the kind of habitat you're dealing with. Down in the southern states, for example, I expect the refuges are more grassland. The cover here is very similar to what you'd see at the Eldorado Marsh area at Fond du Lac."

"What do you do this time of year? What is your seasonal work?"

"Well, this winter, with the amount of snow that we've had, we've been very busy distributing corn to the cooperators. When I say cooperators, I mean farmers, individuals, and members of sportsmen's clubs, feeding the pheasants. Last fall the conditions of harvest were very good, and the bulk of the corn was picked, and some of the fields were plowed. Now, with the snow we've had the birds are having a hard time.

"What we do, we haul corn to a central delivery point, and it is parceled out to the various cooperators from there. For example, there is a sportsmen's club down at Huistesford; they come up here and get the corn and take it down there, and the members distribute it to the birds.

"Got a case over at Beaver Dam where the conservation club is feeding, and then you got a sport shop there; we take corn to them and they find an outlet for it. We've got about eighteen or twenty distribution points in Fond du Lac and Dodge counties, our district.

"We've fed forty-four tons of corn so far, and it's only February. This has kept our field crew very busy. We get the bulk of the corn right here on our wildlife area. We leave some of it standing for the pheasants and the deer, and the rest goes into storage here, or if we have any surplus we send it down to the game farm."

"The farming aspects, then, are under your direction here, too?" I said.

"In the wildlife area we have what we call a share-cropping program. Local farmers do the actual planting and harvesting, and for their efforts with corn grown on marsh land they get two-thirds of the crop. We take the other third."

"What happens in the spring on the marsh?"

"Well, in the spring, we will be planting trees and shrubs. We do extension work with landowners who want to improve their property for wildlife, cover, this kind of thing. The spring is devoted to improvement, and the summer is about the same, posting our wildlife areas, construction of dykes. Those have to be maintained."

I inquired about pesticides. "We never use pesticides," Bell said. "The fall is the busy season. We have to see that the areas are fully posted, make the closed areas plain, and there are areas we flood in the fall of the year for ducks. Throughout the fall, too, we are busy with patrolling, checking into conditions. Our men have warden credentials; they watch for game law violations. And of course we are very busy, have been the past several years, with goose damage. We have a law here in Wisconsin that does pay for crop damage. The first thing we do if we get a complaint is go out there with exploding devices to help the farmer try to get rid of the geese. But if we have a wet fall as we had in '65 and '67 then the geese have already been in there and have caused damage before we can get there. Then we have to investigate the amount of damage and come to an agreement with him, and make out claim forms."

"Are there instances where geese have actually cleaned a farmer out?"

"Yes, we've had situations like that. I think the highest claim we ever had was in 1965, the first year they passed this crop damage law. The damage amounted to some $9,000. Was a large farm called the Flying Dollar Ranch. Recent years we have kept the claims down to an average of about $70 or $80 or a few hundred."

"How do the state men get along with the federal men at the other end of the marsh? Any problems?"

"We don't see eye to eye on goose management," Bell said, thoughtfully, "but we keep it at least on a friendly basis. We aren't at each other's throats."

"What is their point of view that differs from yours?"

"Well, they would like (and so would we) to see fewer geese here on the marsh. What we can't agree on is the method of reducing the number. We would like to see, for example, the possibility of opening the refuge to hunting. And you probably read about the 'hazing' that was done in '66. That wasn't successful. We brought up the hunting possibility at one of our recent meetings. But they were afraid that the geese, driven off the marsh, would only light on the farmers' fields, cause crop damage, and antagonize the landowners. Well, that would be true, except that we would put a concentration of hunters not only in the refuge but also on private land, and maybe with a week of hunting pressure we could drive some of the birds out of here. There was mention of not planting any food in the refuge, except along Highway 49 east of Waupun, where the sight-seers could see the birds. One of the things the federal men propose is draining the marsh, and having very little water in the area. But that would mean that we would have to drain our portion of the marsh, so there really is no concrete suggestion that assures results. No one's in a position to say, 'I know this will work.'

"They think, too, that the state ought to acquire some more areas on the sides of the marsh where we could siphon off some of these birds. Well, we've been doing that. We've got Eldorado Marsh in Fond du Lac County, and Grand River Marsh at Kingston in Green Lake is well along. The dam has been built there, and this will attract a lot of geese. This isn't gonna be right now. It will take several years."

No matter how many years it will take, the Horicon Marsh will remain a fascinating place. Waupun, at the north edge, is already making great commercial good of the marsh and the wild geese by having "Wild Goose Festival Days" in October. The citizens have organized a fine arts council at Waupun, and combine commercial enterprise with art shows and a very unique Middle West sculpture show that attracts more than three-hundred major sculptors.

Sight-seers viewing the birds can go to Waupun and see modern sculpture as well as view the famous "End of the Trail" statue, which conveys the spirit of the defeat of the red man and was the most famous work of the great American sculptor James Earle Fraser (1876-1953). Clarence Addison Shaler, Waupun inventor and manufacturer, who made most of his money through the invention of the cold patch for automobile inner tubes, had a major interest in sculpture. He saw Fraser's "End of the Trail" at the 1914 Exposition in San Francisco. There the work was in plaster, and Shaler asked Fraser whether he could provide a bronze of the figure of horse and Indian for a setting in Waupun. Fraser replied that he could do so. The formal unveiling took place on June 23, 1929. Shaler also commissioned Lorado Taft, perhaps the best known American sculptor of his day, to create a romantic work called "The Recording Angel," which stands above the grave of Shaler's wife, Blanche Bancroft Shaler, in the Waupun cemetery.

VIII. Old Peninsula Barn

IX.  Hilltop at Dawn

# PART THREE -
# OF PLAIN AND HIGHLAND

X. Pacquette Park

# North

Something happens to me when I go up to northern Wisconsin. I seem to expand inside and somehow I become more aware; perhaps it's because the sky and woods and lakes still have an edge of wildness; or it may be that the people seem a little larger in spirit than they do down south. Southern Wisconsin folks will dispute this, of course, and they will point to the broad, fertile fields that have created serenity and stability to some of them and comfortable farm homes and large barns; yet I note that many southern Wisconsin residents travel north, just as I do, and there must be a call that draws them — other than the fishing, I mean, or the deer hunting. I think America does still very much respond to wilderness, and though it is wilderness of a refined kind up north today, still you can definitely experience a feeling that you are alone, and that, for a moment, you do have some intimate knowledge of the secret of solitude.

Then, too, the mementos of the past are keen and poignant in northern Wisconsin.

I visited one day, somewhere in the north, an old man sitting in a wheel chair. The nursing home corridor was dim, and I could not see him very clearly at first. Then I saw that he was very thin, and all his clothing seemed much too large. When he spoke I was hearing an echo of vigor and passion that ninety years could not quite obliterate. I understood that he was yet a woods boss, and that there would always be decision in his voice. He spoke of men and animals and machines as though they were now and they were all his. He saw great wheels holding up the end of a twenty-foot log above the stumps and brush. He called. I heard trees crashing. A cry; laughter; the puff of a donkey engine, a tumble of rolling logs. Then this, this silence of a nursing home and a white-clad, silent woman bringing him a tiny supper on a plastic tray.

Occasionally at least, there is something unusual, breathtaking. I saw evening come once on Moens Lake near Rhinelander; I stood at the end of a wharf while all the shore disappeared in a mist. Then off in the northeast there appeared a rainbow that arched the confines of the lake exactly, fading into the mist at each end. That is when I thought I heard the sighing and a faint drumming from the sky.

I keep coming back to the mystery of memory. I can't get

it out of my head that people who have created a country and have given it its character — the old Indians, the French, the settlers — have really gone. The land they created in spirit is there, though altered, and I create these mystic sights and sounds, for myself of course. In a way, if you can make yourself imagine that the sounds of an older day do haunt the land, the woods, and sky, then what an adventure it is to go, to see, and to mix reality with fantasy.

My third journey takes me north on a clear and still March morning, and as I drive the long windbreaks of willow south of Stevens Point are getting an early springtime chartreuse tint, a smear of color across the wide potato fields, for there is still plenty of snow thick on the earth, and in patches on the hills. The trees seem now to be taking over from the monotony of winter. There is faint color in the aspen and the maples — just a hint of change — and the oaks, which will later add a kind of poetic purple haze, stand black and waiting. On the willows the bud scales open before there is any actual greening; the catkins enlarge and add a faint color; the delicate hairs come on the flower buds, and the deadness of winter is altering the spirit of anyone who will look to see.

There is snow crusting around the tall wheels of the irrigation pipes, left in many fields through the winter. In the summer the pure water will be spraying in spurts of seventy-five feet from the many vents in the pipes, and the earth will accept the water quickly, for the soil is of sand and loose. Across the fields the great lines of pipe move, and the earth, if it could remember, might think of great drought and of the poverty of the folks who farmed it. But no longer, for now the water is everywhere, and the sands are valuable beyond any settler's dreams. Back in the fields are warehouses, sorting sheds for the potatoes that will come from the fields. In summer, perhaps, I will drive this way again to watch the harvest; but now the mechanical potato picker has replaced the lines of colorful migrant workers in the fields, stooping, picking, joking, calling to one another, and in the bean fields the lines of great harvesters, side by side, the whole width of the field, harvest a field in a day . . . oh, less. A half-day or even an hour or two.

Central Wisconsin is plateau, but it seems to reflect the glory of the seasons better than the hill country. The trees, the willows, the hardwoods seem to change more dramatically, perhaps because the clumps and the lines are in the open and can be seen in isolated stands. The feeling there is of the earth, and the fertility and the problems of earth; one gets a sensation of his closeness to earth and of what earth means to man.

A lot of it here is Pole country. When I first came to Wisconsin, just after World War II, there was still a strong Old World flavor in places. Stevens Point, for instance, was using the old town square as a market square, very much like one could see in Finland or in central Europe. On Saturday the farmers came with their trucks loaded with produce, let down a tailgate or set up a sales table, and did business in the old-fashioned way.

The square was a very colorful sight, even in 1945, and how much more colorful it must have been in the early years of the twentieth century when carts and wagons were driven or pushed into the square, and Polish settlers sold chickens, potatoes or almost anything, just as they had in the Old Country. The square was one of my favorite places in Wisconsin, and I suppose I shared the sorrow of others who cherished the folk customs when the Old World disappeared from Stevens Point.

I went through the square the other day and it was full of parking meters, had been for a long time, of course. The old picture was gone entirely, yet the influence of the Old Country still hangs like a faint mist over Stevens Point and the surrounding country and there is still some market activity.

When the Polish settlers arrived during the last half of the nineteenth century, they were searching for a friendly soil that would fulfill dreams of plenty and freedom from oppression and want. They found freedom but for many years there was still want, for the soil in central Wisconsin was not especially fertile. It was sand, the former bed of a vast glacial lake. Good crops were possible in very wet years, but in dry years the grain shrank; the potatoes nubbed in the earth and amounted to little. Livestock became thin, and it was very hard to get the items of produce necessary to sell in the square, to furnish the small number of coins needed for medicine and clothing.

I still hear the old folks talk about those early times. They do so now with humor, but with sadness far back in their eyes, for the times were often hard and desperate for many.

It is hard to believe this now when you drive up Highway 51 and see the "golden sands" pouring forth their plenty; the great wheeled lines of irrigation pipes stretched across broad, beautifully tilled fields; and at times the spouts of pure water pouring forth from an earth that is furnishing its own key to the wealth and the plenty the settlers could never find. I like the sands country, for the story is both sad and happy, gay and beautiful and nostalgic with overtones of tragedy. During the Great Depression of the thirties hundreds of farmers in the sands lost their farms. Many families who had struggled so desperately to stay, to build homes, vanished. Where they went I do not know. To the cities, perhaps, or to other lands in other places. The fortunate ones were those who stayed, somehow lived through it, and, in the end, prospered.

I know such a man in Stevens Point. He is a very old man, still strong though, and very friendly, and though he is an owner of one of the largest potato-growing businesses in the state, he is completely without pretension, finding in his humble background both the strength he has needed and the happiness that his knowledge of want, and finally of success, have given him.

I found Steve Okray in a warehouse near the old square at Stevens Point. At first I was doubtful whether he was the one I had come to see, for he looked nothing at all like a potato king: faded blue overalls, heavy work shoes, a tattered gray sweater thrust inside his overall bib, a wisp of blue work-shirt collar showing above the faded neck of the sweater, a shrewd face, eyes twinkling now, for he was in the middle of a haggle. It was a debate with a young man who had a couple of coon skins to sell, a sale of pennies, really, but to the old man who felt the skins, pointed out blemishes, doubted the prime condition, it was a major deal. He purchased the skins, finally, for a trifling amount, and the young trapper, or whoever he was, went grumbling away. Okray placed the skins on a pile of others with a tender gesture, as though they were gold, or perhaps silver foxes at least. And I wondered how a man who had developed a million-dollar-a-year potato business could find time to haggle over a coon skin. I found out.

I sat on a box, and he on another, or an overturned bucket, I don't recall which, and he told me the tale. He, a small boy in the 1880s; his family, Polish settlers on a poor sands farm. Privation. No schooling. His brother never went to school at all. He himself went to about third grade; then he had to help with a living. It was he who took the family wagon, as he grew older, into Stevens Point, to the square, and it was he who conducted the tiny selling operation — a few potatoes, a chicken now and then — and it was he, the eldest son, who brought the money home to his mother.

He was a born trader, careful, very sharp. He bought and sold, he saved the money. He studied any book he could find, and got the knowledge necessary to keep accounts, to compete. And slowly, very slowly he began to get ahead. Potatoes were what he dealt in most, because potatoes was the crop that did best in the sand soil. He taught his brother the trading business and finally they knew that their market had to be beyond the town square; they risked everything and acquired enough potatoes to load the first boxcar of potatoes ever shipped from Stevens Point to Chicago. It was bold thinking. If it succeeded, there would be many cars of potatoes, and the Okray brothers envisioned themselves purchasing potatoes all through the central parts of the state and shipping them. Unfortunately, instead of success, all was lost.

They knew nothing about packing potatoes for shipment in winter. The cars had no insulation. In the bitter cold, the carload of potatoes froze and was ruined, as were the brothers who had labored so hard to this great turning point in their lives. Okray almost quit then, but the thought of his mother and what she had gone through kept him going. He began again. Small deals over the tables at Stevens Point . . . small sales . . . a few pennies. Saving, saving, and more saving. Haggling deals for skins; finally, another carload of potatoes. This time they were successful in getting them to market. They were on their way. But the land being farmed hard, produced more and more poorly. Its fertility, always small, dwindled to nothing. Quality potatoes became hard to find. And then the depression.

Everybody lost. From two good starts and a lifetime of labor, it seemed that this third catastrophe was the final curtain. Instead, because of the foresight of Steve Okray, the depression became the golden door.

The Okrays stuck with the country. On every side folks were moving out, or the government was relocating them on other farms. It was a period in which the whole central portion of the state was almost given up as lost; the answer was to get out, let the birds and the coons have it. It would never be farming country, that was sure, and there were hundreds of Polish families who would testify to that. They had failed, after two generations of slavery to the sands. Good-by!

But not the Okrays. With what they had they began to purchase the land that others were leaving. Sometimes they would buy an eighty acres for taxes, or once an eighty for $75. They got so much land they suddenly faced defeat again. How to pay the taxes on it? What to do with it? People laughed at Okray, and for a little while Okray laughed bitterly at himself. He had land. Nobody, perhaps, in the Old Country had ever had such an estate, except the richest nobles. Here in Wisconsin, Okray had a nobleman's estate, in size. In worth? Nothing. And he, a poor man again.

Then the revelation. It had been known for a long while that there was water, lots of it, beneath the surface of the sand. But what good was the water under the earth? For a settler's well, fine, for watering the cattle. But what else? They found out.

The Okrays helped to dig one of the early pits. They dug down twelve or sixteen feet and struck unlimited water. The pit filled up immediately. Still, it didn't occur to anyone that the under-the-surface water was the whole key to the land. Irrigation was known, certainly, and some attempts had been made to pump water from the streams onto the land. The state stopped that practice.

But pit water was a different thing. They began to pump from the pits, and the land responded. Seeing the answer to his land problem, Okray acquired irrigation equipment. When the land began to get water, it instantly responded. Many wells were put down, not deep, for the water was plentiful and near. Okray found himself with a vast potato-farming operation of unlimited promise. The fields expanded, were tilled and irrigated, and in the late summer the potatoes poured from the earth, at first picked by hand and then by the harvest machines. In the Okray warehouses the grading machines sorted them, and the potatoes either went to market in trucks or were sacked and stored. The Okray brothers had money. They could do what they wanted. And what did they like best doing?

They liked best to sit in faded overalls in an ancient warehouse where some of their first potatoes were stored in the old, hard days, and haggle with young trappers for coonskins.

"And often," said Okray, "I will look out to the square over yonder, and I will see in my memory the old Poles and their carts and their skinny horses. And I will see myself, a little boy, hoping that somebody will buy a few potatoes scraped from the dry earth of our farm. And do you know what, my boy? I kind of wish the square was like it used to be. Because even then, when they were so poor, people laughed. They do not laugh anymore. And they do not dance and sing in the streets. I don't mean the drunk ones. I mean laughing and singing and dancing for joy because they were alive. That's what I mean. Hard times. Yes. Hard times, my boy. But out of hard times comes a great joy that fills the heart. And to a Pole, this is the joy that will live forever."

# Spirit Rock

The beautiful land of the Menominees. I get a spiritual lift whenever I drive through Menominee County, entering either on 47 near Phlox, and emerging south of Keshena, or on 55 near Markton. The Wolf River country always excites me. There is a place on the river where, from the water, you can see ancient Indian drawings on the cliff. There is strong sunlight this morning and shadow patches on the snow among the trees. It is all very silent. I get an impression of a mighty spirit watching over the land. I pause, listen. I hear the wind in the tree tops. On my way, today, I will stop at Spirit Rock. There the mystic medicine of the old Indians is very strong.

One night, long ago, a Menominee Indian dreamed that Manabush, grandson of Ko-Ko-Mas-Say-Sa-Wow (the Earth) and part founder of the Mitawin or Medicine Society, invited him to visit the god. With seven of his friends, the Indian called on Manabush, who granted their request to make them successful hunters. One of the band, however, angered the god by asking for eternal life. Seizing the warrior by the shoulders, Manabush thrust him into the ground and said, "You shall be a stone. Thus you will be everlasting." The Menominees say that at night kindly spirits come to lay offerings of tobacco at the rock, and that if one looks closely he can see their white veils among the trees. According to the legend, when the rock finally crumbles away, the race will be extinct.

I sat at the kitchen table in the woodland house of Andre and Frances May, north of Keshena, and heard this legend, told as it is written on the historical marker which stands beside Spirit Rock, about four miles north of Keshena on 55. Many Indians do leave offerings of tobacco at the rock today, and since the rock is disintegrating fairly rapidly, many read the fate of the Menominees in its decay.

Wanting to hear more about the Menominees and the rock, I met with Fannie May and Gerti Sennett, Indian women married to white men.

Gerti, very pleasant, very well groomed, and devoted to her people, amplified the legend. "There was this group of hunters," Gerti said, "and they were discussing what they would all like most in life. So Manabush, who wanted to help them, said he would give them what they most desired. Some of the hunters asked for very simple things — a healthy family, a good life, and plenty of hunting and fishing; but one hunter, bolder than the others, asked the god for eternal life. Manabush said, 'All right, you may have your wish and you will have eternal life.' Then Manabush looked at the hunter and turned him to stone. The legend follows that at the death of the last full-blooded Menominee, the rock will have crumbled to nothing, and there will be nothing left of the Menominee tribe."

"Has the size of the rock really diminished since you have lived here;"

"Every year it crumbles," says Andre May, who has entered. He is large, of French descent and is a zealous friend of the Menominees.

"I have pictures somewhere," Gerti says, "from several years back, showing the rock higher than the fence. Now it's way lower."

"The public is helping the old rock to go quick, too," Andre says. "They chisel some of it off for souvineers every summer."

"They would do better to take a Menominee and leave the rock alone," Fannie says. "We would feel safer!"

"When I was working in California," Gerti says, "I came home one time for a visit. I stopped at Spirit Rock and dropped some tobacco on it. I had an envelope with me, picked up some little stones that were around the base, and when I got to California again, I put these stones in a small jar and carried it around with me all the time. When I came back again, I brought the stones with me and dropped them on top of the rock. But many Indians here leave tobacco at the rock all the time."

"Some of the old people," says Andre, "will tell you that they can remember when the rock was real big. It is a very religious thing with them, to go there at almost every opportunity, the whole family, to put tobacco on the rock. When they have a death they always visit the rock."

"It is like an altar," Fannie says.

"Last summer, when I went up to the Rhinelander School of Arts," Gerti says, "on my way up, at five-thirty in the morning, I stopped long enough to put tobacco on the rock."

"We've had two or three deaths on the highway along here," Andre says. "It was reported that one of the policemen, who believes in the rock quite strongly, had seen a strange, flitting figure in the woods behind it. And funny thing is, some of those highway deaths were foretold. Bob Ladd, the policeman, came here and told us one day that something was going to happen. Some bad thing. And Tom Wishkeno was killed right soon after. Bob Ladd believes in the rock!"

"Well," says Gerti, "the Menominees have a right to be afraid that the Spirit Rock legend will come true. Right now we are in a sort of no-man's-land. We're not white, yet we have been terminated as an Indian tribe. We're noncitizen-citizens. That's what we are. As one result, our kids can't get into the Indian colleges any longer."

I guess the Menominees have many serious problems. Alcohol, I have heard, is one. But, as Andre says, with all the frustrations the Menominees have had, can you blame them? The federal government "terminated" the tribe in 1961, when Menominee County was organized. And so, as Gerti says, they are in a no-man's-land at present, not recognized as either Indian or white.

There are some segregation problems with the young people, unfortunately, in the schools, but a higher percentage of the kids are now going to college — twenty-seven from last year's graduating class.

But the biggest problem for the tribe is intermarriage. Only twelve full-blooded Menominees are left in the tribe today. Families are large — more than six per family — and incomes are low. Many of the kids are undernourished. Some are disturbed.

Yet with all the problems, there is a spirit of hope. "Welcome to the Land of the Menominees" reads a sign as you drive into the county. "We Will Make It," says another sign.

My Indian friends believe that when the old rock is worn away completely, and when it is forgotten, there will still be Menominees.

"We'll be mixed," they say cheerfully, "but we'll be there. And we'll be proud of our tribal heritage."

"We absolutely will make it!"

Somehow, my friends, whenever I go to the lands of our red brothers, wherever they may be in Wisconsin, I sense a cry of distilled sorrow. I have heard it at Oneida and Keshena, at Lac de Flambeau and Courte Oreilles. I have heard it near the old Butte des Morts, and from the remnants of the Winnebago at the Dells. Hear it and weep for the sorrows of our red brothers. Hear it in the despoiled woodlands, and in the tainted waters; and hear it from impoverished dwellings where pallid children live.

# Emil

Emil Wanatka, one of the unique characters of upper Wisconsin, is the originator, lord, and master of Little Bohemia. It is a resort, of course, and it is operated now by Emil Wanatka, Jr., a very pleasant young man and host who has a charming wife and a beautiful St. Bernard. But it is Emil, Sr. who has the big stories, the great memory, and the scrapbooks that illustrate his remarkable experiences with practically every U.S. president, sports figure, state official, and FBI personality who has achieved fame within Emil, Sr.'s, working lifetime. He has a talent for knowing famous people and not in a name-dropping way. He really does know them, and they call him Emil with affection for his forthright honesty and his love of his adopted country, the United States of America.

One time Emil was in Washington and felt like calling on Hubert Humphrey, then vice-president. At Humphrey's office, buzzing with about a dozen secretaries and agents, he asked to see his friend Humphrey. When they said that Humphrey was pretty busy and wouldn't have time to see Emil, he whipped out of his pocket a personal letter from Humphrey suggesting that Emil come to call on him when he was over Washington way. They took the letter upstairs, and in a moment Humphrey came down, boomed "Emil! " threw an arm around him, and took Emil up to his private office for an old-fashioned talk.

Another time Franklin D. Roosevelt called up Emil and asked him to come to the White House for a talk and to tell his famous story about John Dillinger, which took place at Emil's Little Bohemia. "In the president's office for about three hours," Emil said:

Little Bohemia, on Highway 51 going north from Minocqua, is a pleasant place on beautiful Little Star Lake. I had been by it often and was, somehow, always in too much of a hurry to stop off for a chat with Emil. When I finally did call him he cried, "Come any time! You will be welcome! Welcome!" The February day that I arrived, Emil had just finished his lunch, and when Mrs. Wanatka, vibrantly attentive to Emil's every wish and movement, had made me comfortable at the pine table with a Little Bohemia special brandy, I urged Emil to tell me his story. He is always ready to tell it, because it shows how a poor boy *can* make it in America; that it is not just a myth that opportunities do grow big in this nation; that a foreign youth with no suitcase can and did find doors opening for him; that the country will give great things as a simple exchange for faith, courage, and work. He also had one exciting experience that he will never, never forget.

"You came to America in 1906," I said.

"Yes. At that time Bohemia belonged to Austria-Hungary, to the Emperor Franz Joseph. At eighteen I was due for the army; my father was an army man and I hated the army. So, if you remember, 1906 was the earthquake in San Francisco, and this country had hundreds of agents all over Europe to hire labor to rebuild San Francisco. They had booklets printed in a dozen different languages. At that time Austria-Hungary had ten different languages. 'Come to America, the land of opportunity!' This country wanted immigrants. So I got hold of one of these booklets, and I wanted to come to America. But how? It cost $18, and I hadn't anything. Finally my poor mother and I had an argument, and I said, 'Why don't you send me to America?'

"So she borrowed money from half-a-dozen neighbors and I paid $18.20 to come to America, from Germany to New York. Seventeen and a half days on the water!

"I came to New York with a dollar and a dime, and no suitcase. God bless America, huh? Only place you can do that is in America!"

"What happened after you got to New York?"

"I stayed in New York, oh, about three or four months. I work in a bakery for $2.50 per week. Delivery boy and kind of a helper."

"How did you get that job?"

"How did I get that job? Well, you could have a long story here. The people who come over . . . if you learn a trade, you get a workingman's book, called in German, *Arbeitsbuch*. In that book is your pedigree, who you worked for, by whom you learned the trade, if you are a bricklayer, carpenter, barber . . . any trade. After you learn your trade and go to the army, then your army record is there. If you were ever in jail, and what schooling you had, it is all there in the book.

"So all the men who came over to America, all the tradesmen, they had these books, and they got shipped to San Francisco. But me, I wasn't eighteen years old, I had no address, and no suitcase. They didn't want me, so I worked on the streets. I got out of the boat, and the first thing I seen was a big six-foot-two black guy. I had never seen a black man before. I followed him. He went to a stand and got some bananas. I never saw bananas. So I give this man a dime and he give me a lot of bananas and give me a nickel back. So I was watching this black guy and he was eating these bananas, but I never saw bananas, and I didn't peel 'em. I tried to eat them with the peeling on and naturally I threw the bananas away.

"So I walked the streets, and a policeman saw me. Now in those days, the police in that part of New York, which had many different nationalities in it, they spoke several different languages. The policeman tapped me on the shoulder and asked me who I was and where was my suitcase. I said to him, 'Verstehe nicht'; and then he spoke to me in German and says, 'What nationality are you?' I says, 'Bohemian.' And he says, 'You want to go in the German-Bohemian neighborhood?' I says, 'I would appreciate that.'

"He walked with me three or four blocks and put me on a streetcar. At that time it was five cents per streetcar, and he told the conductor to leave me off on Seventy-second Street and First Avenue. This was kind of a German-Bohemian neighborhood.

"This was twenty-first of January, snow in New York. Conductor told me to walk a couple of blocks. Showed me on his fingers two blocks that way, and I walked over. I come to this barroom, and there was about a dozen men, all spoke German. With mustaches, with emblems on chains, long chains them days. So I set down at the table like we do in Europe. And the man behind the bar says to me, 'What do you want?' and I says, 'I'd like to have a beer.' and he says, 'Come over here and get it.'

"I got to the bar and a fellow says, 'Where you from?' I answered, 'I come from Vienna.' 'Oh,' he says, 'Vienna!' So he introduced me to everybody.

"Well, they got to talkin' about me, and they says, 'Why don't you get some lunch?' I never saw that there before. Free lunch. There was weiners, ham, and hard-boiled eggs, and two kinds of cheese. I done a pretty good job with the lunch and I had some more beer. Then, this hotel man who worked behind the bar and was the owner also, we got talking, and he says, 'You got any place to go?' and I says, 'No , I haven't got an address.' I didn't want to lie to him, that I didn't have a suitcase. I could have told him I lost it, but I didn't. I says I didn't have one.

" 'You can stay in my attic, and help my men in the

morning to clean up the bar, and a nice boy like you can shovel snow and keep sidewalks clean and you'll make a couple of dollars.'

"So he did introduce me to a very nice boy who spoke German. This boy would go into a house and ask the people if we could shovel the sidewalk. We got twenty or twenty-five cents, and the nice part was we would come to some of these homes and he would say, 'You see this boy? He just came from Europe yesterday, he had no breakfast.' And the people would give us a good breakfast. Then pretty soon I got a job in this bakery, and one thing led to another. I worked for Ringling Brothers Circus, was a sailor. I had many jobs and finally I come to Chicago where I worked in this place on the South Side, and because it is America, I got to be the owner. I called it Little Bohemia, because that was where I come from.

"My place in Chicago was a pretty big one. It was a very famous place for the sportsmen. I had a lot of prize fighters, football players — Red Grange, Gene Tunney, Dempsey had dinner in my place, all during Prohibition days. By the way, that St. Valentine's Day Massacre . . . those were my daily customers! But in Prohibition times things were getting hard in Chicago, killings and everything, so I came out here in 1926. I bought this property on Star Lake — there was nothing here — because I wanted to get out of Chicago.

"I started a little place, and as things went on it got larger and larger. Our business in those days was lumbermen, and we had dances, no closing laws, slot machines — different type life than today. Today we have snowmobiles, skiing. We call the range up here Hurley, Wakefield, Bessmer . . . all these places they used to be dead! Today just a madhouse with skiing and snowmobiling! Originally, before the Dillinger shooting in 1934, (twenty-second of April) when my boy Emil went to school, the little school had eight children. Today we have eighty-eight, and the big business is not only the fishing but also the cranberry business. A million dollar proposition. This country growed up. The real estate value! Unbelievable! It was a fishing country then, however. Up at half-past five, six o'clock! You have breakfast at half-past six. Seven o'clock you went out to fish. Today the fishermen start at ten o'clock.

"First thing they used to ask you about was fishing. Now it's 'What kind of beach have you got? How far to the golf course?' Plenty of fish left, sure. Only now you got to be a fisherman to catch them. The difference in fishing today is that the young fellow don't know anything about fishing. He's restless. He has no patience. He goes out there for a half-hour and he wants to get a prize muskie. Not in the book! I know men who been here for twenty years and never caught a legal muskie. They got a lotta fish. But not a keeper!"

"I tried to catch muskie many times myself," I said, "I never had luck."

"There you are. You know what I'm talkin' about."

"Yep."

"I know men here who have guides for the past fifteen years and they get fish, but never got a keeper. And don't forget today. The traffic here. A madhouse. Even now, on Friday, Saturday, and Sunday, it's like Fourth of July; people go skiing. The mileage don't mean nothing today. What's four hundred miles today? So people don't work on Saturday and Sunday, they come out for the weekend. The property value is 100 percent more! We have fourteen connected lakes, Manitowish Waters. I tried to sell some frontage years ago for two, three dollars front foot. Couldn't sell it. Today, hundred or hundred and a quarter a front foot!

"At the time that Dillinger came here I was the only place open all winter. If people wanted to come out here and do some ice fishing or just come for a few days I was the only place! The big places like Deer Park Lodge or Northern Lights, they required help; and they couldn't afford to keep their help. I could run this place with three, four people, which I did. That's how John Dillinger and that gang happened to come here."

"What triggered this whole thing with Dillinger? Up here, I mean?"

"Every policeman, sheriff, and post office in the country had his picture. Everybody was lookin' for John Dillinger, and he was here. He thought he was in a good hideout. He was! It was a big mistake on the government's part. We had two bridges here, one north of Little Bohemia, one south. This was twenty-second of April. Twenty-second of April is still winter. We still have some snowbanks. Ice is still in the lake. Last week in April. Sometimes first week in May we still got ice. If they had put a car on each bridge, Dillinger would have been on an island. They didn't do that. You remember Purvis?"

"Yes, sure."

"Well, Purvis was the head man from the Chicago FBI

office. The cooperation wasn't very clear. In plain words they thought they had Dillinger hooked. And everybody wanted to get that credit. 'I got Dillinger!' So we had fifty-seven men in our yard; anybody that had a shotgun and a rifle they come over here and shoot! Twenty-seven of 'em was FBI men. Was a big mix-up on the FBI's part. If the FBI had let the local sheriff and the people that live here, alone, Dillinger would never have got away. Anyhow we had here Dillinger, and Baby Face Nelson — real name was Lester Gillis, looked like a young college boy. If he was goin' like this, thumbing, on the highway you would give him a ride. John Hamilton, Pat Reilly, Tommy Carroll, Homer Van Meter . . . six men and four girls. The girls were Marie Conforti, Helen Gillis, Jean Carroll, and Patricia Cherrington. They had three cars, two Fords and a Buick. They were souped up all right. Fast cars. They came in on Friday, not all together. Baby Face Nelson, Homer Van Meter, and one of the girls first . . . one about seventeen or eighteen years old. Marie Conforti. They must have been here before because they called me by my name. 'Emil, how are you?' This was one o'clock in the afternoon. I was outside shoveling snow. 'Can we get some food?'

" 'Absolutely, sure. Come right in.'

"So they walked in. I fix them something to eat. Don't remember what. Don't make no difference. They ask me, 'Look, we're going to Duluth. Is there room here for all of us for three, four days?' Those days I had a pretty big mortgage at six and three-quarters percent. I was very happy to get some customers. I says, 'Why, absolutely I have room.' I took 'em upstairs and they looked the rooms over. I says, 'I got a heated garage.' 'Wonderful!'

"I helped 'em with the baggage, and I took the grip out; it was quite heavy baggage. I never give it a thought. After all, two men and a girl? Why would I care? Anyway I show them upstairs. Was a slot machine. They play slot machine. They never left the place! What makes me think they had this place picked, my place wasn't like it is today. There was just a trail into the place, secluded, and about five, six o'clock two other cars came in. That was Dillinger and Carroll and Hamilton and the whole gang and all the girls.

"I was introduced to Dillinger and it was 'Meet Johnny' and 'Meet Red,' and just like plain people. And Baby Face Nelson he says, 'Boy, you got a nice place! Beautiful rooms and dining room and fireplace, and garage — just terrific!' So they shook hands and we helped 'em, and I had two men working here at that time . . . young fellows, George Basel and Frank Carby. They helped with the baggage. And we took the suitcases out, it was the same thing, heavy. And the boys look at me and say, 'Jesus Christ, who are those people?' I says why. They says, 'Well, feel this.' I lift the bags and they are quite heavy bags.

"I says, 'Well, they could be hardware salesmen.' And after that we got to be like one big family.

"They came in. They play the slot machines. Unpacked the suitcases, and about half-past six, seven o'clock, the one that was just 'Johnny' to me, says, 'How about some food? What can we get? Can we get a steak?'

"I says, 'Sure! We got steaks!'

" 'Put some garlic on,' he says. Real bossy. 'Anyway on mine. Put some garlic on mine.'

"I says fine. So we has dinner. Everybody is jolly. Fine. They like it. After dinner they says, 'You play cards?'

"I says, 'My game is pinochle.' They says, 'Ha! A farmer game. How about a little poker?' I say, 'Look, I haven't got enough money to play any kind of a poker. Kind of poker I can play you wouldn't like.'

" 'Aw, come on. We play dollar limit. Come on.'

"So we start to play cards. And I am sittin' acrost from John Dillinger. To my left is Baby Face Nelson. The first hand there was thirty-four or thirty-six dollars in the pot; I had a six and a king up. Dillinger had an eight and a king showing. So after the last deal I says, 'I'll see you,' and I reached for the money. When I reached for the money, Dillinger says, 'Wait a minute. What have you got?' I says, 'I got kings and sixes.' 'Too bad, Emil. I got kings and eights!'

"He reached for the money and it opened up his coat. And here are two forty-fives in shoulder holsters. Then I got thinking. Who could this be in dead winter, with couple guns on? Never came to my mind it could be Dillinger. Everyday in the papers the headlines, **They Haven't Got Dillinger Yet**, every paper, Ironwood paper, Mercer, all the papers. So I didn't say anything. Just dealt cards; I looked to my left . . . left a card here and a card over there, same thing. Two forty-fives inside Nelson's coat. I deal over here. Sure. All got forty-fives. So I got thinking. Half-hour, Dillinger says, 'Where's the washroom?' So I told him. He got up from the table, and as he walked away I

184

was lookin' at him. He was about five-foot-seven, 170 pounds. Scar on his forehead, sandy hair, and very slow motion. Slow walking. I got thinking, it just come to my mind, 'Who could this be?' So I went in the kitchen, says to the others, 'I will wait till our friend John gets back.' Went to the kitchen and look at my *Chicago Tribune*.

"His was the picture! The profile and the full picture. All the description was there, slow walking and the scar forehead. I says to myself, 'It must be John Dillinger.' So when John come back I look him over again.

"We kept on playing cards, and I got my money back. I was out forty or fifty dollars already, and I guess it was maybe ten o'clock. They started to yawn.

"At that time this was not a modern place like it is today. We cut wood for the stove and the furnace, so I was tired. I says, 'Why don't we go to bed?' So they all got up, and the good night was kind of a cold good night. Wasn't from the bottom of your heart! I never give it a second thought. Anyway I have two good dogs here. I got upstairs and went to bed and the boys who worked for me went to their cottage. So in the morning about six o'clock, when I got up to let the dogs out, the wife says, 'Who are these people? There was somebody walking up and down the hallway all night.' I says, 'Aw, you're dreaming.' She says, 'No! There was somebody walkin' around.' Anyway I got up and took the dogs out, and the first fellow that was out was Carroll. He stretched himself and says, 'Boy! Did I sleep! When do we eat?'

"I says, 'Well, look. You get the gang up and we have breakfast.' So he went into the lodge, and fifteen, twenty minutes they started to come down. Girls come down to help in the kitchen. I have a big kitchen where I used to eat with my help, sits fourteen people, and one of these girls started to fry the bacon and eggs. One big family! Doin' fine!

"At the breakfast table I'm sittin' across from John Dillinger. I didn't have any proof it was him, but I was sure it was. After we had this breakfast I says to John, 'John, I like to talk to you.'

" 'Something wrong?' he says.

" 'No, there's nothing wrong.'

"We walk into my little office near the barroom. He says, 'What you want, Emil?'

"I look him right in the eye. I says, 'Are you John

Dillinger?'

"He says, 'You're not afraid, are you?'

"I says, 'No, I'm not afraid. But look, John, everything I got to my name. Every penny I ever owned, my family, is right here. Every policeman in the United States is lookin' for you. Every sheriff. Every lawman is lookin'. If I don't have to have a shooting match, I sure appreciate it if you move out.'

"John took me around my shoulder. He patted me and says, 'Emil, look, all we want is rest up for couple days. I pay you real well and we all get out! From then on we were like couple of old-time friends. We played cards, and to tell you the truth I learned him how to pinochle. He didn't mind to lose money. I cheated him every hand, and we got to be very friendly. People would come into the yard and he or somebody from the gang would say, 'There's a car driving in! Know them people?'

"I look out of the window and says, 'Yes, this is Dr. Gale. This is so-and-so! This is our neighbor.' They says, 'You know them?' I says, 'Yes.'

"If a car drove in and I didn't know them, then they all went to the lodge. It was one afternoon, Dr. Gale was buildin' a house and ate here. He was from Chicago. He come with his carpenter and his lumberman with him, and they had home-brew and herring on the table. Dillinger walked in and he says, 'What you men eating?' So I says, 'Some herring,' and he says, 'Can I have some herring?'

"I give him a plate and we went to the table. Nobody knew it was John Dillinger. Even after the shooting the FBI men told me there wasn't 250 people in the whole country could say it was really John Dillinger, because of the different clothes and all, different hair. He had his hair dyed a different color. Nobody knew that.

"We was all very friendly. But I could see there was friction between them, like with Baby Face Nelson. He was all the time by himself and always a bossy type. Second day, Homer Van Meter came to me. He says, 'Emil, would you know a place where I could go and get a cottage? There is too many of us here and your place is too public!' He didn't see Baby Face Nelson watchin' us.

"I says, 'Well, I wouldn't really know,' because in those days we had no snowplow service like today. Now we got children going to school in buses, and the towns keep the roads plowed good. At that time there was no such a thing. I says, 'Listen, if you get into some cottage, you never get out count of the snow. Lots of it still in April.' But he says, 'I get out. You let me know.' Nelson was lookin' at us, and when he walked away, Nelson come up to me and says, 'What'd you two talk about?' I says, 'This friend of yours asked me if he could get a cottage somewhere by himself.' And then Nelson looked at me real sharp and pushed his clothes back so I could see the forty-fives. And he says, 'Look, if anybody wants to rent any cottages you tell him to see me.'

"I says, 'I'm not going to see anybody. You do your own business.'

"Anyway, you could see it was not one gang. They were not friendly. And afterward we found out it was two factions and that Dillinger had Nelson to come up with Homer Van Meter to help him out on some robberies they was gonna do up in Duluth. That's what I hear after.

"Well, we went out target shooting. I still have the can. It was a firm in Milwaukee, a gallon can. I have a twenty-two rifle, so I come out with the rifle, and it jammed. So Dillinger says to Van Meter, 'Say, go get one of our rifles!' And back comes Van Meter with a 306 Winchester. They put a clip in there and they give me the rifle. All I had to do was just turn around and let go if I wanted to, but why should I? I'm no policeman. Why should I shoot somebody? They would have knocked me off anyway. I hit the can I think twice. Then Dillinger took the rifle. He never touched the can. Nelson never touched the can. Van Meter did. But they couldn't shoot a rifle. They was all right with the machine gun, but they was not so good at target shooting. So then we went back into the lodge and we played cards and everything was good till Sunday.

"Sunday morning, they paid me. Very nicely. They are going to leave tomorrow. Day goes on. I have some people in the barroom, some neighborly people from here, had a gasman here, Johnny Hoffman from Mercer, I had John Morris, cook from the CCC camp, kind of a family affair. Tom Machirone was here. They all drank home-brew and moonshine, fine! In comes John Hamilton. He wanted to go to the men's room. He walked in, and while he was walkin' in, Machirone, an old-time lumberjack and saloonkeeper says, 'Say, you! I'm Tom Machirone from Winchester,' and he started poundin' his chest. Says, 'How about a drink?' Hamilton turned around and says, 'I'm sorry, Mr. Machirone, I don't drink.' Machirone says, 'Damn you, you will drink with me or I pour it down your neck!'

"I says to myself, 'Here's where it's gonna start.' So finally Hamilton says, 'Emil, you better give me a little beer.'

"And Hamilton says, 'Can I go to the toilet now?' And he pushed him, Machirone did. So when Hamilton come out of the men's room Machirone says, 'Say, are you gonna buy a drink? You know, Emil's a pretty nice guy. He bought uniforms for our baseball team, the Little Bohemia team. We used to play the Flambeau Indians.' So Hamilton fished around and come out with a five-dollar bill, and we all had a drink. Then Machirone sold Hamilton a couple of tickets for the baseball game next summer at a dollar apiece. And Hamilton says, 'Can I go now and finish my dinner?' And Machirone pushed him and says, 'Sure, go ahead.'

"About dark my dog started to bark. At that time the place wasn't cleared out like it is today. The brush was up to Highway 51. The FBI men had flown to Rhinelander, and they commanded cars from Rhinelander and drove up here. They left their cars on the highway and walked through the woods. They had found out some way that Dillinger was here. Everybody looked out but could see nothing. In the meanwhile this cook from the CCC camp, Morris, and another boy from the CCC camp, Eugene Boisneau and Johnny Hoffman, the gasman, they went out to their car, and they got into it. Had had a few drinks, naturally, and the FBI men started to come in. Told 'em to halt! But these guys had the car running and never give it a thought who these people are, just started to drive away. The FBI men mowed 'em down. Put forty slugs into Boisneau. They shot Hoffman and they shot Morris. When the shooting started, naturally the gang got excited. Van Meter got onto the roof from his room, and I went into the lounge and I told the gangsters' girls, 'Get in the basement! Quick as you can!' And I'm in the basement, but I had seen Dillinger go to the front door toward the lake side, and Hamilton walked to the back door.

"While I'm in the basement, Morris and Hoffman, who were with the dead CCC boy, walk back into the kitchen, wounded. My telephone was in the kitchen, and Morris called up Eldon Koerner who lived south down the road. Says, 'Eldon, we're at Emil's! Somebody held up the place! Send some help! They killed Boisneau. I'm shot. Send some help,' and he fell by the telephone right above where I was in the basement.

"So after he fell I says to the gangsters' girls, 'Listen, why don't you give me some help; you go upstairs, and if they need any help, bring them down here.' But they says, 'If you want any help, you go up yourself.'

"So I went upstairs and I'm listening to machine guns. Shooting was still going on. Finally it quieted down and I put up my hands and put on a light in the kitchen so they, the FBI men, could see me. I know by that time what it was. Must have been police. Who else could it have been? I got back to the basement and after about a half-hour I got out to the basement door. In the meantime, Baby Face Nelson got to our neighbors, Paul Lang, about a mile from here on the shoreline. He walked in with a gun — this was an old couple — and told them, 'I gotta have a car. I'm Baby Face Nelson. I gotta make a getaway.' He made Mr. Lang get the car. They started out but the old car couldn't make the hill, so Nelson says, 'Who lives over there?' and Lang says, 'It's the Koerners.' So they walk in. They left the Lang car on the highway, and Nelson held up everybody in Koerner's and says he wanted a car. I come in to Koerner's place in the meantime with my truck and one of my boys. I was after help. I come in and when I open the door, here was Baby Face Nelson behind the door with two forty-fives, holdin' these Koerner people down. So I grabbed for his guns. I says, 'Listen, what you doing here with the guns? People here are friends of mine' He jerked the gun out of my hand, and he says, 'Who is outside?' I says, 'Nobody.' But there was somebody there. My boy, the fellow who worked for me. So Nelson marched me outside with the gun in my ribs. It's about fifty feet from the Koerner's house to the driveway. With a forty-five in my back I was thinking, 'Now what can I do? I know this guy's a killer. Should I wrestle with 'im, or should I obey orders?' I got into the car. He got into the car. He put the forty-five in my ribs, and I don't put the switch on, but I push the starter. He says, 'You son-of-a-bitch, you haven't got the switch on.' I says, 'I dunno. If I haven't, you got me nervous. You got the gun in my ribs.' 'What's the matter with you,' he says. 'I was a pretty good guy for three days, what're you afraid of? Get the goddam car started. I got to make a getaway and you going with me.'

"While we were doing this and talking and while I am getting the car started, up comes Carter Baum, an FBI man from the St. Paul office. He had our constable, Christensen, with him, and another one of the FBI men, Jay Newman. They drove up and Baum had the machine gun on his lap, and he called, 'Halt! We're federal officers!' Just when he said that Nelson jumped out and yelled 'I'll get you above your bullet-proof vest you bastards!'' and shot Baum six different times right in the neck. He shot the other two men who were in the back seat, and while he done that I dive into a pile of snow, and I lay there, playing dead. Nelson threw Baum and his machine gun out of the car, threw the other two men out, and took the federal men's car. But before he left he shot at me. I could see the gun and everything, but I just lay there. He figured he hit me. So he took the federal men's car and left for Flambeau, twenty miles from here. Hid there on the Indian reservation for two or three days with an Indian, Ole Catfish. Then he got a car from some mailman and made his getaway.

"After Nelson left I got up, and I feel my legs and my neck and there's no blood no place. I'm all together. Nervous, naturally. Anybody would. And I come back to our lodge, a mile and a half. I went right to the driveway. And here's all these people from Eagle River, all the men who could get a gun. Fifty-seven men here. And everybody hollered, 'Put your hands up!'

"I had run a mile and a half. And don't forget I was no chicken either. I'll be eighty-one years old next month! My friend Dr. Roberts was here. He was head of all the CCC camps here, and he used to be my daily customer to eat. And Doc says, 'Don't shoot, that's Emil Wanatka. Don't shoot!'

"So the first man come up to me was Purvis. Says, 'What happened?'

'What happened,' I says, 'Why your men up at the Koerner's are dead.' I thought the other two men were dead also. I didn't know there was only one dead, Carter Baum. Newman and Christenson were wounded.

"He says, 'Where?'
"I says, 'Koerner's.'
" 'Where is Koerner's?'
" 'Mile and half south of us.'
" 'What is your name?'
" 'Emil Wanatka.'
" 'How you spell it? Where you get your mail?'
" 'Manitowish.'
" 'How you spell Manitowish?'

"And then I couldn't spell Manitowish. You know what I mean? I couldn't spell it in first place. So we got into an argument. I says, 'Did you come over to get me or Dillinger? All you do is ask me how to spell my name.' I was a little huffy and I was gonna hit 'im. I was mad enough so after I got away from all these shootings ... but I finally told him how to spell it, and right after that the shooting started. Everybody who had a gun they shoot at my windows. The whole thing went so fast. And Bill Summers, of the CCC camps, he was here. And Boisneau, the man the FBI men had killed by mistake, was still in the yard. And I says, 'Bill, how about you and I go into the lodge?' I had seen a lot of money in a suitcase, and I wondered if the gang took that money along. If there was any money left I was gonna get my share, too. I put in some tough hours. So Summers and I walked in. The yard is empty. Everybody is behind the woodpile. The lodge is full of tear gas. The gangsters' girls was still in the basement. We started to open the windows, and I am feeling for this money under the bed, for I knew which suitcase it was, but I couldn't find it.

"So then the FBI men came in, and they told Summers and I to stay out, and they took the three girls to Madison, and from then on we wasn't allowed to go in the lodge anymore. Dillinger, he got away, too, maybe across the ice, I don't know. But you know the next days we had fifty thousand people come here. Still come too! And about a month after the shooting I have an invitation from Franklin D. Roosevelt and Edgar Hoover to come to Washington and explain why the agents didn't take Dillinger and so on. I was Roosevelt's guest at the White House, and later I was the chairman of the Warm Springs dance here. I won't forget it! Come look at my scrapbooks! I got it all in here!"

# The Great Yarn Spinner of Merrill

For a number of years I had heard tales of Walter B. Chilsen of Merrill. He was a well-known publisher, operating the *Merrill Herald*, with his brother, and he had been a prominent member of the Wisconsin legislature. But most of what I had heard about him concerned his prowess as a yarner, a teller of tales. One day, just before I was starting on one of my yarn-collecting jaunts, Don Peterson of the Wisconsin College of Agricultural and Life Sciences Experiment Stations called me to say that if I didn't do anything else, I simply had to see Walt Chilsen.

The day I started north I called Irv Leverenz, Resource Development Agent of Lincoln County, who is a great pal of Walt's. Irv takes Walt out in his car on many trips around Lincoln, which is one great way of learning about it, since Walt probably knows the county and the whole north country for that matter better than any other man. So Irv and I went to see Walt on a winter afternoon. We just walked right in the kitchen door — that is the way you do it with Walt — and there he was in the living room of his charming hundred-year-old house, expectant — one of the most alert men I have ever known — eyes sparkling with welcome and with eagerness to release some of the mighty store of yarns that he has been piling up for eighty-four years.

"Now you listen here," Walt Chilsen says, leaning back in his favorite chair, "you listen and I'll tell you how I once growed a beard like Abraham Lincoln!"

I've heard some yarn spinners in Wisconsin, but I honestly believe that Walt Chilsen has 'em all beat. You can turn him on and three, four hours later he will still be going strong, and he never repeats himself either.

Folks that know Walt will say that it's fun to go with Walt out to what he calls his shack in the woods. The setting there seems to wind him up even more, and he will talk about northern Wisconsin and the people he has known until the Northern Lights fade out with the morning sky. Some people are just programmed into a country. Walt is one. He was eighty-four this year, and in reality he has seen the north grow and prosper. He saw a good share of the big lumbering and he saw the cutover spring up with new growth. He saw the often fruitless struggle to make an agricultural country out of the north, and he saw the rough times of the depression. He saw and had a good hand in the forest coming back. Walter B. Chilsen is northern Wisconsin. When he ran the *Merrill Advocate* he never was tired of plugging the north, and he may have had more than anybody realizes to do with the country becoming the great tourist area it is today.

"About that beard," Walt says, "I had been growing one. When I climbed up a hill backward it looked all right, but when I looked in a mirror frontward, it didn't suit me. So I went into the barber, and it was Lincoln's Birthday. I says to him, 'Can you do anything about this beard of mine?' He says, 'Well, I think I can make it look somethin' like Abraham Lincoln.'

"I couldn't think of anything better, and I couldn't stand that beard, so I told him to go ahead and shoot. He did, and the results were pretty good, if you liked Lincoln's beard. That's what I had.

"Well, a couple of guys come up from Madison. They come to my office and I had swingin' doors like they have in a tavern. I wanted to feel at home when I was in the office.

"I says to these Madison guys, 'Come on in, fellows,' and they says, 'Nope, we haven't got any time.' Then they looked at me and one says, 'Hey! You been growin' a beard and it looks like Lincoln!' He says, 'That can't be. You're homelier than Lincoln, but that beard does look like Lincoln!'

"Then the other guy took a close look and says, 'Now I know why they shot 'im!'

"There was a little Jew lived here in Merrill. A nice guy but queer. Fat. He run a secondhand store. I never could understand how he made enough livin'. And I recall 'im sayin' — his name was Kentucky Joe, 'When I die I want to be buried in a Catholic cemetery. That's the last place the devil would look for a Jew!'

"I went to Tomahawk one fall. It was deer hunting season, and on the way back in the train, the smoking car was crowded. I went to the seat where the newsbutcher was and I sat on the arm of the chair. Along came Martin Foss, who was wearing a black sealskin coat. And he says to me, 'Hello, Chilsen, how are you?' Said, 'This goddam train is too crowded.' He says, 'This smoking car, the decent people that ride on it, like you, can't get a seat.' He says, 'They always have a seat for me.' And he says, 'This train is full of them gol darned hunters . . . up here full of booze and enthusiasm.' Says, 'I was back in the express car and there was three deer and a hundred hunters.' And I says,

'Well, Martin, they ought to be like you that could kill a bear with a fist.' He says, 'Did you ever hear about that?' And I says, 'Yes. Ole Larson told me.'

" 'Well,' says Martin, 'Ole ordinarily tells the truth but sometimes he doesn't get it just right.' He says, 'I'll tell you myself if we got time enough.' Says, 'Takes about an hour to get to Merrill. Guess I can tell it in an hour.' He says, 'You know, Chilsen, I was quite interested in this here Wisconsin Valley Railroad. First we come, on that line, to Garland. It was only a switch. Train didn't even stop there. I remember this man Garland,' he says. 'He was a fat guy. Once he fell off the train and he rolled in a snowbank, and his coat went up and you could see green stretchers put in there so his pants would pull out big enough. Then we come to Irma. Ain't that a hell of a name for a little place named after a woman? The right name is Cloverdale. You go down to the courthouse you will see that the right name is Cloverdale.

" 'Then you come up to a fork. The train stops there, and you know how I got to be a sawmill owner? I was a bridge carpenter for the St. Paul Railroad. And one day a little short man with a cady arm came up and says, 'Pretty good workman.' I says, 'Don't talk to me, because the company don't pay me for talkin'. It pays me for workin'!' He says, 'Well, you are right handy with that saw. Why don't you start a sawmill?' I says, 'What are you talking about?' And he says, 'I am President Erling of the St. Paul Railroad.' And he pictured to me that I should have a sawmill and get that timber and one thing and another. Was a damned good idea, so I started me a place and they called it Foss. Put it on the map, you know.

" 'Now you asked about that bear that I killed with my fist. That's true. I bought me a forty which I could look out of the office and see. One of them Irma hills. A scad of timber on it. And steep! You just cut the logs and slide 'em right down to the sawmill. I never made as much money in my life! You know, son, if you buy flat land, you don't get as much as you do if you buy steep hills. Timber will grow both up and down the sides!

" 'Well, an old man from Merrill come along. George Curtis, Jr. He was so old I never knew why they called him Junior. He says,"Whose timber are you cuttin'?" I says, "Don't ask foolish questions, I'm cuttin' my own." "No you ain't," he says, "Kate Pyle's got a tax title on it." So I went down to the courthouse

194

and I find out that is right. So I don't buy it once. I have to buy it twice!

" 'Well, in the spring of the year I was setting there in my office, and I was thinking that ain't gonna happen to me again! So I put on my jacket of brand new perty mackinaw, and went out to look at my forty. And it would have taken a college professor to count all my trees! But I didn't have a compass man! I had to have a compass man! You know what a compass man is?' I said no. 'Well,' Martin says, 'you go a 125 paces and you say, "Tally one." And your compass man says, "Tally one!" Then you go another 125 paces and you say, "Tally two!" Well, I didn't want to go back and let the crew know that I'd started off without a compass man. And sudden I remember about a Finlander livin' there. I knew exactly where his place was.

" 'So I come to this Finlander, and he had long black hair and a kind of a thin face like you got. So I asks this Finlander if he will be my compass man. And he says, "Yah. Vat will you pay?" Well, of course, it was before those foolish unions came. So I says I will pay a dollar a day. And he jumped at it.

" 'Well, we were goin' pretty good. We was wore out and he was hollering "Tally one, and tally two and tally three," and we'd been out about three-quarters of an hour when he comes runnin' toward me. And I hollers to him "Stop! Stop!" He don't stop at all. He went right by me. And his hair was flapping in the wind. I says, "All right, go on! All Finlanders is crazy!" And I turned around and right there was a big black bear. And he was standing up, you know. Well, I'd heard lots of stories how if you acted sort of friendly toward a wild animal, he'd be friendly too.

" 'So I told him to get out of the way. I don't know if he rightly understood what I was sayin'. He give a couple of "Woofs" and took a couple of steps toward me, and next time he give me a swipe and rips my new mackinaw that had cost me seven dollars. Just tore it all to pieces! And I says, "All right, Mr. Bear, now you're gonna be in trouble," and I was reachin' around, don't you know, to get loose my little ax I had on my belt. But the belt was tight and I was a little bit excited, so I thought I would say "Hello" to the bear again, and he give me a swipe; now I'm mad, and I couldn't get my ax off. So the only thing I could do was to use my fist. So I squared away and I hit the bear right in the middle of the forehead. He went tumbling down one of them hills. And when he got to the bottom he said, "Oof!"

" 'I'm not surprised that he said that because he was goin' pretty hard. Then I had plenty time, so I unloosened my belt and I got out my ax and I says, "Maybe you won't want to be meeting Martin Foss the next time. You might meet somebody who couldn't handle you! So I'm gonna finish you off!"

" 'So I squared his head around, and I took my ax and I split her wide open! And I wiped off the blood from my ax and you know what I did then? You know what I did then?

" 'I went after that Finlander! That blankety blank blank that run away when I was in trouble!' "

Merrill has even been in big-time politics. Chilsen loves to recount the yarn about how Myron McCord got to be governor of the territory of Arizona.

"He lived down in the second ward in what we call the McCord Mansion, about seven apartments now. I remember him very well. Dressed like a congressman. Wore a Stetson hat and a swallowtail coat. He'd been elected to Congress once, but was later defeated, and after his defeat he come back here to Merrill to try to put himself together again. Well, he figured he could do better in Arizona than in Merrill, I suppose, so one day I met him crossing a vacant lot and I says, 'Mr. McCord, I'm sure sorry to hear that you're moving to Arizona.'

" 'Now where'd you get the idea, boy, that Merrill's losing a good citizen?'

" Well, my mother and dad were talking about it, and they were saying what a shame it was that Merrill is losing you."

"Mr. McCord reached into his pocket and took out a quarter. He says, 'Boy, I can't hardly afford this, but here is a quarter for you.'

"McCord went to Arizona and about then there was a big fight between the speaker of the house and McKinley. This fight carried through to the national Republican convention at St. Louis. Meanwhile McCord had got himself made a delegate to the Republican convention, and when he got there he spent his time with the Wisconsin delegation, drinking it up and having a big time. In fact, McCord did so well at the bar that he got the Wisconsin delegation to change to McKinley! McKinley was nominated. McCord was for McKinley because they were both Civil War veterans.

"McKinley come to McCord and says, 'I hear that you supported me in a royal way! And I'm here to tell you that if there is anything in my power to do anything for you, I will!

196

Anything!'

"Well, McKinley is elected, but before the election McCord went to him and says, 'Now, McKinley, I know you're gonna be elected, and you said if there was anything you could do for me you would do it. I want to be territorial governor of Arizona!'

" 'All right,' says McKinley, 'if I am elected, you will be territorial governor.'

"And McKinley went to all the key men and says, 'Now don't forget to vote for McCord for territorial governor, because I'm gonna appoint him.'

"Well, about then McCord was doing a lot of things, divorce and such, which were not so savory. They even sent reporters from New York here to find out about McCord's private life. Well, it goes along, and finally McCord gets into a public brawl in a joint in Phoenix. He knocks a guy out and leaves him in the gutter. The paper picks this nice item up and McKinley sends word to McCord that he is withdrawing his name from nomination for territorial governor. McCord goes to Washington right off to see the president. But McKinley says, 'You're wastin' your time, McCord, because I won't appoint you territorial governor.' He says, 'Oh, I know, it's a kind of a frontier life, morals ain't just the same as they are in the East. I don't care about that. But McCord, you had a common ordinary street brawl, and you left a man lying in the gutter. That I can't overlook. And I won't.'

" 'Well,' says McCord, 'you might listen to extenuating circumstances.'

" 'Extenuating circumstances,' says McKinley, 'Why you beat the guy up to within an inch of his life!'

" 'I know,' says McCord, 'but there were still extenuating circumstances. You see, Mr. President, there was this saloon. There was a bunch of fellers in there that don't like me. But I went in there anyhow and got a drink. And there was a feller there that was talking about carpetbaggers from Wisconsin. And he says, "To think that that son-of-a-bitch McKinley is going to appoint McCord territorial governor!"'

" 'And,' says McCord to McKinley, 'nobody is going to call the president of the United States a son-of-a-bitch in my presence. I'll lick him till he lays in the gutter again!'

"And McKinley says, 'The nomination stands!' And that's how McCord got to be governor of Arizona!"

Once Chilsen introduced John F. Kennedy who was campaigning in Wisconsin. Chilsen kept telling Paul Corbin who asked Chilsen to do it, that, as a Republican, he didn't think he should. "The mayor is a Democrat," howled Chilsen. "Why not him? In fact, we got a lot of Democrats here in Merrill. Get one of them."

"But I didn't convince him," Chilsen said, "and Corbin come back a third time. Finally he come a fourth time and I said, "I hate to have you darken my door so many times. All right, I will introduce Mr. Kennedy. But I was a four-minute talker during the First World War. I only want to use up four minutes, and I don't want anybody to read what I'm gonna say in advance. I'll time it by the clock, so you don't need to worry." Was the hardest thing I ever wrote. Anyway, I was setting next to Mrs. Kennedy at the dinner, and I told her that I was nervous.

"She says, 'Why are you nervous?' and I says, 'You had dinner with Queen Elizabeth and you're familiar with the Waldorf-Astoria, and I didn't dare to go in it when I was in New York. You been the pal of ambassadors and one thing and another; and you really been the 400!'

" 'Well,' she says, 'don't be nervous.' And I says, 'I won't be nervous if you let me tell you a story.'

" 'Oh,' she says, 'I just love stories!'

"So this is the story that I told Mrs. Kennedy. A guy goes to his priest and says, 'Father, I got to make a confession, right now! Right now!' 'Why?' says the priest. 'You don't need to make no confession. If anybody was to ask me who was the best of my parishioners, I would have to say it was you and your wife, your two sons and your two daughters. Nobody can beat 'em. Let's have a cigar and glass of wine and then you can tell me about it.'

"So they had a cigar and a glass of wine and by and by the priest says, 'What's your trouble?'

" 'Oh,' he says, 'I'm workin' for the lumber company and I'm stealing lumber.'

" 'Oh, boy!' the priest says, 'that's bad! Dassn't go and tell your employer 'cause he'll fire you like *that!* You'll have to move out. Maybe you can go to the next town, and maybe your reputation will follow you there and you'll find it hard to get a job. No,' he says, 'we got to think that over. How long do you work for that guy?'

" 'Oh,' he says, 'about twenty-five years.'

198

" 'Just imagine that,' says the priest. 'Fifty years ago all this country was wilderness, just wild animals and Indians. Fifty years this town has grown, and twenty-five years you worked for the lumber company. You played a major part in this town's development. And now we got to think of something. How long have you been stealing?'

" 'Since the first day I worked there,' the guy says.

" 'Oh, imagine that,' says the priest. 'That's terrible!' He says, 'We gotta make a novena.' The guy looks at the priest and the priest says, 'Don't you know what a novena is?'

"The guy says, 'Dadgone it, Father. I don't know. But,' he says, 'you got the blueprints, I got the lumber!'

"You know," Chilsen continued, "I asked to go along to Medford and other places that Kennedy was going. And we hadn't hardly crossed the sixth ward bridge when I said, 'Kennedy, your wife is a delightful dinner companion.'

" 'She has that reputation,' he says.

"I says, 'I agree with you. She likes stories.'

" 'What kind of stories you tell her?' he says, suspicious.

"I started to tell him that story about the guy stealing lumber and he says, 'Stop. Don't go any further. I know that story. I've used it probably a hundred times. Very popular at the Knights of Columbus!'

"And I says, 'Well, your wife even had the courtesy to laugh when she heard that story.'

" 'Aw,' he says, 'rest assured. Because if there's one thing she can't stand, she won't stand, she don't care who it is, she'll say, "I heard that story before" and she'll stop you right away!' And I never heard no yelling from her, and no cries of 'Stop!' So I don't believe she ever heard that story before!"

I asked Chilsen if he had ever known the great Rhinelander prankster, Gene Shepard, who invented the Hodag. Of course Chilsen knew Shepard! And he instantly began to elaborate.

"I first knew Gene Shepard in 1895, but I didn't know it was Gene Shepard. It was Oneida County Fair time. There was a dance and there was a guy with a foghorn voice talkin' about his Hodag, how he captured it on a Sunday morning, how it wouldn't eat anything but white bulldogs. It cost ten cents to get in.

"I stood there holdin' my thin dime I had for helpin' to clean off the fairground. Shepard saw me and he says, 'Listen, young man, do you want to go in here to see my Hodag?'

"I says, 'Yeah, but I only got a dime. If I spend it here, I can't buy anything else.'

"Says, 'Come on in.'

"Well, I saw that Hodag and I was glad I didn't spend my ten cents for it! But I liked the friendly guy. Later on I met Shepard through C. N. Johnson, the writer. He was correspondent for the *New York Herald.* I think Shepard was one of the most versatile fellows I ever knew. He was an artist. He could draw. I always thought he could hypnotize anybody.

"You know, I was in the Wisconsin legislature, and in 1919 I told President Birge of the university that I wanted somebody that could write stories about the lumberjacks and the lumber country, for the *Merrill Poker,* you know.

"Birge says, 'Well, I got a Jewish boy named Perstein in here. He won the oratorical contest for the Big Ten, same one that ol' Bob La Follette won.' He says, 'I think Perstein will fill the bill for you.'

"Well, I brought Perstein up here to Merrill and he didn't do any writing for two weeks. All he did was travel around the country. He had some relatives that lived in Eagle River and he wanted to see them, and on the way to Eagle River, why, we stopped into Shepard's at Rhinelander. Shepard says, 'When you comin' back from Eagle River?'

" 'Tomorrow night.'

" 'All right, boys, come early enough. We'll have some of my golden bantam corn!' He says, 'I'll cook some steaks outside and we'll have a swell feed.'

"When we got back there, I had told Shepard about this Perstein bein' an orator. Said he'd won this Big Ten contest. Well, Perstein was at the end of the table, and Shepard is at the head of the table. Every time that Perstein would say somethin', why Shepard would cup his ear. Finally had Perstein hangin' onto the table and hollering.

"Well, we were about to go home, and we bid Shepard good-by and this Perstein was the last one. And gawd, he yelled, 'I had a wonderful time!'

"Shepard said, 'What you hollering so loud about? I'm glad you had a good time, but you didn't need to bust my eardrums.'

" 'Well,' says Perstein, 'you don't hear very good. So I . . . '

" 'Hell,' says Shepard, 'you was talking so loud I was

coverin' my ear so you wouldn't bust my eardrum!'

"And then in 1912 Governor Pinchot was makin' a campaign for President Roosevelt. He had had a speech in Milwaukee at the Pabst Theatre, and somehow or other he had fallen down gettin' off the stage or something. Wrenched his shoulder. Pained him to beat the band! Well, he come here and stopped off on his way to make a speech up at Rhinelander. He is then going to take the Soo Line over to St. Paul, only the Soo Line don't have a train until two o'clock in the morning. So I got to take him to Rhinelander in an automobile, and put him on the train later. Well, it had froze in October and the roads were rutty and rough, and this jolting hurt Pinchot's arm to beat the band. When we got to Rhinelander, I says to Pinchot, 'I want you to visit Shepard, who invented the Hodag.' Pinchot says, 'Why, Shepard didn't originate the Hodag at all! It was done by a guy in Michigan. Shepard had nothin' to do with it.'

" 'Well,' I said, 'He's quite a guy and you'd like to meet 'im!'

"So he says, 'All right. But only for a minute.'

"Well, Shepard has got that office built in his house over there in the woods; there's a plate glass window and oh, there's a fire blazin' in the fireplace. And we stood outside lookin' in and Pinchot says, 'Oh, if I could only get my sore shoulder up to that fire!'

"So I hollered — there's a swamp down in the back — I yelled as loud as I could. Pretty soon Shepard sticks his head around the corner, says, 'What the hell you guys want here?'

"I said, 'I wanted you to meet Governor Pinchot of Pennsylvania.'

" 'Oh, yes.' Shepard says. And he gets out a key and Pinchot goes in and stands up against the fire. Well, he's supposed to also make a speech at Laona and Crandon. But he didn't leave Shepard's place until five o'clock that afternoon. Shepard kept him fascinated.

"One hot day when he didn't know exactly what to do, C. N. Johnson, a correspondent for the *New York Herald Tribune*, wrote an item: 'There was great excitement in Rhinelander, because the Hodag was gonna have pups.' The *Herald* printed that. Theodore Roosevelt read it, and he didn't call a stenographer or anything, he just wrote in longhand a letter to Shepard, said, 'You're nothin' but a damned nature faker, 'cause there ain't any such animal.' When Shepard got the letter out and showed it to Pinchot, Pinchot says, 'Well, that certainly is Roosevelt's writing! What do you want for that letter?'

"Shepard says, 'If I gave that letter to you, nobody would ever believe that Roosevelt called me a nature faker. I'm gonna keep it myself.' And then he got out his book and read about the Round River Drive, and how Paul Bunyan's cook had put some gunpowder in the pancakes, and the gunpowder went off. They had two black men skatin' around with bacon tied to their feet to grease up the griddle. And when the gunpowder went off, the black fellers went up through the roof, and that's when they had the year of the black snow!

"And on that visit of Pinchot's was the time I saw Shepard kick his priceless silver punch bowl.

"You know, Shepard's wife wasn't well, and in those days they said if you want to get well, go to California. Shepard went to California with her. They stayed in San Francisco at the St. Francis Hotel. She was always talking that she wanted a silver service . . . a punch bowl t-h-a-t big . . . napkin rings, same way, and silverware . . . knives had to be longer and sharper than anybody else's. Well, you know, in San Francisco they got wonderful Chinese workers in silver. So Shepard drew out a design that he wanted on the napkin rings and that he wanted on the handles of the knives and forks, and the coffee spoons; so he hired them to make it. These workers were real pleased when they completed the silver service, and they put it on display in one of their windows.

"Now Shepard was in the habit of taking his wife out for a walk, and he got her to go by this silversmith's store. They stopped and looked at that punch bowl and that silverware there in the window. Oh, that's just what she wanted. It was what she had always wanted and look at the beautiful designs on the napkin rings, and on the knives, and on the punch bowl!

" 'Well,' says Shepard, 'I'm glad we found somethin' that'd please you.' Said, 'Let's go in and find out what it costs!'

"She says, 'Don't be foolish. You haven't got enough money to buy that outfit.'

"Well, it was early in the morning, and the guy who was there said, 'I know nothin' about that silverware. But the boss will be here shortly.'

"So the boss came in and Shepard's wife says to this fellow, 'We are much taken with the silver service in the window. It's beautiful. We want to know what it would cost.'

" 'Ah,' says the fellow. 'Priceless! Can't sell it to you! That's a special order from a wealthy Wisconsin woodsman named Gene Shepard!'

"Out the door goes Shepard's wife! She ran to the hotel and Shepard couldn't catch her. She gets in the elevator and locks herself in her room. And the third day they had to break the door down to feed her!

"Afterward, Shepard would have it, he had to have a walk-in safe. And for guests like Pinchot he would get out the silverware. He had it in two gunny sacks, and he would dump the silverware and the napkin rings all over the floor. Finally he would get out the punch bowl that was badly dented from being bumped, and Shepard would give it a kick like a football. I don't know what ever became of it. It was beautiful and had never been on a dining room table! Shepard says, 'Boys, it's somethin' like my automobile, sets out in the garage there. I got a Winton automobile; fire-engine red! I bought it from an outfit in Milwaukee, I went down to Milwaukee and I learned how to drive it. We didn't have roads to drive it up to Rhinelander. Had it shipped and the freight agent one day told me it was there, so I drove it up to the house. Went in and asked my wife to go out for a ride.

"She says, 'Who wants to go out for a ride today?'

"I says, 'You might. You come out and look what I've got.'

"She come out and she looked at the automobile and she says, 'I'll never set foot in that damn thing.'

" 'So,' Shepard says, 'I drove it in the barn, and the gol damned chickens roost on it. Tires all down flat. Never went a mile!' And he says, 'It cost me five thousand dollars, too!'

"Shepard had a horse named Getaway. The horse had been owned by a man name of Gates. The horse held the world's trotting record and Gates didn't want to kill the horse. It was getting so old. Gates had moved to New York and had no place to keep the horse. Somehow or other Shepard heard about this horse named Getaway, and he wrote to Gates. Gates wrote to the bankers at Rhinelander wanting to know who Shepard was . . . asked if he was able to take care of the horse and if he has money enough so he can keep it. Till it dies. They write back and say okay.

"So Getaway was sent to Rhinelander, and Shepard would

always drive 'im at the Rhinelander Fair. Mark Bellis at Wausau was the announcer, and now is the great day, the last day of the fair, the races. Getaway is going to try and beat the track record. He misses it by about a quarter of a second or some such. And this Getaway, he loved it out there on the track; the band would be playin', and he would arch his neck. He was twenty-eight years old then, but his feet! Gad! He'd lift 'em high and look all around at the grandstand like he knew he was on exhibit.

"So on this day C. N. Johnson and I are up there at the fair. Getaway is going to make his trial mile again. This time he beats the track record by a second. They go out, Shepard with his Stetson hat and his maroon pants and loose shirt and his wide, red suspenders. What happened?

"When he got close to the gate to go out, Getaway rears up and lays down and dies.

"Well, amongst the other abilities that Shepard had was flower raisin'. He had a couple of booths there at the fair of flowers he had raised. Hollyhocks, and all kinds of flowers, snapdragons and all that. So he goes into there and he says to the lady that is in charge of the flower booth, 'I want my flowers.' And this woman — she looked like Mrs. Harding, you know, with a little black ribbon around her throat — and she says, 'You can't get your flowers. You can't have them until tomorrow.'

"Shepard says, 'As far as I'm concerned, all Oneida County fairs are finished.' So he went in, grabbed his flowers by the armful, and went and dropped 'em flower by flower on Getaway.

"So after the people came from the grandstand after Shepard had taken all his flowers and had dropped 'em, there was just a mound of flowers. He had taken away the cart and parts of the harness. Shepard stood there with his Stetson hat against his heart and the tears runnin' like rivers down his cheeks. All people saw was a mound of flowers. They didn't see old Getaway at all."

# how Old Eph Took the Whisky Cure

I was out north of Merrill one day with Harold and Lenore Rusch. As director of the McCardle Cancer Research Laboratories at the University of Wisconsin, Dr. Rusch has done a great deal to advance knowledge of the disease. Along with being a famous scientist, he has a deep love of rural Wisconsin; he was born up in the Merrill country, and he thought I might hear a yarn or so from his Uncle John Franz who had been a lumberjack. We found Uncle John, who is a mighty strong man for eighty-three, out at his place, which he developed from woodlands into a prosperous farm. He took us on a walk out through the fields and he got to talking about this old-time lumberjack named Ephraim McGuire.

"You know," said Uncle John, "They would pile the logs up awful high on the sleighs. They had iced runways so the horses could pull these great loads.

"Well, Ephraim McGuire, he was a teamster, and a good one too. He had got him a load of logs that was maybe twelve feet high and had started it down. To keep the sleighs from running over the hosses when going downhill, they scattered sand on the runways. The sand would hold the big loads back and the hosses would actually have to pull a little, even going downhill. That was all right.

"Only thing that Eph didn't know was that the boys hadn't got around to sanding the runway that day. He clumb on top of the high load of logs and started her moving. Them hosses of his was always full of hell anyhow, and maybe they was skittish that morning. Anyway he didn't notice that the runway wasn't sanded.

"Hadn't gone far, though, when he sure knew what was goin' on, and then it was too late for him to stop. The sleigh run forward onto the hosses and the hosses took off, scared as could be. Old Eph give out a loud holler, and a few of the jacks comes arunnin' to see what is the matter. You gotta remember, friend, that them old jacks was full of piss and fire when the going got rough, and they wasn't about to give it up and quit. Old Eph could have jumped for it all right and easy saved himself, but he didn't. Nope. He stayed up there on top and rode that load of logs! And it was *some* ride! The hosses let clean go. Bolted. You know, you got a sleigh loaded high with heavy logs and a steep and icy slope, it will run fast. Them hosses tried their best to keep in front. Couldn't. Old Ephraim was ahollering and aswearing. He knew what was acoming. It come!

"I expect that old Ephraim was peeing his pants, because you try standing up there on a load twelve feet high and try driving down an icy slope. You will have the same experience.

"Well, they come about half-way down the slope when something gives way. The tongue of the sleigh cracks off and Ephraim knows that Big Bell upstairs has tolled off a few for him. He gives a loud yell, for he feels the timber arisin' up under him, and then the whole load takes off into the air with old Eph aflyin' right along with it.

"Yep, it was snowin' right hard when old Eph took off for them gates of pearl, and Eph could see that St. Peter had got out a big slab of Montello red granite stone and was cutting Eph's name on it. I reckon it was granite from up Montello way, 'cause St. Peter, bein' a judge of stone, wouldn't have had no other.

"Anyhow, them logs and Eph was all mixed up when they landed. Eph give out a kind of high and mournful wail and that was the end of him. Figured the lumberjacks who seen the accident happen would now come arunnin'.' "

"What did they see when they come up to the tumble of logs?" I said.

"Well, sir, one of them jacks says, 'I guess old Eph is hurt some.'

"And another one said, 'It would seem like he is hurt some. I can't see nothin' but a hand and a foot stickin' out.'

"And that's the truth! A hand and a foot. Rest of Eph was buried in amongst them saw logs.

"Well, they uncovered Eph out of that tangle. Lumberjack can handle a thing like that with his peavie and cant hook. I expect they jolted and rolled logs on Ephraim some, but they got him out. Was like everything he had that was of bone was busted, and some things that wasn't of bone too. But old Ephraim was breathin'. He says, 'Whisky, boys! Whisky! I got me a frisky team and I need a drink to handle 'em!'

"Made the lumberjacks think of the hosses, and you know what? That team got not a scratch. Eph was busted up somethin' terrible, but that team wasn't injured. Ain't that wonderful?"

"What happened to old Eph?" I asked.

206

"Now that is somethin' interestin'. The boys got Eph into a sleigh. He was amoanin' and agroanin' something to behold! They got him into this sleigh and two of the lumberjacks was told to carry Eph to a doctor in Wausau. Wasn't a doc anywhere nearer. They was about twenty-five miles from Wausau. So they wrapped Eph up in some blankets and away they went, drivin' Eph's own team.

"Now, I'll have to tell you something about lumberjacks. They was the most kind-hearted fellers in the world. They wouldn't have done a bad thing to Eph, but where there was a saloon, lumberjacks naturally went in. And there were several saloons on the way into Wausau.

"The boys stopped at the first one, leaving Eph out in the sleigh, but they didn't forget him. They brought him out right away all the whisky he could down. And that was quite a bit, even in his condition. They stayed there for awhile, Eph lyin' in the sleigh all the time, then they set out again for Wausau. Went fine until they come to the second saloon. What happened? They stopped, of course. But they didn't forget old Eph. Brought him all the whisky he could drink; they all had a nice time. The two boys inside and Eph agettin' drunk out in the sleigh.

"Happened two more times on the way to Wausau. Took a good twenty-four hours to get there, and when they did arrive all three of them was as drunk as owls, the two lumberjacks and old Eph who was plastered and hollering and singing till hell wouldn't have him.

"And you know, even busted up like he was, Eph got well. Didn't seem to hurt him none. Took him more'n a year to recover, but he was back in the woods drivin' the same team next year. And those three fellers, Eph and the lumberjacks who hauled him to Wausau, were real buddies. Eph claimed that they had saved his life. And he meant it, too! You see, they gave Eph the whisky cure."

# The Big Contest

My partner, L. G. Sorden, who is always collecting old-time lumberjack expressions, says that quite a few of the words the lumberjacks used a lot are rather unprintable. In fact, the true lumberjack seems to have employed a colorful language that contained very few parlor words. Sorden says that one of the nicer terms was the expression for dried apples, a standard item on lumberjack tables; in the camps they called them "pregnant women."

I argue with Sorden sometimes about whether horses or oxen were the best pulling critters in the deep old timber in lumbering days. He says he expects that oxen were the steadiest.

"You ever heard the tale of the famous log-skidding contest between a team of white spotted oxen and a team of brown 'bulls?' " Sorden asks me one afternoon when we are traveling north in his car.

"Heard the famous Wisconsin ballad about the 'Little Brown Bulls,' " I reply.

"Well, the tale," Sorden says, shaking his well-fed stomach and getting ready for the tale, "as it was told to me by Harvey Becker, who was county agent in Oneida County for thirty years . . . "

"Knew him well," I say.

"Well," Sorden begins, "the yarn starts in the office of a boss lumberman named Mart Douglas in the North Woods near Rhinelander country, on the Onion River, Harvey thought . . . oh, about 1880. Mart is sitting at his desk when Bob McClusky, a Scot, comes knocking at his door.

" 'Who's there?' yells Mart.

" ' 'Tis me, Bob McClusky.'

" 'Come in, Bob. How are ye?'

" 'Fine! Fine!' roars Bob. 'And have ye the skidding contract for me, Mr. Douglas?'

" 'Well, sit down, Bob,' says Mart. 'You're the best skidder in Wisconsin, and . . . '

" 'That I am,' says Bob, 'an' me white spotted steers have no equal in all the woods. So if ye'll gi' me the contracts, I'll be signin' 'em.'

" 'Now hold on Bob,' replies Mart. 'It ain't as easy as that. You see, a Mr. Bull Gordon, skidder for a new outfit, called the Goliath Company, was in here this mornin'. Put up a convincin'

208

line of talk, he did.'

" 'Never heard o' the mon.'

" 'Bull Gordon's a Yankee, McClusky. He was askin' for our skidding contract, same as you.'

" 'Where is he?' roars Bob. 'I'll be findin' him and twistin' his ears for him. Askin' for the contract, was he?'

" 'Yes, he was, Bob. And he said he could skid more logs in a season than you can, and for the same price.'

" 'Ah,' says Bob, getting up and pawing the air, 'ain't it a known fact, Mr. Douglas, that I'm the best skidder anywheres? And ain't it known that me white spotted steers are the best?'

" 'Yes,' interrupts Mart. 'But business is business.'

" 'Then, it's no contract you'll be gi'in' me?'

" 'Now hold on,' replies Mart. 'I didn't say that. Here's what I'd like to do. I'll arrange a skidding contest between you and Bull Gordon. Are ye game, Bob?'

" 'You're but wastin' your time, Mr. Douglas. Nobody can beat Bob McClusky. But if it's a contest you're wantin', well, bring on your Bull Gordon.'

" 'Was hopin' you'd say yes,' says Mart. ' 'Twill be a mighty contest.'

" 'And what kind o' steers is this Bull Gordon usin'?' asks Bob.

" 'No steers at all, Bob,' Mart replies. *'Bulls.* He's got a team o' *little brown bulls!'*

" 'What!' hollers McClusky. 'Bulls! It's bulls he's adrivin'?'

" 'We'll see,' says Mart. 'And now, Bob, I want you to come with me. Want you to meet Bull Gordon. Guess we'll find him at the tavern.'

*Not a thing on the river McClusky did fear,*
*When he drew the stick o'er his big spotted steers.*
*They were young, quick, and sound, girting eight foot and*
*three . . .*
*Says McClusky, the Scotchman, they're the laddies for me!!*

" 'Here's Bull Gordon, McClusky,' hollers Mart, 'standin' over here at the bar!'

" 'That little feller?' scoffs McClusky. 'And he's gonna beat *me?'*

" 'Bull,' says Mart, leading McClusky over, 'want you to meet Bob McClusky. Supposed to be the best skidder in the state.'

" 'Where ye from, mon?' hollers McClusky.

" 'State o' Maine. This feller beside me's Kennebec John. My helper.'

" 'Glad to see you boys,' says Kennebec.

" 'Gordon,' McClusky says, 'what do them leetle brown bulls o' yours measure? My white spotted steers girt eight foot and three!'

" 'Well, McClusky,' says Gordon, 'my little brown bulls girt only six and nine.'

*Bull Gordon, the Yankee, on skidding was full,*
*As he cried "whoa hush" to his little brown bulls!*
*Short-legged and soggy, girt six foot and nine.*
*Says McClusky, the Scotchman, "too light for our pine!"*

" 'Bull,' cries McClusky, 'you're sure a sucker.'

" 'Better explain that, Bob,' says Bull.

" 'Why, mon, those bulls're too light for our logs!'

" 'You reckon steers are better, eh?'

" 'Why, mon, I'll skid two to one! You know the terms o' the skid? No more'n three logs to a thousand board feet o' lumber!'

*It's three to the thousand our contract did call.*
*Our hauling was good and the timber was tall.*
*McClusky he swore he'd make the day full,*
*An' skid two to one of the little brown bulls.*

" 'Want to make a little wager on your steers against my little brown bulls, Bob?' asks Bull Gordon.

" 'You're on, mon! What'll it be?'

" 'Twenty-five dollars,' says Bull.

" 'Done,' roars Bob. 'And will ye pay me now?'

*"Oh, no!" says Bull Gordon, "that you cannot do.*
*Though it's well we do know you've the pets of the crew!*
*And mark you, my boy, you would have your hands full*
*If you skid one more log than the little brown bulls!"*

" 'Now,' says Bull, 'what are the terms o' the contest, Mr. Douglas?'

" 'Here are the terms, boys,' says Mart. 'Each outfit will work the same timberland; each of you workin' about half a mile apart. Since this is virgin timber you'll be workin', you'll each have a measured distance of at least one quarter-mile to your respective skidways. You'll work one day — sunup to sunset. There'll be a referee for each one of you to see fair play. I'll furnish the scalers. They'll estimate the number of board feet of lumber in each log, and I'll furnish the judges. Winner will get a contract with my company for the season. All right?'

" 'All right wi' me,' says McClusky.

" 'And with me,' says Bull Gordon.

" 'Contest'll be one week from today.'

" 'I'll be there,' says Bob. 'And say, Bull, see this here mackinaw I'm wearin'?'

" 'Brightest mackinaw I ever see, Bob,' Bull replied.

" 'Right,' says Bob, 'an' I'm cuttin' this mackinaw up, see. I'm makin' a belt from it. A belt o' victory! Fer meself, and me white spotted steers! I'll be seein' ye, boys! Wi' your little brown bulls!'

*The day was appointed and soon it drew nigh*
*For twenty-five dollars their fortunes to try.*
*Both eager and anxious that morning were found*
*And scalers and judges appeared on the grounds!*

"Yes, sir, the day of the contest arrived, and up there in the North Woods a considerable crowd had gathered to watch the fray. 'Twas just before sunup, and Mart Douglas was giving his last-minute instructions.

" 'Folks, this here'll be a skiddin' contest between Bull Gordon, the Yankee, an' his little brown bulls, an' Bob McClusky and his white spotted steers!'

" 'My money's on McClusky,' says one big fellow.

" 'Mine, too,' says a little fellow. 'Hooray for the white spotted steers!'

" 'Hooray! Hooray!' yells everybody.

" 'Judges ready?' hollers Mart.

" 'Ready, Mart.'

" 'Scalers ready?'

" 'Ready, Mart.'

" 'Referees are ready, an' here comes Bob McClusky an' his white spotted steers!'

" 'They're the laddies for me,' hollers the big fellow. 'Three cheers for McClusky!'

" 'Hooray! Hooray! Hooray!'

*With a whoop and a yell came McClusky in view,*
*With the big spotted steers, the pets o' the crew!*
*Both chewing their cuds . . . "Oh, boys keep your jaws full!*

*You can easily beat them, the little brown bulls!"*

"Then came the bulls and Bull Gordon. 'Look at 'em!' yells the big fellow. 'Ain't no legs to 'em! No bigger'n dogs! Give me the white spotted steers!'

*Then out came Bull Gordon with a pipe in his jaw;*
*The little brown bulls with their cuds in their mouths.*
*And little we think when we see them come down,*
*That a hundred and forty could they jerk around!*

" 'Now, boys,' hollers Mart, 'you know the rules. Ready, McClusky?'

" 'Ready an' willin'!'

" 'Ready, Bull Gordon?'

" 'Ready!'

" 'The sawyers and the shanty boys are gettin' your logs down! All right! Go!'

" 'On boys! Gee boys!' cries McClusky. *We'll* fix that durned Yankee!'

*Then up spoke McClusky, come stripped to the skin!*
*We'll dig them a hole and tumble them in!*
*We'll learn the damn Yankee to face the bold Scot!*
*We'll mix them a dose and feed it red hot!*

*Says Gordon to Kennebec, with blood in his eye,*
*"Today we must conquer McClusky or die!"*
*Then up spoke bold Kennebec, "Boys, never fear!*
*For you ne'er shall be beat by the  big spotted steers!"*

*Oh, 'twas up to the logs and fasten 'em on!*
*Hurry up, boys, for it's no longer dawn!*
*The daylight is running, and if you'll take a hunch,*
*You'll hook to the logs and forget about lunch!*

*McClusky, the Scotchman, showed nothing like fear,*
*As he cried, "Whoa hush!" to the white spotted steers!*
*For it's on, boys, and gone, boys! Take hold of the snow!*
*We're hooked to the log and now let 'em go!*

*Bull Gordon he worked with a pipe in his mouth,*
*And the wind blew the smoke from the north to the south.*
*Says he to his helper, "John, I'm scared as can be*
*That those white spotted steers're too much fer me!"*

*The sun had gone down when the foreman did say,*
*"Turn out, boys, turn out! You've enough for one day!*
*We have scaled them and counted, each man to his team,*
*And it's well we do know now which one kicks the beam!"*

"So after supper was over in the camp, the crowd all gathered in the mess hall to hear the results. Bob McClusky had slicked all up and came carrying that belt o' victory he'd made from his jacket.

*After supper was over McClusky appeared*
*With the belt readymade for the big spotted steers.*
*To form it he'd torn up his best mackinaw,*
*He was bound he'd conduct it according to law!*

" 'Well, Mr. Douglas,' roars Bob, 'here I be! Here's me belt o' victory. Gi' it to me when you'll be announcin' I've won the contest. And if ye have the contract I'll be signin' it now. Save some time!'

" 'Hold on, Bob,' says Mart. 'Here comes Bull Gordon, an' we must consider him, too. How do you feel, Bull?'

" 'Fine,' says Bull. 'But I fear me an' my little brown bulls have lost the contest.'

" 'So ye have,' roars McClusky. 'And I'm rememberin' our leetle wager. Twenty-five dollars. Hand it over!'

" 'Gentlemen,' hollers Mart Douglas. 'I'm announcin' the winner o' the skidding contest! The winner, an' the new champ, Bull Gordon!'

" 'Hear! Hear!' yelps McClusky. 'What do ye mean, mon? Me'n my white spotted steers musta skidded one hundred and eight. Maybe more! Mon, nothin'll be beatin' that!'

" 'McClusky,' laughs Bull Gordon, 'if you only skidded a hundred and eight, you only put in a half-day's work! Me'n my bulls musta skidded one hundred fifty. Maybe more!'

" 'Gi' me the count,' bawls McClusky. 'I been robbed! Cheated! Bull Gordon, I'll be breakin' ye in half! Nobody can beat McClusky an' his white spotted steers!'

" 'The count,' says Mart, 'was McClusky: one hundred an' ten. Bull Gordon: one hundred and forty!'*

*Then up spoke the scaler, "Hold on, you awhile!*
*The big spotted steers are behind just one mile!*
*For you have a hundred and ten and no more,*

---

*This refers to the number of logs skidded by each.

*And Gordon has beat you by ten and a score!"*

" 'Three cheers for Bull Gordon,' cries Mart.

" 'Hooray! Hooray! Hooray!' says the crowd.

" 'Well,' says Bob McClusky, 'I canna understand it. But here is your twenty-five dollars, Bull. And lots o' luck may ye have wi' it!'

" 'Thanks, Bob,' says Bull. 'I'll be needin' that twenty-five dollars to marry my gal Suzy.'

" 'Best o' luck to ye then,' says Bob, 'an' to your future missus. An' here! Here's me belt o' victory! Hang it on the little brown bulls! I strike me colors!'

*The shanty did ring and McClusky did swear.*
*He tore out by handfuls his long yellow hair.*
*Says he to Bull Gordon, "My colors I'll pull,*
*So here, take the belt for the little brown bulls!"*

" 'All right, boys,' yells Mart. 'And now we'll have a little celebration!' "

*Here's health to Bull Gordon and Kennebec John,*
*The biggest day's work on the river they done.*
*So fill up your glasses and fill 'em up full,*
*We'll drink to the health of the little brown bulls!*

# Ruth

Coming west on Highway 8 from the junction with 51 above Tomahawk, you quite possibly could be through and away from Tripoli before realizing that anything had happened. There is so little to notice: a tiny red post office, a deserted store with "Stolle" in faded black letters, a filling station, a store-tavern, a strange-looking school building. Not very much. Yet if you are going slowly you may notice some of the names on signs or mailboxes, Finnish names, mostly, here and there a German or Irish name.

Two things are unforgettable after a visit to Tripoli. One is the gay and optimistic spirit of a remarkable woman named Ruth Stolle. The other thing is the undeniable stamp that the residents of Finnish descent have left upon Tripoli and those small and generally visually unimpressive places west: Brantwood and Prentice.

I have known Ruth Stolle for many years. We have exchanged numerous letters, hers always encouraging, perceptive, and philosophic. She is a teacher, trained for teaching only at the normal school at Merrill, but extensive higher education for her, and for the few others like her, is incidental. She and they were somehow born educated, or at least they were endowed with a sensitive understanding so profound that everyone they touch is inevitably changed. It is certainly that way with the youth (many now grown and middle aged) whom Ruth has taught. Her spark changed their lives, and they took fire in turn and burned with a love of art, of nature, of people, of knowledge.

I headed for Ruth's small house at Tripoli and, snow being piled around the front porch and doorway, went to the back door, which I found cleared and hospitably standing ajar. I found Ruth improved. Some years ago she was stricken with the rare disease myasthenia gravis; for a while she could only sit in a wheel chair, but this morning, miraculously it seems to me, she is standing in the kitchen, waiting to escort me into her living room. She has spread a magnificent mid-morning breakfast of Finnish pulla, cheese, ham, cherry pie, country butter, rolls, and coffee on the kitchen table. And, she tells me, two ladies are coming, Finnish ladies who can tell me about the Finns hereabouts . . . at Clifford, Brantwood, Prentice, and Tripoli. Good!

With cups of coffee we talk, and Ruth tells me how she

came to live at Tripoli, a crossroads, when (I say) she might certainly have had any career anyplace she wanted to go.

"When we came here the mill was Dad Stolle's. The Finns were here then, and they were great woodworkers. They worked in the woods and sold their logs to the Stolle Lumber Company. I was educated at a little teachers' college in Merrill, but education doesn't stop after a little while on a campus."

"Not for you," I said.

The two Finnish ladies now arrive: Mrs. Paul Lyytinen and Mrs. Waino Komula. If I expected to see any vestiges of an Old Country peasant flavor, I certainly did not find it in them. They had the forthrightness and honesty of many Finns I have known, but in dress they could have been directly from a Fifth Avenue shop. They were both second-generation Finns, though, whose parents had arrived in late nineteenth century and were among those who carved homes out of a timber wilderness. They told me how the Finns who came to settle in this part of Wisconsin were swayed by ads in the Old Country newspapers: "When a man steps into the grass around Brantwood," the ads read, "the hat on top of his head may be only faintly seen. The lands of Brantwood are better than the gold fields of the Klondike."

And of course the prospect of actually owning such land carried a mighty appeal. Most immigrants had not owned any land in the Old Country. No doubt the lure of "my own piece of earth" explains why so many Finns were happy to get forty or eighty acres and toil on it day and night to clear the forest and brush.

Actually, the ladies said, the farm lands around Brantwood and Prentice were not that good. In the few years after the forest humus was used up, the grass didn't grow tall at all. Still, it was land as good or better than at home in Finland where, it was said, God had been very good to the Finns. He had taken a big sack and had put all the evil things of the world into it and these He distributed to every country except Finland. To the Finns he left the rocks!

Because the fields in Finland are small, the settlers to America had never known big-scale farming, and they had very little to start with except the land itself. Often the twenty dollars scraped together for a ticket on one of the emigrant steamers leaving from the southwestern Finland port of Hanko was all they had. The black bread and sausages they took for the voyage were gone when they got to America.

Some came directly to Brantwood, to take immediate advantage of the lush earth and wealth promised in the papers. Others first stopped off in Pennsylvania or Ohio to work in mills and mines for American dollars or, perhaps, to pay back the twenty-dollar loan for their ticket.

When the first settlers came to Brantwood, the big logging boom was still on. Those who were able to purchase timberland were the fortunate ones, for they could sell the timber to the mills.

Those who settled permanently on farms found it tough going, and, as elsewhere, they were prey to unscrupulous merchants who demanded very high prices for poor goods. Finland, of course, was even then a leader in the cooperative idea, and many discussions over coffee led to talk of a Finnish coop at Brantwood. At one meeting, held at the home of Jacob Suomu early in 1906, the Finns present decided to write to Finland for advice on how to establish a cooperative business.

Victor Wironen, a young man who had attended high school at Prentice was asked to send out a hundred postcards announcing the organization of a coop store. Sixty-one Finns came.

The Finns needed an official charter, but they found attorney fees too high; their combined assets totaled only three hundred dollars. They wrote to a man they thought could help them, Robert M. La Follette, Sr., who immediately replied that he could put them into business with an official state charter for twenty-five dollars, including the filing fee!

They sold forest products, butter, and cream. They sold groceries. In a couple of years the coop made enough money to have its own building and the Brantwood Coop is in operation today.

I was extremely interested, too, to know what traditions and customs the Finns had brought with them to northern Wisconsin. Although they were extremely busy, and perhaps many or most of the folk customs had dropped away, on Midsummer's Eve and Day the northern Wisconsin Finns remembered the homeland.

During Midsummer Night the cattle were put into the barn, the door shut, and an ax driven into the wall beside the door to thwart bad spirits.

On Midsummer Day the Wisconsin Finns had red whey

cheese. It is a cheese the Finns remembered from Karelia, Eastern Finland, since World War II a part of the Soviet Union. The milk is warmed slightly, then curdled. The curds are put in a greased pot and baked in an oven until reddish-brown — a delicious cheese.

For the settler lad and lassie, freckles were disposed of on Midsummer Night by washing the freckles in Midsummer dew; and if Midsummer dew could be collected and placed in bottles, it was a strong medicine that would cure many things.

If a girl wanted a boy to fall in love with her, she would run through the fields of his family on Midsummer Night. When the boy's family made bread of this grain, the boy would begin to yearn for the girl. Apparently many a happy marriage resulted.

A few times a decorated pole was set up on Midsummer's Eve. Vines and flowers from the fields were made into wreaths. The girls' head scarves were used as flags. In the morning there would be gay dancing around the pole.

During Midsummer Night the girls would go to the woodpile, grab an armload of wood, and let it fly out of their arms. On Midsummer morning they would go out to see whether there had been an even or odd number of pieces of wood. An even number meant they would surely be married soon, but an odd number meant they would have to wait at least until next Midsummer.

Nearly all the Finn families had a sauna, and the sauna on Midsummer's Eve was a must. After the sauna seven different colors of flowers were tied together with seven different shades of yarn and placed under one's pillow. What he dreamed would indeed come true, but if one said a word aloud after the sauna his dream would never come true.

Out of such simple customs perhaps, came the salvation of the Wisconsin settlers, for there was joy and simple mystery in them. The Finnish folk customs are much related to the seasons and to saints' days of the calendar; doubtless the northern Wisconsin Finns kept the lore of those days alive as much as they could. It was the often desperate reality of daily life, though, and the dreams of the young people, so difficult to realize, that occupied the time. The Finns still talk with nostalgic awe of the courage required of parents and sons and daughters in those hard, early days.

Mrs. Komula told me how hard it was . . .

"My parents came to Brantwood in 1910. We came on account of my father's sickness. He had, like so many other Finns, stopped off in Pennsylvania on the way west, to work in a big grindstone factory. They made axes, at Glasport, Pennsylvania. He got silicosis. My uncle was living at Brantwood then, and he says, 'You got to get in the wide open spaces, so come to Wisconsin.'

"My father was so sick when he came that in Abbotsford they had to get off the train and put him in a hotel, because they were afraid he was going to die on the train. But my father didn't die. He got to Brantwood in June, and right away, in two weeks, he began picking up. He felt so good he bought this land, forty acres. They had to cut down trees and build a house. My father built one of the first frame houses.

"I remember getting off the train in Prentice. They had a big surrey with fringe on the top, and we rode in that. Oh, how I hated to come there because it was wilderness! I wasn't satisfied living here until I went back to Pennsylvania, to Glasport in 1926; when I saw how dirty it was, from then on I have really loved the clean air of Wisconsin! I was only nine years old when I first came.

"My father lived here only four years, then he died. My mother was a dressmaker in Finland, and she used to make all the wedding clothes for the people who got married. That's how she made a living for us. There was three of us older children . . . I was next to the oldest . . . must have been 1912 or '13 when my grandmother came to live with us, and she says to my mother, 'Oh, if Vianna had of only been a boy, you would of gotten along just fine!' I was twelve years old.

"And you know that hurt me so terribly. My uncle and my aunt, they had a little nine-month-old child, and my aunt was a cook at the lumber camp. Very busy. You know how the lumberjacks ate in those days! So at my father's funeral I went to my aunt and says, 'Can I come and work for you? Take care of the baby?' She says, 'Sure.'

"She gave me fifty cents a month. And the first month's pay I brought it home and stuck it on the table and says 'Now, aren't you happy I'm a girl instead of a boy?'

"Well, I wanted to go to high school the worst way. My sister was going to high school. She had two years. Then the Brantwood area was divided into two parts, one for this Tripoli High School and the other for Brantwood. And the side that we were on, it had no connection with the high school yet. And there was in those days a kind of bus service . . . "

(Ruth Stolle broke in here and said that John Stuart Curry, the first artist-in-residence at the University of Wisconsin, had a painting of one of those old covered-wagon school buses.)

"So they said I would have to pay ten cents a day if I came on the bus. There was no way of going back and forth unless I paid that ten cents; so I inquired if I could stay someplace and work for my board and room.

"I went from one place after another asking, and Stolles they always kept girls."

("Vianna was the cleanest girl in high school," cried Ruth. "She was always cleaning her clothes. One of the girls, Lea, was a kind of different type. She was Irish. I remember Lea going to a dance. She had a hole in the heel of her stocking and she put a safety pin in it. Vianna would have sat down and mended that, I tell you.")

"Then Mr. Stolle told me I could work at the mill office. I don't know whether they really needed me, but I could stay with them anyway. And finally, when one of the other girls left, I became the maid over there. I got up at 4:30 and fixed breakfast, and took care of the milk, separated, washed the milk pails, and I got a whole dollar a week! I would work from 5:30 to 8:30 A.M., and then from 4:00 to 8:00 P.M. Then I would study. That's the way I went to school. And Clarence Stolle, Ruth's husband, he was the first graduate from Tripoli High School!

"I loved school! And I graduated in 1918. I was sixteen.

"Somebody I was visiting one day said they thought I would make a good nurse. I had a chance to go to Chicago to a big hospital there, but I was afraid to go on the train alone. You know, changing trains? And I found out that the railroad went straight from Brantwood to Minneapolis. I wouldn't have to change trains or anything. So I decided to go to a hospital in Minneapolis. They took me, and I finished my nursing training in 1923.

"But I was so homesick, I suppose for the Finns and the land around here, and I came back. There was a hospital at Park Falls just for lumberjacks; the town people wouldn't go near the place. And I went to work there. I cleaned it, got an operating room fixed up and clean, and made it so nice that the Park Falls folks began to come. We had babies there, and I moved all the old men, the old who had no place to go, upstairs. It was a terrible place, but I made it real homey. I fixed up good beds for these old men. They had a good time."

Mrs. Komula's remarkable story included accounts of nursing in many places, but she returned to Brantwood in 1928 and met her husband. They settled down at Brantwood about the time that a number of the Finns were going to Russia. About thirty families were Communists, certain that Russia was the land of golden opportunity.

Mrs. Lyttinen took up the tale then:

"It was depression time. Farmers weren't making too much. Russia was the golden emblem for many. The Finns who believed it thought that if they brought their money and their energy to Russia they could help start the new nation. Our neighbors, the Ahos and the Nurmi girls and Riihimaki ... others too. These people who left at that time weren't so poor that they had to go. It was the ideal. When Pojhonen, one of our neighbors left — he stayed the last night with us — we told him 'If it is such a glorious place, if life is so good, let us know. But if it isn't, don't glamourize it, but tell the truth.' And he said, 'All right. If it's like I think it is you'll hear from me. But if it's like you think it is, you won't hear a word.'

"He wrote only one letter. He sent my husband five cigars. Havana cigars. All he said was, 'We have them here, too!' He didn't say a word about how things were, though. It was the first and the last letter we got from him. I think he expected to have more there than he did here. He expected too much here. But I truly believe that all of the Finns who went would have returned if they had had the opportunity. Some did come back, indeed. They had kept money in America, thinking they might not like it over there. Many, though, who could not guarantee their livelihood here, could never return.

"When Riihimaki went he was so enthused about going that he said they would never return. They said they would throw their passports in the Atlantic Ocean. They must have had money in the bank, though, because it wasn't long before the two boys came back. The old folks escaped from there. And they say when Riihimaki got back he went to the Duluth radio station and he told everything. He was the only one that really come out and said things. But there were others who returned who could not say anything. They had relatives in Russia."

"When the Nurmi girls came back," Ruth said, "they came

over to visit with me. And they said 'Oh, Mrs. Stolle, it's heaven over in Russia.' And I said, 'Well, down through the ages, I've never known a perfect commune. There's always human nature involved.' They tried to talk me into it, that this was perfection. Democracy was a big flop, and they went on and on! Oh, they were well versed. When they left again for Russia I never heard from them. They never came back.

"But you know, that stuck in my craw! I couldn't take it. If democracy really functioned, then, somehow or other, I should have gotten that across to them. I should have made them see that ours is an individualistic state where you have individualistic rights. It bothered me so that when the principal of Tripoli High School asked me to come up and straighten out these high school kids that were getting so rambunctious, I thought, well, here's my link in. I can go back there and say democracy *does* function. But it has to be a sharing thing. So instead of taking a salary, when he says, 'How much do you want, Ruth?' I said, 'Nothing. We'll see if it works.'

"So five years I taught without salary up here. I tried to show the kids how creativity is allowed free reign in America, and how it isn't given much freedom in Russia. I made them work very hard, challenged them every moment. That's what got to them, I think. I was tough, but they knew I loved them. I suppose I am an artist, but I didn't have any academic credits in art. It worried me because I wondered whether I was giving the kids as much as I ought to be. So I went to Aaron Bohrod, the artist-in-residence at the university, and I asked him. He said, 'Ruth, you are doing the greatest job anybody could be doing for these young people. You are opening the doors of the world to them. I wish every teacher had your kind of education.' So I went ahead. It was unorthodox, but everybody accepted it.

"And then I showed them something else. I needed some money up here. You know, small country high schools don't have much money for the arts. A good, stable old Finn farmer thinks art is for the birds . . .yes, and a few Deutsches farmers, too. Anyway I made a contact with Arthur Lougee, then art editor of all the Ford publications. I told him, 'Now, more Fords are sold in our area than any other car. This is a rural community and a rural high school.' I said, 'I know you hire professional artists, Paul Sample, Rexford Brandt, what do you do with their work when it's done?' He said, 'It's stacked up in the archives of our editorial setup.' And I said, 'Why don't you put the pictures out on loan to rural high schools? You're selling cars to rural people, now here's a chance to give the children a rare experience. They never get to see a gallery.'

"'Well,'' Lougee says, 'I am going to Europe this next month, and when I come back I want you to take your high school students and illustrate *This Is Our Town.*'

"We did, and he published the article in the *Ford Times* and he gave me four hundred dollars for it. I took the money and bought brushes, paints, and stuff that the high school couldn't afford. And I saved enough to take the kids down to Madison to see an exhibit in the Memorial Union. We stayed in the Farm Dorms down there.

"Well, that stuck in Vic's craw — he's the administrator. He said 'We need the money for basketball suits. Why don't you give us the four hundred dollars for that?' And I said, 'Because that's all you got in your head! Basketball!' And I said, 'You talk to me about sportsmanship and all that. The lousiest sport you got in the community is the basketball coach!' One day I had this exhibit all ready to send to *Ford Times*, and it was a very good exhibit. The youngsters around here are really talented if you give 'em a chance! I wanted to show the exhibit to the Tripoli High School students. Our art room was right off those smelly toilets, remember? Nobody much went in there except the art kids . . . they had to love their work!

"I called my students and I said, 'I want each one of you' — they were mostly boys — 'I want you to hold these works up; go the main room and we'll exhibit them. And you can tell them why you made these and about our town, and all about it.'

"They said, 'Do we have to, Mrs. Stolle?' And I says, 'What do you mean, you have to?'

"And they says, 'The basketball boys call us sissies, because we're in the art group. "Where's your beret?" they yell at us.'

"My Irish caught fire! By the time we hit the top step to the main room I was ready! I blasted off at those kids, which was unfair, particularly young Saarkinen. He was the captain of the basketball team. I said, 'So! You're cocky!' And I told them about Leonardo da Vinci, who did feats of strength and about Michaelangelo who hung by his heels to paint the Sistine Chapel. I even dragged in Sibelius . . . ! 'If you're looking for he-men,' I said, 'try to match these, any fifty of you!'

"Well, two weeks later the check came from Lougee for

four hundred dollars and I came along the hall and young Saarkinen said, 'Where'd you get that money, Mrs. Stolle?'

"And I says, 'This is a capitalist state, and this is a capitalist company, but they care enough about us here in Tripoli to give us four hundred dollars.'

"Then Lougee, that's the Ford editor, says, 'When you come over to Ft. Dearborn, you come to see me. I want to meet you.' By then he had built that Ford Rotunda at the World's fair, and the only student work housed in that rotunda was the kids from Tripoli, Wisconsin."

"All right," I said to Ruth, "what's the follow-through? What's the result of all this fight between democracy and communism that tore this community apart? And what's the result of Ruth Stolle and her work here?"

"Well," said Ruth, "I don't know a Finn farmer that doesn't insist now that his kids get art in school!"

# Archie

The Adams County Courthouse stands on a little knoll in the small town of Friendship, so named by settlers from Friendship, New York. Frankly, Friendship folks are lucky that the courthouse is located there. It almost wasn't. Back in the early years of the twentieth century, the Chicago & North Western Railway was being built through Adams, just a mile south of Friendship. The Adams folks had big ideas. Their town was going to be one of the greatest in the north, maybe a million citizens, eventually. Naturally, the county seat ought to be moved to Adams from Friendship, which wouldn't ever amount to anything anyhow. Once Adams had been called South Friendship, because Friendship was the older place, but the citizens of Adams appealed to the railroad and got the name changed to Adams, "because it was short."

I like Adams-Friendship, or Friendship-Adams, very much. Rarely have I met more outgoing and genuine people. We worked hard at my Department at the university, with the Friendship citizens, to try to get "some culture" going in their town, and, thanks to some sturdy workers, succeeded. Even the restaurant keepers are interested in art in Friendship; Mary Grignano, who owns the Friendship Cafe, displays many original paintings and drawings on the restaurant walls.

Adams-Friendship folks want their kids to have the breaks, same as in New York City. Some time back Harold Le Jeune, the young and imaginative "resource agent" of Adams County, told me that the county woods were just full of fine violinists. I never inquired how they came to be there, but Harold said there were enough musicians of concert quality living out in the bush to man a fine symphony orchestra. His idea was to get these fine players together and invite Leonard Bernstein to come out to Friendship and conduct a great concert.

Mr. Bernstein was actually contacted, without our having had any face-to-face meeting with the bush-country orchestra. Perhaps Mr. Bernstein had some doubt about the range of talent available, for he gracefully declined. But the desire to have the best characterizes the people up in Adams County. Shirley Temelis, who with her husband used to skate professionally in the Sonja Henie ice shows, decided the young folks in Adams-Friendship really ought to know how to skate and how to perform. Singlehandedly she taught about one hundred kids to do spectacular things on ice. They now put on a ballet every winter that local folks, at least, feel would shame the old Henie shows right off the ice!

Liking Friendship so much, I was very interested to know just how the New York State folks got up in there originally.

Harold, who knows everything and everybody in Adams County, asked Archie Crothers if he would come up from his home at Big Spring down in the south end of the county and visit with me. Archie was, of course, delighted, and we met in Harold's office in the basement of the Adams County courthouse.

Archie is eighty-two. His thin white hair is combed straight back, very neat, and his face is angular and weathered. On his nose, a little prominent, are old fashioned gold-rimmed spectacles. He is very erect, full of pride and information and happy to share it.

He sits down across from Harold's desk, while I occupy the boss's chair. I don't need to do any pump priming. Archie is off to the races! Before I know it he is telling me about the early arrivals at Big Spring.

"You see," said Archie, "it was very interesting the way folks got into this part of the state. My folks came up here to Adams County from Jefferson County, not far from the city of Jefferson, now. Some of them were from New York State and some from the state of Maine. So they came first to Jefferson County and lived there for some little time. The federal government at that time didn't have money to give away to everybody, like they do now. But the government thought they did have unlimited land, all the way from here to the Pacific Ocean. So when they wanted to be good to somebody for any reason, they usually gave him a land grant.

"It so happened that this area in here between the Wisconsin and the Fox rivers was taken over by the government from the Indians some time immediately after the Black Hawk War about 1836. It was a piece of land that probably wasn't considered very valuable because you could go over the first hill and maybe find another patch of land — wasn't flat and good for big farming. There was an army officer who left a widow at Mineral Point, and the government thought they owed that man something, so they gave the widow a grant of this land around here. Don't know how much. In order to get title to their land, my folks and the other settlers from New York State had to go eventually to Mineral Point to get her to sign them their title. Guess this must have been about 1846.

"Well, the York people settled at Big Spring, down in the south part of the county. Among them was a family by the name of Landt. Some of their descendants still live in Wisconsin Dells. Well, some of those folks were from Friendship, New York, and I guess they was the ones that gave Friendship, Wisconsin the name 'Friendship.'

"There is a story about how they came to leave Jefferson County and come here to Adams. You know, in those days there were no places to keep the insane, or anything of that kind. Now these Landts had more worldly goods than their neighbors. Among other things, they had a house built out of sawed lumber, boards . . . probably boarded up and down, with battens over the cracks. They had a little furniture, too, manufactured furniture. Not homemade. And then they had a cast-iron cookstove, which was rare.

"And they were educated people. Smart people. Real intelligent. The whole outfit of 'em, far as that was concerned. And across the field from there, possibly half a mile, there was another farm, and living there was a man that had 'crazy spells.' Certain days he would have those berserk spells come on. They built a jail for him out of logs, and when he felt a spell comin' on he would tell them and they would lock him in for about twenty-four hours and it would pass over. He was a good worker, and in every other way he was all right.

"They had a school and the teacher boarded with these Landts. So happened that on a Saturday Mr. and Mrs. Landt were going to town, and these neighbors that the crazy man lived with thought they would like to go along. The two couples started off to town, leaving this man who had the spells at home. They didn't think there was any reason why he would have a bad spell or anything . . . wasn't time for one anyway. So he was at large and working, and it happened that this teacher who was boarding with Landts was around home that day. She could look after the children. They had a little orphan boy, too, that stayed with 'em. And he was small. Undersized. Landts had taken him in when his folks died. Made a home for him.

"Well, along some time during the day this teacher looked out the window — they had a real glass window, too — and saw this crazy man comin' with an ax over his shoulder. She knew that it meant trouble. She wondered what to do. There was no place to go. All open around there. No place to hide. She had those children. Kinda on the spot. Well, there was a closet built into the corner of the house, somewhere, made of twelve-inch boards. The teacher herded these children all into that closet, barricaded the door in the inside, and thought that was her best chance. Well, the man came in and he wrecked everything in the place, including the cast-iron cookstove. He busted that to little bits with his ax and he wrecked the Landts' furniture, just chopped it all up to kindlin' wood. But the teacher, she managed some way to get a board loose at the bottom and pry it off far enough so she could push this little orphan child out, and she sent him after help.

"Well, that little fellow run as fast as he could to a neighbor's quite some distance away, and they come. Got there just as the crazy man was choppin' down the closet.

"And you know, that whole deal so discouraged the Landts that they wanted to get out of Jefferson County. Wanted to leave if they could find a place to go. Just at that time they heard about his Indian land up here — this side of Fort Winnebago at Portage. My grandfather and another man by name of Dick Roach walked up here in the month of June, about 1845 or '46, and Grandfather told me that Big Springs was the prettiest country he ever seen. Big Springs was the place! And you know, that spring bubbles out right to this day. It is right beside County Road G where there is a little bend in the road. Can see it from the road. The whole country is full of springs.

"Anyhow, this grandfather of mine and this man Roach come up in there. My grandfather told me the flats looked like one vast orchard . . . white oaks, and the June grass, he said, was right up to their knees when they walked up through there. Hay as far as the eye could reach! Beautiful! And under the oak trees great numbers of deer feeding, other kinds of wild things too, of course. Turned out, after they got there, land was stony. Rocky. I handled thousands of cords of rock myself. Getting now so it's pretty decent, but them days it was awful. They didn't know it was rocky because of the grass! Saw some stone around the springs, but they were used to some stone back east. Wasn't as bad as what they were accustomed to. Turned out this country was full of hardheads. Glaciated area, you see.

"So they walked in there and went back with such a rosy report that most all of those people sold their claims down in Jefferson County and moved up here, fast as they could.

"This land hadn't been surveyed then, and folks were coming in from every side. Hundreds of 'em. All squatters. In order to hold the piece of land that he wanted, Mr. Landt made arrangements with an Indian chief named Pretty Man. I knew him. Tall, fine looking. I knew him when he was a very elderly man. Was Winnebago. Was a good Indian. Well, the settlers made a deal with Pretty Man that there would be friendship among them for all time. And do you know, to this day, the Winnebago Indians know I am descended from those early folks, and we have wonderful relations. They can come to my place any time for anything they need, and I can go to them. They come to my place right today for Big Spring water. They will only drink the water from that spring. They say it is the only water that has been blessed by the Great Spirit. Haul it all the time. Won't touch the water over to the Dells if they can help it!

"I like the Indians. I been a member of the school board for years over at the Dells and other places, and we had less trouble with the Indian kids than the whites. You know, there was a certain kind of white man called renegades in the olden days, because they were exploiting the Indians. That's the reason the Indians learned to scalp people. White Eagle, who lives over by me, over on the hill by Big Spring, tells me that some of those traders, reprobate people that came in advance of civilization, actually paid so much a scalp for certain kinds of scalps . . . white men and Indians they didn't like or something. Just pay 'em so much a scalp like a bounty on gophers!

"White Eagle claims that that's where the Indians learned to scalp people . . . white man is to blame for it. 'Course, the Winnebago Indian, by and large, not all of course, is improvident. He sees no reason to provide for next week. Never did. Never had to. This whole area lent itself to the Indian way of life in a superb manner. These streams were all full of fish and the woods full of game. All they had to do was go get some sticks or cut down a tree and they had a fire. Deer skins covered their lodges. Everything was here. All they had to do was step outside and take it. Any day. So for generation after generation that's the way they did it. Didn't provide any space to store up anything. Western Indians made dried meat, pemmican. These Indians, to best of my knowledge, didn't do that. To this day, my neighbor White Eagle, he's one of the most resourceful people you ever seen in your whole life. Many Indians are. They can do anything. This man's skillful. Right now, after this heavy snow, there's some dead timber on his place, but it's uphill from the house, and when this bad weather struck, how was he gonna get wood? He had a truck, but you couldn't get a truck up into that woods at all.

"So he took a big sheet of steel roofing and made a toboggan. He takes it up on top of that hill, loads it with a cord of wood, and lets her go. Slides right down to his house!

"White Eagle isn't a chief. We don't call him chief. Most of the Indians gotta be chief. Not him.

"Indians, the Winnebago, work at the Dells in the summer. Indian ceremonial. Winter, they get along as they always did. Best they can. If they have any money they get an old car and do a lot of driving. Darnedest people to move around!

"We don't know who made those Indian mounds over around Jordan Lake and Parker Lake and all through that area. I seen lots of those mounds. Got a trace of a mound on my farm yet. I didn't recognize the darn thing. It was a long shaped mound. Reptile or something like that. The mounds, you know, boys, headed toward the northwest, just like the early wagon roads that came into this country. Know why? Because the ridges run to the northwest. Land drains into the Fox River. Early roads, all on them ridges. And such trouble we had getting the modern roads straightened out! All followed the old settler roads. And the Indian mounds always point toward the setting sun on the longest day of the year. Ain't that curious? Every one of 'em I ever seen in this area does.

"An immense white oak tree grew on top of that mound on my place. Biggest tree seen around here. How old? Who knows. Bet it was several hundred years old, and growing on top of this mound. Makes those mounds pretty old. I and another man sawed that tree down.

"Right down below Germantown — a big rocky gorge runs through there — was where the Indians crossed the Wisconsin River. They stole a baby down in our end of the county once, years ago. Lots of blueberries in there. Folks had this baby asleep near some wagons they had in the woods. Indians come through there, Chippewas, I reckon. Like boy babies. Took him along.

"Folks come back and found baby gone. Was some scene of worry and sorrow. Figured, I guess, that the Indians had took him. So they put a man on a horse and sent him to Big Springs to see Chief Pretty Man. Rider was one of my father's brothers.

He had a faster horse than most of 'em, so they sent him after the Indians. Pretty Man told my uncle, 'Chippewa in here on visit.' Says, 'They will cross the river at Germantown and you better head 'em off before they get there. 'Crost the river, they'll be long gone.'

"Well, my father's brother took off after the Chippewa, and he headed 'em off. Told 'em that they better give him the boy, because Pretty Man and his Winnebago Indians and the white people would come and kill all the Chippewa if they didn't give the baby back. He got the baby, brought him back.

"I heard that yarn when I was a kid, and here back a few years or so ago — might have been longer, was still using horses — I was cultivating one day out in the north field when I seen a man coming up through the corn. Stopped. Come up to me and says, 'Your name's Crothers?' I says, 'Yep.' He says, 'Well, my name's Landt.' He says, 'I am Warren Landt.' We all called him Warry. He's got a son buried down to Big Springs.

"He was a geologist and miner from Idaho and he had come back to the old stompin' ground, come to see me. Told me, out there in the corn, this story of the kidnappin'. And he was the boy! The baby.

"The folks down around Big Spring have changed greatly today, of course. Was an awful lot of strength and resourcefulness in them early days. 'Course, we're modernized now. We still have plenty of good people in there, though. Unfortunately, at the moment the dairy farming is being squeezed out. That was the thing that provided the best part of the economy for the past fifty years.

"You know that the consumer is getting very fussy. We're overly regulated. I question whether any man can live a week in Wisconsin without breakin' a law, at the present time. We have plenty of regulation on this milk. Makes it mighty expensive to produce. Have to have a lot of things, particular kinds of milk houses and such. I question, if I was a young man, if I would try it. We're not on Grade A, because of the cost. A man come and told me 'You ought to be on Grade A.' He enumerated all the things would have to be done. I was looking over his shoulder. He figured $7,000 and something. Was too much. My boy's milkin', though.

"In the early 1860s every farm had a hopyard. That went belly up. Is an old hop building on my own farm.

"Big Springs is just a wide spot in the road now. Was a big

center in the old days. I can still find traces of the old ox trail from Fort Winnebago north. All the settlers come that way. I can show you traces of the old ox roads right on my farm.

"But if you will come down to Big Springs, you will see what wonderful works some of the early settlers left. There is a Congregational church down there, still standing. Has an unusually high steeple! Very tall. The building itself is sturdy looking. I often wondered how that old church stood against the hard winds that blow through there. I have gone by it in storms years ago, drivin' a team, when I would have swore the old thing would go over. But it never did. And a few years ago it fell to my lot to go up into the old church and do some repair work, put a new railing around. I found out why it was so sturdy. I found out why she stood all these years! The wonderful joining of those timbers! The ship couplings they put in the timber — wonderful work. I found that my wife's grandfather, a stonemason from Maine, built the foundation. His two brothers did the carpenter work. And they were ships carpenters from Maine, also. No wonder the thing stands. Now if they build something down there, come a heavy snow, have to get help to hold it up! Old church is at the crossroads! Looks like Congregational churches world over! New England!

"Those people who come in there were accustomed to small streams and power sites. So when they came to Big Spring they said, 'Ah, here we have three power sites, chance for small factories.' And they came in and built all kinds of things at the start. Folks named Clough. Original patriarch come over on the *Mayflower*.

"Well, boys, some interesting things have took place in Adams County. The railroad. Now that was a big event here. In 1912 the Chicago, North Western was finished. Farmers all around from here, my section too, hired out to do it. Had mules from Missouri, too. Great big mules. They used to haul freight from old Kilbourn . . . Wisconsin Dells, now. I see them down there with a whole yard full of them freight wagons, four big mules to a wagon. Interesting to me. Didn't know how they hooked 'em in at all. Would go there, and the four mules would stand with their four tails as far from the wagon as they could get 'em. The driver would take a chain tug down and beat that mule over the ribs and make him get in there. Way they did it. Every one of 'em. All the same. From Missouri. And they were Missouri mule skinners, too. Was quite a boom on here at that time. Big thing, and that's when the courthouse was almost moved to Adams from Friendship.

"One day some folks from Friendship come down to see my father. He was quite a man. Lots of force. Says, 'Jim, if somethin' ain't done to stop it, Friendship is gonna lose the county seat.' 'That so?' he says. 'Yes, they're trying to pull it away both ways.'

"So my father took a team and went up the east side of the county; golly, some way he convinced folks that that courthouse ought to stay here at Friendship. Adams folks wanted it right down by the railroad track. He told them, 'You don't want the courthouse any closer to the railroad! Now that nice little knoll up there in Friendship is the place for it.' It was. 'Course if a railroad came through you wanted to be almost in the railroad yards with everything. Even churches! Can't blame the Adams folks none.

"Well, we had the Irish, mostly down toward the Dells. They come in to help build the Milwaukee Road in the 1860s. Wonderful people. Sixty families come. Most stayed. And the Norwegians! Fun loving. But once in a while a fellow would turn the tables!

"When the first farm telephone cooperative was being organized; everybody chipped in. One evening a meeting was held at the old Badger schoolhouse. That's right down on the county line. Meetin' was for the purpose of hearing the merits of the telephone on the farm. Number of old fellers who had never seen a telephone come to hear the discussion. A speaker told 'em all about the joys of Mr. Bell's invention and told 'em that through the telephone you could talk to a neighbor even though the neighbor lived a mile or so down the road.

"After the meeting a few of these Norwegians were talking the meeting over, and one said, 'We forgot to ask him whether we could talk Norse on this machine!'

"And one said, 'We'll ask Clough! He'll know!'

"So they did.

"He told 'em, 'Why no! For Norwegian you got to use a machine with a hollow wire!' That was my wife's father. He was a joker, you know!

"This joke delayed the organization of the coop for several weeks, and several meetings were held to clarify that hollow wire business. Took it for gospel!"

233

# The Witch o' the hills

The Baraboo Range, once called the "Irish Hills," then the "Scotch Hills," is some of the oldest land in the world. In the fall those hills are a sight to see! Drive west from Portage and take Highway W up to Owen Park, and up there you can see for thirty or forty miles. Never have I seen a finer view than that from Owen Park looking south, especially when the fall color is riding high. Then you come down, and there is this antique shop sitting right on a little trout stream, not far from Durward's Glen. Mr. O'Shea, who ran the place for thirty years, would tell you some queer and strange stuff about the hills and the hills people. The last time I was up there, it was a slow day in late October. Slow, I mean, because life runs slow in those hills. No hurry except for a slug or so of moonshine, if a fellow is dry enough to hurry for it; I guess you can find some moonshine stills in those hills if you are a mind to. Last time I was there Mr. O'Shea says to me, "You ever heard of the witch o' the hills?"

"I never heard of a witch before in Wisconsin," I say.

"You are young, my boy, and you seen very little as yet," says Mr. O'Shea. "You see this Kentuck rifle?" he asks, taking one off the wall.

"My great-great-granddaddy, Jacob, carried one in the War of 1812," I say. "Would like to have this gun, Mr. O'Shea."

"You ain't having it," says Mr. O'Shea. "And this gun has seen aplenty of things and has pointed at a few things, too, I'm thinking. It ain't talkin', but I can talk and I have seen too."

"I've seen no witch," I say.

Mr. O'Shea gets up from a Boston rocker, starts for the door, and I am following him. When Mr. O'Shea starts for somewhere he goes fast.

We climb up a hill behind the shop to a white ramshackle farmhouse, an old place — been there seventy-five years, maybe longer. We see an old, old lady chasing cows up the hill. She is whacking them with a switch, because they aren't going rapidly enough for her. A brown dog is yapping but not helping her much, and she takes a kind of gentle cut at him too. She is hardly five feet high and is wrinkled some, but she is bright and saucy and not breathing hard at all from chasing those cows.

She gets the cows into the pen. The brown dog stops yapping at the cows and comes over to yap at Mr. O'Shea and me. Mr. O'Shea says something in a gentle voice and the dog yelps and takes off fast for the timber. Four white geese march around from behind the house and start honking at us; ten or twelve cats, big ones and kittens, rub around our legs. The old lady motions for us to come into the kitchen and sit. She goes to the wood range and lifts the lid of a lone, simmering kettle. She sits down at the round table, not tired at all. She says, "Well, boys, set down now and don't get so excited. I been chasin' them cows. Them critters won't come much when I call to 'em. Voice ain't what is used to be. Now, boys, what'll it be for you? I'm eighty-one, would ye think it? Am in good health."

"Now, Mrs. Bacon," says Mr. O'Shea, "we come to hear 'bout the witch woman of the hills."

"Her?" says Mrs. Bacon. "Her? That woman better not come 'round here. I won't have her suckin' dry my cows."

"She's long dead and gone, ain't she?" says Mr. O'Shea.

"Well, she's dead, that's right, but what a time my husband's father had with her! Them was awful times, boys . . . afrettin' and afrettin' and causin' that old man the misery. Oh, he knowed she was a witch, wasn't any doubt. Day he found out he was cookin' an old rooster right here on this stove. Same as I am now. Sudden that old rooster knocked the lid off of the pot and began to crow. Right there, my husband's pa, he grabbed the kettle and throwed it out in the yard, rooster and all, said, 'It's that old woman up on the hill, she's been awitchin' me.'

"Then it got worse. His misery got bad, and his horses took so they wouldn't cross the bridge over the crick. Just went up to the edge of the bridge they would and stood there alatherin!

"Pa went over to old man Wolf. Wolf lived couple miles over yonder side of the hill. Said, 'You got to help me. Old woman Kranz got a witch on me.' Oh, I'm tellin' you, boys, young folks thinks I'm crazy. But I ain't. Them things happened!

"Said to old Wolf, 'What'll I do?'

"Wolf says, 'I got the Seventh Book here. I'm afightin' her with the Seventh Book. She's got the Seventh Book, too, and she's fightin' you. But I'm fightin' her.

" 'Now I tell you what to do. When you come to that bridge you take a broom and sweep that bridge good! Sweep her hard. The dirt'll fly up into the witch's eyes and blind her. Then you can drive across.'

"Pa done as he said.

"Horses quit latherin' and pulled the wagon across. Pa kept a broom in the wagon all the time.

"Why, boys, I seen it myself. Food, right here on this table, disappeared when a body went to pick it up! She done that!

"Witch of the hills she was. Our cows never give no milk. She sucked 'em dry. And our pigs, they got thinner and thinner. Neighbors' hogs got waddlin' fat. She was out to get us. She loosed the devil hereabouts, and she did it with the Seventh Book!"

"Well, we got hard times now, too," says Mr. O'Shea.

"You said it," the old woman cried. "I'm eighty-one and still chasin' cows, and milkin' cows, too. My daughter milks two and I milk three. My daughter, she answered an ad in one of the novel romance magazines and she got her a man. He comes here and soon they had a child. But this man wasn't no good! Stole our chickens, he did, and stole my canned fruit and sold it. Well, he come back one evening, wouldn't come to the house, dodged into the privy out yonder to hide, but we seen him.

"Went out and says to him, 'We don't want you here. Git!' He says he was changed, but he wasn't. Went to stealin' chickens right away. So one night we loaded him into the car and taken him out north of Portage. Shoved him right out into the road, my daughter done. Shoved him hard! Says, 'Now git!' and we come on home. Ain't seen him since. Witch woman put him on me, I suppose.

"But you see that trailer up yonder on the hill, boys? I got eight grandchildren in that and another on the way. Lots of kids and cats around here!"

"Well, we got plenty of trouble," says Mr. O'Shea.

"We got trouble, sure," the old lady says.

Suddenly the lid that was on the big cookin' pot bubblin' on the wood range flew off and clanged onto the floor. The old woman whirled around, and I'm telling you true, boys, a big rooster that was stewin' in that pot, or so it looked to me, stuck up his head and crowed.

The old woman grabbed the pot off the stove and heaved it out into the yard and hollered: "By God, she's back! Lord, she's at me again! Causin' me more trouble!"

And she reached for her broom and went to sweepin' lickety-split.

# The Portage

I am up in a small roadside bar out north of Portage. It is a dim place and pretty quiet, though there is a whistle of winter wind and the rattle of a window behind me. I sometimes like to drop in at such places and have a quiet glass of beer, and just listen to talk. A lot of the talk I hear is about places, and generally each place name has a sound, as it is spoken, that goes far, far into the past, into warm memories of home and people and love, and events that are pulled out of the memory and live again in the sound of the name and the feeling of the name and the meaning of the name ... even if the name may have faded out of the present, forgotten, let lie, erased, by-passed ... a shadow on a rotted board.

"Recall once," a fellow says, standing by the bar, leaning with the small of his back against it, and back of him an empty beer glass, "Recall once ... " and then he stops and you can see the memory going into gear and a creative force take hold of his entrails, and the name comes busting out: "Recall once, at the Portage ... " He doesn't say just Portage, as most of us would, but *the Portage*, and he means just that, speaking of the "carry" between the upper Fox and the Wisconsin rivers. "Recall once at the Portage," he says again, and the door yawps open to the winter night and a couple of farmers come in. One is named Henry and the other is Wally. Farmers around here don't hand-husk corn any more, but their hands are like the corn huskers' hands I knew as a boy; large, red. Hanging sore. They have been in weather. Henry has on a bill cap with the flaps pulled over his ears. He slaps the cap on the bar, and out of the shadows comes a woman who draws two beers and slides them down the bar. The two farmers reach and swallow together.

"Down to the Portage, yeah!" says Wally, with his back against the bar. "I seen the last boat come through the old canal before the U.S. jerked out the Fox River end locks in '56. Wasn't no profit keepin' a lock man down there. Wasn't nothin' but a few little pleasure boats. Ain't even a basin there now, just a little waterfall."

"Big carp in around that old lock site," his pal Henry says. "I've drawed out many an eight or ten pounder around there."

"Well," Wally says, "I seen a lot. And my pa seen more than I seen, and my grandpa seen more than my pa seen. We have lived, my folks, in around the Portage for more'n a hundred years. A feller come up not long ago to our farm. We got us one of them centennial farms, you know, been in our family over a hundred years. Come to see me since Pa ain't here no more. Says, 'You McBride?' I says, 'Yes, sir, I'm McBride.' I seen he was from the State Historical Society down in Madison, had a station wagon, Ford '69, with Historical Society painted on the door. He says to me, 'Well, Mr. McBride, I come to ask you a few questions.' 'What about?' I says. He says, 'We was talking about you down in Madison and we figure you might know quite a bit of local history.''

"Darn fool," Henry said.

"Well, lookin' at it one way I expect I do know quite a bit . . . more'n most, maybe. He says, 'We're out getting dope on the Portage. Some fellers is going to make a report because they are talking about rebuilding old Fort Winnebago. You know, that the army built where Moore's house is over on the hill east of town . . . back . . . must have been 1827.' ''

"Ought should have come to me," Henry says, "I been over every inch of that Fox River. Know where to get good crappie any time."

"*The Portage*," Wally says, "now *that's* really something. Was a trader and interpreter there in the 1830s named Pacquette. I heard all about it because once Joe Kerwin from Madison come to see us. Joe had a whole folder full of clippings and such. Said his great-grandpa was this Pacquette. Said he was the strongest joker ever seen. Said his flesh was hard like a gas pipe. Said he'd easy hoist up a keg of lead weighin' more'n eight hundred pound. Said he'd sometimes get himself under a big hoss's belly and just carry away that hoss on his shoulders, and the hoss fightin' and bawlin' but not able to do nothin'. Never was certainly heard of such a man."

"I heard of Pacquette," Henry says. "Was immune, complete, from snake bite. Would let a old rattler up and fang him any old time. Kinda liked it. And town of Poynette, down the road here, was supposed to be called Pacquette. Some government clerk in Washington messed it up."

"I heard that, too," says Wally. "And I heard also that Pacquette would let any old snake up and chaw him anytime the snake felt like takin' a chaw. And Pacquette never stopped walking, even to scratch the bite or anything."

"Well," Henry says, "there's a explanation. I heard that too. Old saying around the Portage: you take a neck of a crow

238

and dry it and beat it up to a powder. Then you rub this powder onto you wherever you figure a snake might like to set his fangs, and that snake won't bite you. You ever hear of that?"

"No, but I heard plenty about the Portage. All my life," Wally says, "I heard yarns about the Portage. Mighty strange, come to study on it, how the Fox River rambles north and the Wisconsin pours over west, to the Mississip . . . only that portage mile between them rivers. And in early days that mile was just a swamp, I heard. Water often between the two rivers!"

"Old Pacquette," Henry says, "had him quite a business hauling them boats acrost the Portage with oxen and big wagons. Wagons twenty-seven foot long! If an ox happened to give out, bust a gut or somethin', Pacquette he'd set the yoke onto his own shoulders and pull along. Done his full share, too. Heard that Pacquette would be up ararin' to go while the ox would be down in the mud on his knees aslobberin' and abellerin' for mercy."

"You ever hear how Pacquette up and died?"

"I heard he was murdered," Henry says, "all I know."

"Was shot in the belly by an Indian," Wally says. He reached around behind him, wrapped his fingers around the empty beer glass, took a long swig of nothing, and says, "This Indian was name of Iron Walker. Was kin of Chief Black Hawk. You know that?"

"Nope," Henry says.

"Well, so it was. And Iron Walker had it in for Pacquette. What the hell, whenever Pacquette seen Iron Walker he would drub the hell out of him."

"Can't blame Iron Walker none for feeling sore," Henry says.

"Well, one night after a big powwow or something, Pacquette come to Iron Walker's campfire. Had a squaw there and she seen it all. Maybe Pacquette had hoisted a few . . . likely. Anyhow, he pushed this Iron Walker over backward into the brush, and when the Indian gets up he was steamin' and afumin'. He says to Pacquette, 'You knocked me down, but I get up.' So this Indian runs over where his shootin' iron was standin' against a tree. Was one of them flintlocks, I suppose. Wasn't nothing else in them days nohow. And old Iron Walker got his old trusty centered on Pacquette's chest. About right *here* I suppose. And old Pacquette he just laughed and grabbed his shirt and ripped it open and hollered, 'Shoot, and see how a brave man can die!' Never had no buttons on shirts then, just let her rip."

"He really say that?" Henry said.

"What my pa said his pa said. I expect Pacquette didn't think the Indian had the nanny to let him have it. But old Iron Walker he did let him have it. Killed the Wisconsin Giant right there.

"Joe Kerwin says this here Pacquette was quite a feller. Owned about twenty-two sections of land hereabouts. Got that land from the U.S. government for fees, and money they owed him for interpretin'. And do you know, when Pacquette come to die, they gotten all that land away from him? Way I heard it told, his two kids, a boy and a girl, was found later barefoot in the snow over in Iowa. Wasn't even enough of Pacquette's money left to buy 'em a pair of shoes."

"I heard that, too, that Pacquette he left a treasure buried hereabout," says Henry. "Had him a farm over at Belle Fontaine. Maybe the money is buried over there. I heard tell there was at least seventeen nail kegs full of gold. Somebody seen it under Pacquette's bed the night before he was murdered. Nobody ever found what became of that gold. I reckon it's hereabout yet."

"You got the facts all wrong," Wally said, "Pacquette had gold all right. He was a rich man. But when the Black Hawk War come along . . . that's when Pacquette buried the treasure. To keep them hostile Indians from gettin' hold of it. I figure he buried the treasure over at his old house . . . you know, just acrost the river bridge."

"Pacquette he built the first Catholic church here," says Henry. "That much I do know. Little log church he built for Father Mazzachulli, who was the early priest around this part of Wisconsin. And when Pacquette was kilt he was buried under that church."

"Old Joseph Crelie," says Wally, "now there was a man! Was Pacquette's father-in-law. Joe Kerwin says he was the oldest ever heard of in these parts. Was a pioneer mail carrier. Died in 1868. Was over a hundred and forty years old. That's honest fact. I heard my daddy tell it too. Old Crelie drank whiskey like hell all his life. Chawed tobacco, ate any kind of grub he could get hold of. Helled around with the women whenever he could; twelve squaws one night, I heard, when he was a hundred and fifteen! Don't know nothing definite that he helled around with women, but who wouldn't? Walked all his life. Walked all the time. Carried the mail from Green Bay to Prairie du Chien. Some walk. All winter he done that. Made him strong and virile!''

"Well, them things ain't the only ones happened at the Portage," Henry says.

"Who says they was? And anyhow them crappie is still pretty good in the river," Wally says, "if you can keep the carp away."

"What I heard," Henry said, "they buried old Pacquette up in town, where Portage town is now. Right in the middle of where Adams Street is now; and when they come to build streets around there they had to move 'im. I heard my pa say that he seen Pacquette's bones when they dug him up and they was really huge. A real giant's bones. He seen them."

"Joe Kerwin said that too," Wally says. "But you can knock over a giant with a bullet. Another beer here, Jessica! And include this stranger, too," he says, looking at me.

Looking back over the notes I took on this random conversation at this bar north of Portage, I might now say that we later researched this yarn about these seventeen kegs of missing gold and found it wanting. I had talked to Pacquette's great-grandson, Joe Kerwin, about the matter. A retired Madison fireman, Joe has done about forty years of research on Pierre Pacquette and all the details of Portage local history. Joe and I went up to Portage one day to look over the land, thinking that we might go after the Pacquette treasure, which Joe still thinks does actually exist. Why wouldn't he, when it was reputed that Pacquette was the richest man in the whole territory at the time; that he possessed twenty-two sections of choice land, some of it where the city of Madison now stands; that he had government contracts; that the U.S. government owed him $20,000; that he was a fur trader; that he had all kinds of chances to make money. Why wouldn't Joe think that there was a screw loose when, after Pacquette's death in 1836, there wasn't enough money left to keep Pacquette's kids out of the snow?

Joe told me that his grandmother, Pacquette's daughter, said that Pierre remarked often, "None of you will ever have to worry after I'm gone. There's plenty."

However, there wasn't plenty. Hercules Dousman, executor

of the Pacquette estate, allowed hundreds of claims against it. These are on record in the manuscript division of the State Historical Society. Anybody can look at them. I have.

The main point remains: what became of the gold that Pacquette was said to have possessed just before his murder? Here's how we tried to find out.

Bill Steuber, assistant state highway engineer, is very much concerned with local history; his job demands that he be. Nothing can bug the highway department as much as the destruction of a historical site, or a historical landmark. The old Pacquette house at Portage was one such landmark that Bill had to deal with.

The house, built in 1834 by Pacquette just two years before his murder, stood across the old Wisconsin River bridge at Portage, exactly where the ferry that Pacquette established used to come out on the south side of the river. In 1968 the Pacquette house faced destruction by the State Highway Department, which was replacing the old bridge with a new one that would emerge exactly at the location of the old house. It was a touchy situation and Bill knew it.

It so happened that at the same time I was certain that Portage was at last going to realize its illustrious heritage. I thought that very soon there would be a new revolving theatre at Portage, fashioned after the Finnish Revolving Theatre at Tampere (where I borrowed the idea), doing Portage history drama. A big play at Portage might draw thousands of people each week, just as Paul Green's "Lost Colony" had done for thirty years at Roanoke, North Carolina. At about the same time, the man who was promoting the revolving theatre at Portage called me. This was Bob Guilbert, advertising expert from Connecticut, who had moved to Portage to get the theatre going. He had made a fine start. R. Buckminster Fuller, internationally known architect, had drawn the plans. The land had been acquired through a local committee and "theatre corporation," which succeeded in gaining possession of some of the property along the canal and near the canal-Fox River junction where the theatre was to stand. This land acquisition alone is rapidly becoming Wisconsin folklore.

The U. S. government had pulled out of management of the old canal in 1956. In 1963, it turned over the canal and the locks to the state of Wisconsin, which in turn passed them on to the city of Portage, which, not wanting them, gave a lease on the property to the theatre corporation. The theatre corporation gave a lease to Guilbert and his group, "Portage Park, Inc." Everything looked rosy for a time. The only thing lacking, as the whole plan unfolded, was money. Lots of it. And this was hard to get. Perhaps that's beside the point, too.

Anyway, Guilbert asked whether I could help to get the old Pacquette house saved, that he would see that it was moved to the site of the proposed revolving theatre; of course, I thought this a very good idea. The old house was a landmark, and, properly fitted up, it could be quite an attraction. I called Bill Steuber at the state engineer's office.

Bill responded instantly. The project, he said, had a lot of romance attached to it. Also, if the old house could be saved, the highway department might come out with a halo instead of a slap. I thought of Bill imagining headlines: "Kindly Highway Department Saves Old Pacquette House in the Face of Vast Difficulties . . . "

Bill called a meeting of several individuals, publicists, and engineers, and it was at this meeting that I related the tale of the Pacquette gold.

"Yes," I said, "it was true. There were stories about a lost treasure. Pacquette, on the night of his murder, was indeed supposed to have had possession of a large shipment of gold, part of which, at least, was meant to pay the Winnebago Indians for a treaty. Pacquette was the interpreter. And there was the fact," I went on, "that there wasn't much cash in Pacquette's estate after his death. Something happened to the wealth that the Pacquette family said he possessed. Where was it?"

"Buried," someone cried.

"Perhaps, yes. Buried."

"But where?"

"Near the old Pacquette house. Naturally he'd bury it nearby, wouldn't he?"

"Sounds reasonable."

I went on to relate the yarns that Joe Kerwin had told me and about which, so far as specific location was concerned, Joe was fantastically vague. Joe had said, however, that he thought the old Pacquette house was a good bet, and this was enough for our eager bunch of treasure hunters gathered in Bill's office.

Bill set a date for the great "dig" and promised, "In order to lay these buried treasure legends to rest for all time, the contractor will put a front loader out there. We'll strip off the dirt and see what is really what."

The idea was received with immense cheers, except from the Historical Society representatives who were rather glum. They didn't like front loaders — a spade and some brushes to work over each inch of earth would have pleased them better. But when you are after seventeen barrels of gold, what chance does a poor anthropologist have? The historians were put to humiliating flight.

Practically everybody was there on a morning in late September, 1968. A warden from the forest service who had been at the house the evening before with an army mine detector reported several very exciting readings. At one place the needle almost went crazy, jumped all over the dial, practically came out of the glass, and pointed a shaking finger down to where a large mass of metal was resting. This kind of talk made us all very bubbly, and, as we drove to Portage early on the morning of the great day, we discussed what could be done with the vast wealth. Bill thought the federal government would surely get it, since they had prior claim, if it was really treaty money. I thought the state of Wisconsin would get it. George Bechtel, P.R. man for the Department, thought maybe the former owners of the old Pacquette house might have a chance. And Joe Kerwin thought that the Pacquette family sure needed it.

The day didn't start well. The warden was there with his mine detector, and the darn thing suddenly wouldn't work at all. The needle lay inert, flat against a side of the dial. Nobody could fix it. Fortunately, when it looked as though we were going to have to fly blind, an interesting couple from Janesville came along. Quite a crowd had gathered and these good folks just happened by, saw the crowd, and stopped to investigate the excitement. It turned out that both husband and wife were metal detector nuts, and each had a detector in the car much more sensitive than the army piece. They didn't need much of an invitation to run to their car and bring the detectors. And we found metal!

Cans. An old baby buggy wheel. Nails. A piece of something that might have been part of a still. A hunk of radiator. An old auto hub cap.

But we put on a very good show. Bill had passed out crash helmets from the highway department to a chosen few. I had one and strutted around trying to look like a straw boss, as much as I could anyway. And we all took turns directing where the great front loader should dig. And we dug plenty! We dug up the front yard, the back yard, the side yards, and down in the crick. We went deeper and deeper. Once we discovered what looked like part of an ancient well  with sand of a different color than the river sand nearby. We gasped! The gold would be there, under that sand in the old well. Nope.

After a day of suspense, with the Portage folk standing around cheering or jeering, we did turn up a hoard: a squirrel had made a cache of hickory nuts at one corner of the house. These we got. Finally at the end of the day we admitted defeat. The saddest of all was Joe Kerwin, who had already spent a lot of the Pacquette gold. We all had a fine lunch, though, out at the new restaurant on the "I" road.

Just as we were quitting for the day a letter was handed to me. It was from Bob Guilbert. The letter said that, with real regret, Portage Park, Inc. could not move the old Pacquette house as promised. The expense would be too great.

And that is why, next day, the bridge contractor's machines drove against the old Pacquette house, built 1834, and ground it to splinters.

XI. Abandoned Farm

# PART FOUR -
# The
# NORTHWESTERN QUARTER

XII. Hills of Vernon County

# Mrs. Salter

My secretary, Arnita Ready, made most of the arrangements for my journey north and west. She had it all laid out, where I was to go, where to stay, and who to see. "But Arnita," I said, "I'll never connect with all those places. You've got me going night and day!"

"Well," she said tartly, "perhaps so, but you don't want to scant the northwest, do you?"

And indeed I didn't. Folks down in southern Wisconsin seem, too often, never to get to the northwest. It's pretty easy to stay south, or to go over to Milwaukee, or to another city on the lake shore, or to head north through the center of the state. Yet it's a mistake to scant the northwest. The country gets into you and stays there. The roads through the woods and swamplands have a beauty that comes from the solitude and the wild flowers, from the old orchards way back in that earlier settlers planted there . . . gone to the wild, now. It is a beauty of the open expanses through the sand country; of the hills and great, lone bluffs; of streams that were once so important to logging; and of coulees and the great river. And the tales . . .

Starting, late one afternoon, I drove up Interstate 94, which heads out north and west of Madison toward St. Paul, as far as New Lisbon. Arnita didn't have the item on my list, but Archie Crothers over in Adams County had told me about a terrible murder of Civil War times that had happened up north of New Lisbon, so I turned off on Highway 80 and stopped about four miles north at a little place called the Airport Tavern. Sure. They knew the yarn . . . not far from here where it happened. A marker there — rude, concrete slab, very close to the highway. One end rests on a block of wood. Inscription on the concrete, too.

Mrs. Salter
Killed Here by
the Indians
June 13, 1863
Two Indians
Jo and Jim Dandy
Killed by Salter
and Buried Here
This Ax Handle
Killed Two Indians

246

and Mrs. Salter
Puck-A-Chee

After the railroad reached New Lisbon, about 1857, the highway between New Lisbon and Necedah became a main current of travel. During the fifties and sixties, many lumberjacks went down the Wisconsin and Mississippi rivers on rafts, to return by boat to La Crosse, then by train to New Lisbon, and finally by stagecoach or "shank's mare" to Stevens Point, Wausau, and other centers in the pineries. Many of the rivermen walked the remainder of the distance after reaching New Lisbon, for by so doing they not only saved their fare but frequently made the journey in less time than the coaches, which had to cope with the abundance of sand in that region.

By the side of this highway, a little more than a mile north of the bridge spanning Yellow River, Mr. and Mrs. George Salter operated the Halfway House, midway between New Lisbon and Necedah. The region was sparsely settled at that time, and many Indians roamed over the undeveloped countryside.

Salter's Halfway House was a favorite stopping place for travelers, especially those who walked, for liquor was sold there, as at most taverns of the time.

On the fatal day, June 13, Salter was away from home. Apparently, two Indians came to the place and demanded liquor of Mrs. Salter, which she refused. What transpired between the landlady and the unwelcome guests will never be known, but it is surmised that Mrs. Salter's refusal infuriated the Indians, who killed her. When the husband returned he found his wife dead and the two Indians intoxicated to insensibility. Near the dead wife lay an ax handle, which appeared to have been the weapon used to kill her.

When Salter fully realized the situation, he killed the two Indians with the same ax handle that had been used on his wife. He severed the heads from the bodies and placed them on hop poles by the side of the highway as a warning. Later the heads were removed from the poles and buried with the bodies near the scene of the tragedy. Mrs. Salter was interred in a cemetery not far away.

Salter, who later married a sister of Mrs. Salter, died about 1905, and now all three rest in the same burial ground.

The memorial slab was made in Necedah and hauled to the place through the efforts of Gus Nooney, a friend of the family. There is an impression of the ax handle in the block.

All traces of the wayside inn are now gone.

I drove on to see the marker. Only the top was sticking out of the snow. All I could read was:

Mrs. Salter
Killed Here by
the Indians

# Bog People

Going northwest on Interstate 94 toward Eau Claire, and about at Camp Douglas, there are many isolated, rocky hills that to me resemble the ruins of castles I have seen in Europe. There are crags of sandstone, irregular bluffs, and a flat plain that gives a sense of great space and openness. Scrub oak and dwarfed evergreens cling to the rocky slopes. The soils are sandy, and spiny plants and dwarf trees always make me think of certain parts of the Far West. There is monotony here, but strange formations come suddenly to light the monotony and fill it with great poetic atmosphere.

All through the Driftless Area, that mysterious section of Wisconsin where the glaciers did not penetrate, are strange erosional remains. The Driftless Area contains about 13,000 square miles; bounded on the west by the Mississippi River, the area then extends up the Wisconsin River to north of Wausau and terminates on the Black River between Neillsville and Black River Falls, and on the Mississippi between the Trempealeau and Chippewa rivers.

Much of the lure of Wisconsin for me comes from the odd-shaped rocks in the Driftless Area: Stand Rock at the Dells; Turks Head and Devils Door at Devils Lake; Monument Rock south of Viroqua; Devils Chimney and Picture Rock in Dane County; Roche à Cri and Friendship Mound in Adams County; Mosquito Mound in Portage County; Pilot Knob, Rattlesnake Rock, and Petenwell Peak all in Adams and Juneau counties; Gibraltar Rock in Columbia County, and Necedah Mound.

Erosion has made natural bridges, too. Eight miles north of Richland Center is Rockbridge, and about two miles northeast of Leland in Sauk County is another fine natural bridge. There is also a small one in Dane County near Devils Chimney in the town of Primrose.

At Millston I stopped to visit with old friends, Betty and Lou Epstein. I first met Betty when she showed up at the first Wisconsin Regional Writers meeting about 1950 and said, with emphasis, that she meant to become a selling writer. Her very first article, which she instantly sold, was about the mansion built by William T. Price, a Black River Falls lumber baron and congressman. Thereafter Betty went from literary sale to sale, and almost everything she wrote was based on life and legend in her part of Wisconsin: the Millston-Black River Falls area.

Around Betty today persists the same feeling of achievement and interest in others that she had back in those days. The older people around Millston and Black River are her special charges. She is forever carrying a meal to Charlie Pitts, who is pretty badly crippled with arthritis now and lives alone in a small shack plainly labeled "Charlie's Shack." Sometimes Betty will pause to sweep him out a little, or just sit and gossip with Charlie and his pal Claude, who lives a few rods away in another bachelor dwelling. Betty would like to go in and clean up Claude, too, but she doesn't quite dare. He likes it the way it is.

Claude and Charlie are bosom pals, and although Charlie can walk hardly at all, Claude comes to get him and the two of them toot off fishing or berry picking, or in season hunting and fishing, for Charlie has a permit to hunt from the seat of a car. They know every good berry-picking site in Jackson County, and they mark these places with little streamers of cloth so they won't forget where they are. There are numerous old orchards around in the bush, too, for once many farm families lived out there. The depression got most of them, and the government moved them away to better places. But the old fruit trees still bloom and bear fruit, which Charlie and Claude pick and can. They are great canners and mostly they live off the land.

Charlie's father, a pioneer blueberry shipper, sent most of the berries from Millston to a Chicago wholesaler, C. F. Werner, who placed a standing order for as many or as few blueberries as Pitts could ship. Indians and settlers both worked out in the burned-over lands picking berries, which were then very plentiful. The berries were sold by the pound and shipped in crates specially built so that the bottom of the crates extended out over the sides. In this extended section of wood, holes were bored in each corner. About ten crates were then stacked on top of each other, a cover was placed on the top crate, and stakes driven down through the holes to hold the berries in place for shipment. Charlie got very adept at making these crates!

A while back Claude got a pair of walkie-talkies so he and Charlie could keep closer track of each other, and now they can talk back and forth wherever they are; I guess either one would lie down and die for the other, or for Betty, too, as far as that goes. She took me over to Charlie's shack, and while we were waiting for Claude I was shown some neatly painted signs that said, "Millston This Way." It seems that Claude and Charlie got the idea that not enough folks knew how to get to Millston, so the Chamber of Commerce (there really is one in Millston!) commissioned them to make and paint a lot of signs and put them up out in the brush. I guess Millston is the best marked town now of any up in the Black River parts.

As we sit in the shack, Betty is telling a yarn about how Long John Fleming got pulled in by the law for illegal hunting during the depression. "But," Betty said, sitting on one of Charlie's special chairs, which sink down a little in the middle, "I'll bet there wasn't a single Millston family that didn't have some deer meat out of season in those years. How else could they stay alive? Anyhow, Long John was arrested, and they carried him off to jail. And in jail he simply couldn't eat the food. Just wasn't what he was used to. So he asked 'em if he could bring some of his own chuck up to the jail — that was before we had the new one in Black River. And of course they couldn't see why Long John shouldn't have what he wanted. So they let him go home and get it, he got his venison that he had shot and canned out of season and brought it back to the jail."

"Judge and all was eatin' Long John's venison," cried Charlie. He is short, and rather plump, has a large kind face, crewcut hair, and bright twinkling eyes.

"Course, we got better control of the season now, and that's better," said Claude. "But some other things are not so good. They are killing off the oak trees, did you know that?"

"What is killing the oak?" I asked.

"Conservation men. Sending boys out to band the oak trees, and then they put poison on the band and the tree dies. Just like that! Why, squirrels can't live without oak trees. They kill 'em so more pine can grow. Deer eats the acorns, too. No grass will grow under pine trees. No deer food!"

"Even bluejays need acorns," Betty said. "Charlie, do we still have snowshoe rabbits around here?"

"In the swamps is all," Charlie said. "Very few. Used to be so thick hunters was shootin' them rabbits like crazy, puttin' 'em in barrels and shippin' 'em to Chicago. One time a La Crosse professor come up here and wanted to go huntin'. So I took him out to City Point. It was lousy with rabbits! It was New Year's time . . . couldn't have got in there if it hadn't been froze. We got a hundred and ten rabbits! I took my dogs along. Was told, don't take your dogs. Leave 'em in the car. And I found out why. Why a dog would go crazy! Wouldn't know which rabbit to take off after! We got into one of those potholes with the trees all fallin' down and all, and Ellis, he was a cranberry man, and these two fellows from La Crosse, we went way out in there, and they says to me, 'You get up on one of these windfalls, Charlie, and we'll go around the other side and chase 'em out.' Well, I'd like to have a picture of that! Was just like a flock of sheep comin' through! 'See 'em comin'!' Ellis yells, 'See 'em comin'!'

"My God, mostly snowshoes! Well, I was standin' up . . . had got up on quite a big windfall . . . easy for me to stand there . . . I shot five times and got twelve rabbits! . . load gun again . . . and they was runnin' this way and that way; couldn't shoot fast enough. Finally used my shotgun like a pistol, just pointed her and let go . . . kicked a little but did I get rabbits!"

"Dadgone it," Claude said, "I sold my rifle!"

"Just this year," Betty said, "Claude sold his pet rifle. What was the year of it, Claude?"

"1884," Claude said. "Winchester. 1884."

"Feller come along and looked at that gun of mine . . .three different people kept askin' me. A doctor from Winona, and a conservation man, and this doctor from Illinois. 'Got the gun yet?' 'Yep.' 'Well, when you get ready to sell her let me know.' I didn't know it was an old saddle gun, see, 38:40, 12-shot carbine. This feller was a collector, and he stayed at my place, and he says, 'You want to sell that gun?' And I say, 'Well, if I keep it I'll just go ahuntin'.' 'What you want for it?' 'Well, what you give me?' When I got the gun I had traded a little gas engine for it, cost me $10. Well, this feller looked at it, and says, 'I'll give you $110 for it.' 'You can have it if you want it,' I hollers. Same time another feller come along, bow hunter. Says, 'How much did you get for it?' '$110!' 'You damned fool, I'd have give you $150.' Gun was a relic!"

"I sure remember the depression," said Betty. "Lou and I married, he was taking $2.50 a week out of the moss business . . . that's all it could afford. And some weeks it couldn't afford to pay Lou even that. I can remember picking wild strawberries in the fields for supper one night. It was all we had. Depression times were real bad up here. We married on absolutely nothing. And no one else had anything either. Everybody was in the same boat. I picked lilacs and sold them to the Chicago flower market to buy my wedding dress."

Charlie, sitting in a corner, had taken an old scrapbook off a shelf. He was already laughing even before he found what he was looking for in it. Claude, with his hunter's cap, mackinaw, and boots still on, was across the tiny room still going on about how hard it was to get along in the depression. "Everybody was a violater," Claude says loudly. "Everybody had venison!" By this time Charlie had discovered the scrapbook item.

"Edward Bundy," Charlie cried. "When they arrested Edward Bundy!" Charlie roared a great laugh and I laughed too, not knowing exactly what was so funny about arresting Edward Bundy. We all waited.

"He was a feller ran the store here in Millston. First day of trout season he always had trout. Fishermen come there, and Edward, he wasn't above doin' a little illegal fishin', and sellin' 'em a few fish.

"Anyhow Edward has a big icehouse out behind his place, and the night before the trout season opened the game warden came down — this was about 1930 — and they raided old Edward's icehouse. Had a search warrant and went in and dug around, and they found one trout. Just one. They wasn't looking for venison, but anyhow they also finds a big piece of venison in there. So they had old Edward nailed, and they arrested him. They taken him up to Black River before the court and he plead guilty. What else could he do? The court kept the venison and that one trout. Had a feed!

"Well, the Black River paper come out the next week end. Edward he had a letter in it addressed to the people of the town of Millston. He knew who squealed on 'im."

Betty had taken the old scrapbook from Charlie and now she read aloud what Edward Bundy had written to the folks of Millston:

"I think you know," wrote Edward, "that I have enough common sense to take the worst of it without squealing when I have been made a victim. Fighting people who plot in the darkness is hard and the only way to meet that is to take your medicine and get set to trap the trappers. I want to say the game warden who was compelled to take action against me acted like a gentleman and only done his duty. There wasn't nothin' else for him to do after he was tipped off. The finding by the warden of one lone trout in my icehouse will be good enough evidence to my friends that it was planted there. Anyone who knows old Edward Bundy knows that if I had gone after trout before the opening of the season I would have gotten plenty. Not just one! The story is too thin for anyone to believe. I pleaded guilty because I knew very well it would be impossible to prove my innocence. Nobody saw what was done in the dark of that night! But don't think that because I have taken the worst of it in this that I'm not gonna fight. I am working fourteen hours a day now, and I will work twenty hours a day to put a stop to this persecution. This is just a gentle hint intended to be read where it will do the most good! In the future, skulking around my yard and my outbuildings will be unhealthy. If anyone hears that I caught somebody, don't be surprised!"

"Well, everybody was doin' it," cried Claude. "I recall a fellow around here had an old hearse, you know, one of them kind with them little draw curtains at the sides? Well, he loaded that hearse up regular with venison and drove her into Chicago. Nobody was gonna stop a hearse. Sold plenty of deer to Chicago restaurants that way."

Betty and Lou Epstein met in a very curious way. Although not acquainted at the time, they both were raised on the South Side in Chicago. One went to a Catholic school, the other to a public one, a block or two apart, but they didn't really meet until they both came to Millston.

Millston doesn't seem to be a very likely place for two young strangers from Chicago to romance, but that's the way fate figured it, and their meeting greatly affected the whole life and economy of Millston and the area. Nowadays, Millston isn't one of the larger communities of the state. It's chiefly Charlie Pitt's shack, Claude's shack, a filling station, a town hall (small and white, it was, I think, a former one-room school), Grandma Smakars' restaurant, which is a favorite tourist stop just off I-94, a few other houses, a slightly larger school building, and across the North Western Railway tracks the warehouses of the Mosser Lee Company, which processes and sells sphagnum moss. The Mosser-Lee Company is, of course, Lou Epstein and his brother, Max, and, in the background but casting a spell over it all, Betty Epstein.

Lou's father was selling fish around Millston and Black River Falls in about 1930. His brother had a fish business in La Crosse, shipping tank cars of rough fish that had been seined out of the Mississippi River. Business was definitely not good. Lou's father became aware, while he was at Millston, of the possibility of reviving what once had been a mildly flourishing

254

business: taking moss out of the extensive swamplands of the area and selling it to florists. The elder Epstein managed to persuade a local farmer to let him take a few bales of the moss down to Chicago to try to sell it. He took about forty bales of moss and the Chicago florists snatched them up instantly. Naturally, the price was very small, about forty cents a bale, but it was a sale! Mr. Epstein, Sr., came back to Millston with his eighteen-year-old son, Lou, and they went to work, grubbing out and baling moss. Lou became the salesman.

They needed a place to stay, and one day they came by Betty's mother's house at the edge of Millston. Recently widowed Mrs. Lee had been forced to move her family to Millston to the frame house that Mr. Lee had purchased with the hope of starting a summer resort. The house was large, and the Epsteins, father and son, were taken in by Mrs. Lee. Betty gave up her own room to them, and Mrs. Lee fed them, often letting the board bill run because the Epsteins just weren't able to pay right then.

And out of these incidents came the Lee-Epstein merger, carved right out of the teeth of the depression, which has led, finally, to the Mosser-Lee Company, one of the largest sphagnum moss companies in the world. It is a real Wisconsin success story and is especially good because it was all founded in unselfish help to one another. Even today, Betty's mother, whom they fondly call "Sis," does most of the cooking in the Epstein house because she loves it. She is a darn good cook, and almost any stranger (who looks as though he deserves it) can get a square meal from Sis Lee.

Lou's older brother, Max, also lives with the Epsteins. It was Max who put up the money early in the business. As a commercial artist, he didn't have so much but it was enough to get them going. During World War II when Lou was away in the service, Max moved up to Millston to run the business, and he just never went back to Chicago. Life is too good up in the moss country.

The marsh land is leased from the Wisconsin Department of Natural Resources, and the state collects ten cents per bale "stumpage" on each bale of moss taken out. The mossers can harvest only about every two years. The moss grows without planting and requires the wet moss beds for growth.

About fifty years ago, the moss suffered a terrible setback when an effort was made to drain the wet land region to create farm land. If this had succeeded, there would be no Mosser-Lee Company today. The operation began when a Chinese man named Hip Lung leased 15,000 acres of moss land from a realtor named Burke. Burke showed him the land when it was all frozen over and covered with snow. He painted a marvelous picture of how productive the land was, and how the man could raise enough vegetables to "feed the world."

Betty told me that, instead, they couldn't even raise enough to feed themselves, and at the end of one year the project was a disaster. The fifteen Chinese families who had arrived in Millston went after Burke with knives, and he took refuge in the house of a Mrs. Smith. They didn't get Burke, but the dredging operation killed most of the moss. It took a long, long while to recover.

The mossers who work with the company today are a hardy and interesting lot of men and women who do unusual things. Bill Tollefson, for example, got acquainted with a shy girl of about fifteen who was wandering around in the woods and invited her to come and share their one-room, one-bed shack. The wife thought it wasn't quite nice, somehow, for all three to sleep in the same bed, which they had been doing. So she said either she goes or I go, and Bill said *you* go. That was it. Eventually Bill married the little girl. They live together now. Happy.

Bill is quite a lady's man. Once he got friendly with a girl down the road and she became pregnant. He had a sort of goofy feller working for him at the time, so Bill made a deal with this feller that if he married the girl he would give him ten dollars and three quarts of whisky. By golly, the guy took Bill up on it. Married the gal! 'Course he was simple to begin with!

One family in the moss area has twenty-two children. The welfare worker who came out to urge them to take a few precautions got thrown out on her ear. As the husband explained, "Judge, some folks goes to the movies. Some goes to have fancy dinners and to dances. Some goes out for car rides. We don't do none of those things. We just stays home and has kids."

I asked Lou Epstein to explain just what happened out in the woods . . . in the mossing, that is, not the other.

"First thing you do, you got boots on and you wade into the water, and you use what we call a 'hook.' It is really an eight- or ten-tine fork with the points bent. They pull the moss with this, and shock it.

"The moss is allowed to drain there in piles for several days, then we come out with what we call a crawler — a tractor with cat tracks and thirty-inch two-by-fours about eight inches apart. This keeps the tractor from sinking. They come out with this crawler and a stone boat like a large sled with oak runners. They load the moss on this stone boat and haul it out onto dry land, what we call the drying bed. Then the moss is spread and shaken, and after the sun and wind have dried the top of it, they go over it with a wooden rake and flip it over so the sun will dry the bottom, too. Then the moss is bunched up together and stacked; then it's baled. The baling, incidentally, all has to be done with hand pressure. If we used a hay baler, for instance, the pressure would destroy the fibers. This would make the moss lose its water retention value, which is the great thing that the moss can do, of course. That's why florists use it to protect the roots of plants and shrubs. A bale is about 12 x 14 x 43 and weighs about 15 pounds. If this same bale is thoroughly saturated with water one man can't lift it.

"Originally the moss was harvested with oxen; then they started to use horses with special clogs on their feet, to keep them from sinking into the bog, you know.

"Now we have a number of products made from this moss: one that keeps worms alive for fishermen; a seed germinater; a soilless growing medium. You know, hydroponic gardening — growing without soil — has produced amazing results when moss and chemicals usually found in soil get together. Why, giant-sized tomatoes harvested with stepladders! Radishes as large as turnips! carrots so big you practically have to dig them with a crowbar! And moss as foundations for wreaths. That's big now. Over the years we have had a lot of business shipping carloads of moss to the nurseries. But we were forced into this diversification because we awoke one day to discover that they weren't using sphagnum moss any more. They were using cheaper substitutes. Years ago any shrub shipped out had to have this moss. Now they have new techniques, packing in polyethelene bags and so forth . . . "

This conversation was interrupted by Sis Lee calling us all to supper. Among the good things served was a large bowl of local cranberries. Betty said that at Grand Marsh, which is south of Spaulding, there was once over five hundred acres of wild cranberries and that early settlers employed more than three hundred Indians to harvest them. The berries were put in grain sacks and hauled to market by ox team. So nature provided well for the bog area. Cranberries, wild at first, then the wild ones developed into fine domestic varieties that are widely used today. The area is part of a cranberry center in the United States; only Massachusetts produces more cranberries than Wisconsin. The blueberries are about gone now. You can still get pie berries or some for canning, but the great days when blueberries were shipped every day to Chicago, Milwaukee, and many other cities are over.

Betty took me over to the nursing home at Black River Falls, a very pleasant place, where we visited with some remarkable folks: Jennie White, 99, and Jane Spaulding, 94.

With Betty doing most of the prompting, the two charming ladies, both with memories clear and intact, told us about Black River Falls when it was the high society place of northwestern Wisconsin. Both the Spauldings and the Prices had mansions on "Price Hill." Miss Jane Spaulding and her twin sister, Mary, who lives with her at the nursing home, remembered well the wedding of their older sister, Julia, who married Clark Osborn in December, 1881. Guests used sleds and the river to come to the social event of the year.

The bride, who had met her husband in Chicago where she attended school, chose a floor-length wedding gown of red velvet styled with a bustle in back. The Spaulding twins were only six when their sister was married in the beautiful new Spaulding home (it burned in 1961, with the original wallpaper from Marshall Field still on the walls). The pièce de rèsistance at the wedding was something never before heard of in Black River. Angel food cake! The cake was imported from Chicago and served with homemade ice cream!

Jennie White told us about *her* wedding in 1890. "It was short and sweet! I married a doctor and he was very busy. They wanted him to come and treat somebody just before the ceremony, but he said no! Wait a few minutes! Right after the wedding he took off in a buggy to see a sick person. He didn't return till the next day!"

Betty asked Jennie if she remembered the wedding of William Levis and Mary Elizabeth Blanchard Miller, a couple that really started a trend in weddings in the Black River section. The wedding was performed with about a tenth of the guests present, because a bad storm had delayed the others. Not wanting to disappoint anybody, the young couple had the wedding performed again for more guests when they could come, then for more and more until the knot had been tied maybe ten times or so! Frontier hospitality! Got so that a wedding wasn't considered much of an occasion unless the preacher said the words a few extra times.

I simply couldn't get over the atmosphere that this small woodland community generated in those days. Jacob Spaulding, Miss Jane's grandfather, actually founded Black River in 1838, and started the "age of elegance" for Black River. Price carried it on.

William Thompson Price was born in Huntingdon County, Pennsylvania, June 17, 1824. When he came to Wisconsin he brought only an ax and twenty-five cents in cash. His great will power and integrity were demonstrated when, after the panic of 1857, he found himself $25,000 in debt. Although he was not legally responsible for the debt, he felt a moral obligation and paid every penny of the money to creditors, during the next several years.

After a fabulous career during which he was lawyer, banker, lumberman, deputy sheriff, bookkeeper, miller and stage line operator, judge, state senator, and congressman, Price became known as the largest single lumber operator in the state. He built a "castle" for his wife, the former Julia Campbell whom he married in 1851.

The three-story "castle" was 58 by 68 feet and had a basement and twenty rooms. The front was of cream city brick, the rest of red brick. Marshall Field of Chicago had the contract for the furnishings, and six artists and paper hangers came from Chicago to decorate the palatial home.

The soft blue tapestry that covered the dining room walls was imported from Italy and reportedly cost more than $2,500. The front hall featured carved maple woodwork, its price: ten thousand dollars. The balance of the woodwork in the home was of solid oak.

Green marble, also from Italy, was used in the six fireplaces. Imported stained glass was used in the conservatory windows. And there were two bathrooms, in a day when even one was considered luxurious.

The house was razed in 1950 to make room for a church.

Black River Fall's era of elegance was only a memory.

I suppose you might say that there were two or three "kings" that had something to do with the Black River area. First was "King" Price; then there was King James Strang. I didn't know that he had a relationship to the region until Betty told me about it, but it seems that Strang, the Mormon leader who competed with Brigham Young for leadership of the church after the death of Joseph Smith, in order to confirm his high pretension, found it necessary to produce some kind of evidence that he, indeed, was chosen.

The new "prophet" claimed that an angel from heaven visited him one Sunday evening, as he was strolling along on the east bank of White River, and that his spirit was taken out of his body and conducted, by the angel, to a ledge of rocks some eighty rods distant, which was covered with earth and trees. The angel informed him that under a certain oak tree, some four feet under ground and just on the top of the rocks, there were deposited three copper plates, which were placed there by the last surviving prophet of the ten lost tribes of Israel. He was then informed what was written on the plates, and who to select as his apostles, and that they should be witnesses when he should take the plates from the earth. The angel told him where to erect the Holy Temple, and how to proceed with the Latter-day Saints, when they should come together and acknowledge him as the great prophet and leader. His spirit was then taken back to its "house of clay," and the angel departed.

Strang called his apostles to the spot of earth containing the sacred plates; the earth was removed, and, sure enough, there was found a box of blue clay, six inches square and twelve inches long. The box was duly opened, and the plates exposed to the astonished "twelve," who subsequently swore to everything necessary to confirm the farce. Strang led his followers to Voree near Burlington, Wisconsin, where a village was constructed. The colony didn't stay very long, however, and soon removed to Beaver Island in Lake Michigan. In 1850 the leader had himself crowned "king," King James, actually. The coronation was complete with regal red robes and crown, and he had made it quite plain previously that the Lord had commanded him to institute polygamy.

Well, the king got himself shot because he was too dictatorial and tried to get the ladies to wear costumes they didn't like. A husband shot the king partly as a result of a beating the king had administered to the fellow, and that was the end of his reign. But it wasn't quite the end of the Wisconsin story, for two of Strang's five wives brought him back to Wisconsin and one of these was Betsy McNutt.

While we were driving back to Betty's house from the nursing home, she told me the story of the old Mormon cemetery near Knapp.

"Although he wasn't a Mormon," Betty said, "old Jacob Spaulding, grandfather of Miss Jane, leased them land. And one of Strang's wives was Betsy McNutt whose original home was Warrens, which is in a little section of Monroe County . . . adjoins Jackson. After Strang was shot they brought him to Burlington in Racine County where he died and was buried. After that two of his wives, Phoebe and Betsy McNutt, came back here and settled out in the township of Knapp; it adjoins Millston. I believe they farmed. Anyway, there is an old Mormon cemetery out near Knapp. It's too bad that it's in such terrible shape. Cattle run through it . . . the stones have fallen over. In the early days any Mormon who came through this area knew that they could stop over at Knapp. The country was full of McNutts, but I have never been able to find out what relationship Betsy McNutt was to the others. Anyway, one of the Mormons was an inventor. He invented a mop wringer and a hand washing machine with a spring plunger. When he died they decorated his grave with his inventions; there were still pieces of spring from this washing machine out there some time ago. Incidentally, did you know that the Mormon Temple at Navoo, Illinois, where Joseph Smith was murdered, was built of Jackson County timber?"

"Nope."

"Well, it was. And I do wish somebody would keep that old cemetery in condition. It's a shame! Poor Betsy McNutt!"

There is one more "king" I ought to mention. Betty told me about him like this:

"A monument stands in Dexterville, a crossroads place in Wood County, a lone sentinel proclaiming the grandeur that once surrounded the life of 'King' George Hiles, truly a self-made man and one of Wisconsin's pioneers in the lumber industry. The shaft of marble, over forty feet tall, peers over the denuded land rising from the Dexterville cemetery, which was once filled with virgin timber.

"The miniature Washington monument is unusual enough to cause tourists to stop on Highway 54 in central Wisconsin and inquire what it is for. A stop at the small cemetery proves that today, as in the century before, the Hiles family is something special.

"The five-acre Hiles family plot, enclosed by a heavy iron fence, is dominated by the marble monument. It had been rumored that Hiles ordered the monument before his death and left a sum of $25,000 for the upkeep of the family plot and the village cemetery, yet no one today remembers that story as a true one.

"The Hiles section is maintained today by Dexter and Samuel Hiles of Dexterville, two great-grandsons of their bearded patriarch, just as their fathers did before them.

"One queries how such a large monument could be transported into the cemetery at the turn of the century after Hiles's death in Milwaukee in 1896. A railroad spur was built to the cemetery to carry the monument, a special favor to the man who built a great portion of the Green Bay, Winona, and St. Paul Railroad. He later built two of his own railroad lines, which were sold to the Chicago, Milwaukee, and St. Paul Railway for $800,000 in 1890.

"But building railroads was a small part of Hiles's business interests. 'Everything he touched turned to gold,' said Mrs. Samuel Hiles, 84, wife of the king's grandson. Mrs. Hiles and her sons, Thomas and Samuel, live in Dexterville today.

" 'From the stories I heard of George Hiles, he was always good to people, but they took advantage of him,' she said. Mrs. Hiles recalled that when Hiles operated a furniture factory here people used to drive their teams and wagons to the factory at night and load up the ornamental furniture legs to use for firewood.

"A factory in Dexterville? In this tiny rural village in the midst of the vast cutover region with no apparent means of income for his residents? It seems incredible today when one views the tiny village. But the furniture factory was one of many enterprises proposed by Hiles, who truly had the Midas touch, turning virgin timber into a multimillion-dollar fortune.

"He built railroads to move the lumber from his five sawmills; he did extensive fur trading with the Indians and shipped his fur to Milwaukee markets, a distance of twelve days.

"Hiles was perhaps one of the state's first cranberry growers. His obituary details his many activities, stressing cranberry growing as one of his first business interests in Dexterville. Later he added a general store, a planing and shingle plant, and the manufacture of tubs, staves, laths, and pails, in addition to furniture.

"Another story of Hiles, which has been handed down in this community, is that Hiles came to Dexterville with $1.50 in his pocket and a mule named Dexter and that he named the village for his mule. The story seems highly unlikely since the *Weekly Wisconsin*, a Milwaukee publication, stated in its March 14, 1896, issue, that, with three yoke of oxen, he moved from Baraboo to Dexterville with his wife and possessions.

"It also seems unlikely that even if Hiles had a mule named Dexter, he would hardly name members of his family the same name. It is more reasonable to believe that Dexterville was already named when he came or was named for a grandson, one of James or Frank's sons who carried the name.

"The ancient newspaper account, included in Hiles's obituary and filed at the State Historical Society, also stated the terms of Hiles's will, which gives an idea of his wealth. His wife was given the family home at 88 Farwell Street in Milwaukee and $75,000 cash. His two sons, Frank and James and his daughter, Mrs. Phoebe Brown, each received $318,200 stock in the George Hiles Land and Lumber Company, which was worth $7 to $8 for each share of nominal value.

"The money was to be left in the company for a term of twenty years, with the interest providing an income to his family. His grandchildren, Dexter, Samuel, Willie, and Kittie, received $10,000 in stock, as did many relatives, valued helpers, and servants.

"What happened to the wealth of George Hiles and his sons, James and Frank, who were reputed to have lighted fat cigars with $10 and $100 bills and rode in private railroad cars? What happened to the Dexterville in which Hiles invested $70,000 worth of improvements, including a complete electric plant?

"What happened to his $500,000 worth of property in Milwaukee and Chicago, the mineral spring at Arcadia, the 100,000 acres of Florida pine land, the Nebraska ranch, lumber interests in the state of Washington, as well as his 70,000 acres in Wood, Jackson, and Clark counties?

"No one seems to know. Today, one slows to go through Dexterville only because state highways 54 and 80, which slice through the village, will it so. The barren cutover land is mute testimony of Hiles's grasp for power. Only the marble monument, worth about $30,000 today, pays tribute to the king and attests to the position he once held as a lumber baron over a century ago."

# Fishing Journey

July Progress Days at Viroqua are just getting started. Forty thousand farmers are in town, and the merchants have put their best wares in the windows. Banners across Main Street belly against the wind, and half a hundred bands are lining up for the big parade. It is a blast of color in Viroqua. A rocket of excitement. Over on a hill beyond the fairgrounds they have set up an 1860 threshing machine . . . horsepower. Some sight! Six horses tramping around and around and the chaff aflying! Careful Joe! Don't start them hosses too sudden! Break them shafts! Too bad the boys don't know more about hossflesh these days!

"Come on, son," says my friend, Neil Greene, to me. "Come on, boy. I'm goin' fishing. You're comin', too."

Tomorrow I will produce the big show for Progress Days, "Jeremiah Rusk," the show is called. Based on Uncle Jerry Rusk, once of Viroqua, first U.S. secretary of agriculture. Big man. President Benjamin Harrison appointed him. Two hundred seventy pounds, Uncle Jerry was, and tall to boot. Coined the phrase, "I seen my duty and I done it," when as governor he quelled those riots in Milwaukee in 1887.

But today I am free. "Come on, boy," Neil says. Neil calls me boy, though I'm not such a boy anymore. I've known Neil for twenty-five years. He's head of the teacher's college at Viroqua now.

"Where we going fishing?"

"Genoa."

"You got tackle?"

"You know that."

In that second while we are standing there on Main Street in Viroqua, I recall a night on the Wisconsin River with Neil back in '59. It had been a still and a misty evening when I got to Wauzeka where the Kickapoo enters the Wisconsin. We pick up some others, and we are seven in two boats, and the props kick foam as we head upriver. I am in the bow and Neil is in the middle, with his brother-in-law in the stern. We are heading three miles up the Wisconsin where there is a shack, a table for poker, a couple of bunks, a kerosene lamp.

The Wisconsin seems almost a wild and primitive stream along its lower reaches. At least it gives one that feeling. It's a solitary river anyway, a mysterious river with many sandbars and swift channels, which have milky ripples in the long, still evenings.

The Wisconsin is a river of great beauty and deep history. Of all the rivers in mid-America it is the one that seems to flow most inside and outside of a man, and it pulls at one again and again, drawing one to its breast. And now, on the Viroqua street, I am remembering that night trip up the river in the slow dark, how we put in the set lines, tying each to a root or a branch, and used for bait a hunk of hog liver as big as our fist. I remember climbing the river bank in the darkness with soft men's voices guiding us, and seeing the faint yellow light coming from an open door. I am thinking of night on the Wisconsin and how, in the darkness during a break in the poker, I slip outside to listen to the river sounds in the silent moments before dawn, and how in the morning I take a thirty-five-pound catfish on one of the set lines.

"That was a good night," I say to Neil. And he nods, perhaps not knowing exactly to what night I am referring, but there have been many good nights. What matter?

"Let's go fishing," I say, so we leave Main Street where the Farm Progress parade is already starting, and four queens come down toward us, each one riding on top of the back seat of a white convertible. Must have borrowed every white convertible in Vernon County. We wave to those queens, or they wave, because all of the Vernon County girls are friends of Neil's. We pick up our car and toss in a little tackle and head west out of Viroqua, not speaking much, but enjoying the coulee country, feeling a security in the land and the people, for back in these hills and in these valleys live a sturdy people.

They have been sturdy since 1855 when Mrs. Lucy Stone came out here. Lucy had "Blackwell" tacked onto her monicker, too, but she didn't care about that, since she was working for the cause of woman's suffrage and wanted her own identity, not her husband's. (As I get older I see more and more of these younger women sort of rebelling at being Mrs. Jerry Jones or Mrs. Henry Adams. Nope. Wants to be *Harriet* Jones or *Jenny* Adams.) She and her husband drove up to Viroqua to look at some land, yep, drove a buggy up from Chicago. And while Mr. Blackwell was looking over the land Mrs. Lucy Stone set out to make a speech. She found out there was going to be a big picnic in the grove north of town, so she invited herself to make a mighty lecture on "Slavery, what are we going to do about it, and what about women's rights?"

They fixed up a speaking platform for her and she set right in to talk. Was going along good, scorching the slaveowners, when all of a sudden the platform busted down, and Mrs. Lucy Stone was lying there on the dirt. But Mrs. Lucy never stopped talking. She just lay there and yelled, "All right, folks, and so must this nation go down to perdition 'less we abolish slavery!"

Well, there was a newspaper fellow there that day, editor of the *Viroqua Times*, and he wrote a piece about Lucy. Said: "After the platform collapsed, the speaking continued. Mrs. Stone was listened to. She is an excellent speaker and she whipped the stuffing out of the slavery question. But we can't accept part of what she said about women. Women will never demand universal suffrage and accept the responsibilities and unnatural hardships inseparably connected with man . . . "

"They're a sturdy people out here," I say aloud. "You bet they are," Neil replies. I don't need to tell Neil what I'm thinking, often. He seems to be able to just pick up a thought like that. "You know," he says, "there was a really big cyclone hit out here in 1865. The boys were just coming home from the Civil War. Frank Minshall was marshal, and he was so popular that the boys wouldn't let him run for sheriff. Wanted to keep him marshal. On the day of the cyclone, Frank was standing in front of the hotel looking south. Suddenly Frank saw a man grab a horse by the neck, and the wind, which came up mighty sudden, whipped that fellow out like a ribbon. Was lying out flat in the wind with his feet akicking and him hanging onto the horse's neck. Frank thought that was a pretty funny sight until he looked up and there was a roof from the First Baptist Church flying overhead. Frank figured it was time to move then, so he threw down his toothpick and took off for a picket fence and grabbed hold of one of the pickets of that fence.

"Wind blew off the pickets and so, holding onto a few pickets, Frank started down the hill with that wind behind him. The wind was travelin' more'n eighty miles an hour and Frank was going so fast that he stumbled over a rabbit that was also steamin' full out. Frank ran right through a window of the tavern and would have been going yet if he hadn't dove head-first into a barrel of wine.

"And you know, half an hour later a rug blew into a house down at Hillsboro twenty miles away, which the woman in that house recognized as a mate for hers, and which belonged to her sister up at Viroqua."

"Seems like she must have known something was wrong up at Viroqua," I said.

"They are a sturdy people hereabout," Neil said, "and get messages in strange ways."

We go on west through tobacco-growing country. A white house, where my friend Ada Allness lives, looks like an old southern plantation with neat tobacco rows running right up to the white-pillared front porch. ("My husband told me I could grow me a crop of tobacco and pocket the money," Ada once told me, "so I planted the big front yard. Saves mowin' grass, and I can keep an eye on the crop all day long!")

It always startles me to see fine tobacco growing here in western Wisconsin. Got started around Stoughton and Edgerton in the sixties and seventies and spread west. Folks found that it would do well in certain areas, and there used to be a lot of small cigar factories out here, many of them in homes where two or three workers would turn out many fine cigars. Not anymore. Can't compete. But there is still a lot of tobacco in western Wisconsin, far cry from the pioneer days when settlers grew only enough leaf for their personal use.

Anyhow, we are going west, and the hills are getting steeper and the coulees deeper as we get closer to the Mississippi. Don't know why it always thrills me to be driving west to the Mississippi. Ever since I was a kid I am loving the Big River, imagining how it looks, and seeing the whole length of it in my mind . . . past and present . . . carrying the canoes of the explorers, the steamboats 'round the bend, echoing the blasts of Civil War cannon, seeing the modern barges and power dams and the jam of industry along the banks. Hearing the roar of duck guns of a clear morning, and knowing that the river folk live along the river pretty much as they always have. I am afraid of the Big River, too, for mystery lies in its deeps. Who knows really what the river is, or what monsters inhabit it?

"Down yonder is Genoa," Neil says, as the Ford heads down a steep grade.

Genoa is a tiny town, a real river town above the Burlington railroad tracks. There is one main street along the river, some houses up the hill. At a tavern we stop and buy eight or ten beers and some crackers and Wisconsin cheddar.

We park the Ford and Neil leads me, carrying tackle and beer and a minnow bucket to the river bank. We slide down a steep sand path, cross the railroad tracks, follow a path to the river beach, and wade deep sand to the river's edge.

When you look at the Mississippi from high up above on a bluff it is sometimes blue and far away and quiet. But when you are standing on the edge, it is brown and restless and it pulls at you ceaselessly. A black man and a white man are fishing, casting weighted bait far out so that it sinks near the bottom, and as we stand a moment the black man catches one, a big cat, and the white man who is not doing so good reels in and rebaits.

Down the shore fifty yards a whole family is fishing. Grandma is sitting in an old rocking chair she has fetched along. Every once in a while she yells, "Henry! Somethin's aplaying with my bait. I can feel him. It's a big something, Henry!"

"Ain't nothing," the old man beside her replies.

"We fishing here, off the shore?" I ask Neil.

"Nope," Neil says. Behind us, stuck into the sand is a long pole, an unbarked sapling, and on this pole is a lanyard and a strip of blue cloth . . . might have been a lady's petticoat or maybe a pair of bloomers. Neil hauls on the line and the blue petticoat or whatever it is runs up to the top of the pole. The wind, usually strong in the river valley, whips the blue rag out, and over across the river about three-quarters of a mile a fellow standing on the shore shades his eyes as we can faintly see, and points across at us.

"They'll be coming over to fetch us," Neil says.

A boat sets out from the far shore, and when it crosses we see that an old man is driving it and a kid is sitting in the bow. She is a flat-bottomed boat, fifteen feet long, wide, and a good river craft. She slides into the bank, and the boys fishing on the shore don't care much for the disturbance. But we pile in, and off we go toward the west bank, which is Minnesota right at this point. We pull into a strange wharf.

The wharf is built right out over the Mississippi for thirty or forty yards, and it is almost under the power dam. There is a space of eddy at the north side, and on that side five or six farmers are fishing. They are using minnows, and they are hauling in big crappies. At the other edge of the wharf there is a couple, a fat lady sitting on the wooden bench built at the side of the wharf and a little guy who is there principally to bait her hook. I know because she was always saying, "Roger, you ain't got this worm on very good. If you would bait better for me I would be catching more good fish. Ain't you got any purpose in life, Roger?"

"I am baiting your hook, Corrine," Roger says. He mops his bald head and wipes his hands on his overall legs.

"I wonder what Harriet is doing," Corrine says.

"Harriet is restin' in bed, I expect," Roger says.

"She's lazy, that's a fact," Corrine says. "She's too lazy to even set with a fish pole in her hands."

"Fishing is hard work," Roger says, and baits up Corrine's hook again.

"Where'll we fish?" I ask Neil.

"We'll try it down here by this lady," Neil says, and sits down beside Corrine.

"There's fish in this river for all," Corrine says, "but I ain't catching them. I got me a misery-poor hook baiter."

"Why don't you bait up yourself?" Roger says.

"Don't give me no back talk," says Corrine. "You back talk me, I will personally bait you onto my hook and drop you in where a garfish will nibble you. Wouldn't anything but a garfish take a piece of you."

"You sure don't like me none," Roger says.

"You was pretty near the last human male thing there was left when I hooked you," Corrine says.

"Hooked is an absolutely correct word," Roger says. "If you wasn't such a good punkin pie maker I would leave you settin' right here and go off and find myself a kinder woman."

"Wouldn't do much good," Corrine says. "I would just come and fetch you back on a leash."

Roger sighs and baits up her hook and we all fish silent for a few minutes. Then Corrine gets a bite and it is a big one. She gives a loud beller and starts to reel in, but whatever it is on her line sets off down the Mississippi and don't want to come home. She yells out for Roger, but he don't move.

"I got me a big fish," Corrine yells. "You come and git him in for me, Roger."

"Nope," Roger says. "You're a big girl. You are bigger'n me. Pull him in yourself."

She has a light tackle, and the big fish or turtle, or whatever it is, is bending he pole about double. Roger don't stir from his bench. We sit there, watching the woman play the fish, wondering with dignified interest what it is she has hooked into.

"Might be a big river sturgeon," Neil says. "There are a few around." Corrine has now decided that she'll get no help and she is playing the critter with some real skill. Roger pretends that he isn't much interested.

"Where you from?" Neil asks Roger.

"Mormon Coulee."

Now Neil knows more about names of places than anybody I know. He knows especially well these names over in western Wisconsin. But he says, "How come Mormon Coulee gets a name like that?"

"Why it's a good name," Roger says. "Ain't so many folks knows about it anymore. Mormon Coulee ain't nothin' but a name anymore."

"Yes it is," cries Corrine. "He's agittin' away, Roger," she yells.

"No he ain't," Roger says. He takes a nice pinch of Copenhagen out of the can and puts it back under his tongue. "Mormon Coulee?" Roger says, "I suppose ain't so many asks about Mormon Coulee anymore. Was a spell awhile back when we had a real rash of Coulee askin' people come from all over. 'What's this here Mormon Coulee?' they'd say. 'Who'd ever want to name a place Mormon Coulee? Was there some Mormons around here sometime?' Well, I'll just bet you there was some Mormons! Come in '43, 1843, that is.

"Wasn't poor folks neither. Was well off, so they tell me. Had them a place over Nauvoo, crost the river from Keokuk. Nauvoo had more'n two thousand folks then, was only a town three year old, too, and Joseph Smith, the prophet, said he seen a beautiful temple in a dream, temple that was to be built over there in Nauvoo. And where was the Mormons to get the stuff to build that temple? Here in Wisconsin, of course. Anybody in Nauvoo them days could see the lumber rafts afloatin' past on the Big River, and most of them rafts come from Wisconsin pine woods.

"Well, was two elders come here, Miller and Wight. Come with a bunch of men to work out some timber for that temple, spring of '43 it was. Wasn't nothin' much here then. Anyhow these elders come and stayed in La Crosse a few days, then they went up the Black River in canoes. Rented them a whole lumber mill, they did, Spaulding and Son, Lumber Mill, sawed timber there all summer. Didn't have no money, the Mormons didn't. Paid for grub and outfit with sawed lumber. Myron Myrick and Scoots Miller run the store them days.

"Come summer of '44, the Mormons'd cut themselves enough timber and went home to Nauvoo. La Crosse folks figured they'd seen the last of 'em. But 'twasn't so. No it weren't.

"They come back. A whole crowd, women and kids and men and two elders, Wight and Bird. Was there to settle down. They liked La Crosse right well. Was right many pretty gals along with 'em, so I heard.

"Picked out a coulee, lower end of a prairie, and set out to file claims on that. Put up some cabins and was serious about settling down. You know now, fellers, how Mormon Coulee got its name. But that ain't the end of the story. Them pretty gals cause a barrelful of trouble.

"I guess you know how it is in a new country . . . ain't much different now, either, far as I can see. Men like women, ain't that so? Specially, ain't it so when there are a whole lot more men than women? Down to the university at Madison the professors been studyin' stuff like that, I heard. One reason I wouldn't let my boy go down to the U. What I heard, them gals at Wisconsin got only one thing in mind. They're there to nail a man. Ain't that so? It ain't?"

"It ain't hard to nail a man," Corrine hollers. "But I'm having a hell of a time with this fish!"

"Anyhow this country hereabouts was full of lumberjacks and farmers who was mighty gal hungry. Elder Wight's flock of ewes, mostly English and Welsh, I heard, looked mighty temptin' to them lumberjacks. You know how it is with a lumberjack and a woman. So every night was a big shindig with young fellers comin' in and out of the woods fifty, sixty mile away. Made them Mormon men right sore. Wouldn't blame them none myself. What do you think? Supposin' you brought maybe fifty good lookin' fillies along with you to a new country, expectin' to keep them fillies for your own pasture, for your own use, and supposin' . . . well you know what I was going to say. What would you do?"

"I would get me a shotgun and stand at the gate," Neil says.

"I figured you would. And that's what the Mormons done too. Wouldn't allow no more sparkin'. None. Gals done what the elder said in them days. Don't know how they'd act now. Expect they'd do some bawling and asquealin', anyhow. Caused some real bad feelin'. Local folks always done what they wanted. Didn't like it when the Mormons shut the door on their pen of ewes. Folks about here was fixin' to come and let them gals out by force. Even if the gals didn't want to come out, they was fixin' to do it.

"Sure. That's right. Mormons decided to leave. Made plans to leave, and kept it all real quiet. Nobody outside the Mormons knowed they was leavin'. Got all fixed to go when the ice went out in the spring of '45. Loaded up their stuff on some boats that was froze into the ice on the river. Didn't make no difference that the boats wasn't theirs.

"Roger," Corrine says, tugging hard and puffing hard too. "When I get you home I will lard you down and put you into a crock for winter fryin'."

"You're doing fine," Roger says. "Just don't let him get out too much line. Well, come spring, out goes the ice and out goes the Mormons with all them gals, all of 'em ridin' down the Mississippi on them borrowed boats. Gals and all, that's right. A real waste. Astandin' up there in them boats they was, them gals, faces right into the wind. A pretty sight — 'course it was night.

"Only one thing. 'Fore they sailed away they set all their houses in Mormon Coulee afire. Didn't want the local folks to have no good of them houses. Can't say I blame 'em. Wouldn't want nobody takin' over my house, was I to up and leave. Rather burn her for sure.

"Folks down in La Crosse saw them flames. Most everybody in the village come in a body to help fight the fire. Guess they didn't want nothin' to happen to them gals. Anyhow, when they come to the Coulee the Mormons was long gone. Guess they owed quite a bit of money in La Crosse for grub and supplies. You know how it is . . . everybody runs bills in a new country. But the La Crosse folks was mad and set out chasin' them Mormons. Didn't lose no time.

"Wouldn't never have caught up with them, hadn't been a little steamboat tied up on the river. Got aboard her and set down river, crowded on the steam. Course they caught up with the Mormons. Made them settle up right there on the river. Wasn't takin' no nonsense. Took most everything them Mormons had. Guess the La Crosse boys would have took some of the English gals in trade, but there wasn't no offer like that made . . . not as far as I heard anyhow.

"Now the Coulee's a right nice place. But I always kind of wished them Mormons had stayed. You know why? You don't? I'll tell you, feller. My grandpa was the only lumberjack busted the fence. He carried off one of them ewes. Married her, of course. My grandma. Anyhow, I'm a Mormon myself. How about you? What's your religion, feller?"

Just then Corrine gets her fish up. It is a big carp, weighing maybe twenty pounds. Roger goes over and lifts it out onto the wharf.

"I knowed it was somethin' big," Corrine cries. "Ain't he beautiful?"

"Carp's no good," Roger says. He unhooks the fish and shoves him into the river.

"Bait me up, boy," Corrine says. "Maybe I can hook him again!"

# Country Tales

I was up near Eau Claire in a tavern and this Neillsville man was there. He was a talker, everybody could see that. Those that liked noisy chatter were up around him, and some were well away at the far end of the bar drinking a quiet beer. Sometimes a beer needs to be inhaled quietly, and I was feeling that way myself. I was sliding along toward the quiet end when this Neillsville man reaches out and hooks me by the arm. "You heard of it?" he says.

"Heard of what?" I says.

"What I'm agoing to tell," he says.

"I ain't heard of it," I says, "because you ain't told it."

"No, I ain't," he says. "But I'm agoing to tell it, and I don't want a lot of movin' around while I'm atelling it. You stand right still, because I am a man that likes a still-standing audience. Don't mind no laughin' at the right places. Anybody here that figures he don't want to hear it? Huh? Speak up. You?" he says to me.

"Nope," I says, "not me. I wanta hear it!"

"There was this black man named Carter," says the man from Neillsville. "He was a good man, had lots of friends, but those days it wasn't like it is now. A black man could have him a right hard time in certain parts of the state. I heard tell of one town in Wisconsin, and I'm mentioning no place names tonight, boys, that wouldn't let a black man stay in town overnight. That's no lie. That was what they said, I heard it.

"Anyhow there was this feller named Carter. And he figured that if he could only be white skinned, all his troubles would be ended. Only a matter of the color of a man's hide. That's a hell of a thing to judge a man by, now ain't it? Anyway, this man Carter he disappeared from town. Didn't tell nobody where he was going. Was away for a long while. And you know, I'm telling you straight stuff now, and anybody out in Neillsville will tell you it's gospel true, when Carter come back he was white. And I mean white. Just like you or me. Bowled us over. Couldn't understand it.

"Well, we asked him about it. We was kind of embarrassed, he didn't seem like himself some way, and he says that he'd been studying about being white for a long while; whites had the best of it and so forth, and finally he decided to do something about it. So he just went into a church and asked the

Good Lord God to make him into a white man. Was an Episcopal church, so I heard. And by golly He done it. That's what Carter said. He done it right there and then.

"Funny thing about it, though, Carter never got along near as well when he was white as he did when he was black. When he turned white it made him into just another white man and folks treated him twice as mean. At least that's the way it looked to me. Always figured the Good Lord God changed him for a joke, so he would appreciate it, that he was born black.

"Ain't that some story?

"Now I got another strange one," the man from Neillsville said. "It's too strange. Nobody believes it. But, my friend, it's true, gospel, sure as I have two plates upper and lower. And that's another story."

"What about them upper plates?" says a pea-sized rounder about halfway down the bar.

"Well," says the man from Neillsville, "this is a digression but it's one hell of a good yarn. You want to hear it?" he says to me.

"Sure, sure." (What else could I say?)

"I was in this hotel, see," says the Neillsville man, "remember it was up at Hungry Holler or some such flea-infested place. And cold! Them cowardly little organs of mine retreated clean up to my bellybutton and stayed there. Wouldn't come out for nothin! Was afraid to. Well, this hotel keeper he says for me to go up and occupy a room and I done it. Me an another feller. And boys, we slept cold! Wasn't no heat in the whole buildin'. Everything froze.

"Come mornin' I was so cold my legs was froze stiff. Like I was walking on stilts. I takes hold of the water pitcher and starts for the door and the other feller yells, 'Where in hell are you goin' with the pitcher?'

"My upper plate's froze into this damn thing," I yells back, "and I'm going outside and bust the hell out of it so I can eat breakfast!"

The Black River Road, or what is now Highway 27, was so called because it extended from Prairie du Chien beyond La Crosse to the Black River. It is now known as "The Old Indian Road." Traveling over this road, noting the peaceful dairy farms along the way, it's difficult to imagine the country as it was one hundred years ago: the hills and bluffs were forest covered; settlements were miles apart. There was a trading post at Prairie du Chien, on the Mississippi River, a handful of houses at Viroqua, then on to La Crosse. The mail was carried along this route on horseback.

About one-fourth of the way from Prairie du Chien, in Crawford County, lived a young Englishman named William Boggs and his family. Their nearest neighbor was at Eastman, sixteen miles away. Mr. Boggs was known and respected for his integrity. He was termed "the friend of every man." His latch-string was always out for the stranger, and seldom a week passed but some friend or stranger ate at his table. His log house, which stood on a knoll in his clearing, was well made, with a slant porch over which he had trained vines brought from his father's estate. The rich virgin soil and his knack for gardening made his fruit and vegetables the talk of the countryside. As a background for his home stood a large mound named "The Mound of Sterling."

It is no wonder that the weary mail carrier always guided his horse up the knoll to the Boggs house with a feeling of contentment and security. He exchanged his tired horses there for fresh mounts, had his dinner, and relaxed by the fireplace having a chat with the young Englishman.

For two years he carried the mail through to La Crosse without mishap. But suddenly letters and packages containing money began to be missed from his sack. He tried to be more diligent than ever in guarding his mailbags. Whenever he entered a house he would ungirth his horse and carry the heavy sacks into the house with him. But greater and greater were the losses, so the government ordered that on the next trip a package of money should be placed in the bag and the bag examined just before arriving and after leaving each stopping place.

As he neared the Boggs place on this mission, the mail carrier thought how useless and unnecessary it was to carry out the government precaution at the Mound of Sterling. But, being a man of duty, he carefully looked in the bag; the money was still there. Arriving at Boggs' he took the bag in the house and threw it down by the fireplace. He felt so secure that he left the bag and went out to attend one of the horses that had picked up a stone in its shoe. Later, while eating his dinner, it seemed to the mail carrier that the Boggs' were even more sociable and friendly than usual, and he departed with his mailbag with a warmer feeling for them than ever.

Accompanying the mail carrier on this trip was an officer of the law who rode on ahead but waited to be present at the opening of the bag. This arrangement avoided revealing to anyone at the stopping places that an officer was accompanying the mail carrier.

After riding a few miles along the trail beyond the Boggs home, the mail carrier took down his bag and examined its contents.

The money was not there!

He couldn't believe it. He searched the bag again and again, but the money was gone. The officer ordered the horses turned back toward the Mound of Sterling.

When the wife saw the mail carrier accompanied by a stranger ride up the knoll, she hastily drew a package from her deep skirt pocket and threw it on the roaring blaze in the fireplace. Her husband observed her act but thought nothing of it. Busy with his mail, he had not noticed the reappearance of the mail carrier. When a rap was heard at the door, Boggs opened it and, seeing the mail carrier, merely supposed he had failed to deliver some message.

The officer, however, stepped forward and told Boggs about the loss of the money and how they knew it had been in the bag that was brought into the house. Mrs. Boggs stoutly denied that the theft had been committed in their home. Mr. Boggs usually a calm and gentle man, seemed suddenly the more agitated of the two. This attitude the officer mistook for certain evidence of guilt. Mr. Boggs indeed had great cause for concern, for now he knew what the action of his wife had meant when she threw a package into the fire.

The officer searched the room without success until, stepping to the mantle to look behind a pewter plate, his attention was attracted to some scraps of paper that had blown outside the grate. He rescued some of the pieces. Enough was recognizable to tell the story of the stolen money. Mrs. Boggs denied the theft. Her husband, neither admitting nor denying guilt, stood mute. Finally the officer laid his hand firmly on the young settler's shoulder and turning him about, slipped handcuffs on his wrists and mounted him on an extra saddle horse outside.

One can imagine the horror the husband felt on leaving his family, his home, and his freedom for a crime he had not committed. Yet he must have weighed the consequences. If it was terrible for a man to be imprisoned, what would it be for a woman? He allowed the officers to take him away. Boggs was placed in the prison at Prairie du Chien to await trial. While there he contracted a severe cold, from which he never fully recovered. From its effects he lost his speech, and when he returned to his home, finally, after serving a term of twenty years in prison, he could only speak in a whisper. His hair was white, and his figure was bent and stooped like that of an old man.

He quietly took up his home life again. No one ever heard him utter a word of reproach against his wife for her part in the tragedy of his life. He became known in that part of the state for the fine quality of his apples and grapes. In addition, by diligent study and personal observation, he became one of the best informed men in the state on the history of Wisconsin.

# Fortune hunt

When I want an entertaining hour or two, I go up to Eau Claire and visit with Doris Friedman at the Eau Claire Public Library. Personally, I think this fine library has one of the best staffs in the whole state, and one of the friendliest. They will knock themselves out for you. I was met at the front door by a girl who told me, without my even asking, how many of my books they had listed in their card file! That always makes an author feel wanted somehow. Someday they hope to have a new building. They desperately need one.

And Doris! She's something else! Steeped to the brim with facts about Eau Claire. She is very bright and attractive, with a sharp sense of humor, and before you know it she will take you down to the rare materials vault and relate yarns that can make a collector's mouth moisten and his stomach draw tight with the excitement of discovery. She never seems to be too busy to give personal attention to a reference problem, no matter what it is. While I was there she got a call from a lady who wanted Doris to write a play about the history of Eau Claire for a club performance. Doris said, very sweetly, that of course she would do it. It might take her a day to write the play, but would the lady call back please? And Doris meant just what she said. But, of course, I don't know whether she wrote the play or just showed the lady how to do it herself. That's the best way anyhow. Without my asking, Doris seemed to know what kind of material I was looking for, and down in the vault she told me the fantastic yarn about the disputed Astor wealth. Maybe this incident couldn't have happened anyplace except Eau Claire where so many interesting and curious events have taken place.

"There is a very interesting old trunk," said Doris, "in the museum of the Eau Claire Historical Society. The trunk has a fascinating history. It once concealed the will of John Nicholas Emmrick, the wealthy fur trader. Here's the tie between Emmrick and Astor:

"When John Jacob Astor, father of the American Fur Company, came over from Europe in 1784 he was a fellow passenger with John Nicholas Emmrick, who had been in Europe with a shipment of furs. Astor was young and very poor, and in conversations with Emmrick the older man said that he would grubstake Astor if he wanted to go west and try for his fortune.

"Emmrick was apparently very fond of young Astor, but

not at all fond of his own Emmrick relatives. He had two living brothers, Christopher and Valentine. John Emmrick made out his will in such a way that his relatives would not receive anything for ninety years. He also appointed as executor of his estate his friend John Jacob Astor.

"Since exceedingly large amounts of money were involved, a lawsuit was inevitable. The eventual lawsuit was based on the terms of the partnership agreement between Astor and Emmrick and on Emmrick's will, copies of which were finally found in the old leather sea case now in the Eau Claire museum. The trunk had been lying around in an attic in Eau Claire since 1862.

"The Emmrick heirs, in their lawsuit, claimed that Astor's heirs failed to make an accounting to the Emmrick estate, such as the trust agreement called for, and that a division of the total Astor holdings should be made among the Emmrick heirs . . . of which quite a few developed during the ninety-year period. They asked for an accounting of the estate from the time of the death of John Nicholas Emmrick, December 16, 1816, up to the time of filing the will, and that two-thirds of the whole Astor estate be distributed to the Emmrick heirs, descendants, and legal representatives of Christopher and Valentine Emmrick.

"Why did John Nicholas Emmrick tie up his estate in trust for this period? The question was answered in Eau Claire by Mrs. Edna Astor Carnahan, one of the three active plaintiffs in this tremendous litigation, which threatened to involve at least a half-billion dollars. Mrs. Carnahan, a descendant of the fourth generation of Christopher Emmricks, was the owner of the trunk in which the partnership agreement and the will were found.

"A violent quarrel between John Emmrick and his brother Valentine on a ship dock in New York was the cause. John had landed there after a visit in Germany at the home of his father, Conrad Emmrick. He brought back from Germany a sum of money sent by the father for his two other sons. Valentine met John at the boat dock to get the money, and, as Mrs. Carnahan explained, John refused to give any of the money to Valentine. The quarrel was a loud one, and finally John Emmrick walked away, vowing that neither of his brothers, Christopher or Valentine, would ever inherit any of his property. John Emmrick was himself a very wealthy man by this time. He had made money in the fur business.

"To make his threat good, Emmrick left his whole estate in

trust to his business partner, Astor, to be divided among remaining Emmricks after ninety years. Mrs. Carnahan could not say what really caused the original quarrel.

"It was Mrs. Carnahan's great-grandmother, Mrs. Nancy Emmrick, who brought the mysterious old sea trunk to Eau Claire about 1862. It's a bit tough to follow the genealogy now, but here it is: Nancy was the widow of George Emmrick, a son of Christopher. George and his wife moved from their home in Lysander, New York, some years after John Emmrick's death. They came to Walworth County, Wisconsin, where they lived for many years on a farm, and where George died in 1849. Their daughter Lucinda first married Henry Jones in New York State, and after his death remarried, this time to a Thomas Jones, no relation to her former husband. Thomas had a farm in the town of Washington near Eau Claire. Lucinda Emmrick Jones died there in 1901, and her daughter, Ann Jones (by her first husband), married Ben Cassel, Civil War veteran and one of the last survivors of the cavalry unit that captured Jefferson Davis. Mrs. Carnahan, nee Cassel, plaintiff in the lawsuit, was a daughter of this union. Her parents died in Mrs. Carnahan's home in Eau Claire. When the lawsuit against the Astor estate got really going, more than ninety heirs joined together to press the claim."

Doris Friedman got involved in the yarn when a company from Phoenix, Arizona, a genealogical concern, wrote her and asked that she help find the Joneses. She found them over in Colfax and gave the firm their address.

"It had been common knowledge among the Emmrick heirs away back that a partnership agreement between the old Emmrick and Astor existed, and that there was a will. But these had never been discovered. Search for these documents was pressed in every section of the United States where there was a living Emmrick. There was even a search made in Germany, for it was thought that the papers might have been deposited with some other family member there. All efforts failed.

"In 1927 the long searched-for documents were found at 316 Sixth Avenue, Eau Claire. It all reads like a detective story. Years before, one of the Joneses had remembered that a man named Emmrick had once come to the house, and had asked to examine the contents of an old sea chest in the attic. This investigator found nothing that he considered to have any bearing on the will. However, Mrs. Carnahan by chance delved again into the old chest in 1927 and there discovered a letter from old John Emmrick to his brother Christopher in "the bonds of brotherly love," seeming to indicate that the old quarrel had been patched up.

"The chest was then taken to the Eau Claire National Bank for safekeeping, where they noticed that inside was an old snuffbox, the cover of which was rusted tight. No attempt had ever been made to open it. Mrs. Carnahan suggested that the lining ought to be cut and this was done. Edward Lindmark ran his hand under the lining on all sides and pulled out a number of papers. One of these was dated New York, April 10, 1815, and signed by John Nicholas Emmrick. It read as follows:

" 'To my lawful heirs: I have left in trust with John Jacob Astor, my estate, personal property, together with my business, which is a very prosperous one; and of which I am two-thirds owner.'

"Two notebooks in John Emmrick's handwriting were also found; they disclosed the detailed story of how it all happened. It was after the Revolutionary War when the two remarkable men met — a fateful meeting that led to the creation of one of the greatest fortunes in American history. Emmrick had taken a shipment of furs to Europe and was returning home. John Jacob Astor, a penniless German youth who had spent some years in London, had shipped for America to seek his fortune. When the ship carrying the two men arrived in Chesapeake Bay, the Bay became frozen in, and the crew and passengers were marooned on board ship for two months before they could land in Baltimore. Emmrick and young Astor became well acquainted, and, when they finally landed, Emmrick took Astor to New York City where he got him a job with Robert Baun, an old furrier. For three years Astor worked there, and, according to one of the Emmrick notebooks, Astor worked well in the business.

"In 1787 Emmrick and Astor entered into a partnership in furs and other business, the agreement being that the proceeds of the said business would be divided two-thirds to John Emmrick and one-third to John Jacob Astor. These documents were written in brown ink; the signatures were authenticated. The ink was dim with age, and a magnifying glass was needed to read it.

"In 1865 James Parton wrote a biography of John Jacob Astor. The meeting on board boat is described, but Emmrick is never mentioned by name but called only 'a Young German.'

"Sometime later Mr. Carnahan pried up the lid of the old

snuffbox and found the original partnership agreement with John Jacob Astor, along with the trust agreement in which Astor was made trustee for ninety years.

"For a time excitement ran fever-high among the Emmrick heirs. A half-billion dollars is a lot, even when split ninety ways. Celebrations were held. However . . .

"Yes, it is a disappointing ending. The court dismissed the suit in December, 1928, and declared the trust to be void. Too much time had elapsed.

"All was not quite over, however. In the spring of 1930 the American heirs received word from the European heirs that in 1849 Linneus Emmrick of Eau Claire received a court decree ordering the Astor heirs to pay the Emmrick heirs their share. The heirs claimed that Linneus sold the whole ball of wax to Astor interests for $50,000, and then bribed a court clerk to give him the original records. This court decree and other documents were reported found in Europe. The American heirs then tried to force the possessor of the documents to release them, so that the decree would then be in force. Nothing, however, was ever made public. The pot at the end of the rainbow faded before it was ever found."

# The Eagle

When I started out to collect materials for this book, I told myself that one episode I would not include would be the story of the famous Wisconsin eagle, Old Abe. The story has already been told a lot of times, and I couldn't see why I should do it again. I knew, of course, that it was certainly one of the most famous of all Wisconsin tales, one that school kids and adults alike knew well. It had glamour, historical importance, and emotional warmth, and it was so much a part of the Civil War that you simply couldn't mention Wisconsin and the war without mentioning Old Abe . . . but I wasn't going to tell it again, anyway. But then I went up to Eau Claire and got swept into the wealth of activities that still go on there relating to Old Abe.

I met Mrs. David Barnes, who told me that each fall she and her husband take the new teachers in the Eau Claire school system around town and show them historical sites.

One of the things the Barneses point out is the steamboat landing at the foot of Gray Street on the Chippewa River, the place where Old Abe went off to the Civil War with Company C of Eau Claire.

"The boys had evidently fixed Old Abe up with colored streamers on his perch, and he was a proud little eaglet that went with them down to Camp Randall at Madison. The teachers are always interested in this because inevitably there is some young man who is going to be helping with the athletics at Memorial High School and is very glad to learn why the team there is called 'The Old Abes.'

"And one other trip that my husband and I make is to Cornell, Wisconsin. On the way, we go along the highway beside the Chippewa River and past the place where the historical marker says that 'This wayside is part of the old McCann farm, childhood home of Old Abe, the War Eagle.' This is about a half-mile north of Jim Falls, on Highway 178 in Chippewa County.

"Only a couple of months ago our newspaper took a picture of the stuffed eagle that we have in the Eau Claire museum, similar to what Old Abe was, and wrote the story again. You'd be surprised how often somebody comes by wanting information about that bird. We have a lot of material in the museum files, and the public library does too."

Mrs. Barnes went on to relate how her grandmother, Mrs. Judson, went to the Centennial Exposition at Philadelphia in 1876. She was from central New York, and one of the things she wanted most to see at the big fair was Old Abe. The eagle conveniently dropped a feather, which she eagerly picked up.

There are three Old Abe feathers in Eau Claire, at the univerisity. They were the property of Mr. Demerest, who used to carry Old Abe. The feathers are framed and Mr. Demerest's daughter, Mrs. Scott, had them in her home until she gave them to the university.

I finally figured that if the Eau Claire folks thought Old Abe's feathers were still important, then I really ought to tell his story again. So here it is, as told by Earle D. Rounds. His granddaughter, Evelyn, works in the university library.

On the morning of September 6, 1861, the little steamer *Stella Whipple* churned out from the steamboat landing at the foot of Gray Street, for a trip down the Chippewa River as far as La Crosse on the Mississippi. Sacks of wheat were piled on the lower deck. It was a rainy morning, but hundreds of people were gathered on the bank to see her start. Some were shouting loud good-byes and waving caps and handkerchiefs; many looked through tear-dimmed eyes, but could find no voice to call out a last farewell to son or brother or sweetheart. For it was not the sacks of wheat that had drawn the crowds to the river bank in the rain, but Eau Claire's first offering of a company of her own daring boys, enlisted to fight for the nation and for freedom.

A band on the upper deck helped to offset the sadness of parting with martial music; out in front on a rude perch between two little flags stood a bewildered eaglet starting on a career that was destined to make him the most famous eagle in American history.

Some Indians making maple sugar up on the Flambeau River in Chippewa County had found this eaglet's nest in the top of a tall pine. Not without a thrilling fight with the old birds, they had cut down the tree (some people still point out the stump) and rudely brought to earth the two little eagles. One was badly injured, but one they saved and brought down river when they came to sell their sugar. Dan McCann had a little farm and a "stopping place" at Jim Falls, and here the Indian, O-go-ma-ke-shik, tried to sell his eaglet.

Now the eaglet had a marvelous eye, and it may be that

Mrs. McCann "fell" for him because of that, or it may be that she wanted to get rid of a persistent trader. At any rate, she pointed to a sack of corn and offered to trade, and before she knew it she had a young eagle on her hands. The eaglet was kept in a barrel at McCann's, which was just across the bridge from the village of Jim Falls. As he grew, his appetite increased — and also his desire to fly, while beak and talons came more in use. He used to hop away through the woods and had to be chased and caught, and by September the McCanns were good and ready to part with the youngster.

Mr. McCann, who saw the young eagle as an appropriate military symbol, tried to sell him to a company recruiting at Chippewa Falls for the First Wisconsin Battery, but he couldn't interest them. When he heard that Captain Perkins was organizing a company for the Eighth Wisconsin Infantry at Eau Claire, he took his eagle down there. Some boys in the company at once accepted the idea of having an eagle for a mascot. Others liked him because he showed fight on the least provocation. A subscription was started among the men of the company and the businessmen. One tavern keeper whom the boys had been patronizing at first refused to subscribe, and Lt. Victor Wolf collected a few fellows out in the street in front of his place and gave him a "boo." When the tavern keeper understood what was up he brought the bird and presented it to the company. Some ladies rigged up a perch and nailed two little flags at the sides. The company voted to change their name from the Eau Claire Badgers to the Eau Claire Eagles.

Who knows what instincts stirred in the wild heart of the young captive as the boat backed out into the current, and he caught with darting eye the panorama of moving tree and hill and shore. Did the loud band behind him remind him of the thunder and the storm in his high nest in the pines? It is certain that, as he shook the raindrops from his plumage that September morning, he had reached a certain philosophy of life that made him ready for his remarkable career of comradeship and service in the great war for freedom — a career in which he was destined to play a part more fittingly than any other bird or beast has ever done at any time.

Partly through petting and teasing, and partly no doubt by an instinct that animals seem to have, he learned very soon to like some of the soldiers and to take a lasting dislike to others. Years after the war some of the company went to see the eagle at Madison, and he showed very plainly that he knew them and was glad to see them. On the other hand, an old soldier, Tom West, said in 1923 that he never could get near the eagle: "I plagued him too much."

As the boat steamed down the river, past Durand the beautiful Round Hill and Shoo Fly, out into the Father of Waters at Read's Landing, past Wabasha and Alma and Winona, the young eagle was getting acquainted with the men and was also watching the land and water and sky. We don't doubt that his eagle eye caught sight of his own kind soaring high above the hills, for eagles were common along the Chippewa. They still nest at Read's Landing; regrettably, one was shot not many years ago on the shores of Lake Pepin — the same species of the great Bald Eagle to which our eaglet belonged.

Word had gone ahead of the boat that the company had a live eagle with them, and crowds gathered wherever the boat stopped, and recruits joined the Eau Claire Eagles. As the boat whistled for landing at La Crosse, the guns of the First Wisconsin Battery fired a salute. This was a new sensation for the eagle, and the soldiers were delighted to find that cannon held no terror for their king of birds. Dwight Hazen, a fourteen-year-old drummer boy with the band on the *Stella Whipple*, told how the repeated firing of the cannon after the boat had landed got on the nerves of some of the band, but seemed to delight the eagle. Never in the long years ahead could the thunder of cannon or bursting of a shell send a shiver of fear through his stout heart — nor do aught but rouse in him a fierce spirit of combat; for with flashing eye and spreading pinions, above all the noise of war, he would shrill forth his eagle scream of defiance and his delight in battle.

But it was as the company was marching through the gate at Camp Randall at Madison on September 9 that the eagle won fame overnight. The Seventh Wisconsin and several companies of the Eighth were in camp, and seeing the Eau Claire boys and their eagle marching up the hill, the band started "Yankee Doodle." Music had come to affect the eagle, and the cheering soldiers apparently stirred his pulse. With a dart of his piercing eye to the flag floating above him, the eagle seized one end with his beak, and, spreading his wings with a continuously flapping motion, he held the flag aloft as they crossed the grounds through the excited crowd until they reached Colonel Murphy's headquarters. The *State-Journal* in Madison carried a colorful account of the incident on September 10, and all the North soon knew of the war eagle of Wisconsin.

Captain Perkins, six-feet-four, and with a long face like Lincoln's, named his new recruit "Old Abe." At the state's expense, Quartermaster Billings had a new perch made, a shield in the shape of a heart, on which was drawn the stars and stripes; painted along the base was 8th Reg. W. V. A few inches above the shield there was a crosspiece for the roost, with three arrows at each end to represent war. The staff was about five feet long, and the eagle bearer wore a belt with a leather socket so that the eagle on his perch could be carried high above the heads of the men. The company was mustered in as "C," the color company of the regiment, so Old Abe always marched beside the regimental colors.

It was no easy task to care for Old Abe and to carry him in battle. Young McGinnis had asked the privilege, and he proved a faithful keeper. With only a month and three days drill, Company C of the Eighth Regiment, started for the front. At Janesville an immense crowd greeted the Eagle regiment. The *Chicago Tribune* of October 13, speaking of the reception tendered the regiment in that city, said:

"A noticeable feature among them was the Chippewa Eagles — Captain Perkins' company — a company of first-class stalwart fellows. The live eagle which they brought with them was an object of much curiosity. He is a majestic bird and well trained. When marching, the eagle is carried at the head of the company, elevated on a perch at the top of a pole. The eagle was caught on the headwaters of the Chippewa River by an Indian. The men were offered a large sum for it in Madison, but they will not part with it. They swear it shall never be taken by the enemy. No doubt the Chippewa Eagles and their pet bird will be heard of again."

The next day at St. Louis, a crowd of southerners, seeing the eagle, called out, "A crow! a wild goose! a turkey buzzard!" As if to avenge this insult, Abe sprang from his perch with such force that he broke his tether, and flapping the caps off some of his tormentors with his powerful pinions, he soared up, while a thousand voices called after him. He lit on the chimney of a southern mansion, and the regiment did not march further until the eagle was secured. Here Governor Gamble, Sec. Simon Cameron, and General Thomas addressed the regiment, complimenting them on their soldierly appearance and their mascot. On the very next day the soldiers were ordered out after the enemy, and Old Abe got his initiation in cross-country marching — a pastime that was to be common in his life the next three years. At Big River the enemy had burned the bridge, and the soldiers had to wade waist deep. Abe noticed the fish and whistled shrilly as he was carried through. On October 21 — only a month and a half after leaving Eau Claire — the eagle, after an all-night march, saw his first battle at Fredericktown, Missouri. Company C was held in reserve, and from the top of the courthouse Abe watched with keen interest the long lines maneuvering for the attack, the charge; and as the roar of musketry reached his ears, with "the tumult and the shouting," he became wild with excitement, screeching and clawing at his perch.

After wintering at Sulphur Springs, Missouri, the regiment saw service at Point Pleasant, New Madrid, and Island No. 10, but it was on May 9 at Farmington, Mississippi, that our war eagle got into the thick of the fighting and won his right to share cover as well as peril with his soldier comrades. As the firing became severe, the men were ordered to lie down. Seeing his comrades hugging mother earth, Abe sprang down from his perch, but McGinnis, thinking he should stay up with the colors, put him back with orders to "stay put." Repeatedly he flew down after being put back, until finally the bearer, in disgust, threw the perch down and crouched down with the rest; then the eagle quickly crept up to him and lay flattened out. But when the bugle sounded the charge he leapt up with the men and stayed up through the fight. It was here that the kindly Captain Perkins was mortally wounded and buried nearby. Lt. Victor Wolf succeeded him in command of the company. The body of Captain Perkins was later removed to the national cemetery at Shiloh.

When the Confederate General Price attacked Corinth, Mississippi, on October 3, 1862, the Eagle regiment stood at the base of the hill in the front line with the eagle beside the colors. "a sentinel of liberty." Price saw him there and gave orders to capture or kill him at any cost, saying, "I would rather capture Old Abe than a whole brigade."

As the troops drew near, several men in Company C heard a Confederate officer shout, "There he is — the eagle — capture him boys!" In the midst of the din of battle, the eagle made a desperate lunge and gained his freedom, flying for a time over the heads of the soldiers, a target for thousands of rifles, his shrill battle scream sounding above the cannons' roar. Once he was seen to career as if struck, but he came swiftly down to his own line, giving his whistle of satisfaction as though having added another deathless deed to his growing fame as a fearless leader.

It was soon afterward that someone clipped Abe's wings and tail so that he wouldn't get lost. The whole regiment, officers and men, resented this, for Abe had always carried himself with regal dignity as became the king of birds, and now he cut but a sorry figure. David McLane of Menomonie, then Old Abe's bearer, became so disgusted that he resigned; Edward Homaston, a native of Vermont and a lifelong lover of eagles, gladly became his carrier and beloved comrade.

Since he grew up on the banks of its tributaries and spent much of his life within the sight and sound of its waters, it was fitting that our eagle should serve the valley of the Father of Waters. In transports he had sailed up and down on its broad waters, had watched the ceaseless flow past its bluffs and forests and plains, had spent many days on its shores at Point Pleasant. In the campaigns at Point Pleasant, New Madrid, and Island No. 10, he had helped to clear the rebels out. But now they had stretched great chains across the mighty stream at Vicksburg and erected strong fortresses to command the channel. It was fitting that Old Abe should have a part in the task of clearing a path for the commerce of freedom on the Mississippi.

As a preliminary, the Eagles under Sherman, in the midst of a great thunderstorm, on May 14, 1863, helped to drive the Confederates from Jackson, the capitol of Mississippi. Strangely stirred by the thunders of the heavens mingling with the thunder of cannon, with piercing eye while the lightning played on his plumage, Old Abe saw the rebel flag hauled down and the stars and stripes raised over the Capitol on whose steps thousands of human beings had been auctioned into slavery. It was in this campaign that General Sherman, observing the soldierly qualities of the regiment, said to them, "You are worthy to carry the American eagle."

He hurried them on to Vicksburg, for just eight days later, the regiment took part in Grant's desperate assault. In this charge, Homaston tripped and fell, and at the same instant a rebel bullet struck Abe's breast a glancing blow, for he made an upward plunge, dragging his bearer to his feet just as a rebel shot struck where he had lain. Hurrying to rejoin the colors,

Homaston planted the perch beside the flag in plain sight of the enemy's battery under a large tree. A shell cut off the top of the tree and burst with terrible havoc, killing several and tearing many holes in the flag. Abe made another lunge but was held fast and remained in the scant shelter of the fallen tree until they were ordered into a ravine. As the broken companies gathered into this shelter, a soldier caught a frightened rabbit and threw it to Abe's perch, saying, "Here, Abe! You've earned this fellow." And while the eagle was enjoying his meal, heedless of his narrow escapes from death and of the roar of battle, Homaston took several canteens to fill at a nearby spring,, exposed to the enemy guns. A piece of exploding shell hit the canteen he held under the spring, but he remained to fill the others, and his first concern was to find his eagle safe. So when Vicksburg surrendered on July 4, and the Union troops marched into the city, celebrating the greatest victory of the war and the opening of the great river to the sea, at the head of the column beside General Logan — called the Black Eagle of Illinois — rode our famed war eagle of Wisconsin.

We have not space to tell of his further service in the ill-starred Red River Expedition; or how his sharp whistle led to the capture of the courier in a fifteen-mile night march on Henderson's Hill, making it possible to learn the countersign and capture the fort by surprise attack; of his return on furlough in June, 1864, and his noisy welcome at Madison and Eau Claire, and his celebration of the Fourth of July at Chippewa; of how his head-feathers turned white at this time, so on his return to the regiment he had an added dignity in appearance which he carried through his remaining years.

We can only mention his presentation to the state by Captain Wolf when mustered out of service; his great help in raising money for a soldiers' widows and orphans fund; and his reception at the Philadelphia Centennial in 1876 and at state and county fairs. Old Abe had an untimely death in 1881, having been exposed to fumes in a fire; finally, his stuffed body burned in the Capitol fire at Madison in February, 1904.

# The Cranberry Men

A cranberry bog, to a stranger at least, is a fascinating place. One day at the original Lewis bog at Shell Lake in harvest time I watched the clever, small harvesting machines enter the bog water and the brilliant berries come pouring out the chute into the boat floating alongside.

"We used to do it with hand scoops," Chuck Lewis, Jr., said. He took one of the clumsy-looking part-fork, part-basket implements and showed me how the scooping was done: swing the heavy tool downward into the water and with a sharp, upward pull bring out the bright fruit.

"Hard work," Chuck said. "Took practice and a strong back!"

Chuck has been in the cranberry business with his father almost since he graduated from college — he went to the University of Minnesota, just as his father did. Ever since he has been in the business he has talked, breathed, eaten, and lived cranberries, and lately he has taken to flying his own plane on business trips to save time, so he can grow more berries!

I tried to picture how it was in the days when the harvesting was done by hand, with the scoops, and the rugged work it must have been, wading in the water, swinging the scoop, bringing up the berries, and down again for more. I tried it, with Chuck looking on and laughing at my ineptitude. It did indeed take skill, strong arms, and a strong back.

The older Lewis bog is very picturesquely located. The sorting sheds and the foreman's house are on high ground; down below in the valley are the bogs, with the water ditches and the flood gates — to me a sort of wild sight, cultivated, yet somehow not cultivation like any other kind of farming. Back and higher up is the pond, with a few old stumps sticking out of the water, and back farther the woods and the hills come down. I think I can see why cranberry growing has a fascination for an outdoor and imaginative man like Chuck Lewis. There is definitely a feeling in the process and the fruit, of an earlier, wilder and more primitive day.

After the trucks had been loaded at the bogs, I followed them up to the sorting sheds, where the trash was removed and the berries graded. I watched while the stream of berries poured from the machine into the Ocean Spray trailer to be transported to the canning factory. Most growers belong to the Ocean Spray

Cooperative these days, and they really see nothing more of the berries after they have left the grading machine. Ocean Spray does the rest.

I have always been greatly intrigued by the cranberry operation, partly because cranberries have always been a favorite food of mine, and partly because I sensed that the preparation of a bog must entail a fantastic amount of work. I wanted to know, from a pioneer, just how it was done.

I got the yarn from Chuck's father.

Charlie Lewis, Sr., is a man of perseverance who believes that you have to go all the way if you want to make a difficult idea take root. When the local citizens were trying to raise money to build the Indianhead Art Center at Shell Lake so the kids and adults in northwestern Wisconsin could have opportunities in the arts, Charlie Lewis, Sr., was one of the first to come forward. He said, "You are trying to do a difficult thing. It's going to take you several years to make the center a success. You have a struggle. I like hard challenges. I will contribute."

At eighty, Charlie still manages one of the two large Lewis bogs. This, in his own words, is how the cranberry business developed at Shell Lake.

"My father encouraged me to go into the cranberry business after talking to somebody who was interested in cranberries. It sounded good to my father, who had an agricultural background (he was a member of the Minnesota Supreme Court at the time).

"When I graduated from the forestry school of the University of Minnesota in 1910, I went to Massachusetts, which is the leading cranberry state. I had been in the class of a Professor Franklin who came to Minnesota from Massachusetts and taught entomology in the ag college.

"I had talked to him about going into cranberries, too, because he was from the cranberry state. Later he returned to Massachusetts to start a cranberry station and was made the director of that station. When I got off the train at Middleboro, Massachusetts, be hanged if I didn't meet the professor on the street!

"I hadn't been too good in his entomology class because it came right after lunch and I was on the football team and, well, that was that. Anyway I asked him if he had a place for me in his experiment station in Massachusetts. I thought it would be wonderful if I could get in that.

"Well, he hemmed and hawed and said that it was his first year and he had a small budget and he had all the help hired that he needed. He wouldn't be able to use me that summer.

"I said to him, 'How about next spring?' I think that in the back of his head he thought that I wouldn't be anywhere around the next spring, so he said, 'Oh sure, if you're here next spring, I'll be glad to take you on.'

"Well, I found a job working down there in Massachusetts, just a common laborer. There were two classes of laborer: Negroes from one of the islands off Portugal, who were paid $1.50 a day, and then there were Finlanders, and they got $1.75 a day.

"I found a summer job on the cranberry marsh and I worked there from the first part of July until the harvesting was finished about the first of November. Then I contacted a man at Yale in the forestry school. He recommended that I see a fellow who ran the American Forestry Company. I got a job with him working up in the Berkshire Hills bossing a crew that was thinning out a stand of timber.

"I stayed there all winter, and every once in a while I would drop a note to Dr. Franklin. I told him I was still expecting to come and work for him. He finally, after I had worn him down, said that I could come the first of May; that's how I happened to go down to work for Dr. Franklin. It was a wonderful experience.

"I had previously worked at the cranberry experiment station in Wisconsin between my sophomore and junior college years, so I had a little bit of experience. I took care of the weather station, got nineteen dollars a month, and I had to do the cooking for three men. So that was good background for what I had to do in Massachusetts with Dr. Franklin. I took care of the weather station, which was established while I was there, and worked with him until July. We became very close friends, and the friendship lasted during his lifetime. He became the leading scientific authority on cranberries in the country.

"Then, in July, I came back to Wisconsin and started looking for a location. I was determined that I was going to have my own cranberry bog. I found this place out here at Beaverbrook. My father knew a real estate man in Spooner. This man mentioned places that might be suitable and I went out and looked them over. I thought this Beaverbrook place might be a good location. I didn't have any money, so I borrowed five hundred dollars from my dad and then I tackled pretty near everybody I knew, to form a stock company, and sold stock. Among my stockholders were two of my professors at the university.

"Well, I started in. Came up to Shell Lake in August, 1911. I had just a team of horses I had bought in South St. Paul, and I had the help of the professor of livestock at the university in picking them out. I drove this team out to Shell Lake, and out to Beaverbrook which is about five miles east. I had to cut a road to get them in there, and set up a tent. I hired a carpenter to build me a little shack for an office and to live in. I did my own cooking and I hired a Finlander whom I knew in Massachusetts. I thought he would made a good foreman. I got him to come out here with his family. John Makki was his name.

"He came out and lived at Beaverbrook, and that winter was the coldest winter we have ever had — winter of 1911-12.

"I didn't know enough to bank up my little shack. When I got up one morning and looked at the thermometer I kept on the floor under my bed, it was eleven below zero . . . under my bed!

"I had a dish of prunes I had put to soak on the stove when I went to bed. That pot of prunes was frozen and some of the prunes stuck out of the ice.

"That morning the foreman came over. I saw him stop and look at the thermometer on the outside of the house near the window. I had a little airtight stove in the office, about two feet square; it wouldn't burn very long, you know. I was monkeying with that stove when he came in. I says, 'John, how cold is it?'

"He says, 'Dat tam thermometer don't know nothing this morning.'

"I didn't know what he meant, so I went outside and looked. The thermometer registered forty below and the mercury was all down in the bulb!

"Well, we got about fifteen acres developed, that is, scalped and leveled, and we sanded it in the wintertime on the ice. One thing that was rather funny — I woke up and I thought it was daylight. Gee, I had to go down and feed the horses and harness them because I was driving team then. I rushed down to the barn and fed the horses and put their harness on; then I ran back to the house and grabbed a bite to eat. I looked up and there was the full moon. Then I looked to see what time it was. It was two-thirty in the morning!

296

"We planted the first marsh the next spring — that was the spring of 1912. We bought the plants from another grower. You see, the Wisconsin cranberries all came from the wild cranberry, and at that time many growers were planting the native cranberry; but this man, Mr. Sarles, who was one of the oldest growers in the cranberry business in Wisconsin, had done some selection from the wild cranberries, and he had developed a variety that he called the Sarles Jumbo. They were a large, attractive berry, a much better berry than the native berry. Now that's one of the principal varieties grown in the state. We've always planted that same variety since.

"We planted the marsh by hand. All we had to work with was horses to plow the upper surface of the sod. We had to take that off, and we built the dikes with that sod, because the levels were different and we had to divide the bog into fields. We planted with a little "dibber," that is, we would take a few pieces of cranberry vine and place the end of this dibber on them and push the vines into the soil. We had put on about four inches of sand, so we had to plant the vines about four inches deep.

"The first year about all cranberries do is take root. We planted them fourteen inches apart, which is too far for Wisconsin. The second year they start to send out runners. The third year they will send up uprights, and the fourth year the plants will start to bear.

"My wife and I were married in April of 1914, and shortly after we were married, her father, who was U.S. district attorney in Minnesota, came up to see what the heck this cranberry business was. He was a little skeptical. Understandable.

"I explained how the first year they took root, second they got runners, third uprights, and fourth, they started to bear fruit. Fifth and sixth year the crops keep increasing.

"He says, 'My God,' he says, 'that is a great exhibition of faith!'

"And the plants did pretty well for us. They took longer than it would have if they had been planted closer together.

"But while the first plants were developing, we were getting more land ready. We kept on planting until we had about sixty acres planted. I lived for the first five or six years on a thousand dollars a year, and saved some money!

"Both my wife and I were born in Fergus Falls, Minnesota. I claimed that the way we met was that my mother was wheeling me out in a buggy, and her mother was wheeling her out, and they stopped to talk, and I had a bottle and handed it over to her and says, 'Have one on me!'

"Then we both went to the University of Minnesota. I used to take her out, and we became engaged in the spring of my senior year. Then I went east. I always told her it took me four years to save up enough money to buy the license and pay the preacher! She was just as interested in cranberries as I was!

"We picked the berries by hand the first two years they bore. Got a bunch of people from Shell Lake and gave them fifty percent of the berries they picked. And we had a lot of Indians from Coudery. The Indians came down with their whole families and pitched their tents on the hill. It was really quite a sight in the evening to see their campfires burning. They had a bunch of kids, you know. And there were some wonderful people among them. Some of them were wonderful workers and wonderful characters, too. So we had to have a store and a bunk house, sort of like they had in logging camps. We had as high as eighty-six men working there. They were doing construction for the bogs. They had to do all the work with wheelbarrows, hauling sand and leveling. Some parts of the bog were so soft that we got what we called "bog shoes," which are hard maple, about an inch and a half thick and about nine inches square with a leather shoe to put the horses' hooves in, then you would just buckle them on.

"We had to use the horses to pull the plow, and if we didn't have those bog shoes on they would go into the soft places clear up to their bellies. Once in a while one of them would get down with even the bog shoe on. Then you would have to dig and dig to get the horse's leg out . . . some of the trials we had.

"We worked ten hours a day, and we started out with a wage of twenty-five cents an hour. We started the bog in 1914 and didn't get anything back until 1918.

"In 1918 we had a pretty good crop, but we hadn't built a warehouse so we shipped all the berries to Minneapolis. John Makki, my Finn foreman, went back to Massachusetts the third year. He missed the Finnish baths. The way he had to take baths out here . . . he used to heat water and fill a barrel up with water. They would put the kids in the barrel first, then he and his wife would bathe in the same water!

"In 1918 we started hand scooping — large scoop which

actually scooped the berries out of the bog. Hard to do it well. We had to learn how to hand scoop. Luckily one of the Indians had seen it done and showed us how. John Harrington. I started out, and finally John said, 'Hold. Let's try it a different way!' I could see right away that he knew what he was talking about. We hand scooped for many years until machinery came in. Now all the cranberries are harvested by machines. In those days when we started harvesting, we would sometimes have as many as a hundred men there looking for work. The wages got up to forty cents an hour in a few years, for harvesting . . . hand scooping. Now, the contrast! We have about twenty now. And to get twenty is a hard job.

"This relief problem has gone completely haywire. So many men you ask if they'll come to work say no. They're getting relief; if they work, they'll lose their relief! I had one young fellow . . . I guess, the way I summed it up, he must have worn out his welcome somewhere, because the man he was staying with brought him over and asked if I could use a good man. I says yes, I could always use a good man. He says, 'My nephew here would like to work.'

"Well, he came the next morning, and I put him under another man in the highland helping with a machine. Next morning I needed more men on the bog. I told him to go to a certain man and get a pair of boots. 'Boots,' he said. 'I wouldn't like to work in the water.'

"I said, 'Well, there're about sixteen people down there who are wearing boots and working in the water. They don't seem to mind it.'

"Oh, I wouldn't like that."

"Don't you ever do anything you don't like to do?"

"No, sir."

"I said, 'Well, you can come up and get your check. I can't use you.'

"But, oh, nothing was like that terrible time in 1959. Set the industry back five years. I was out hunting pheasants in South Dakota not long after it happened. We were waiting for twelve o'clock — season opened then. A fellow came by, said he had a place up on the hill that was alive with pheasants. We were welcome to come and hunt there. Well, I had some Lewis cranberries in the back of my car. I went and got two or three pounds of cranberries and says, 'Thank you. Here are some cranberries. Maybe you'd like to have these.'

" 'Cranberries,' he says, 'cranberries! Oh, no. They're poison!'

"That's the way the public took it."

I remembered something of the cranberry disaster of 1959, and Chuck Lewis, Jr., repeated his father's statement that 1959 was the worst year the growers ever had. That year the U.S. Department of Agriculture approved a herbicide called Amino-Triozol, or shortened up, just A.T. It was used to get rid of certain weeds that are always a problem to cranberry bog men. The growers were not supposed to use this chemical after July 1, but, unfortunately, a few of them did.

The chemical was put on with a spreader, like fertilizer, so much per acre, and it was very effective. It took out a lot of weeds the growers had been fighting for years.

When A.T. was cleared for cranberries, evidently the Food and Drug Administration must not have had complete reports from their pathologists, because they issued information that there was zero danger from cancer-causing elements.

The scientist from American Cyanamid who had done the original experimenting fed cranberries to rats, cranberries he had sprayed with this weed killer. Nothing happened. He then gave them doses of about ten times the amount anyone would ever get from cranberries grown where the chemical was used. Nothing happened. Then he gave the rats a hundred times what they would get from normal spraying, and the animals got swellings in the neck. He made slides of this rat tissue. Although there was considerable disagreement, some of the scientists who examined the tissue thought the chemical did cause cancer. However, when the scientists stopped using the chemical, the swelling in the rats went away.

The growers then always felt that the disaster that struck them was caused by pretty shaky proof. It finally came out that a human being would have to eat two tons of cranberries a year for ten years to get as much A.T. as one of the experimental rats had had. Nevertheless, word came to the press that the whole cranberry crop was suspect, that any person eating cranberries might get cancer.

It happened just two weeks before Thanksgiving. Lewis was worried. His operation had used the chemical, and he was fearful that his berries would show some traces of it. He didn't realize just how the whole thing happened. They had used the chemical according to the label; Lewis had sent samples of their berries to the university where they were tested. The report came back "All clear."

In November they were just beginning to ship the cranberry crop. Lewis had shipped one load to Duluth. That same night he was watching a movie on television when an announcement came through that showed a clerk putting cranberries out again on a store shelf. The clip said: "This particular lot of cranberries has been tested and found to be completely free of any contamination by A.T." "Furthermore," the announcer said, "The berries are from the Badger Cranberry Company at Shell Lake, Wisconsin!" The Lewis outfit!

Chuck Lewis thought he had it made! Unfortunately the public at that point was terrified, and Lewis didn't sell another cranberry, despite the announcement on TV.

Nobody bought cranberries. Actually only six lots of cranberries out of the thousands of tests made showed any contamination. One of these lots was in Wisconsin, one in Oregon, one in Washington, and one or two in the East. However, there was nothing to be done. It was a catastrophe for the cranberry growers.

The two Lewises, father and son, dug a great trench and poured in their whole crop and covered the berries with earth. That wasn't the end of the bad time, because the next year they couldn't sell any berries either. The public just wasn't taking a chance. For three years the growers dumped their berries. The fourth year, 1962, they sold almost everything — not always at a good price — and the fifth year the incident was apparently forgotten and the cranberry market returned to normal.

Since 1963 the market has been fine, only now that cranberry producing has become mildly profitable, everybody and his brother, as Chuck Lewis says, is planting cranberries. There may be a surplus. Chuck got an ulcer from the 1959 trouble. No matter what the market does he doesn't figure that he will get another one. Nothing could be as bad as that terrible fall of 1959.

XIII. Coon Valley Farm

# PART FIVE -
# SOMETHING OF
# OLD MILWAUKEE

XIV. Milwaukee Waterfront

M any Milwaukee tales have been told to me by many people. One that I have heard told or referred to repeatedly, is the story of the wreck of the *Lady Elgin*. How could it be otherwise when so many relatives of those who went down on the *Elgin* still live in Milwaukee? The wreck worked profound changes in many personal lives and, indeed, in the whole political complexion of the city, the large majority of those who lost their lives were Irish and thus vital to the Irish flavor of the city and its politics. One elderly lady, who sang me the sentimental ballad of the *Lady Elgin*, said that the tragedy broke the Irish rule in Milwaukee!

Sometimes, after reading or hearing so many times the narrative of such an event, I get the feeling that the people involved in it are really there, in the shadows, and that I am failing them, somehow, by not letting them tell their own story. A writer has license to call characters out of the past, and I have chosen to do that with the *Lady Elgin* and her passengers, rather than to choose one of the living narrators. I think it is first necessary, though, to present some of the facts.

*"Lost on the* **Lady Elgin***"*
*Up from the poor man's cottage*
*Forth from the mansion's door,*
*Reaching across the waters,*
*Echoing 'long the shore . . .*

*Caught in the morning breezes,*
*Borne on the evening gale*
*Cometh a voice of mourning--*
*A sad and solemn wail.*

*Lost on the* **Lady Elgin**
*Sleeping to wake no more;*
*Numbered with that three hundred*
*Who failed to reach the shore.*

In 1860 the side-wheel steamer *Lady Elgin** was one of the

---

*Lady Elgin, after whom the vessel was named, was the wife of Lord Elgin, Governor General of Canada from 1847 to 1854.

largest and finest boats on the Great Lakes. Owned by G. S. Hubbard, A. T. Spencer, and F. A. Howe, she carried freight and passengers on Lake Michigan and Lake Superior.

On the morning of September 7, a large excursion party got aboard at Milwaukee to go to Chicago. The excursion was under the auspices of a Milwaukee military company, which was trying to raise money to purchase arms, as the country was at that time fired with talk of the impending war. There were about three hundred of the excursionists, mostly members of the military company, with their families and friends. The boat was to start the return trip to northern lake points at 8 P.M., but because of the excursion she didn't leave the dock at the foot of La Salle Street until about 11:30.

The exact number of passengers on board is uncertain. There was no list of those bound for Milwaukee; in addition, some had boarded for northern points. Some accounts place the number, including members of the crew, at 393; it is certain that there were about 400.

About 2:30 A.M., September 8, at a point some ten miles out from Waukegan, the schooner *Augusta*, bound for Chicago with a cargo of lumber, collided with the *Lady Elgin*. The schooner showed no lights, and responsibility for the accident was placed upon her officers. The schooner struck the steamer forward of the paddle wheel on the starboard side with such force that her jib boom penetrated the steamer's cabin. The captain of the *Augusta* called to the steamer, asking if she needed help, but the officers, not realizing how badly their boat had been damaged, declined. The schooner then continued on her course, her officers thinking that they were the worse sufferers for the collision. On arriving in Chicago the next morning they learned of the loss of the *Lady Elgin*.

Crew members immediately lowered three boats and attempted to stop the hole in the steamer's side, but the lake was so rough that they were unable to accomplish anything, and soon their oars were broken and lost. About a half-hour after the collision the boilers and engine broke through the bottom of the boat, and it went to pieces rapidly. In a few minutes all the passengers were struggling in the water. Many of them seized pieces of the wreckage and drifted toward shore with a strong northeast wind. Many persons even kept afloat by clinging to the bodies of cattle that had been in the cargo.

One of the first to reach shore was Fred Rice, the steward.

He landed near Waukegan and immediately gave the alarm. News of the disaster spread rapidly, and soon crowds of people from Chicago to Waukegan gathered on the shore. During the early morning a boat was sent on a special train from Chicago to Winnetka, but because the bluffs there were so high and the lake so rough she could not be launched. After several vain attempts that plan of rescuing survivors was abandoned.

All day the watchers on shore could plainly see the victims. Although they had been in the cold water for hours, many of them retained their holds on pieces of wreckage and drifted safely. When they reached the breakers, however, they would almost invariably be wrenched from the objects they clung to and the undertow would wash them out again, lost before the eyes and within hearing of the persons on the shore.

Edward W. Spencer, a young divinity student from Northwestern University, was the hero of the day. Only 30 persons came through the breakers alive, and of that number Spencer saved 17. Some 60 others were picked up by a tug, which was sent to the scene of the disaster from Chicago. Of the approximately 400 passengers, 2 or 3 less than 100 were saved.

Captain Wilson of the ill-fated *Lady Elgin* gathered a number of people on a large piece of the deck that had held together when the boat went down. These passengers drifted toward the shore at Winnetka and seemed to have just reached safety when the raft struck on a sandbar and most of those on it were drowned. Captain Wilson was among those lost; at the time he was trying to save a small girl, and undoubtedly gave his own life in the attempt.

For days the wreckage and bodies drifted to shore, and all bodies that were not identified and claimed by friends or relatives were given a decent burial. The last body to be recovered was that of a deck hand, found on October 27 at the mouth of the Calumet River.

Spencer wrote his own account of the tragedy:

On the morning of the wreck a number of us students went out to the lake shore for a walk and were met by Henry Kidder, riding down from his place near Gross Point, who told us of the disaster. Supposing the *Lady Elgin* had been blown ashore and that we might assist in rescuing those aboard, we hurried along and came to the dead body of a woman close in, with no vessel in sight, but plenty of wreckage. This impressed me that the disaster must have occurred far out in the lake. I hurried ahead through an open field on the high bluff. Between the field and the lake was a narrow strip of thick brush and timber. Coming to an opening, I saw out in the breakers what appeared to be a human being. With my coat I waved to the students behind me, jumped down the bank and made my way out just in time. I grasped the chilled and helpless woman just as the breakers washed her from the wreckage, to which she had clung for weary hours. Then the struggle began, the huge breakers forcing us much of the time, and the strong undertow tending to carry us back out into the lake. It was a struggle, indeed, and I was gaining but little, when two tall, stout biblical students, to whom I had signaled, came to our relief. One named Chadian was from Indiana. The other was the Rev. W. S. Harrington. With the angry surf pounding us against the shore, we fastened a shawl, thrown down to us, under her arms, and then a rope, and as we let go her feet those on the bank above grasped her hands and lifted her to safety.

Two other incidents will illustrate the labors of that eventful day. As yet few persons were coming in shore. Later they came in great numbers.

Going north about half a mile, I saw another person, a man, coming in on the long swelling waves out on the lake, into the breakers. While not an expert swimmer, I was born and raised on the Mississippi River and had learned to be at home in the water. As I reached this man far out from shore, his raft hit my head, seriously hurting me, but chilled as he was, and helpless, I succeeded in getting him ashore. Thereafter, for my own safety, I had a rope tied to me with someone on shore to play it out. Several times during the day I came up through huge breakers just missing heavy timbers and wreckage that endangered my life. Of the lighter wreckage, I carried bruises for two or three months, and the postmaster at Evanston told me that he saw, at one time, my feet sticking out of the top of a breaker.

About 10 A.M., while standing on the bank by a fire and covered with blankets, and after going into the lake many times, I saw someone coming into the breakers apparently supporting something partly submerged by his side, and it came to us that someone from the wreck was trying to save a companion in distress. This was an inspiration to me. I rushed into the lake to the end of the rope and waited while Dr. Bannister, who held the rope, and who had been standing with me at the fire, tied on another, which enabled me to reach them after a tremendous struggle. The high bluff back from the shore was covered with a great multitude looking on with intense interest. I remember now, after nearly forty-eight years have passed, that when the pilot of the *Lady Elgin* and his wife were rescued the storm of cheers from the thousands on shore drowned the roar of the storm raging about us.

The body of Captain Wilson was picked up by a tug a week after the wreck and taken to Chicago.

Among those lost were Sir Herbert Ingram, a member of the English Parliament, and his wife and eldest son. The body of the father was recovered and taken to Boston, England, for burial, but the son was never found. Sir Ingram was the founder of the *London Illustrated News.*

Another was the proprietor of the *New Orleans Picayune.*

Demonstrations against the officers and crew of the *Augusta* occurred in both Chicago and Milwaukee after the disaster. The name of the schooner was finally changed to the *Colonel Cook*, and she sailed on the lakes for many years afterward under that name.

Captain Malott of the *Augusta* was drowned a few years later when the bark *Major* was wrecked.

The owners of the *Lady Elgin* started suit against the owners of the *Augusta*, but the latter sent all the members of the crew out of the country so that no witnesses were available. The suit never came to trial.

Among the rescued was John F. Hartranft, who later became governor of Pennsylvania.

Now, here before me in my study, I have assembled a grim little group . . . leading figures in the drama of the wreck of the proud *Elgin*. First, here is Captain Wilson . . . a large man. A sad man.

"I'm Captain Jack Wilson," he begins. "The *Lady Elgin* was my ship, and I lost her there on that terrible night, with the Michigan waves rollin' wild in the teeth of a nor'east gale!

"Aye, she was a proud ship. Named, she was, after Lady Elgin, wife o' the Governor General o' Canada. Pride o' Lake Michigan we called the *Lady Elgin!* Three hundred feet long she was, with twin paddle wheels. But she was a death ship, my boy. A thing o' doom!

"Aye! And even now when the lake rolls high of a September night, you'll hear my voice whisperin' out o' the mighty rollin' waters:

*Lost on the* Lady Elgin
*Sleeping to wake no more:*
*Numbered with that three hundred*
*Who failed to reach the shore.*"

It was on September 8, 1860, that the *Lady Elgin* met her doom. 1860! The war guns would soon be booming, and men would soon be marching. Union or disunion! Free or slave! And here, beside Captain Wilson, is another captain who failed to make the shore: Captain Barry of Milwaukee.

"How'd you happen to be aboard the *Lady Elgin*, Captain Barry?"

"It's a curious story, my friend," says the Captain. "It's part of the whole story of where Wisconsin stood in relation to the rest of the Union."

"How's that, Captain?"

"In 1860 Governor Randall of Wisconsin and some members of the Wisconsin legislature were extreme Abolitionists. Threats were made that Wisconsin would secede from the Union unless slavery was abolished. You see, I was captain of the Union Guards — a mighty proud Milwaukee company — and one day the adjutant general of the state stopped me and said, 'Barry, in case of war between this state and the United States — in the event we should secede and should take up arms against the nation — where would you stand?'

"Sir," I replied, "My Guards and I would stand with the United States of America. Any other course would be treason!"

"In that case, Barry," says the Adjutant General, "We will immediately disband your company. I order you to give up your arms, and the arms of the Union Guards!"

"And did you, Captain?"

"I was forced to give up the arms," says the Captain. "But the people *wanted* the Union Guards in Milwaukee. Congressman Larabee tried to get us arms from the United States government. He failed because we were no longer part of the state militia. The only course left was for us to purchase our own arms. Congressman Larabee found muskets for us at two dollars apiece!"

"And how did you plan to pay for 'em, Captain?" I ask.

"We planned to pay for them by conducting an excursion to Chicago. I looked around, found an excursion boat that'd take us all from Milwaukee to Chicago and back. The name of that boat was . . . "

"It was the *Lady Elgin*, Captain."

Fate played many strange tricks in this famous disaster. In the group before us is a well-known Englishman:

SIR HERBERT: I'm Sir Herbert Ingram, founder and publisher of the *Illustrated London News*. In September, 1860, I was visiting the United States. Some of my friends in England said I was making that trip to escape a curse . . . maybe I was; maybe the whole story of the *Lady Elgin* disaster was because of me. You see, many, many centuries ago, there was a priest of ancient Thebes in Egypt. On his deathbed he supposedly said . . .

PRIEST: Place my body in the pyramid of my fathers. And let it be inscribed with my body that whosoever touches my tomb or desecrates my form will be cursed by the triple curse of Isis and Osiris. Let it so be known and written down for all the ages to take warning!

SIR HERBERT: And my father, on a trip to Egypt, assisted in the excavation of the mummy of this very priest. Yes, and he purchased this very mummy which was sent to the British Museum in London. And one day at the museum, an Egyptologist examined the body . . .

EGYPTOLOGIST: I found a curious thing, sir, that might interest you: a roll of papyri in the mummy windings. Freely translated it says: "Let a curse destroy him who touches my sacred remains. May his children, and his children's children, suffer the fate of untimely death."

SIR HERBERT: And not long afterward my father died, and my younger brother was trampled to death by an elephant while hunting in Somaliland. The curse was working, you see. And while I myself scoffed at the curse, my friends thought — when I took the American journey — that I was running away from my fate. Well, on September 7, 1860, my wife and I were in the city of Chicago. We wished to journey up the west shore of Lake Michigan, to visit Milwaukee and other points along the way. On the morning of September 7, while I was reading the paper, my wife . . .

LADY INGRAM: When do we leave Chicago, Herbert?

SIR HERBERT: It says here, my dear, that an excursion steamer will leave the foot of La Salle Street tonight for Milwaukee and points north. I think we should take that steamer.

LADY INGRAM: I'm afraid of those small boats, Herbert.

SIR HERBERT: Nonsense! They aren't small boats! The lake steamers are quite large! According to the description, this boat is an especially fine one!

LADY INGRAM: I can't say I particularly like the idea. But if you think we should go . . .

SIR HERBERT: I think we should. Definitely.

LADY INGRAM: Very well, dear. What's the name of the boat?

SIR HERBERT: Why . . . it's called the *Lady Elgin!*

Here is a couple who loved each other very much. Their name is Eviston, Mr. and Mrs. John Eviston of Milwaukee. You see, on the evening of September 6, 1860, the Evistons were having supper.

MRS. EVISTON: John . . .

EVISTON: Yes, dear . . . ?

MRS. EVISTON: John, do you know what day tomorrow is?

EVISTON: Why . . . September 7, 1860.

MRS. EVISTON: I mean, what *great* day?

EVISTON: Well, it's not the Fourth of July . . . or Washington's Birthday . . .

MRS. EVISTON: You've forgotten again! Darling, it's our anniversary!

EVISTON: Why, it is! Sure enough. Let me see, how many is it?

MRS. EVISTON: Oh, don't count them. Every anniversary's been happier than the one before. Darling, do you love me as much as you did last year?

EVISTON: I love you more than I did last year.

MRS. EVISTON: I love you more too. I love you so much it seems nothing in the world could ever separate us. Nothing!

EVISTON: I know. When I think how happy we've been, I believe I could fight and whip the strongest thing in the world!

MRS. EVISTON: John, there's a steamer excursion to Chicago tomorrow. It's been arranged by Captain Barry and the Union Guards. It's to help them raise money to pay for their new muskets. Could we go, John?

EVISTON: Why, I suppose so. Certainly!

MRS. EVISTON: There'll be dancing and singing. We'll have the whole day in Chicago together.

EVISTON: I'll get the tickets first thing in the morning.

|             | Say, what boat's making the excursion? |
| MRS. EVISTON: | Captain Wilson's boat. The *Lady Elgin*. She's the best boat on the Lake! Oh, John, I love you so much! |
| EVISTON: | Darling, here's to the happiest anniversary yet! |
| MRS. EVISTON: | Here's to *you*, John! |

And there is one more vignette, arranged by Fate, setting the scene for the disaster. In a dormitory room at Northwestern University at Evanston, Illinois, a slender young fellow named Edward Spencer talked with his brother on the evening of September 7, 1860.

"Seems like we never do anything except study anymore," said Spencer.

"Sure does, Ed," replied his brother. "This theological course is gettin' me down. We ought to take a holiday. Go for a long hike! Remember how we used to hike along the Mississippi River out home? I'd like to go for a long walk tomorrow — out beyond Winnetka and right on up the lake."

"Then let's do it," Spencer said. "Maybe we could stop some place along the lake and take a swim. I don't get enough swimming anymore."

"You used to be the best swimmer along our whole part of the river out home," replied his brother.

"I *was* pretty good. But I'm rusty. Would like to try swimming in Lake Michigan though. Big waves kind of challenge me. Well, tomorrow we'll have an outing!"

"It's a bargain," said the brother.

Now from the vignettes to the proud boat herself. There's the *Lady Elgin*'s whistle as she stands at the pier at Milwaukee on the evening of September 6, 1860, a proud white ship, black smoke funneling out of her stacks, her big paddle wheels beginnin' to churn in their housings.

There's Captain Wilson on the bridge; there's Captain Barry of the Union Guards, looking over his men. There's John Eviston and his wife, arm in arm, there up in the bow! And lined up along the decks are a whole lot of Milwaukee folks — mothers, fathers, kids, grandparents — off for a fine day in Chicago on the pride of the lakes: the *Lady Elgin!*

"How's the weather, Captain?"

"Weather's fine today," shouts Captain Wilson. "*Ain't* exactly *liked* the feel o' the air, though. Like there might be a storm comin'.

"Cast off there!" he shouts suddenly. "Steady now!"

And there she goes — the *Lady Elgin* off on her trip to Chicago. We won't worry about her on the way down. She had a fine run to Chicago, tied up at the dock on La Salle Street in mighty good time. Yes, the folks from Milwaukee all had a grand time in Chicago that day. They were sightseein'. Captain Barry's Union Guard company marched through the streets, band playin', and flag wavin'! There was a big banquet that evening, and Captain Barry made a speech.

BARRY: And so, thanks to the loyal support of the people of Milwaukee; and thanks to the excursion on the *Lady Elgin*, the Union Guards have now accumulated enough to pay for the muskets! On behalf of the Guards, I thank you. Thank you all!

There were plenty to cheer Captain Barry's speech. Everybody was having a good time. Nobody knew, or cared, that far up Lake Michigan that evening was a small lumber schooner, the *Augusta*, heavily laden and wallowing through a lake that was already beginning to turn sullen. On the *Augusta*, the mate was muttering . . .

MATE: Don't like the look of the sky. Comin' on to storm. Storm before midnight sure's shootin'. Have to keep a sharp lookout tonight.

And in Chicago, about the same time, the excursion party heard the whistle of the *Lady Elgin*, and they knew it was time to get aboard for the return trip to Milwaukee.

There they go up the gangplank — a tired but happy bunch of holidayers. And along with those Irish lads and lassies from Milwaukee are a few new passengers just getting on at Chicago for the trip up the lake. There's F. A. Lumsden, editor of the *New Orleans Picayune.* He's bumpin' into the Englishmen, Sir Herbert Ingram.

"Excuse me, sir," says Mr. Lumsden, "didn't go to shove you. Didn't expect such a crowd!"

"Nor did I," replied Sir Herbert. "Which way are the rooms?"

"Up thataway, I reckon," says Lumsden, pointing.

"These American boats confuse me."

"I'm Lumsden. *New Orleans Picayune.*"

"Ingram," says Sir Herbert. He turns to his wife. "Are you all right, dear?"

"There's such a crowd," replies Lady Ingram nervously. "Do you think it's safe to go aboard this boat, Herbert?"

"Certainly, my dear."

"These lake steamers are first class, Ma'am," says Lumsden.

"I've had a strange feeling all day," replies Lady Ingram, "as though we shouldn't make this trip."

"Nonsense," retorts Sir Herbert.

"Look sharp there!" bawls a voice. "Let the Union Guards through!"

"Here comes that Guard company from Milwaukee," says Lumsden. "Excursionists."

"All right, dear," says Sir Herbert. "Let's try to get through to our cabin. Follow me."

"Herbert, I feel rain on my face," says Lady Ingram. "We're going to have a storm."

"Won't make a bit of difference. This is a sturdy boat."

"All aboard!" bawls the captain. "Move sharp there!"

"They're loaded, Captain," answers a voice.

"Then gangplank in!" roars the captain. "Cast off there!"

"Hawser loose, Captain!"

And there they go, slippin' out into Lake Michigan; a long, white ship, ghostly there in the rain-filled dark; white faces dim along the rails, most of 'em takin' their last look at the Chicago shoreline. Tragedy a long way from the minds of most of 'em too. But up there on the bridge Captain Wilson's anxiously peerin' into the dark, and listenin' to the risin' wind. Captain Wilson's not goin' to be lonely on the bridge tonight. Here come John Eviston and his wife.

"Good evening, Captain Wilson," says Mrs. Eviston.

"Good evening, madam."

"I'm Mary Eviston, Captain. This is my husband, John."

"Good evening, sir."

"We . . . we wanted to thank you, Captain," says Mrs. Eviston, hesitating a bit.

"For what, madam?"

"Well," replies Mary Eviston, a little bit embarrassed now, "this is our anniversary, Captain. It's been such a splended day. We wanted to thank you for a pleasant trip to Chicago. I knew we wouldn't get a chance to say anything when we got to

Milwaukee, so . . . "

"You're welcome, I'm sure, madam."

"The *Lady Elgin's* a fine boat, Captain," says John Eviston. "How far are we from Chicago now?"

"Well, sir, we're just about opposite Winnetka, Illinois, now. Lake's roughened up considerable. We won't make such a fast trip back to Milwaukee."

"Just hear the wind," remarks Mary. "And it's so dark on the lake! Put your arm around me, John dear. I feel cold all of a sudden!"

"We'll go below," says Eviston. They start below but on the way they bump into Lady Ingram who's comin' up, followed by Sir Herbert.

"Captain, is everything all right?" cries Lady Ingram.

"Don't mind Lady Ingram Captain," says Sir Herbert. "My wife couldn't rest until you'd assured her the trip would be uneventful."

"Everything's shipshape, ma'am. Not a thing to worry about."

"Forgive me, Captain," says Lady Ingram. "But I'd been upset all day. I started this morning thinking about the Ingram curse, and I . . . "

"It's nothing," scoffs Sir Herbert. "There's an old story about a curse that's supposed to haunt my family. Something about an Egyptian mummy. It's nothing."

"The wind frightens me," says Lady Ingram. "Dear! how it's blowing!"

"Ahoy, Captain!" shouts a voice from the bow.

"Ahoy, lookout!"

"Schooner on the port bow, Captain! She's making toward us!"

"How far is she?" bellows the Captain.

" 'Bout three hundred yards."

"Hail her!"

"Ahoy, schooner!" bawls the lookout.

And from out there on the black lake, the answer comes back.

"Ahoy, steamer!"

"You're makin' toward us," bawls the lookout. "Alter course."

"We're trying, steamer!"

"There," says Sir Herbert. "I see the schooner now. I say,

she's quite close!"

"Steamer!" comes the bellow over the dark water.

"Schooner?"

"We can't alter course. Sea's too strong!"

"They'll crash us!" cries Lady Ingram.

"Nonsense," replies Sir Herbert. "There's plenty of room to alter course."

"They'll crash us," cries Lady Ingram. "I know they'll crash us!"

"Hush, dear," says Mary Eviston. "There's nothing to be alarmed about. Captain Wilson knows what he's doing."

"All the same," says John Eviston, "I don't like the way that schooner rolls. Like there was no steering to her."

"Hard starboard!" shouts Captain Wilson.

"No use, Captain. She's runnin' too high!"

"Keep trying, man! Harder! Harder!"

"I knew we shouldn't have come," sobs Lady Ingram. "I knew it!"

"Keep calm, old girl. Nothing's happened yet."

"But it will. It will!"

"John," says Mary Eviston, "hold me tight. If anything should happen tonight, we'll stay together, won't we?"

"We'll stay together," says John Eviston. "I'll look after you. Remember what I said yesterday? I love you so much, we're bound to come out all right."

"I remember, John."

"Look sharp, Captain," comes the voice from the bow. "She's comin' down on us!"

"Steamer," bellows the voice from the schooner, "we'll crash you!"

"Can't you pull her over, man?"

"Can't do it, Captain!"

"Then," bellows Captain Wilson, "stand by for crash! Stand by for crash!"

"Herbert! Herbert!" cries Lady Ingram.

"Let me have your hand, John," says Mary Eviston calmly and quietly.

"Here she comes! roars the captain. "Get set! Look out! *Now!*"

*Lost on the* Lady Elgin,
*Sleeping to wake no more;*

*Numbered with that three hundred*
*Who failed to reach the shore...*

And there goes the proud *Lady Elgin* on her last trip: to the bottom of Lake Michigan! As she goes, we hear the cries of women and children. The despairing calls of men who've lost their families in the mad crowd. As she goes she breaks in pieces, and we see people clinging to the wreckage swirled here and there in that wild lake. There's Captain Wilson on a part of the deck with a baby in his arms; women are there, too, and they disappear into the night. There's Sir Herbert Ingram trying to keep his wife afloat. There's the drummer boy of the Guards. His drum's still strapped to his back and it's keeping him above the water. He's a smart lad. There's Miss Rivers trying to keep her friend Mrs. Walters floating.

Yes, there are heroes aplenty there in that icy water. There's Captain Barry, a good soldier, helping people right to the last; and there he goes now, swimming after a woman who's slipped off her bit of wreckage. There's little Willie Pomeroy trying to save his friend Willie Barry. Over there, almost out of sight, is John O'Neill with Alderman Crilly on another bit of deck. O'Neill is giving his coat to his friend. And there — over there to the right — is John Eviston. Yes, his wife's still with him; they're together holding onto a beam.

They're floating away rapidly, all those who've been able to find wreckage to cling to. Some of 'em will survive. Others'll slip off there in the dark waters. Good luck. Good luck to 'em all!

It's morning now, a mighty grim, lowering morning. The folks on the *Lady Elgin* have been in the water quite a few hours. And down at Northwestern University, Edward Spencer and his brother have risen early and are walking along the lake shore.

"Stormy morning," says Spencer. "But I'm glad we decided to come anyway."

"Yeah," replies his brother. "I figured if I studied theology any longer my brain'd bust. Say, Ed, what is that thing lyin' over on the shore there? Part in the water. It looks like a body."

"It sure does... it *is* a woman," shouts Spencer and he begins to run. "She's dead," he says after a minute, kneeling down beside the body. "Been drowned, I guess. There's a board or somethin' here underneath her. Got some printin' on it."

"Yeah," says his brother, taking the board and turning it. *Lady Elgin.*"

"There's been a shipwreck."

"Look, Ed. There's wreckage coming in! There're people out there!"

"They 'll never get through the breakers," says Spencer. He begins to unfasten his clothes.

"What are you going to do, Ed?"

"You go and get some help. Get everybody! Lots of ropes! I'm going out there!"

A man never knows when he's going to be called on to be a hero. Young Spencer happened to be on the spot and he could swim, so he jumped in. Almost the first people he saw were the Evistons, John and Mary, still together, holding onto a beam. Mary Eviston was mighty weak.

"Hold on, Mary. We're almost in. Hold on a little longer."

"I can't make it, John," says Mary. "You let me go. Save yourself."

"If we go, we go together. Wait! There's somebody swimmin' out to us! Help!" he shouts. "Over here! Help!"

Spencer battered his way out to 'em, and he told John he'd help 'em. But they'd have to help *him*, too. And finally he brought 'em in. But you can bet the love John and Mary Eviston had for each other helped. It helped a lot!

Yes, Spencer got his fill of swimming that morning. They tied a rope around his waist, and time after time he went into the lake. He saved seventeen people. Sometime, if you're ever at Northwestern University, take a look in the library. You'll see a tablet there in memory of his bravery. But there were about three hundred souls on the *Elgin* that nobody could save. Among 'em was Captain Wilson.

WILSON: The *Elgin* was my ship, boys. Pride o' the lakes she was. But she was a death ship. A thing o' doom!

And Captain Barry and the flower of the Union Guards went down. Those muskets did 'em no good. But they were carried by other Milwaukee lads in the Civil War who remembered the *Lady Elgin*, you bet.

Yes sir, and on the Northwestern University grounds, the body of a man was found washed ashore. When they turned him over they said, "This is Sir Herbert Ingram."

There was a curse on you, Sir Herbert. A curse of old

Egypt. You are proof it it. And we wonder: is there Fate in such things? Was it the voice of that ancient priest of Thebes who caused the wreck of the *Lady Elgin* when he said so many centuries ago, "Let it be inscribed that whosoever desecrates my tomb shall die, and his children, and his children's children."

We don't know. But sometimes of a September night, if we listen closely, we may hear the voice of Lake Michigan sighing

*Lost on the* Lady Elgin
*Sleeping to wake no more . . .*

XV. Stage Door at the Pabst Theatre

Northwest Country

SHELL LAKE

MANITOWISH

RHINELANDER

Northern Highland Country

WASHINGTON ISLAND
ROCK ISLAND

MERRILL

STURGEON BAY

KESHENA

EAU CLAIRE

STEVENS POINT

GREEN BAY
DE PERE

Ridge and Water Country

NEILLSVILLE

WINNECONNE

PORTAGE

HORICON

VIROQUA
GENOA

Southern

Old Milwaukee Country

PRAIRIE DU CHIEN

LONG ROCK
ARENA
SPRING GREEN
DODGEVILLE

Uplands

MADISON

Country

MONROE